T0247930

Karolinum Press

Václav Havel's Meanings:
His Key Words and Their Legacy

Edited by David S. Danaher and Kieran Williams

VÁCLAV HAVEL SERIES

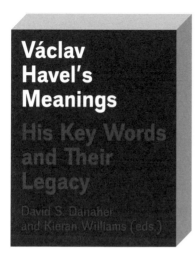

Václav Havel's Meanings

His Key Words and Their Legacy

David S. Danaher
and Kieran Williams (eds.)

KAROLINUM PRESS

KAROLINUM PRESS is a publishing department of Charles University
Ovocný trh 560/5, 116 36 Prague 1, Czech Republic
www.karolinum.cz

Cover and graphic design by 3.dílna
Set and printed in the Czech Republic by Karolinum Press
First edition

Cataloging-in-Publication Data is available from the National Library
of the Czech Republic

ISBN 978-80-246-4941-2
ISBN 978-80-246-4942-9 (pdf)
ISBN 978-80-246-4943-6 (epub)

The original manuscript was reviewed by Milan Babik (Colby College, Maine)
and Craig Cravens (Indiana University, Indiana)

TABLE OF CONTENTS

David S. Danaher and Kieran Williams: Editors' preface:
A word about Havel's key words **9**

Jiří Přibáň: At the Garden Party of Moths and Butterflies:
a foreword to Havel's keywords and imaginaries **16**

David S. Danaher: Appeal: *apel, výzva* **29**
Kieran Williams: Truth: *pravda* **60**
Irena Vaňková: Home, homeland: *domov* **91**
Jiří Suk: Prison: *vězení* **126**
Barbara Day: Theater: *divadlo* **162**
Kieran Williams: Hotspot: *ohnisko* **192**
Delia Popescu: Power: *moc* **224**
Barbara J. Falk and Daniela Bouvier-Valenta:
Responsibility: *odpovědnost* **254**
David S. Danaher: Indifference: *apatie, lhostejnost* **282**
Aspen Brinton: Civil society: *občanská společnost* **309**

About the authors **337**

EDITORS' PREFACE: A WORD ABOUT HAVEL'S KEY WORDS

David S. Danaher and Kieran Williams

Lying in a prison hospital bed in September 1981, Václav Havel wrote to his wife of his conviction that life has meaning. "We wade in transience, we are sinking in it," he told her, "And if we do not wish to surrender entirely—that is, to give up on our journey (and thus on ourselves)—we must feel that 'it is all for something,' that it has a direction, that it will not all pass away irretrievably, enclosed in its own momentary randomness." We may never determine exactly what that meaning is, but it would be enough to feel that "our lives are heading somewhere and mean something, are not—from 'the cosmic point of view,' so to speak—overlooked or forgotten, they are 'known about,' and somewhere are valued and given meaning."[1]

Since his death 30 years after writing that letter, many efforts have been made to ensure that Havel is not overlooked or forgotten, and that he is "known about." If anything, his life has taken on an urgent timeliness, owing to developments in his home country and worldwide. He has served posthumously as an ally against a range of perceived maladies, be they messianic populism,[2] Chinese brutality in Hong Kong,[3] or "identity politics."[4] In addition to commemorative events on the anniversaries of his birth and death, and of the

---

1   Letter 94, in Václav Havel, *Spisy 5: Dopisy Olze* (Prague: Torst, 1999), 370-71; in English as *Letters to Olga: June 1979 – September 1982*. Trans. Paul Wilson (New York: Henry Holt, 1989), 230.
2   Daniel Brennan "Reading Václav Havel in the Age of Trump," *Critical Horizons* 20:1 (2019): 54-70. See also Kieran Williams, "Václav Havel's 'Leaving' and the Toxic Aging Narcissist in a Baseball Hat", *Medium*, December 6, 2017, https://medium.com/@KDWIlliams7/v%C3%A1clav-havels-leaving-and-the-toxic-aging-narcissist-in-a-baseball-hat-f8e006fbb3ee.
3   Štefan Auer, "Power and Violence, Hope and Despair: Václav Havel's Political Thought in 1989 and 2019," November 5, 2019, Lingnan University, Hong Kong.
4   Jeremy Carl, "Douglas Murray Challenges Us to Oppose Identity Politics and 'Live in Truth'," National Review, October 17, 2019, https://www.nationalreview.com/2019/10/douglas-murray-challenges-us-to-oppose-identity-politics-and-live-in-truth/.

1989 revolution with which he is intimately associated, there has been a longstanding public display, "Havel in a Nutshell," with companion book,[5] and a steady stream of publications from the Václav Havel Library, including reminiscences of Havel by friends, associates, and acquaintances.[6] Most of the contributors to this volume in Karolinum's Václav Havel Series have written their own monographs about him, and others are available in numerous languages.[7] He has been the subject of numerous documentary films and, in 2020, the dramatized biopic *Havel*. Novel ways are found to reassemble his words to inspire new generations of readers: a collection of 100 quotations has been compiled to preserve and promote Havel in aphoristic form (as was done for an earlier president, Tomáš Masaryk),[8] while interviews he gave between 1964 and 1989 have been reissued under the title *Má to smysl*—"It makes sense," "It has meaning," "It has a purpose," or simply "It matters."[9]

5   Nina Rutová, *Havel v kostce: 14 lekcí o jedné osobnosti a každé době pro učitele a studenty* (Prague: Knihovna Václava Havla, 2011).

6   Anna Freimanová (ed.), *Příležitostný portrét Václava Havla* (Prague: Knihovna Václava Havla, 2013); Jan Dražan and Jan Pergler, *Náš Václav Havel: 27 rozhovorů o kamarádovi, prezidentovi, disidentovi a šéfovi* (Prague: Zeď, 2016); Rosamund Johnston and Lenka Kabrhelová, *Havel v Americe: rozhovory s americkými intelektuály, politiky a umělci* (Brno: Host, 2019).

7   Martin C. Putna, *Václav Havel. Duchovní portrét v rámu české kultury 20. století* (Prague: Knihovna Václava Havla, 2011); James Pontuso, *Vaclav Havel: Civic Responsibility in the Postmodern Age* (Lanham: Rowman & Littlefield, 2004); Daniel Brennan, *The Political Thought of Václav Havel: Philosophical Influences and Contemporary Applications* (Leiden: Brill, 2017); Dirk Mathias Dalberg, *Der "Versuch, in der Wahrheit zu leben": Václav Havels Politikbegriff und politische Strategie in den Jahren 1969 bis 1989* (Stuttgart: Ibidem, 2014); Martin Bermeiser, *Václav Havels Reden: Aspekte einer holistichen Rhetorik* (Stuttgart: Ibidem, 2017); Geneviève Even-Granboulan, *Václav Havel, président philosophe* (La Tour-d'Aigues: Éditions de l'Aube, 2003). For biographies, see Carol Rocamora, *Acts of Courage: Vaclav Havel's Life in the Theatre* (Hanover, NH: Smith & Kraus Global, 2005) and Michael Žantovský, *Havel: A Life* (New York: Grove Atlantic, 2014). For review essays of biographies of Havel, see Miloš Havelka, "Úspěchy a neúspěchy v nejednoznačných konstelacích. Pět biografií Václava Havla", *Soudobé dějiny* 22:3-4 (2015), 474–502, and Václav Sixta, "Václav Havel a jeho zápletky", *Historie - Otázky - Problémy* 8:1 (2016), 159–170.

8   Pavel Kosatík, *100x Václav Havel: Jak rozumět jeho myšlenkám* (Prague: Universum, 2019).

9   Anna Freimanová and Tereza Johanidesová, eds. *Václav Havel - Má to smysl: Výbor rozhovorů 1964 – 1989* (Prague: Knihovna Václava Havla, 2019).

Just as he was certain that life had meaning, Havel felt no less certain that he must try to impart the meaning of his own but was doomed to fall short because of the inability of language to capture the mystery of Being.[10] Despite the inevitable frustration, language enchanted Havel and was at the center of all his efforts:

> Another thing I should perhaps mention here is an interest in language. I'm interested in its ambivalence, its abuse; I'm interested in language as the architect of life, fates, and worlds; language as the most important skill; language as ritual and incantation; the word as the bearer of dramatic movement, as an identity card, as a way of self-affirmation and self-projection.[11]

With words Havel built a corpus of texts that stand as his legacy, a body so rich that it will probably be the only work of a Soviet-bloc dissident that will still be read long into the future, because its meaning is not confined to the circumstances of its creation. But Havel himself warned in his 1989 essay "A Word about Words" that no word's meaning is limited to its dictionary definition: "Each word contains within in it also the person who pronounces it, the situation in which it is pronounced, and the reason why it is pronounced."[12] That applies to Havel himself, famous for his frequent use of certain words that upon inspection turn out to possess layers of meaning, sometimes idiosyncratic, which offer the keys to understanding why he still matters and still speaks to people in diverse situations as well as to the modern condition in general.

Our volume builds on the approach set out in Danaher, *Reading Václav Havel* (chapter 4) of focusing on key words. A key word is

---

10   Václav Havel, *To the Castle and Back*, trans. Paul Wilson (New York: Knopf, 2007), 347.
11   Václav Havel, *Spisy 4: Eseje a jiné texty z let 1970-1989. Dálkový výslech* (Prague: Torst, 1999), 902; in English as *Disturbing the Peace: A Conversation with Karel Hvížďala*, trans. Paul Wilson (New York: Vintage, 1991), 193.
12   Václav Havel, "Slovo o slovu," in *Spisy 4*, 1135.

one that occupies a central position in a work—or even over the entire oeuvre—of a given thinker because it exhibits special organizational and semantic potential for that work or for that thinker's whole system. While Raymond Williams and Anna Wierzbicka pioneered the investigation of key words in culture,[13] Mark Edmundson, among others, emphasized their role in philosophical thought: "[I]t is not surprising that to every philosopher of consequence we attach a word list, a central vocabulary. We think of the words and phrases they have invented or those that they have bent themselves over for long periods, minutely shaping and polishing, like expert gem cutters."[14]

Key words in Havel's oeuvre are not particularly difficult to identify. They are running motifs in his writing that cut across genres and time periods (his pre- and post-1989 incarnations); as central elements of his core vocabulary, they serve as intellectual touchstones around which many of his larger ideas take shape. The meanings of Havel's key words may also be found in works where the words themselves are absent—that is, in his plays, where we might speak more productively of Havelian key concepts. We should also note that often these words defy simple translation into English and thus require linguistically sensitive analyses, and some chapters in this volume focus on those aspects of meaning that may be lost in translation.

The contributors to this volume are drawn from a range of academic disciplines and countries, and approach Havel in varying ways. As editors, we have not insisted on a single method for analyzing the key words they have selected. That pluralism is a strength, a reminder of Havel's own talents in multiple fields—essays, plays, speeches, letters, interviews, poems, diaries—and done in the spirit

---

13 Raymond Williams, *Keywords* (Oxford: Oxford University Press, 1976); Anna Wierzbicka, *Understanding Cultures through Their Key Words* (London: Oxford University Press, 1997).
14 Mark Edmundson, *Literature against Philosophy; Plato to Derrida* (Cambridge: Cambridge University Press, 1995), 13.

of collage, which he experimented with in his plays (such as *The Increased Difficulty of Concentration*) and memoirs (*To the Castle and Back*). It is our hope that this mixture of methods will open up dimensions of Havel's writing that non-Czech readers might not appreciate from translations, or even that Czech readers may find do not tally with customary, everyday usage. Havel, after all, started out attempting to make it as a poet, and a poet's mission is to disturb settled language and make the familiar strange, which he strove to do even after abandoning poetry in early adulthood.

The first key words we have chosen to present relate to the ideas of the appeal or challenge, as the whole of Havel's work represents an exhortation to everyone—not just to those normally considered powerful—to reflect critically on the state of the world and what we can do to repair it. As he told his country at the beginning of his second year as its president: "A year ago I closed my New Year's address by paraphrasing Comenius's famous sentence, 'Your government, o people, has returned to you!'. Today I would follow this sentence with: 'It is up to you, o people, to show that the return of government into your hands made sense [*měl smysl*].'"[15] That words without action are meaningless was the premise of one of his lesser known early plays, the one-act *Butterfly on an Antenna*, about an overly intellectual couple who cannot cope with the pressing task of shutting off a running faucet but fixate instead on its abstract, technical hydraulics and symbolism as a "metaphor of apocalypse."[16]

The idea of speech as an appeal, in particular an appeal to arrive at one's own truth and act upon it, frames the progression of the chapters, as we move through several chapters relating to place and space (to which Havel, as the son and grandson of builders, was very

15   'Václav Havel, "Novoroční projev," in Havel, *Spisy 4: Projevy z let 1990-1992. Letní přemítání* (Prague: Torst, 1999), 331.
16   Václav Havel, "Motýl na anténě," in Havel, *Spisy 2: Hry* (Prague: Torst, 1999), 231.

sensitive), before arriving at power, responsibility versus indifference, and the collective action of civil society. We have asked Jiří Přibáň, one of the most prominent Czech public intellectuals of the post-1989 era, to introduce these chapters with a foreword, but there is no last word: we hope that this collection will appeal to readers to think with Havel on their own terms and engage with his many key words not covered here, such as *autentičnost* ("authenticity"), *bytí* ("Being"), *dějiny* ("history"), *demokracie* ("democracy"), *Evropa* ("Europe"), *fanatismus* ("fanaticism"), *identita* ("identity"), *intelektuál* ("intellectual"), *katarze* ("catharsis"), *naděje* ("hope"), *samopohyb* (usually translated as "automatism"), and not least the multiple meanings of *smysl* ("meaning, sense, purpose").

Notes on the volume's citation format and translated texts

Citations of Havel's collected works refer to Václav Havel, *Spisy* (Prague: Torst, 1999); citations will indicate volume and page numbers.

Havel's prison letters, *Letters to Olga*, will be cited by reference to the letter number. The Czech version of this work is found in Václav Havel, *Spisy* 5 (Prague: Torst, 1999), and the English translation (by Paul Wilson) is Václav Havel, *Letters to Olga* (New York: Henry Holt,1983).

His essay "The Power of the Powerless" will be cited by reference to chapter number. The Czech version of this work is found in Havel, *Spisy* 4, and the English translation (by Paul Wilson) is in Václav Havel, *Open Letters* (New York: Knopf, 1991). Wilson updated his translation for a special edition of the journal *East European Politics and Societies* (32: 2, May 2018, eds. James Krapfl and Barbara J. Falk) devoted to the essay, and a full text with an introduction by Wilson is available there. Other full-text versions in both languages are also readily available on the web.

Presidential addresses by Havel will be cited by title and year. Texts of these addresses are available on the website of Prague Castle, the seat of the Czech presidency: the Czech versions may be found at http://old.hrad.cz/president/Havel/speeches/index.html, and the English versions (of those addresses that have been translated) are at http://old.hrad.cz/president/Havel/speeches/index_uk.html. Czech versions of the presidential addresses also exist in various volumes of Havel's *Spisy*, and English translations for some of the major addresses from the early-to-mid 1990s are available in Václav Havel, *The Art of the Impossible: Politics as Morality in Practice* (New York: Knopf, 1997).

Havel's plays are cited by name. Czech versions of most of the plays may be found in Havel, *Spisy 2*; for *Leaving*, see Václav Havel, *Spisy 8: Projevy a jiné texty 1999-2006. Prosím stručně. Odcházení* (Prague: Torst, 2007). English translations of certain plays may be found in: Václav Havel, *The Garden Party and Other Plays* (New York: Grove Press, 1994); Václav Havel, *Vaněk Plays*, trans. Jan Novák (New York: Theater 61 Press); Václav Havel, *Leaving*, trans. Paul Wilson (New York: Theater 61 Press); Václav Havel, *The Memo*, trans. Paul Wilson (New York: Theater 61 Press); and Václav Havel, *The Beggar's Opera*, trans. Paul Wilson (Ithaca: Cornell University Press, 2001).

The editors of this volume have collaborated with the authors on translating two chapters in this volume ("home, homeland" and "prison") from Czech into English.

AT THE GARDEN PARTY OF MOTHS AND BUTTERFLIES: A FOREWORD TO HAVEL'S KEY WORDS AND IMAGINARIES

Jiří Přibáň

One of the most typical hallmarks of political modernity is Thomas Hobbes's view that *auctoritas non veritas facit legem*, usually shortened as the 'might is right' statement invoked by self-declared political realists. Against this view, political idealists argue that *veritas non auctoritas facit legem* and call on the authority of reason to guide our political life by guaranteeing truth in politics. For them, the political sovereign's might depends on the mightier rule constituted by the sovereign power of reason.

While the legacy of Hobbes still dominates political and social theories and definitions of politics through the exercise of sovereign commands, the general habit of obedience and the state as the monopoly of power within a given territory, the tradition of identifying legitimate politics with truth is much older and its modern imaginary is typically associated with the Kantian view of public opinion governed by reason. The persuasive force of reason manifests itself in the public sphere of civil society, which is expected to facilitate free discussion transforming diverse opinions into rational judgements and political consensus. Public participation and rational engagement are then expected to constitute specific control of political authority, in which the sovereign reason rules the state and its legal constitution.

These conceptual and ideological distinctions between political realism and idealism, or power and truth, are usually mastered by political, legal, and social scientists in early stages of academic development despite their gross simplifications of political and legal reality as well as a failure to describe the complexity of modern society. It is therefore very important for academics, as much as citizens, to encounter and explore political and legal constellations in which the keywords of *auctoritas*, *veritas*, and *lex* cannot be simplified and summarized in typical formulas, conceptual distinctions and intellectual clichés.

Realism of idealistic visions

For me, this moment came when I was invited to a private meeting of constitutional law experts with President Václav Havel in the Lány castle residence in 2000. It was the time of the most serious constitutional crisis since the split of Czechoslovakia, one that threatened the whole system of separation of powers. The crisis was triggered by the 1998 parliamentary election leading to the political pact, the so-called "opposition treaty," between two major parties, ODS (the right-wing Civic Democratic Party) and ČSSD (the left-wing Czech Social Democratic Party) and their leaders Václav Klaus and Miloš Zeman. The treaty included proposals of constitutional changes that would shift power to the executive branch of Government and, even more importantly, eliminate smaller political parties from Parliament.

Havel opposed this move to concentrate parliamentary and executive powers in the hands of two major political players. When general goals of the opposition treaty materialized in the form of a new electoral system proposal that meant to transform the existing proportional system into a *de facto* majoritarian one, he, therefore, wanted to discuss his options with some senior judges and constitutional law experts. When he entered the room and pulled out his worn copy of the Czech Constitution from his blazer pocket to point to a particular section, it, nevertheless, was clear that he already had a strong view and critical assessment of the whole situation.

Havel's knowledge of the Constitution's letter was impressive and his commitment to the spirit of constitutionalism dominated the discussion of specific rules and techniques on that evening. The election reform proposal was enacted by Parliament later that year in June 2000.[1] Havel's early assessment of the proposed changes and his determination to refer them to the Constitutional Court were overwhelmingly supported by constitutional experts. His arguments that the new electoral law was a legal technique of effectively introducing a majoritarian system of voting and would violate the constitutional rule that the lower chamber of Parliament be elected by proportional representation, were ultimately accepted by the Court, which declared the electoral law unconstitutional in January 2001 and thus fundamentally strengthened the new Constitution's fragile and evolving fabric.[2]

This first working encounter with Václav Havel, however, also had a strong symbolic and intellectual meaning for me because it illustrated that the relationship between *auctoritas*, *veritas*, and *lex* was a lot more complicated than the two formulas defining the distinction between political realism and idealism.

Havel was sometimes labelled an idealist, yet he realistically judged his political moves and made powerful strategic decisions that successfully weakened his adversaries and fundamentally strengthened the emerging system of democratic constitutionalism and firmly placed the Czech Republic in European and transatlantic structures despite the notorious Czech Euroscepticism and anti-NATO sentiments. After all, it is hard to imagine anyone but a pragmatic and realist politician leading the country for over thirteen years marked by the most profound political, economic, and social transformation.

---

1 Act No. 204/2000 of the Collection of the Laws of the Czech Republic.
2 Judgement of the Constitutional Court of the Czech Republic No. 64/2001. In his speech before the Court, Havel summarized: "I am a big supporter of the majoritarian system myself. This is why I welcomed its implementation for the Senate elections. Nevertheless, this incorporation of majoritarian elements to the proportionate representation system not only attacks foundations of this proportionality, but also brings no advantages of the majoritarian system. Should majoritarian elements prevail, the very existence of bicameralism could be questioned ...". For the Czech transcript, see https://archive.vaclavhavel-library.org/File/Show/158529

Havel's politics used ideals as tools of achieving realistic goals. Even his most famous quote "Truth and love must prevail over lies and hate" is a blend of idealism and realism because truth and love are taken as carriers of specific policies and modes of political judgement. However, this realistic use of truth's power was always framed by Havel's idealistic vision of politics as a meaningful human effort and not just a professional vocation.

Theatrum politicum v. noble lies

The idea of collecting essays on Václav Havel's keywords, therefore, is a praiseworthy and original contribution to the growing body of literature on this person's life, work, ideas, and politics. Havel's notions of truth, power, civil society, and responsibility are inseparable from his understanding of theater and prison or indifference and appeal. His thinking is impossible to categorize and organize as a lexicon, and this collection of essays successfully argues against any such attempts. It actually invites its reader into the most complex, even contradictory thoughts and intellectual and artistic reflections in Havel's works.

It should not be surprising that the centrality of Havel's arguments from the perspective of human authenticity and living in truth goes hand in hand with constant use of the theatrical aspects of politics in both his dissident and presidential actions. For Havel, politics was always dramatic, but this *theatrum politicum* does not mean that, as Plato argued, it would be just the world of mimetic acts, illusions, and appearances obstructing our access to the truth. Havel's notion of living in truth integrated drama as an intrinsic part of authentic human creativity. However, Havel was always critical of the political idea of legitimation by a "noble lie" originally formulated by Plato and subsequently adopted by ideologues of all kinds from conservative traditionalists to revolutionary Marxists.

In his *Republic*, Plato imagines the ideal polity founded on "one single, grand lie which will be believed by everybody including the rulers."[3] The lie was to function as a fiction of the common descent of the city's population from the earth that, nevertheless, is accompanied by a fiction that the citizens' souls contain different metals and their bearers therefore belong to different social classes.

Plato's assessment of the ideal city as a polity to be ideologically integrated by a lie was replicated by many different theories and philosophies of politics. According to this view, the need to balance concurrent expectations of commutative and distributive justice is impossible to satisfy by real political acts and therefore must be answered by idealizing metaphors, fictions, and symbols. These symbols of power must guarantee acceptance, unity, and general consensus, and their main function is to eliminate internal conflicts, contradictions, and dissent potentially emerging in society.

Karl Mannheim described this function of ideology as stabilization of a political order by blurring the pluralistic and conflictual reality of society. In "The Power of the Powerless," Havel described the legality of the communist regime as a façade functioning exactly like this ideological machine, using abstract and empty notions of the legal system to cover the regime's real repressive character. He did not just criticize the regime's official lies and the role of legality in masking its brute power.[4] He also highlighted its legitimizing function of presenting the total and only representation of society while suppressing societal pluralism and the structural conflicts between those who rule and those ruled by them.

Havel's dissident call for living in truth thus should be interpreted as a delegitimation strategy unmasking all ideological lies, noble or

---

3 Plato, *The Republic*, Book III, 414b-c (Cambridge: Cambridge University Press. 2000) 108-10.

4 Václav Havel, "The Power of the Powerless" in Václav Havel et al., *The Power of the Powerless: Citizens Against the State in Central Eastern Europe*, ed. John Keane (London: Hutchinson 1985), 74-75.

poor, and their total images of society. Its social function is to reveal specific gaps in ideological claims of total legitimacy.[5]

Legality and legitimacy

As regards the *lex* of the communist regime, political dissent exposed its ideological function of concealing the *veritas* of the state of politics and thus operating as a tool of filling the legitimation gaps in the regime's *auctoritas*. Rather than the simplistic distinction between truth and lies in politics, the dissident strategy thus reveals the basic problem of modernity in which the original question of legitimacy *by* legality was gradually transformed into the question of legitimacy *of* legality itself. The relationship between power, truth, and laws thus has to be reconceptualized because modern history offers many examples of the worst atrocities and crimes against humanity committed by legislated laws and court judgements.

Every power calls for legitimation. In modern democratic statehood, this legitimation, however, is extended from the power-holders to the whole polity described as the constituent power of the sovereign people. Nevertheless, this concept of popular sovereignty as self-rule must be strictly limited to the system of politics. In this sense, the totalitarian state failed because it was constituted by the ambition to govern the totality of society beyond politics. Totalitarianism is thus best described as the political goal of creating a state with one official ideological opinion on everything—something contradicting the very nature of modernity differentiating between politics and society and generating its legitimacy from the distinction between the public and private spheres of social life.

The modern democratic state governed by the laws, the democratic *Rechtsstaat*, operates on simultaneous limitation and expansion

---

5   Jiří Přibáň, *Dissidents of Law: On the 1989 Velvet Revolutions, Legitimations, Fictions of Legality and Contemporary Version of the Social Contract* (Alershot: Ashgate 2002), 145-51.

of the state power by legality. Power is legitimized by legality as its limitation but the same legality expands it. The problem of legitimation is thus extended from the political system now legitimized by legality to the legal system and its internal constitution.

Despite all references to living in truth, political dissent and its critique of communist ideology paradoxically proved that modern *lex* cannot be subjected to the higher-legitimacy test of ultimate *veritas*. The *auctoritas* of law is neither in its higher truth as claimed by idealist philosophers, nor in its efficiency as argued by realist political scientists and sociologists. Legality in the democratic state is actually legitimized by its internal capacity to minimize potential risks of injustices produced by the system of positive law.

Apart from controlling political power by its constitutional limitation, the rule of law legitimizes it by intrinsic legal values such as clarity, consistency, and coherence of rules, judgements, and decision-making. These values of legality have profound external effects, and their general societal validity recursively turns positive law into commonly accepted practices and the ultimate authority of legitimate politics. Neither the sovereign power, nor reason make laws. It is the law's internal morality that self-constitutes its authority and functionality beyond the ideological façade of repressive consent. And dissidents showed that the absence and systemic breaches of this internal morality delegitimizes both law and power.

In this respect, it is interesting how this internal morality of law was present in Havel's thinking in his dissident as much as president years. When he reflected on post-1989 constitution-making, he remarked that:

Lawyers have their own vocabulary, and I think I understand most of what is said or written on these matters, but it's not just about me. The language of the constitution should be as clear as spring water, and it should be immediately and fully understandable to every student. It should, in short, be the real property of the people, as it is in the United States.[6]

It is also noteworthy that this remark on the clarity of law is closely connected to Havel's lifelong critique of legal formalism and positivism. In the following sentence, he states: "I am no friend of an overly formal, positivistic notion of the law, because I know how much injustice can flow from a mindless and literal cleaving to the letter of the law."[7]

The struggle of a political dissident meets the ethic of a democratic president in these words.

Values and the meaning of politics

The legacy of political dissent primarily consists of negative warnings and comes close to Blaise Pascal's view that political reality is constituted by earthly power conflicts and struggles, not divine entitlements.[8] According to Pascal, it is human fear and fragility that constitute a political order and the sovereign ruler, therefore, should fear power of the ruled people. Similarly, any dissent reveals a paradoxical truth about the totalitarian state—it is based on fear and noble lies, yet its rulers constantly fear the ruled in their poverty and powerlessness.

These lessons from dissident politics show the impossibility of eliminating the language of values from either the system of positive law or politics. The ultimate point of the legitimation of power is neither its efficiency, nor its principled limitation. It is the very meaning of politics as a valuable human enterprise.

However, modern history shows that human values are formulated as transcendental foundations of our society by both professional

6   Václav Havel, *To the Castle and Back* (London: Portobello Books, 2007), 191.
7   Havel, *To the Castle and Back*, 191.
8   Blaise Pascal, *Pensées* (New York: Dutton, 1958), 85.

politicians and their dissenting critics, yet they operate as just momentary outcomes of different legitimation strategies and operations. Values are expected to be universal, objective, and socially stable, yet they suffer from profound instability, subjectivity, and particular conflicts.

The problem of values in modern politics and society is that there is no chance that they could be generally shared and accepted as universally valid. Modern society is by definition morally pluralistic, and different people share different and conflicting values. All categorical and absolute value imperatives are challenged by the plurality of existing values.

Reflecting on this immanence and plurality of legitimizing values, Max Weber stated that the most important aspect of authority is that the ruled believe that they "had made the content of the command the maxim of their conduct for its very own sake."[9] It means that they believe in objective validity of values behind the subjective will and power to which they are subjected.

Weber concluded that this paradox of subjective beliefs in objective validity does not have a definitive solution because politics, like the economy or science, cannot be founded by a system of universal values expressing the true human existence and responding to the most essential question of the meaning of life. According to him, the only existential meaning of politics is its recognition that neither politics, nor science or philosophy, can open access to universally valid principles and values of humanity. In short, Weber believed that the vocation of politics, law, science, or any other intellectual discipline or social activity, consists of the recognition that objective legitimacy by values is paradoxically both necessary and impossible.

---

9   Max Weber, *Economy and Society 2* (Berkeley CA: The University of California Press, 1978), 946.

Dissident *potentia* of delegitimation

The paradox of values as necessary yet impossible sources of legitimation of politics and law is well illuminated by dissident struggles to both unmask the true mechanisms of communist power and formulate valuable alternatives to the existing rule. In this context, Havel's conceptualization of the power of the powerless needs to be revisited and reformulated in light of Spinoza's distinction between societal force—*potentia*, and institutionalized political power—*potestas*.[10]

The distinction between societal force and political power has been popular among critical theorists and philosophers contrasting repressive power of the political system to the repressed multitudes striving for self-determination. However, the strategy of dissent hardly can be reduced to these simple dichotomies and alternatives between state repression and societal liberation. It escapes apocalyptic imaginaries of political sovereigns controlling the bare lives of their populations.[11] Despite Havel's distinction between the intentions of life and the intentions of the system and its similarity to critical philosophers such as Jürgen Habermas's criticizing the alienating and automatic working of the system of politics and society without any meaningful purpose,[12] these thoughts call for a more radical rethinking of Havel's concept of power and its dichotomies.

Havel's dialectics of power and powerlessness can be reformulated as a problem of the difference between the productive societal *potentia* and the reproductive political *potestas*. Havel is more fascinated by the problem of power as a constellation and effect of

---

10   See, for instance, Etienne Balibar, *Spinoza and Politics* (London: Verso, 1998).
11   Giorgio Agamben, *Homo Sacer: Sovereign Power and Bare Life* (Stanford CA: Stanford University Press, 1998), 44.
12   For this comparison and further analysis, see Jiří Přibáň, "Resisting fear: on dissent and the solidarity of the shaken in contemporary European and global society," in Francesco Tava and Darian Meacham, eds., *Thinking After Europe: Jan Patočka and Politics* (Oxford: Rowman and Littlefield, 2016), 39-56.

societal forces and less concerned with more conventional analyses of institutions of power and their repressive strategies and apparatus. He notices the actual decline of ideological explanations of "metaphysical power" and focuses on surveillance techniques and societal discipline of the automatic "physical power" of the system.[13]

Havel was interested in the power of social discipline and subjugation, and he formulated his living in truth as a microphysics of the power of the powerless that can disrupt the physics and metaphysics of state power. He was less interested in localization of power and identifying those responsible for its use and more focused on its functions and circulation in social systems and networks. Havel thus looked beyond the concepts of repression and alienation or consensus and participation and, similarly to Michel Foucault,[14] explored how power, rather than being applied to individuals, effectively passes through them.[15]

In this respect, the power of the powerless consists of the *potentia* of societal delegitimation of the political system that officially ruled by the code of law and factually governed by the discipline of social normalization. It is a counter-productive force to the official language of productivity and efficiency of the communist system of power. This force operates as a dense system of societal formations and multiple relations that, despite some shared keywords and concepts, cannot be reduced to the philosophy of existentialism with its calls for authenticity as a true alternative to the corrupted system built on lies. This power of the powerless remains unfounded by some ultimate values as sovereign sources of a meaningful life itself.[16]

---

13 See note 4 above.
14 Přibáň, *Dissidents of Law: On the 1989 Velvet Revolutions, Legitimations, Fictions of Legality and Contemporary Version of the Social Contract*, 53-56.
15 Michel Foucault, *"Society Must Be Defended": Lectures at the College de France, 1975-76* (London: Penguin, 2003), 29.
16 Michel Foucault, *The Archaeology of Knowledge* (London: Routledge, 1972), 76.

Poietic politics in autopoietic society

This assessment of political dissent, its societal force, and value may seem minimalist. To this question, one, however, can respond by recalling that the delegitimizing strategy of dissent turned out to be indispensable in bringing down the communist regimes in Central and Eastern Europe in 1989.

Contrary to Weber's value scepticism, freedom and democracy certainly can be optimistically seen as transcendentally valid and giving the fundamental meaning to human existence. Nevertheless, the paradox of the community of values claiming transcendental validity but depending on their immanent enforcement and legitimation manifests itself even in Havel's keywords of transcendental truth and love which, if not realistically enforced through specific and immanent policies, would remain just empty moral promises on our political waiting lists.

If there is a moral lesson from Václav Havel's political life as both dissident and president, it is exactly this knowledge that, in politics, we are always dealing with waiting lists of values and the most valuable is the very act of waiting. Optimists are convinced that their values will materialize one day. Pessimists do not believe it. And sceptics act as if these values are coming despite circumstances and experiences indicating that it may not be possible.

Havel was a hopeful sceptic who, despite circumstances and experiences, always acted as if these values were coming and depended on our will. I realized this during our conversations with Zygmunt Bauman when he was awarded the Vize 97 Prize by the Dagmar and Václav Havel Foundation in 2006. After a roundtable discussion with Czech and Slovak sociologists, Havel came to informally greet Bauman, and we ended up talking about social sciences, politics, art, and language in general. While discussing a number of different topics, it was clear that society was imagined by Havel as primarily a community of values.

Modern society is described by social theorists as functionally differentiated into so-called autopoietic systems that are normatively closed, self-constituted and operate by self-references and without interference by external values and judgements. Unlike this theoretical image, Havel's work and life remind us that the same autopoietically organized society also keeps its poietic character in the sense that it is always open to different interpretations and retains the possibility of living a meaningful and valuable life.

The last time I met Havel in person was at a public discussion commemorating the Velvet Revolution in London in November 2009. To my provocative question about his biggest political nightmare twenty years after the revolution, he responded by playing with *noční můra* ("nightmare"), which is a homonym for "moth" in Czech, and saying that he believed moths were the same species as butterflies and should be treated in the same way.

I am sitting and observing all sorts of moths in the night garden in the summer of 2020 while looking forward to the morning with its butterflies. I am thinking of Havel's *Garden Party* and the Čapek brothers' play *Pictures from the Insects' Life* while imagining society as a garden party of moths and butterflies and, apart from Havel's keywords, immersing myself in the poietic world of his artistic and political metaphors.

APPEAL: *APEL, VÝZVA*
David S. Danaher

> For me, the notion of some complete and finite knowledge
> that explains everything and raises no further questions is
> clearly related to the notion of an end to the spirit,
> to life, to time and to Being. Anything meaningful that has
> ever been said in this matter (including every religious
> gospel) is on the contrary remarkable for its dramatic
> openness, its incompleteness. It is not a confirmation
> so much as a challenge [*výzva*] or an appeal [*apel*] [...]
>
> — Václav Havel, *Letters to Olga*[1]

Introduction

That Václav Havel was an appeal-oriented writer and thinker ought not to be controversial. By the late 1960s, he had established an international reputation as the author of absurdist plays written in the style of "theater of the appeal" (*divadlo apelu*), which is a kind of theater that aims, in the words of Ivan Vyskočil, "to engage the intellect and the imagination of the spectator in order to force him to agree, disagree, compare, and view a subject matter from various angles."[2] Jan Grossman adds that this is absurdist theater of a special kind "in which the techniques associated with absurdism are deployed to provoke—and thereby 'activate'—the audience by creating within the play an empty space for audience self-reflection."[3] In my 2015 book *Reading Václav Havel* (Toronto: University of Toronto

---

1 Václav Havel, *Letters to Olga*, trans. Paul Wilson (New York: Henry Holt, 1983), letter 92.
2 Cited in Paul Trensky, *Czech Drama Since World War II* (New York: Columbia Slavic Studies, 1978), 105. For more on "theater" as a key word, see Barbara Day's chapter in this volume.
3 Jan Grossman, *Texty o divadle I* (Prague: Pražská scéna, 1999), 71.

Press),[4] I argue that the appeal component of Havel's thought should not be seen as limited to its dramatic incarnation. The concept of the appeal instead permeates his oeuvre as a whole: the meaningfulness of Havel's literary and political engagement arises precisely from its anchoring in the appeal form.

In the conclusion to that book, I make a preliminary attempt to analyze the words Havel uses to reference the notion of the appeal, chiefly *apel* and *výzva*, and I note that while the second of these words might be considered a key word in Havel's thinking, it presents challenges to the reader of Havel in English given the multiple pathways that exist for its translation. One Czech-English dictionary, for example, gives five possible translations for *výzva*: "call" (e.g., to begin boarding a plane), "appeal" or "plea," "summons" (in the bureaucratic sense), "prompt" (on a computer screen), and "challenge" (e.g., to a duel).[5] Given, then, the contextual difficulties involved in translating *výzva*, it represents a key-word motif in Havel's thought that is partially obscured in English (and no doubt other languages).

Here I will endeavor to flesh out that preliminary analysis in considerably more detail. I will first demonstrate more systematically the key-word status of words related to the notion of the appeal in Havel's writings with a primary focus on *výzva* (along with the related verbs *vyzývat/vyzvat*) and a secondary focus on *apel* (and the related verb *apelovat*), and I will then use the Czech National Corpus (CNC)[6] to develop a semantic-discourse portrait of these words and compare this portrait to Havel's own usage. The latter work entails both determining translation equivalents for these words in the CNC as well as in works by Havel (that is, in those that have been professionally translated into English) and also examining

---

4   Also published in Czech translation as *Číst Václava Havla*, trans. Stefan Segi (Prague: Argo Publishers, 2016).

5   Josef Fronek, *Velký česko-anglický slovník* (Prague: LEDA, 2000).

6   See https://korpus.cz.

collocations associated with these words in both the CNC and Havel's oeuvre. Taken as a whole, this detailed analysis will allow us to see more clearly the import of Havel's understanding of the "appeal" and to point to those ways that Havel embellishes or extends the basic sense of this concept (at least as this sense is reflected in the CNC). It will, as a result, enable us to recover the significance of the key-word motif turning on the notion of the "appeal" that is necessarily obscured in English translation.

The appeal motif in Havel's thought

Extrapolating the idea of the dramatic appeal to Havel's other genres,[7] we might note his tendency in many of the genres he engaged in to explicitly "activate" the reader's consciousness in completing the message of the work (the visual poetry of the anticodes and the collage-like framing of his political memoir *To the Castle and Back* are prime examples of this, but it runs arguably through all of his genres), his propensity to write political-philosophical essays in the form of open letters (sometimes called *apelativní dopisy* in Czech), and his prolific engagement, both prior to 1989 as a dissident and especially after 1989 as president, in the writing of various kinds of formal addresses (conference presentations, exhortations to protesters, political speeches), which could be taken as open letters that are spoken. On both macro- and micro-levels, Havel is a decidedly appeal-oriented thinker and writer, and I have already explored aspects of his literary and political engagement from this perspective in my book.

It should not, then, come as a surprise that words related to the appeal frequently occur in Havel's writing, and this cuts across both genres and time periods. For the purposes of this study, I analyzed

---

7   For a discussion of Havel's genres and the necessity of a mosaic-like approach to reading him, see Danaher, *Reading Václav Havel*, chapter 1.

a sampling of 60 Havel texts selected from a variety of genres from 1965 to 2006 for occurrences of appeal-oriented vocabulary.[8] Across all texts, I found a total of 181 instances of appeal-oriented vocabulary. Nine texts from the 1960s yield 25 instances; six texts from the 1970s yield 15; six more texts from the 1980s add 51 more (with 27 of those in the *Letters to Olga* alone); 33 speeches as president from the 1990s yield 66 examples; and one text from the 2000s (his presidential memoir) adds 24 instances to the total. The distribution of appeal-oriented words across these texts is the following:

Word	Instances	Total frequency
výzva (noun)	88	48.6%
vyzývat/vyzvat (verb)	50	27.6%
apel (noun)	28	15.5%
apelovat (verb)	11	6.1%
apelativní (adjective)	4	2.2%

As we can readily see from the chart, *výzva*-oriented words predominate (76.2% of the total) over *apel*-oriented ones (23.8%) and nouns (with 64.1% of the total) take precedence over other parts of speech.

While these numbers are not overwhelmingly significant against the background of the total number of words represented by these texts, the steady recurrence of appeal-oriented vocabulary is remarkable. Moreover, not all texts in my sample contain an appeal-oriented word (e.g., the 1985 essay "Thriller"), but a case could be made that even these (handful of) texts exemplify the appeal-orientation of Havel's thought, each in its own way—much like the plays themselves, which also do not contain explicit appeal vocabulary.

8   For a list of texts in my sample, see the appendix to this chapter. Most of these texts are available in their original Czech in Havel's collected works (*Spisy*, Prague: Torst, 1999) with speeches available online. I have cited Czech titles where English translations are not, to my knowledge, extant.

In sum, then, there is enough evidence to suggest even at the level of word usage that the concept of the "appeal" is a strong motif in Havel's thought, and that this motif is lexically instantiated in particular through *výzva* and related terms. What, however, do these words mean in Czech? Do they translate easily and consistently into English? If not, what might be obscured in the process of translation?

Translation equivalents for appeal-oriented words in both the CNC and Havel's writings

To seek answers to these questions, I first searched for translation equivalents for the nouns *apel* and *výzva* using the Treq tool in the CNC,[9] and the results provide both an initial impression of the semantic-discourse portrait for the Czech terms as well as a baseline summary of translation pathways.

Treq results for *apel* yield 88 results with approximately 77% of those rendered into English as, not surprisingly, "appeal." Approximately 7% of these instances have "call for" or "roll call" as translations, and indeed a military-style roll call is a secondary meaning for *apel* as listed in Czech dictionaries[10] with Fronek's Czech-English dictionary (cited above) listing this meaning as primary; we can also surmise that the "roll-call" meaning was uncomfortably familiar to Havel given the time he spent in prison (see Suk, this volume). More interestingly, a number of one-off translations via "challenge," "urge," "message," or "claim" also occur, and I list the first three of

---

9 Treq makes use of the InterCorp corpus, a parallel corpus containing over thirty languages and almost 1.5 billion words, to provide a database of translation equivalents. For more on Treq, see M. Vavřín and A. Rosen, *Treq* (Prague: FF UK, 2015) at http://treq.korpus.cz as well as M. Škrabal and M. Vavřín, "Databáze překladových ekvivalentů Treq", *Časopis pro moderní filologii* 99, no. 2 (2017): 245–260; for InterCorp, see https://intercorp.korpus.cz. Note that all searches in this study are based on lemmas, an approach which generates all possible grammatical forms of the given word.

10 See, for example, the 1966 edition of *Slovník spisovného jazyka českého*.

these contexts here to give a sense of the range of possible translation pathways:

(1) *Zkusme ji proto pochopit jako lekci či školu, jako zkoušku, jako apel, který možná přišel v pravou chvíli.* "Let us, therefore, understand it as a lesson, a test, a challenge that may have come just in time."

(2) *Odstavec 149 zprávy pana Catanii o situaci v oblasti lidských prav v Evropské unii chapu jako apel na členské státy, aby zajistili rovné zacházení s pacienty v systému zdravotní péče také ve vztahu k drogově závislým.* "I interpret paragraph 149 of Mr. Catania's report on the situation of fundamental rights in the European Union as urging Member States to ensure that the equal treatment of patients within the healthcare system also includes addicts."

(3) *Je mnohem důležitější tuto službu co nejdříve zřídit a vidět určité hmatatelné výsledky její činnosti, protože jedním z důležitých apelů Lisabonské smlouvy je požadavek, abychom Evropskou unii ve světě více zviditelnili.* "It is much more important to have this service set up as soon as possible and see some progress with it, because one of the most important messages of the Treaty of Lisbon is that we should be visible in the world."

The related verb *apelovat* occurs more frequently in Treq (515 contexts) with the following distribution of translations: "appeal" (58.1%), "call" (27%), "ask" (1.2%), "challenge" (.6%), "highlight" (.4%), "encourage" (.4%). In other words, while "appeal" may be the path-of-least-resistance and therefore predominant translation pathway for Czech *apel(ovat)*, the Czech term has a range of meaning that sometimes requires contextual specification via other English words, and this serves as valuable insight into Havel's conceptual starting point.

There are 8,789 instances of *výzva* as lemma in Treq, and translation equivalents prove both different and more varied:

Translation	Raw frequency	Proportional frequency
"challenge"	5764	65.6%
"call"	1676	19.1%
"invitation"	509	5.8%
"appeal"	348	4%
"notice"	108	1.2%
"request"	53	.6%
"dare"	41	.5%
"summons"	21	.2%
"plea"	19	.2%
"message"	14	.2%
"encouragement"	14	.2%
"signal" (among animals)	13	.1%
"urge"	10	.1%
"demand"	7	.1%

Other less well-represented translations are: "ask," "reminder," "warning," "exhortation," "provocation," "advice," and "command." Specific contexts for some of the less well-represented translation pathways, which give us a better picture of the potential meaning of the Czech term, are the following:

(4) *Poslední* <u>*výzva*</u> *na nástup do autobusu I-95 směrem na jih.* "Last <u>warning</u> for bus I-95 towards the south."[11]

(5) <u>*Výzvy*</u> *se opakovaly, stejně jako jejich podkreslení.* "The same <u>exhortations</u> were repeated, like punctuation also."

(6) *Začala se skrytymi* <u>*výzvami*</u>. "She started with veiled <u>provocations</u>."

(7) *Uposlechl vlastní* <u>*výzvy*</u>, *my rozněž.* "He responded to his own <u>commands</u>, and we followed suit."

11 Needless to say, some translations here are disputable: the last "call for boarding" would be better English than "warning."

(8) *To je nehorázná a pro Českou republiku i nesplnitelná <u>výzva</u>.* "This is an outrageous <u>demand</u> and one that cannot be fulfilled by the Czech Republic."

(9) *A na <u>výzvu</u> Velké Ley mnozí naši studenti vstali od svých počítačů, her a blogů.* "At Lea's <u>urging</u>, and under her supervision, many of our students left their computer games and blogs."

(10) *Grit, energický advokát najatý Mary Ross Phelanovou Jackmanovou povstal a pronesl válečnou <u>výzvu</u>.* "Grit, the feisty litigator hired by Mary Ross Phelan Jackman and her husband, stood and made a <u>plea</u> for war."

(11) *Myslíš, že odpovědi na <u>výzvu</u>?* "Will they answer the <u>summons</u>, think you?"

(12) *Hlas z megafonu <u>výzvu</u> opakuje.* "The voice from the megaphone repeats its <u>request</u>."

Data for the related verbal forms *vyzývat* (4,298 instances in Treq) and *vyzvat* (8,012 instances) provide an even more varied list of possible translation pathways. For the former, we observe "call" (43.6%), "invite" (19.7%), "ask" (7.7%), "urge" (5.2%), "say" (5%), "challenge" (4%), "encourage" (3.4%), "appeal" (2.7%), "request" (1.7%), "require" (1.3%), and "tell" (.9%) as well as one-off translations via "direct," "demand," "summon," "order," "dare," "suggest," "instruct," "exhort," "beckon," and "enjoin." For the latter, we have most of the above plus "recommend," "implore," "incite," "warn," "insist," and "charge."

If we summarize this data to begin to sketch out a semantic-discourse portrait of the concept of the appeal in Czech, we should first note that *výzva*-words are much more prominent than *apel*-words, and this fact helps to focus our analysis. We may also note that *výzva* and its related verbs are used in a wide range of domains from the personal (an "exhortation" or "plea") to the official (a "summons" or formal "notice"), and as a result our contextualized translations into English run the gamut. This makes good sense when we consider that a "challenge," the main translation for the noun *výzva*, is something that may also "ask," "invite," "encourage,", or even "dare" us to confront it. More strongly, perhaps, a particularly imperative challenge may "implore," "enjoin," "require," or even "order" us to take it up: it may "call out" to us to take a stance, if not also to take action. Here, then, we should also note the close relationship in Czech between the noun *výzva* and the verbs *vyzývat/vyzvat*: a *výzva* is implicitly understood as a context-specific verbalized "call" (like English "challenge" in "I challenge you to a duel"), and this call may be personalized in various ways or depersonalized in the sense that it is institutionally generated. English lacks a similar noun/verb pair that is both high-frequency in common usage and also freely crosses domains of human experience, which is another way of understanding why we have multiple pathways for translation of *výzva*-words.

Given this general background provided by data from the CNC, we are in a good position to examine translation equivalents for appeal-oriented vocabulary in texts by Havel that are included in my sample, and I limit myself here to those texts that have been professionally translated, which yields a total of 141 contexts. In these texts, we note 74 instances of the noun *výzva* with 28 uses of *vyzývat* or *vyzvat*, which is about 72% of the total of appeal-oriented vocabulary; there are 26 uses of *apel*, nine of the verb *apelovat*, and also four uses of the adjective *apelativní*,[12] which represents about 28% of the total vocabulary. In terms of distribution of vocabulary, then, Havel is more or less in conformity with general usage as represented in the CNC with the increased prominence of *výzva* words.

Indeed, translation pathways in Havel's writings also largely agree with the data in the CNC—with some significant differences to be discussed below. The main pathway for translating *apel* and *apelovat* is via "appeal" (about 67%) while the main pathway for translating

---

12 Note that *apelativní* is not represented in the CNC's InterCorp, which means that we do not have a baseline reading from Treq for translation equivalents.

the noun *výzva* is via "challenge" (about 60%). Examples of these primary translation pathways, which are from a range of decades and give us an initial sense of Havel's understanding of the terms, are the following:

(13) *A přesto jsem nakonec znovu kandidoval! Jako v minulých případech a jako ještě v jednom, který měl následovat, zvítězil i tentokrát <u>apel</u> na mou odpovědnost nad mými osobními zájmy.* "And yet I ran for president again. As in the previous election, and as it would also be in the one to follow, the <u>appeal</u> to my sense of responsibility won out over the pull of my private interests."[13]

(14) *Argumentaci Vašich odpůrců si dovedu živě představit: především asi zneužívají Vaší komunistické víry—zdůrazňují zájem strany, zájem hnutí, zájem socialismu; <u>apelují</u> na Vaši stranickou disciplínu; a to, co od Vás žádají, žádají jako službu věci, která Vám je nejdražší a které jste zasvětil svůj život.* "I can readily imagine how your opponents will argue. First and foremost, they will probably exploit your communist faith, stressing the interest of the party, of the movement, and of socialism. They will <u>appeal</u> to party discipline. And they will demand all this from you in the name of a cause that is dearest to you and to which you have devoted your life."[14]

(15) *Ježíšovu zvěst přijímám jako <u>výzvu</u> k vlastní cestě.* "I accept the Gospel of Jesus as a <u>challenge</u> to go my own way."[15]

(16) *Když před deseti lety začala vážně praskat ve švech a posléze se hroutit železná opona a když se pak spolu s ní začal propadat do historické minulosti i sám komunismus, málokdo z nás asi tušil, jak velké otázky se tím před lidstvem otevírají a jak velké <u>výzvy</u> tyto děje přinesou.* "Ten years ago, when the Iron Curtain began to crack and

13 Václav Havel, *Prosím stručně* (Prague: Gallery, 2006), 87 and Václav Havel, *To the Castle and Back*, trans. Paul Wilson (New York: Knopf, 2007), 170.
14 Václav Havel, "Dopis Alexandru Dubčekovi" in *Spisy* 3 (Prague: Torst, 1999), 914–915 and Václav Havel, "Letter to Alexander Dubček," trans. A. G. Brain, in *Open Letters: Selected Writings 1965–1990* (New York: Vintage, 1992), 39.
15 Havel, *Letters to Olga*, letter 41.

eventually crumbled and took Communism with it in its fall, probably few of us discerned the far-reaching questions that the human race became confronted with, or the great <u>challenges</u> that would be generated by these developments."[16]

(17) *Podle mého přesvědčení tento stav věcí obsahuje naprosto jasnou <u>výzvu</u> nejen euroamerickému světu, ale celé dnešní civilizaci. <u>Výzvu</u> k tomu, aby sebe samu začala vskutku důsledně chápat jako civilizaci multikulturní a multipolární, jejímž smyslem není ničit svébytnost různých kulturních či civilizačních okruhů, ale umožňovat jim naopak, aby byly lépe samy sebou.* "It is my belief that this state of affairs contains a clear <u>challenge</u> not only to the Euro-American world but to our present-day civilization as a whole. It is a <u>challenge</u> to this civilization to start understanding itself as a multicultural and a multipolar civilization, whose meaning lies not in undermining the individuality of different spheres of culture and civilization but in allowing them to be more completely themselves."[17]

Three examples of where the translator has chosen less typical pathways that are also represented in the CNC data—"urge" for *apelovat*, "invite" and "invitation" for *vyzvat* and *výzva*, and "warning" for *výzva*—are the following:

(18) *A tak jsem napsal obsáhlý veřejný dopis dr. Husákovi, v němž jsem se pokusil rozebrat smutnou společenskou situaci v naší zemi, ukázat na hloubku duchovní, morální a sociální krize, která se skrývá za zdánlivě poklidným životem, a v němž jsem na adresáta <u>apeloval</u>, aby si uvědomil míru své odpovědnosti za tu celkovou mizerii.* "So I wrote a long open letter to Husak. In it, I tried to analyze the sad situation in our country; to point to the profound spiritual, moral, and social crisis hidden behind the

---

16 Václav Havel, "Address to the French Senate," 1999.
17 Václav Havel, "Harvard University," 1995.

apparent tranquility of social life. I urged Husak to realize just how much he himself was responsible for this general misery."[18]

(19) *Má tvářistická éra začala, až když mne nová redakční rada (prý na návrh Jana Lopatky) vyzvala, abych se stal jejím členem. Tato výzva nebyla zcela prosta věcného kalkulu.* "My real association with *Tvář* began when the new editorial board, apparently at the suggestion of Jan Lopatka, invited me to join them. This invitation was not entirely free of ulterior motive."[19]

(20) *Buď strčit hlavu do písku, globálními a dlouhodobými problémy se nijak osobně netrápit v naději, že za našeho života se nás ještě nijak katastrofálně nedotknou, a starat se o tento den či o zítřek, případně— jsme-li politici—o svůj image dnes či zítra v televizi či o své vítězství v nejbližších volbách. A na varovné výzvy či dotazy těch, kteří se tím vším trápí, odpovídat prostě tvrzením, že moderní věda nepochybně přinese další vymoženosti, které tyto problémy vyřeší. Druhou možností je přemýšlet o celé situaci vskutku vážně, byť s vědomím rizika, že se naše přemýšlení či výzvy, které z něho vzejdou, nemusí dočkat žádné odezvy.* "We can take the ostrich-like approach, disregarding the long-term global problems in the hope that they will have no fatal effects within our lifetime and concerning ourselves instead just with today and tomorrow, or—when we happen to be politicians—with our momentary image on television or with our chance of winning the next elections. We can dismiss the warning appeals or questions of those who are worried with a simple answer: that modern science will undoubtedly produce new achievements to solve these problems. The other alternative is to give the situation a truly serious consideration, even risking the outcome that our thoughts or warnings may go unheeded."[20]

18 Václav Havel, *Dálkový výslech* in *Spisy* 4 (Prague: Torst, 1999), 825 and Václav Havel, *Disturbing the Peace*, trans. Paul Wilson (New York: Vintage, 1991), 122.
19 Havel, *Dálkový výslech*, 777 and Havel, *Disturbing the Peace*, 76.
20 Václav Havel, "The Latin American Parliament," 1996.

These examples give us a sense of the variety of contexts in which Havel uses appeal-oriented vocabulary, and we also see the beginnings—in examples (15), (16), (17), and (20)—of an expanded understanding on Havel's part of the concept, in which we leave the domain of the everyday "appeal" (or "invitation" or "urging") and are confronted instead with a sense of existential urgency in the given situation. The "appeal" for Havel, in other words, begins to take on philosophical contours.

Perhaps more interestingly, Havel does use appeal-oriented vocabulary in ways that differ from the data in the CNC. I would note, for example, that the sense of *výzva* as an official "summons" or formal "notice" is downplayed in Havel's usage except for an occasional reference to a public document, like Charter 77, as an "appeal" (*apel*). He also sometimes uses both Czech words, *apel* and *výzva*, side-by-side in the same context for added emphasis, and we see this both in the epigraph to this chapter, which I will return to in due course, and in this example in which Havel is writing about human consciousness of death:

> (21) *… je ovšem i zde, na rovině existenciální, smrt v nás přítomna nikoli jako to, s čím je třeba se identifikovat, ale naopak jako to, čemu je třeba čelit, co je třeba nějak překonat, překlenout, popřít. Lze říci, že vědomí smrti je ve struktuře lidské existence něčím jako <u>výzvou</u>, hozenou rukavicí, <u>apelem</u>, provokací, zkrátka něčím mobilizujícím a probouzejícím.* "On the existential level, too, death is present in us not as something with which we must identify, but which must be defied, overcome, spanned, denied. We might say that in the structure of human existence, the awareness of death is something like a <u>challenge</u>, a gauntlet flung down, an <u>appeal</u>, a provocation, in short, something that has the power to mobilize and arouse."[21]

---

21 Havel, *Letters to Olga*, letter 97.

This example, in addition to the context of the epigraph, again pushes the implications of Havel's appeal-orientation into the philosophical domain.

Another difference that becomes clear when professional translations of Havel's texts are examined is the greater frequency of translation (of all words) via English "challenge." For contexts with *apel* in the CNC, "challenge" is the pathway in only one of 88 examples (less than 1% of the total), but in Havel's texts the percentage of the total jumps to 19% (five examples out of 26 in total). The verbs *vyzývat/vzyvat* are rendered as "challenge" in 4% of the contexts in the CNC, but in 25% of the contexts in Havel's texts. Two examples of this tendency are the following:

(22) *Lze říct, že tento absolutní horizont je v nás tedy přítomen nejen jako předpoklad, ale i jako zdroj lidskosti a <u>apel</u> [...]* "It might be said, therefore, that this absolute horizon is present in us not only as an assumption, but also as a source of humanity and as a <u>challenge</u> [...]"[22]

(23) *To všechno je neskonale důležitější, než si asi většina lidí myslí. Klade to totiž zcela zvláštní nároky nejen na stavbu hry, ale vůbec na všechny zákonitosti jejího světa, který musí být na takto daném půdorysu cele rozvinut a kontinuálně pochopitelným způsobem obsažen; který musí být vybudován tak, aby se to dalo vydržet (čili: aby na to vůbec někdo přišel, aby tedy divadlo vůbec mohlo být) a aby o sobě samém něco víceméně zřetelného řekl, aby vůbec něco určitého vyvolal; hra musí být prostě napsána tak, aby tu „dobrodružnou stezku" vůbec stihla v takto ohraničených podmínkách naznačit a k cestě po ní <u>vyzvat</u>, přičemž publikum musí v takto omezeném čase získat jakous takous představu, proč vůbec mělo vynaložit tu námahu a přijít na start (tj. do divadla).* "All of this is far more important than most people suppose. It makes special demands not only on the structure of a play, but on all the laws of its world, which within the given plan, must be fleshed out in a way that is

---

22 Havel, *Letters to Olga*, letter 95.

consistently comprehensible. It must be constructed in a way that can be tolerated, that is, so people will actually come to see it, so the theater, in other words, can exist at all. A play, quite simply, must stake out that 'adventurous trail' and challenge people to go down it, and in the limited time available, the audience must be given an inkling at least of why it should make the effort to show up at the head of the trail (i.e., come to the theater) in the first place."[23]

In (22), Havel is musing philosophically on what human responsibility (understood here as an orientation toward the "absolute horizon") means, and in (23) he is discussing the intellectual and spiritual significance of theater as a genre. In both instances (and in more like these), Havel's English translators have gravitated toward the "challenge" reading, which is undoubtedly prompted by the contexts—philosophical and theoretical—in which Havel uses the words.

Another deviation from the CNC data is the presence of translation choices that do not appear in Treq. I will mention only two words here, that is, "opportunity" for *výzva* and "impel" for *vyzývat*. Examples of these are:

(24) *Čili: nenavštěvovat jen generální štáb, ale pořádat i krátké přepady jednotek. Teď máme jednu rotu kousek od Sarajeva. Není to přímo* výzva *k tomu, abych ji tam na půl dne navštívil? Dřív než se rozhoupe Zieleniec či Baudyš?* "In other words: we shouldn't visit just the general headquarters but arrange brief, unannounced visits to individual units as well. Right now, we have a company based a short distance from Sarajevo. Doesn't that provide an opportunity for me to visit them for a half a day, before Zieleniec or Baudys swing into action?"[24]

(25) *Mám jeden nápad související s povodněmi. Bylo zničeno mnoho ošklivých domů postavených špatně, draze a na nesprávném místě.*

23 Havel, *Letters to Olga*, letter 114.
24 Havel, *Prosím stručně*, 14 and Havel, *To the Castle and Back*, 28.

Povodeň je <u>*výzvou*</u> *k tomu, abychom dali naší zemi tu a tam trochu lepší tvář. Hrozí však pravý opak: lidé budou pospíchat a budou stavět ještě větší potvornosti, než jaké měli dosud.* "I have one idea related to the floods. Many ugly buildings, badly and expensively constructed and in the wrong place, were destroyed. A flood is an <u>opportunity</u> for us to give our country a slightly improved appearance here and there. But the danger is that exactly the opposite will happen: that people will be in a hurry and build something even uglier than they had before."[25]

(26) *[O]kolnost, že mám čest mluvit v tak slavném středisku evropské vzdělanosti, jakým je Oxford, a na tak slavné univerzitě, jakou je ta zdejší, mne přímo* <u>*vyzývá*</u> *k tomu, abych se tu zamyslel nad tématem 'intelektuál a politika'. Tedy nad tématem, o němž jsem nucen často přemýšlet a na které jsem často tázán.* "The fact that I have the honour to speak in such a famous centre of European education as Oxford, and at such a renowned university, virtually <u>impels</u> me to dwell here upon the theme of 'the intellectual and politics'—a subject that I have often had occasion to think about and to discuss."[26]

Translation via "opportunity" in the first two contexts (both of which represent different kinds of political or public-policy "opportunities") suggests that Havel reads the world through an appeal-oriented lens: certain external developments might "call out" a different approach than might normally be considered, and these then become "opportunities" for a new strategy. The third context with "impel" is similar in that the "opportunity" to speak at Oxford strongly suggests to Havel his choice of topic. In neither of these contexts could the translator have opted for translation via "challenge," which leads us to conclude that the Czech words have a semantic-discourse range that is not matched by any one English word-root.

25   Havel, *Prosím stručně*, 74 and Havel, *To the Castle and Back*, 103.
26   Václav Havel, "Address in Acceptance of an Honorary Degree from Oxford University," 1998.

More interesting are several contexts in Havel's works featuring uniquely contextualized translations that highlight the (potential) urgency of the given "appeal," and this aspect of Czech appeal-oriented vocabulary is already implied in some of the translation pathways we have seen in the CNC data. Examples here include:

(27) [What were your expectations when you finished the letter to Husák?] *Hlavní, co mne zajímalo, bylo, jestli ten text je dobrý, totiž jestli má hlavu a patu, jestli není příliš abstraktní a nudný, jestli je z něho cítit i určitý apel—jinak by to mohla být esej a ne dopis.* "I was mainly interested in whether the text was good, that is, if it made sense, if it wasn't too abstract and boring, if it radiated a certain sense of exhortation, of urgency—otherwise I might as well have written it as an essay, not a letter."[27]

(28) *Byl jsem nedávno na jedné docela spontánní a žádnými disidenty neorganizované manifestaci, protestující proti výprodeji nejkrásnějších částí Prahy nějakým australským milionářům. A když tam jeden řečník, bouřlivě proti tomuto projektu vystupující, chtěl posílit svůj apel na vládu zdůrazněním, že za záchranu svého domova bojuje ve jménu socialismu, začal se shromážděný dav smát.* "I was recently at a spontaneous demonstration, not dissident-organized, protesting the sell-off of one of the most beautiful parts of Prague to an Australian millionaire. When one of the speakers there sought to bolster his stormy denunciation of the project by declaring that he was fighting for his home in the name of socialism, the crowd started to laugh."[28]

(29) *Není pravda, že dík televizi, filmu, videu a jiným velkým vymoženostem této doby ztrácí divadlo na významu. Řekl bych, že je tomu právě naopak a že právě divadlo je lépe, než co jiného, způsobilé odkrývat*

27 Václav Havel, "It Always Makes Sense to Tell the Truth," trans. Paul Wilson in *Open Letters*, 85.

28 Václav Havel, "Slovo o slovu" in *Spisy* 4, 1134 and Václav Havel, "A Word about Words," trans. A. G. Brain, in *Open Letters*, 383.

vskutku <u>apelativním</u> způsobem vše temné, čemu svět propadá, i vše světlé, v čem spočívá jeho naděje. "It is not true that because of television, film, video, and the other great achievements of this era, theatre is dwindling in importance. I would say that exactly the opposite is true, that theatre is better-suited than any other medium to reveal, in genuinely <u>compelling and challenging</u> ways, not only all the dark forces that are dragging the world down, but also everything bright and luminous, in which its hopes are contained."[29]

(30) *Posílám projev k 17. listopadu. Nejsem s ním zcela spokojen, zdá se mi být trochu kostrbatý, málo <u>apelativní</u>. […] Uzávěrka připomínek v pátek v poledne, neboť v sobotu to budu definitivně redigovat.* "I am sending the speech for November 17. I'm not entirely happy with it. It seems to me to be a little rough and <u>does not have a strong enough message</u> […] The deadline for remarks is noon on Friday, because I intend to do the final edit on Saturday."[30]

In each of these cases, which come from a variety of genres (an interview, an essay, a speech, a memoir) and which span the 1989 divide, the translator has clearly felt that a path-of-least-resistance translation does not suffice to convey Havel's intention. Something extra must be done to underscore the urgency of the original-Czech "appeal." In (27), then, *apel* becomes a "sense of exhortation, of urgency" and in (28) the same word is elaborated to imply a "stormy denunciation" of the project that is being described; in (29) the adjective *apelativní* is rendered as "compelling and challenging" and in (30) the phrase *málo apelativní* (literally, "only a little appellative") is translated as not having "a strong enough message."

A final difference concerns a number of contexts in the Havel corpus where appeal-oriented vocabulary in the original Czech is

29 Václav Havel, "International Theatre Day," 1994.
30 Havel, *Prosím stručně*, 26 and Havel, *To the Castle and Back*, 32.

simply left out in English translation.[31] Two examples of this, one with *výzva* and one with *apelativní*, are:

(31) *Důvod tohoto smutného stavu je prostý: tkví v pocitu, že výzvu dějin lze obelstít, a v pštrosím přesvědčení, že nutnost velkorysého a obětavého angažmá lze nahradit pouhým smiřováním bojovníků a ustupováním jejich nárokům.* "The reason for this sad state of affairs is simple. It lies in the belief that we can somehow outwit [not translated] history and in the ostrich-like belief that the place of the need for generous and dedicated commitment can be taken by the appeasement of warring factions and by giving in to their demands."[32]

(32) *Izolacionismus se Spojeným státům nikdy nevyplatil. Kdyby bývaly dříve vstoupily do první světové války, zdaleka by za ni nemusely zaplatit tolika oběťmi. Totéž platí o druhé světové válce: vzpomínám si, že když se Hitler chystal přepadnout tehdejší Československo a provést tím poslední zkoušku nestatečnosti západních demokracií, psal váš prezident našemu prezidentovi apelativní dopis, v němž ho žádal, aby se, proboha, nějak s Hitlerem domluvil.* "Isolationism has never paid off for the United States. Had it entered the First World War earlier, perhaps it would not have had to pay with anything like the casualties it actually incurred. The same is true of the Second World War: when Hitler was getting ready to invade Czechoslovakia, and in so doing finally expose the lack of courage on the part of the western democracies, your President wrote a [not translated] letter to the Czechoslovak President imploring him to come to some agreement with Hitler."[33]

In (31), the "call" of history is rendered simply as "history" and in (32) the adjective that Havel insists on in the original Czech is left out in translation. These examples illustrate that even a professional

---

31 In the CNC, we cannot, of course, determine when these words are not translated, so we have no good way to compare how often lack of translation occurs on a wider scale.

32 Václav Havel, "Council of Europe Summit," 1993.

33 Havel, "Harvard University," 1995.

translator struggles in certain contexts to maintain Havel's invocations of the concept of the "appeal," and this despite the range of possible translation pathways that we have seen in the CNC data.

Collocates for *výzva* in the CNC

Translation equivalents go a long way to sketching a semantic-discourse portrait of Czech appeal-oriented vocabulary in comparison with English, but we can further refine this portrait by examining collocates, that is, words that typically co-occur with a given lemma in discourse. According to Paul Baker, analysis of this kind "elucidates semantic preference,"[34] which means that it indicates a possible relationship between a given lemma and a set of semantically related words. Baker goes on to note that when two words frequently collocate, then there "is evidence that the discourses surrounding them are particularly powerful,"[35] and he gives the example of the word "rising" in the British National Corpus, which co-occurs with "incomes, prices, wages, earnings."[36] Unlike Baker, I am less concerned here with statistically significant collocates and more with the overall picture that emerges from collocational analysis—and, indeed, a coherent picture does emerge.

Here I limit the scope of analysis to Czech and specifically to the noun *výzva* as lemma in both the CNC and in Havel's writings. In examining each of these sources, I relied on manual analysis of the discourse contexts. For data in the CNC, I searched *výzva* as a lemma using the concordance tool KonText with a specification of plus or minus five places, and this yielded over 6,000 contexts; my analysis focuses on a randomly generated sample of 500 of these contexts. In examining my subset of Havel's texts, I looked at all 88 contexts

---

34 Paul Baker. *Using Corpora in Discourse Analysis* (London: Continuum, 2007), 86.
35 Baker, *Using Corpora in Discourse Analysis*, 114.
36 Baker, *Using Corpora in Discourse Analysis*, 86.

with *výzva* and also focused on which words co-occurred five places before and after. For the CNC data, I divided collocates into groups largely by part of speech and noted the most frequently co-occurring words in each group. Given the large amount of data present in the CNC, I will eschew lengthy exemplification and present instead a summary of the overall picture that emerges, and then compare this to Havel's usage.

We might first note that some of the collocates in the CNC make reference to *výzva* as an official call (e.g., to solicit proposals for a competition), a meaning that we noted is not emphasized by Havel. Thus we have five contexts with the adjective *vyhlášená* (some kind of call that has been officially "announced") and 14 with the verbs *vyhlašovat/vyhlásit* ("to announce, declare"). Other data in the sample point to a more general tendency for the "call" or "appeal" to originate with some kind of (presumably) authoritative voice in one domain or another, and we might then understand the official *výzva* as a special kind of authoritative "call" that emerges from an administrative/bureaucratic domain.

Data in the CNC also capture quite vividly that *výzva* is regularly used in a wide range of domains from the personal through the interpersonal to the cultural and political, and we can chart this by looking at contexts where *výzva* combines with the prepositions *pro* (that is, an appeal or call "for" some entity), *k* (an appeal or call "to" or "for" someone or something) as well as in contexts where *výzva* is modified by a noun in the genitive case (that is, the appeal or call "of some entity"). In contexts with *pro*, we have the following data: *pro mě* ("for me") occurs eleven times, *pro nás* ("for us") seven times while *pro člověka* ("for [generic] man"), *pro církev* ("for the church"), *pro cyklisty* ("for cyclists"), *pro čtenáře* ("for readers"), and *pro oblasti* ("for [administrative] regions") each occur twice; there are 26 other one-off contexts with *pro* that invoke domains ranging from individual people (e.g., "for Mirek") to more generic categories (eg, "for employers, for actors, for the future"). The

67 contexts with *k* suggest even greater diversity: we see three occurrences of both the phrasal construction *k tomu, aby*... (a call or appeal "to do something") and the administrative *k podání nabídek* (a call "for sending proposals") and two occurrences of the phrase *k boji* (a call "to battle, arms"), which is likely a fixed phrase; the remainder are one-off contexts that instantiate a wide variety of domains (e.g., *k toleranci* ["for tolerance"], *k bojkotu* ["for a boycott"], *k zákazu filmu* ["to ban the film"], *k vytvoření tajné společnosti* ["to create a secret society"], *k evakuaci lodi* ["to evacuate the boat"]). The modification of *výzva* by a noun in the genitive is much less represented in the data with only 26 instances, but the same tendency for the "appeal" to cross domains of human experience—as well as to originate from a domain-specific authority figure—is present, for example, *výzva policisty* ("of/by the police officer"), *výzva radnice* ("of/by city hall"), *výzva teoritiků* ("of/by the theoreticians"), *výzva majitele bytu* ("of/by the owner of the apartment"), *výzva iniciativy* ("of/by the initiative"), *výzva průvodčího vlaku* ("of/by the train conductor").

What emerges from this data is that *výzva* is used as some kind of prompt in a given domain, and that we can seemingly interpret just about anything as an "appeal" in this sense, although we typically register the "appeal" by sight or hearing. I would also highlight here the large number of collocates that suggest the process of interpreting, understanding, or perceiving something as *výzva*, and these are most readily evident in verbal collocates: we have six contexts with the verbal phrase *brát/vzít jako výzvu* ("to take something as an appeal"), five with *představovat* ("to represent" something), four with *chápat/pochopit jako* ("to understand something as"), four with *vnímat jako* ("to perceive as"), and a number of discursively similar one-off collocates such as *identifikovat* ("to identify"), *interpretovat jako* ("to interpret as"), *považovat za* ("to consider something as"), *vidět jako* ("to see as"), *znět jako* ("to sound like"). The CNC data, then, seems also to emphasize the very process by which something is ascertained as a (genuine) *výzva*, and much more often than not the word is used to note the acceptance of this "appeal," although we have a handful of negated contexts where the existence of the "appeal" is denied.

Adjectival collocates further imply that *výzva* is often modified by a word that intensifies it. The more or less synonymous adjectives *velká/veliká* ("big") occur in combination with *výzva* 15 times in the CNC data, which is the most frequently occurring adjectival collocate. Other adjectives synonymous with *velká* that are present in the data include *obrovská* ("huge"), which occurs six times; *největší* ("the biggest"), which occurs four times; *ohromná* ("enormous"), which occurs twice; and *větší* ("bigger"), also occurring twice. We note adjectival collocates that emphasizes the genuineness of the "appeal", for example, *opravdová* ("real, genuine") and *skutečná* ("real, true"), each occurring three times. There are a number of adjectives that refer to the large scope of the "appeal": the twice-occurring *globální* ("global") in addition to *celospolečenská* ("society-wide"), *osudová* ("fateful, crucial"), *všeobecná* ("general, universal"), and *značná* ("significant"), each of which occurs once. Other adjectival collocates bring out the urgency of the given "appeal" for the present day or for other implied specific reasons (e.g., it is a moral imperative), and these include the twice-occurring *aktuální* ("topical, current") and *morální* ("moral") as well as the one-off adjectives *každodenní* ("everyday"), *barbarská* ("barbaric"), *bojovná* ("militant, combative"), and *mimořádná* ("exceptional, extraordinary"). The adjectival collocate in second place in terms of frequency in the corpus with fourteen instances is *nová* ("new"), which implies that the "appeal" is something perhaps unexpected that we try to take in and understand: it breaks us out of conventional ways of seeing the world. A final point in regard to adjectival collocates is that they reinforce the impression that usage of *výzva* spans a considerable range of experiential domains, for example, the (inter)personal domain (*osobní* ["personal"] occurs twice along with all possessive modifiers, each at least once), the domain of science (*onkologická* ["oncological"], *ekologická* ["ecological"]), the domain of business (*ekonomická*, ["economic"], occurring twice, and both *manažerská* ["managerial"] and *pracovní* ["work, occupational"], each of which occurs once).

A final point about usage of *výzva* that is discursively highlighted in the CNC data is its status as a provocation, large or small, that we are expected to react to in some way: we accept it (or not) as a "challenge," we position ourselves in reference to it in some way, we confront or ignore it, we struggle with it. Verbal collocates that serve to create this strong impression include *reagovat na* ("react to") and variant forms with 14 occurrences, *přijmout* ("accept") with five, *odpovídat na* ("respond to") and variant forms with four, *čelit* ("confront") with three, *odmítnout* ("deny") with three, *postavit se* ("adopt a stance toward") with three, *ignorovat* ("ignore") with two, *podporovat* ("support") with two, and a large number of one-off verbs that include *adresovat* ("address"), *bojovat s* ("struggle with"), *konfrontovat* ("confront"), *necouvnout před* ("not back away from"), *nenechat bez odpovědi* ("to not leave with an answer"), *stavět se k* ("to position oneself in relation to"), *ustoupit od* ("step back from"), and *zapomenout na* ("to forget about"). To further reinforce this point, we also have 17 contexts in the CNC data where *výzva* is combined with active constructions that indicate what should, in fact, be done in terms of a reaction: in Czech these constructions are rendered as *výzva, aby…* and *výzva, ať'…*

A collocational analysis of Havel's conception of *výzva*

The CNC data fills out the semantic-discourse portrait coherently, and we are now in a better position to consider Havel's works in light of it. Quite simply put, Havel eagerly builds on the semantic-discourse base as it is represented in the CNC in order to endow the concept of the "appeal," as we have seen in examples above, with philosophical force. While he himself may not emphasize, for example, the bureaucratic meaning of *výzva* that is present in the CNC data, he does rely on the word's association with a domain-specific authoritative voice of some kind, although often that "voice" is much less literal than it is metaphorical. Indeed, commanding voices of one sort or another arguably abound in Havel's works (for example, the authorial voice that interrupts action in his last play *Leaving* or the voice of conscience that compels Havel to pay his fare on the empty night tram[37]), and this even without the explicit presence of an appeal-oriented word.

In terms of appeal-oriented vocabulary, however, we note a commanding voice, most literally and prosaically, in example (19) where the authority figure appealing to Havel is one of the members of the journal *Tvář*. Metaphorically speaking, we see the same process at work in example (16) where Havel asserts that the human race will be confronted with "great challenges" resulting from the fall of the Iron Curtain: history itself is, then, the voice of authority that harkens to us to heed its call. Examples (17), (20), and (25) are similar: in the first, the "voice" challenging us is the historical rise of a multicultural, multipolar civilization; in the second, it is the collective "voice" of historically unprecedented global challenges currently facing humanity; and in the third, it is the historical event of mass flooding that seems to "call out" to Havel to try something different. Example (21) is unambiguously spiritual: death is metaphorized as the authoritative voice that "throws down a gauntlet" to challenge us to think more deeply about how best to live, a provocative idea that is obviously not unique to Havel.

Havel also relies on *výzva*'s usage, as we saw in the CNC data, across domains of human experience. He himself views small things in his own personal and official life in terms of the "appeal," but

---

37 Václav Havel, *Leaving*, trans. Paul Wilson (New York: Theater 61 Press, 2012); the night tram is described in Havel, *Letters to Olga*, letter 137.

then extrapolates outward to larger-scale events to the point that, as we saw just above, the state of the world itself becomes a grand *výzva* for humanity. Indeed, this is a strongly recurring theme in his post-1989 presidential addresses, each of which, in its own way, seems to present an aspect of humanity's then-current condition as an "appeal" or "challenge" to the listener. In this respect, *výzva* is not a unique keyword in Havel's thinking: the baseline usages of many of Havel's keywords tend to span domains of human experience from the (inter)personal to the cultural, and Havel has a tendency to apply these concepts to ever larger-scale domains (e.g., politics and philosophy). I am thinking particularly here of *svědomí* ("conscience"), *klid* and *neklid* ("tranquility" and "restlessness"), and *lidskost* ("humanity, human[e]ness"), but we could add, from this volume, *domov* ("home[land]"), *pravda* ("truth"), *odpovědnost* ("responsibility"), and *moc* ("power").[38]

Given that conventional usage of *výzva* already spans domains of experience, Havel's extension of its import to the political-philosophical domain is a natural one. In fact, one main point of difference between collocates in the CNC and in Havel's usage is the strong presence of political-philosophical vocabulary in the latter. Collocates that illustrate this include: *doba* ("era"), which occurs seven times; *svět* ("world"), six times; *přemýšlení* ("thought, thinking"), *odpovědnost* ("responsibility"), *demokracie* ("democracy"), occurring three times each; *transcendence* ("transcendence") and *lidstvo* ("humanity"), occurring twice; and one-off words and phrases such as *lidský rod* ("the human race"), *dějiny* ("history"), *zásadní rekonstrukce* ("fundamental reconstruction"), *krize* ("crisis"), *varování* ("warning"), *dialog* ("dialogue"), *postkomunismus* ("post-communism"), *pokora* ("humility"), *slušné chování* ("decent, moral behavior"),

---

38 For *domov, svědomí,* and *(ne)klid),* see Danaher, *Reading Václav Havel,* chapter 4. For *lidskost,* see David S. Danaher, "Revolution with a 'Human' Face: A Corpus Approach to the Semantics of Czech *lidskost*" (in *Taming the Corpus: From Inflection and Lexis to Interpretation,* eds. Masako Fidler and Václav Cvrček, New York: Springer, 119-144).

přítomnost ("the present day"), *dnešní člověk* ("contemporary humanity"), *autenticita* ("authenticity"), *sebereflexe* ("self-reflection"), and *solidarita* ("solidarity"). Words with a political-philosophical import make up almost a third of all collocates for *výzva* in Havel's texts, which represents a substantial departure from the CNC data. We might note, however, that in many of these contexts Havel relies upon *výzva*'s association, as documented in the CNC data, with an intensified or large-scale experience, genuineness, newness, and urgency as a conceptual starting point underlying the political-philosophical twist he gives them.

In relation to Havel's extension of the concept of the "appeal" to the philosophical domain, we should also point out that the text with the most instances of appeal-oriented vocabulary (15% of the total in my subset of Havel's writings) is *Letters to Olga* (1979-1983). Here Havel develops his understanding of the "appeal" by embellishing the standard definition of the word and raising it to the level of a philosophical concept. These were prison letters, written ostensibly to his first wife, Olga, but we know now that Havel was also addressing a group of Czechoslovak intellectuals who engaged with him in a philosophical back-and-forth.[39] In my book, I argue that these letters function as *explications du texte* for the rest of Havel's writings: they are meta-versions of his other texts, the underlying code for the more concrete or genre-specific manifestations of his thinking, and they act as a mediating frame or grid, a philosophically schematized reduction of Havel's understanding of human identity.[40] It is no surprise to note, then, that appeal-oriented vocabulary forms a strong motif in them.

---

39 For more on this group, known as Kampademie because it gathered on the Prague island of Kampa, see Daniel Kroupa, *Dějiny Kampademie* (Prague: Václav Havel Library, 2010). See also Martin C. Putna and Ivan Havel, *Dopisy od Olgy* (Prague: Václav Havel Library, 2010). For more on "prison" as a key word, see Jiří Suk's chapter in this volume.
40 Danaher, *Reading Václav Havel*, 47-48.

We might summarize this motif by suggesting that Havel tends to view the world as an aesthetic object of sorts, one that has a strong appeal component. He "reads" the world around him in the same way that he urges an audience to interpret one of his appellative plays. As an aestheticized object, the world is replete with signs that we should understand as "prompts" for serious reflection and sometimes even urgent action, and our response to these signs imbues our lives with a kind of transcendent, and perhaps even cathartic, meaning. In this scenario, then, it is Being itself whose voice "appeals" to us, calling us out to engage with it.[41] Indeed, Havel's ultimate philosophical position is that if we read the world as an appeal, then we have an obligation to react, which is another aspect of the meaning of *výzva* in the CNC that Havel takes as a fertile jumping-off point. In this regard we should emphasize that the two most frequent collocates with *výzva* in Havel's texts are the preposition *k* (present in 43% of the contexts) and the active construction *aby* (present in 17%), each of which is used considerably more frequently in Havel's writings than in the CNC data and each of which presents the "appeal" in terms of an end-goal reaction. The focus is, in other words, on our response to being called out: a *výzva* expects an appropriate *odezva* ("response, echo").

These considerations, then, bring us back to the epigraph to this study, which is, not surprisingly, also from Havel's prison letters. Here Havel adds an additional component to his extension of *výzva*'s meaning, which is that the appeal-oriented framework for thinking about and being in the world ought simultaneously to serve as an antidote to ideological petrification.

---

41   For more on this reading, see the conclusion to Danaher, *Reading Václav Havel.*

Conclusion

A semantic-discourse portrait of Czech vocabulary related to the "appeal"—especially as compared, at least partially, to English—enhances our understanding of Havel as an appeal-oriented writer. By way of concluding this study, I mention several central ways in which it does so.

(1) Havel uses appeal-oriented vocabulary, especially *výzva* and its related forms, throughout his intellectual and political career(s). The idea of *apel* is, moreover, a cornerstone of his theatrical style, and we can say that his plays as performances enact the very concept of the "appeal" that we have examined here lexically.

(2) In using this vocabulary, Havel both relies on and strategically embellishes the baseline meaning(s) captured by the CNC data in order to endow the concept with philosophical force. Havel takes a word that has wide usage in Czech across a variety of experiential domains and situates it as a key philosophical concept for thinking through what it means to be human in the late 20th and early 21st centuries. We must, Havel urges, learn to hear and heed the world's authoritative "appeal" in order to solve the problems that confront us.

(3) At least some of Havel's thinking in this regard risks being distorted or even lost in translation, given that English concepts of "appeal" or "challenge" are not translation equivalents in the strict sense. Havel's conceptual starting point is, then, different from those of his English-speaking readers, who may not be in a linguistic position to fully appreciate the import of this motif.

(4) We might conclude by noting that *výzva* is a key word that calls out to other key words in Havel's thinking, many of which are analyzed elsewhere in this volume. Indeed, we might best understand Havel's key concepts as collectively forming a network: they intersect and interweave with one another, likes roads on a map.

Appendix

The texts in my sample, listed chronologically, are below; I also indicate the genre as well as the number of instances of appeal-oriented vocabulary in each.

"Address at the Conference of Writers" (address; 1965; 2)

"Address to the Congress of Writers" (address; 1967; 2)

"Falešné dilema [A False Dilemma]" (essay; 1968; 1)

"Výzva spoluobčanům [A Call to My Fellow Citizens]" (appellative text; 1968; 2)

"Pět rozhlasových projevů ze srpna 1968 [Five Radio Addresses from August 1968]" (address; 1968; 6)

"Czech Destiny?" (essay; 1969; 2)

"Zvlástní příhoda [A Strange Event]" (essay; 1969; 1)

"Letter to Dubček" (open letter;1969; 3)

"Vystoupení v Československé televizi [Appearance on Czechoslovak TV]" (address; 1969; 6)

"Dear Dr. Husák" (open letter; 1975; 1)

"It always makes sense to tell the truth" (interview; 1975; 2)

"The Trial" (essay; 1976; 3)

"Power of the Powerless" (essay; 1978; 1)

"Zpráva o mé účasti na plesu [Report on My Participation in a Dance]" (report; 1978; 7)

"Reports on My House Arrest" (report; 1979; 1)

Letters to Olga (letters collected in a book; 1979–1983; 27)

"Anatomy of Reticence" (essay; 1985; 2)

Disturbing the Peace (collaborative book; 1985–1986; 16)

"Projev k demonstrantům [Speech to Protesters]" (address; 10 December 1989; 1)

"Projev k demonstrantům [Speech to Protesters]" (address; 25 November 1989; 1)

"A Word about Words" (essay; 1989; 4)

"University of California" (address; 1991; 1)

Summer Meditations (book; 1991; 3)

"Conference on Comenius" (address; 1992; 1)

"The Onassis Prize for Man and Mankind" (address; 1993; 3)

"Council of Europe Summit" (address; 1993; 2)

"The George Washington University" (address; 1993; 4)

"The Indira Gandhi Prize" (address; 1994; 3)
"World Congress of the International PEN Club" (address; 1994; 1)
"International Theatre Day" (address; 1994; 2)
"The Philadelphia Liberty Medal" (address; 1994; 2)
"Jackson H. Ralston Prize" (address; 1994; 1)
"Chulalongkorn University" (address; 1994; 1)
"National Press Club (Authority and Democracy)" (address; 1995; 5)
"1995 Geuzenpenning" (address; 1995; 1)
"Harvard University" (address; 1995; 4)
"The Future of Hope Conference" (address; 1995; 1)
"Technical University of Dresden" (address; 1995; 1)
"Victoria University of Wellington" (address; 1995; 1)
"The Latin American Parliament" (address; 1996; 2)
"Vilnius University" (address; 1996; 3)
"Státní svátek" (address; 1996; 1)
"Acceptance of an Honorary Degree from Trinity College" (address; 1996; 1)
"Europe as Task" (address; 1996; 5)
"Address before the Members of Parliament" (address; 1997; 3)
"The State Holiday of the Czech Republic" (address; 1997; 1)
"Taras Shevchenko National University" (address; 1997; 3)
"Speech at the University of Warsaw" (address; 1998; 1)
"50th Anniversary of the Universal Declaration of Human Rights" (address; 1998; 2)
"Address in Acceptance of an Honorary Degree from Oxford University" (address; 1998; 1)
"Address to the French Senate" (address; 1999; 2)
"Speech in Acceptance of the St. Adalbert Prize" (address; 1999; 3)
"Address at the Congress of the United States of America" (address; 1999; 1)
To the Castle and Back (memoir; 2006; 24)

TRUTH: *PRAVDA*
Kieran Williams

Introduction

Like many people, I have associated Havel with truth ever since
I bought my first collection of his writings, the Faber and Faber
Living in Truth collection that included "The Power of the Powerless."[1] But only much later did it occur to me to ask about the truth
in which he wanted (us) to live. Taking an approach that is both ge-
nealogical (tracing a line from writers who directly influenced Havel) and archaeological (retrieving the Havel of his formative poetic
phase), I will lay out three ways in which Havel thought about truth,
and how he brought them together in one of his first analytical pieces, a 1957 lecture on Edgar Lee Masters' *Spoon River Anthology*.
I will conclude by confronting Havel's conceptions of truth with the
challenges of fanaticism and science.

First, however, it is worth eliminating one possible understanding
of truth: it cannot be reduced to just a matter of "correct" or "accurate" facts and information, because then Havel's legacy outside
of the context of authoritarian censorship would be very limited.
Such a view of truth would also succumb to the technocratic fallacy
that the world can be improved simply by the free communication
of data.[2] One of Havel's many reasons for rejecting the temptation
to emigrate in the 1970s was that it would allow him only the freer
pursuit of information, whereas he could still seek truth behind bars
and behind the Iron Curtain. Indeed, he feared, emigration would
be a flight away from truth, not toward it, if it allowed him to avoid

---

1   Jan Vladislav, ed., *Living in Truth. Twenty-two essays published on the occasion of the award
of the Erasmus Prize to Václav Havel* (London: Faber and Faber, 1987).
2   Václav Havel, *Letters to Olga*, letter 92: Havel is referring here to the philosopher Josef
Šafařík. All translations are mine unless otherwise noted.

potentially difficult introspection.[3] And while in prison Havel noted that truth is not just *what* is said, but also by whom, to whom, why, in what circumstances—as in many of his plays, when characters deliver fine speeches but not in good faith.[4]

Avouching and veracity (Rádl, Fischer, Šafařík)

Havel's willingness to go to prison several times rather than leave the country or renounce his dissident activity is itself an illustration of the first and most fundamental of his understandings of truth, as a personal avouching:

> Putting it very simply and succinctly, truth for me is information but at the same time is something more. Of course it is information which, like all other kinds of information, is clearly shown or confirmed or verified or is simply convincing in the context of a certain system of coordinates or paradigms, but at the same time it is information for which a human being avouches their entire existence, their reputation, their honor, their name. [...] [Tomáš] Masaryk's stance [on the forged Královédvorský and Zelenohorský manuscripts] shows that really standing for truth means not looking at whether or not it benefits a person, whether they are esteemed or cursed by the public, whether their struggle ends in success or in derision and finally in oblivion.[5]

A cluster of related words features here, all derived from the Czech word for "hand" (*ruka*): the verbs *ručit* [*za*], *zaručit* [*se za*] and *zaručovat* ("to avouch," "vouch for," "guarantee," "ensure," "pledge," "safeguard") and nouns the *záruka* ("guarantee,"

3   Havel, *Letters to Olga*, letter 94.
4   Havel, *Letters to Olga*, letter 138. For more on "prison" as a key word, see Jiří Suk's chapter in this volume.
5   Václav Havel, "Acceptance of an Honorary Degree from the University of Michigan," 2000.

"assurance," "surety") and *ručitel* ("guarantor," "bondsman").[6] Havel acquired the idea of truth as something personally avouched from the two men who exerted the greatest influence on his philosophical development, Josef Ludvík Fischer (1894–1973) and Josef Šafařík (1907–1992). They in turn owed the idea to Emanuel Rádl (1873–1942), who taught Havel's father and supported his efforts to create a Czechoslovak YMCA.[7]

Rádl was a historian of science (especially biology) and observed that many breakthroughs in science were made as a result not of methodical ratiocination but of visceral conviction, and often required going out on a limb with an intensely personal defense before the corroborating evidence became available (if it ever did). He cited as an example the biologist Ernst Haeckel, who subscribed not to narrowly specific teachings but to a doctrine in its entirety, regardless of the consequences: "he believed and would vouch for his conviction at any time [*ručil za své přesvědčení kdykoli*]." Haeckel's science may have been "crude and empty" but it was also "forthright, without caginess and without fear."[8] For Rádl, truth was not a matter of factual correctness—which Haeckel's science lacked in many regards—but a personal "living truth" that kicks in once the person who holds that belief draws the appropriate conclusions and makes the necessary changes in how they live their life; only people living by truth (*pravdou žijící*) are bearers of truth (*nositeli pravdy*).[9] Rádl worked from a notion of truth as something requiring active engagement with fluid, ever-changing reality (*skutečnost*) rooted in deeds (*skutky*) and natural events, from which the observing person is inseparable—Rádl was thus neither objectivist nor subjectivist,

6 I have derived these translations from the Treq database of the Czech National Corpus, accessed July 18, 2019; see http://treq.korpus.cz/.

7 V. M. Havel, *Mé vzpomínky* (Prague: Lidové noviny, 1993), 142.

8 Emanuel Rádl, "E. E. Haeckel," *Naše doba* 15:9 (1908), 663.

9 Zuzana Škorpíková, *Rádlovo pojetí pravdy* (Prague: Filosofia, 2003), 30 and 65.

but a critical "realist."[10] Interested not so much in the validity of a theory as in its impact and reception, Rádl gave the example of Copernicus's heliocentric model:

> On one pope it had the effect that he praised it, on another that he had it placed on the Index; on Galileo it had the effect that he discovered Jupiter's moons; on Kepler that he arrived at the laws of planetary motion; on thousands of people who heard this truth, it had no effect at all.[11]

Toward the end of his life, as a bedridden shut-in under German occupation, Rádl turned back to his first subject, theology, and to belief in a "sovereign, invisible Lord" who through the ages "vouches for one moral order in the world."[12] In his final work, *Consolation from Philosophy*, his language of avouching flowed from a nostalgia for the fabled chivalry and organic harmony of the Middle Ages.

The next generation was often critical of Rádl for his association with the First Republic that was thought to have failed at Munich, but nevertheless respected his conception of truth; as Josef Ludvík Fischer recalled, Rádl insisted on "personal avouching for every decision taken [*osobní ručení za každé učiněné rozhodnutí*]" and Fischer himself "had no other criterion other than personal avouching for a professed truth [*sám neměl jiného criteria kromě takovéhoto osobního ručení za vyznávané pravdy*]."[13] As a young man in the 1920s Fischer had asked in an essay on truth and lies, "Is the life in truth not just an ideal, but also an unconditional command?" He did not answer the question, but struggled with the problem of the subjectivity of truth and the search for something objectively

10   Jan Patočka, "Význam pojmu pravdy pro Rádlovu diskusi s pozitivismem," in *Češi I. Sebrané spisy Jana Patočky sv. 12*, eds. Karel Palek and Ivan Chvátík (Prague: Oikoymenh, 2006), 37. Patočka in turn rooted Rádl in a tradition going back to the physiologist Jan Evangelista Purkyně (1787-1869), and he likened him to contemporaries such as Henri Bergson.
11   Quoted in Škorpíková, *Rádlovo pojetí pravdy*, 49.
12   Emanuel Rádl, *Útěcha z filosofie* (Prague: Čin, 1946), 52.
13   Josef Ludvík Fischer, *Listy o druhých a o sobě* (Prague: Torst, 2005), 150.

true.[14] Fischer borrowed from an eclectic range of sources, including Anglo-American pragmatism, whose approach to truth he liked because it was "an appeal for constructive truths [*výzvou k činorodým pravdám*]" and it "demands of each person an avouching for his truth: it is an upbringing for bravery [*žádá na každém ručení za jeho pravdy: jest výchovou k statečnosti*]." Pragmatism, Fischer claimed, does not devalue truths, just insists that the ones you want to espouse are avouched by a "vital truthfulness [*vám ručiti životní opravdovostí*]."[15] As he put it in 1921, a truth claim must be "redeemed by the whole person," so that it be done

[…] with a seriousness that knows no respite or repose until our truth has grown from the very root of our essence; for only then, when there is no difference between me and my truth, when I can vouch for it with every fiber of my being [*dovedu ručiti za ni celým svým žitím*], when it has become the blood of my blood, my everything, only then can I dare to say that it has become the truth. No matter however partial, however imprecise, always my entire truth. Encountering various truths in life, I will respect only those that were gained in this way, and I bow to them even when my agreement with them is withheld. Then will truth stand against truth as rivals full of respect for each other, and thus of equal value. I do not know to which side the scales of victory will tilt; but defeat, even my defeat, will be an honourable one.[16]

Fischer tried to come to terms with the pluralism of truths that this gave rise to, as both inevitable (if truth is regarded as the work of humans) and good (if it contributes to a democratic environment).[17]

14   Josef Ludvík Fischer, "O pravdě a lži," in *Výbor z díla I*, eds. Sylva Fischerová and Jan Šulc (Prague: Academia, 2007), 28.
15   Fischer, "Traktát o pravdách," in *Výbor z díla I*, 333.
16   Fischer, "Filosofie, její podstata a problémy," in *Výbor z díla I*, 207.
17   Lubomír Valenta, *J.L. Fischer: Osobnost, dílo, myšlenky* (Olomouc: Univerzita Palackého, 1990), 30.

At other moments, however, he was uncomfortable with its potential slide into an undue emphasis on social efficacy and contingency on consensus or majority opinion, to the detriment both of individual discovery and of something more fixed to guide and restrain behaviour.[18]

As an adolescent, Havel got through Fischer's dense, longwinded works,[19] and absorbed something of their pragmatic emphasis on truth as an appeal to bravely fruitful action (not just contemplation). But it was from Josef Šafařík, especially the 1948 book *Seven Letters to Melin*, that he most strongly absorbed the language of truth as personal guarantee.[20] Not a treatise but a fictionalized meditation on an artist's suicide, *Seven Letters* confronted humanity's enduring need for truth and salvation, which it will find in neither traditional religion nor theosophic spiritualism nor the sciences. Šafařík viewed Nazi racialism and the war crimes then on trial as the fanatical but logical climax of modern Europe's culture of depersonalized science and reliance on externally generated standards of right and wrong, which had resulted in a society of pliant spectators only too willing to follow orders.[21] Since the moral "scaffolding" and "balustrades" that modern man constructed had clearly failed, Šafařík advocated a radical individualism following the voice of conscience, "of one's own accord, at one's own risk, on one's own responsibility."[22] The detached spectator would be replaced by the active participant, a *ručitel*—someone willing to avouch a belief, even unto death—in place of the scientific explicator, who

18 Fischer, "O budoucnosti evropské kultury," in *Výbor z díla I*, 397.
19 Pavel Kosatík, *"Ústně více": Šestatřicátníci* (Brno: Host, 2006), 78.
20 Vladimír Just, "Příspěvek k jazyku experanto aneb Dramatické neosoby Václava Havla," *Divadelní revue* 15:3 (2004), 3-13.
21 Josef Šafařík, *Sedm listů Melinovi* (Brno: Atlantis, 1993), 190, 193, and 230. On the circumstances in which the book was composed, see David Drozd, "Dobové kontexty *Sedmi listů Melinovi* Josefa Šafaříka," *Estetika* 42: 2-3 (2006), 149-87.
22 Šafařík, *Sedm listů Melinovi*, 175.

tries to prove a point with impersonal facts. Šafařík likened the participant-avoucher to the tightrope walker in Nietzsche's *Thus Spake Zarathustra*, a person who has to keep moving above the abyss, living in the here and the now, relying on a balance and resolve that comes entirely from within.

Some of the concerns that troubled Fischer were allayed by Šafařík's assurance, probably informed by the recent experience of war and occupation, that life regularly provides the tests and exemplary individuals who will distinguish truth from casual, subjective assertions: "Thus life will choose for us those whose voices are worthy to be heard," in whom we detect "strong and uncompromising avouchers [*ručitelé*]." Let each go about according to his conscience and undergo a "test of viability."[23] For the individuals who subscribe to a truth, it will have the feeling of absoluteness, for which they would be willing to sacrifice their lives as the "personal guarantee [*osobní záruka*], the certification of truth by life and death"; "maximum avouchers [*ručitelé*]" such as Socrates, Jesus, Bruno and Jan Hus, had done so to put the "stamp of certainty" on their teachings.[24] Šafařík thus rephrased the Pontius Pilate question, "What is truth?," into, "For what can I vouch, for what do I vouch [*zač dovedu ručit, zač ručím*]?"[25] Martyrdom in itself did not make a person's pronouncements objectively correct for all; truth for Šafařík was "vertical," within a person, not "horizontal" as a dictate binding on others. Each martyr appeals for others to follow his truth, but would do better to urge them to follow his example as a *ručitel* and to arrive at their own truth. The salvation for which people hanker would come from this personally avouched truth and its attendant morality, not from a church or other religious institution, which Šafařík said (citing William

23 Šafařík, *Sedm listů Melinovi*, 213.
24 Šafařík, *Sedm listů Melinovi*, 216.
25 Šafařík, *Sedm listů Melinovi*, 217.

James, a prominent pragmatist) only wants you to "surrender your own responsibility."[26]

Šafařík was, inadvertently or not, paraphrasing something Rádl had said 30 years earlier, at the end of another great war:

> However we may express our ideal (by word and deed) differently from Hus, from Socrates [...] nevertheless we know that we have the truth and so do they, an absolute truth, and that those who are against our ideals do not have the truth. Absolute Truth lies not in the formulation, but in the conviction of people; people, not their words, have or do not have truth.[27]

Rádl, and by extension Šafařík, Fischer and Havel, respected a life lived not so much in truth (*pravda*) as genuineness (*opravdovost*), by which Rádl meant the "consistent searching for truth," a yearning and striving without actually attaining it. Someone's *opravdovost* could be a challenge or appeal (*výzva*) to seek the truth in what they say, even if at first it is just a matter of understanding their truth without endorsing it.[28] As Rádl put it, "Is not that consistency already a guarantee [*zárukou*] if not of the truth, then at least of the philosopher's approximation to the truth?"[29]

Havel on avouching

The language of avouching pervades Havel's writing, be it his philosophical and political essays, prison letters, or his presidential addresses; its presence is lost in translation, as the cluster of

---

26 Šafařík, *Sedm listů Melinovi*, 221. Šafařík's view of religion and morals was influenced by James's *The Varieties of Religious Experience*, and he was quoting from the lectures on "Saintliness." Fischer also expressed an undying respect for James; see *Listy o druhých a o sobě*, 97.

27 Quoted in Škorpíková, *Rádlovo pojetí pravdy*, 69.

28 Škorpíková, *Rádlovo pojetí pravdy*, 234. On *výzva* as a Havelian keyword, see David S. Danaher, *Reading Václav Havel* (Toronto: University of Toronto Press, 2015), 216-22 as well as the chapter in this volume.

29 Emanuel Rádl, "Masaryk a Kant," *Masarykův sborník* 1: (1924), 97-105 (at 102).

ruka-derived words takes so many unrelated forms in English. In his inaugural speech as president in 1993, setting out the virtues on which he wanted the new Czech state to draw, he topped the list with "faith in a truth for which it is necessary to vouch personally [*víra v pravdu, za kterou je třeba osobně ručit*]."[30] In presidential addresses Havel extolled individuals who had avouched their truths, such as Thomas Jefferson (when putting his fate on the line by drafting the Declaration of Independence) and Tomáš Masaryk (when exposing ancient manuscripts as forgeries or defending Jews accused of child murder).[31] Havel also elevated avouching to something that could or should operate in a group or community, citing the examples of the Plastic People of the Universe, who had spoken a truth that was "personally experienced and avouched [*osobně zakoušená a zaručovaná*]"[32]; Soviet-bloc dissidents who offered their bare skin as the only way to affirm the truth for which they stood, compelled by an inner force that did not allow them to live in falsehood[33]; and resistance groups in the Second World War, which had constituted a moral community of solidarity and mutual vouching (*ručení*).[34] The idea of guarantee (*záruka*) was one of Havel's political keywords in his 1968 essay "On the Theme of Opposition," and then again in 1989–90, especially when defining his presidency as a guarantee of free elections and of democratization generally. In his *Summer Meditations* (1991), he couched his ideal of a "spiritual state" (*duchovní stát*) in the language of avouching:

30 Václav Havel, "Projev k občanům po inauguraci," in Václav Havel, *Spisy* 7 (Prague: Torst, 1999), 40.
31 Václav Havel, "Kongres USA" in *Spisy* 6 (Prague: Torst, 1999), 72; Václav Havel, "Výročí narození T. G. Masaryka," in Havel, *Spisy* 6, 92; Václav Havel, "Odhalení pomníků T. G. Masaryka," in Havel, *Spisy* 7, 67; Václav Havel, "150. výročí narození T. G. Masaryka," in Havel, *Spisy* 8, 64.
32 Václav Havel, "Hovězí porážka" in Havel, *Spisy* 4 (Prague: Torst, 1999), 449.
33 Václav Havel, "Anatomie jedné zdrženlivosti," in Havel, *Spisy* 4, 558.
34 Václav Havel, "Geuzenpenning," 1995.

Building a spiritual state does not mean building an ideological state. An ideological state is not a spiritual state. It means the very opposite: extricating a human being from the carapace of all ideological interpretations and rehabilitating it as an autonomous subject of individual conscience, of one's own thinking avouched by one's own existence [*vlastní existencí zaručované*], of individual responsibility and an altogether non-abstract love for one's neighbor.[35]

Elsewhere, he advocated a single-member electoral system so that candidates "personally vouch [*osobně ručí*]" for their campaign promises, and on a visit to Athens he appealed for a democracy based on integrated persons "personally vouching for the fate of the community [*osobně ručící za osud obce*]."[36]

These last examples direct us to the nexus between avouching a truth and personal responsibility that can be found in several of Havel's texts. At the Fourth Writer's Congress in June 1967 he advised his peers—many of whom had once been Stalinists and were now turning into fierce critics of the regime they had served—to be more circumspect when making pronouncements: it was better, he said, to commit to 100 words and stand by them rather than sign up for 1,000 and have to renounce 900 of them later. The fundamental question, he said, is "whether we are all truly capable of bearing to the end full responsibility for our words, whether we simply are truly and without reservation capable of vouching for ourselves [*zaručovat se sami za sebe*], of vouching for [*ručit za*] our proclamations

35 Václav Havel, "Letní přemítání," in *Spisy* 6, 544. Compare my translation of this passage to Paul Wilson's version in Václav Havel, *Summer Meditations* (New York: Vintage Books, 1993), 128 where the Czech phrase *vlastní existencí zaručované* is rendered as "backed up by [one's own] experience" and in which the vouching motif has been effaced.
36 Václav Havel, "Vystoupení ve Federálním shromáždění," 1992; see also "Projev k občanům před začátkem předvolební kampaně," 1992; Václav Havel, "The Onassis Prize for Man and Mankind," 1993.

with all our practice and its continuity."[37] Havel was very impressed at the time by the "authenticity" of Aleksandr Solzhenitsyn's May 1967 open letter to the Soviet Writers' Congress, because it had not one word less than was necessary for a complete statement of truth, but also not one word more than the author could "avouch by his whole life, without exception and to the very end [*beze zbytku celým svým životem a až doposledna zaručit*]."[38]

On the other side of the "Prague Spring," in his own Solzhenitsyn-style letter to Alexander Dubček in 1969, Havel urged the former first secretary not to succumb to pressure to validate the Soviet-led invasion, but instead to vouch for the thwarted reform program, despite its inadequacies. Even though Dubček could no longer influence the country's trajectory, he had a residual responsibility to "vouch personally for his truth [*osobně ručit za svou pravdu*]" lest he left his countrymen feeling that everything attempted in 1968 had been for naught. He was not asking Dubček to be a scapegoat or sacrificial lamb, but to set an example that would be like a bolt of lightning on a darkened landscape.[39]

Havel practiced what he preached by going to prison ten years later, when he often reflected on the connection between avouching, responsibility, and the continuity of identity. In a letter to his wife Olga, he states:

If I know what I have done and why, what I do and why, if I truly vouch for it [*za to skutečně ručím*] and if I declare myself [*se k tomu… hlásím*] for it (albeit perhaps in secret), that means that I continually relate to something stable, which I "gain" in my "unstable" surroundings, and thereby myself become "relatively stable"—something graspable, continual and integrated—I am, in short, "someone", that is, someone identical with

37 Václav Havel, "Projev na IV. sjezdu Svazu československých spisovatelů," in Václav Havel, *Spisy* 3 (Prague: Torst, 1999), 783.
38 Havel, "Projev na IV. Sjezdu," 784.
39 Václav Havel, "Dopis Alexandru Dubčekovi," in Havel, *Spisy* 3, 926.

myself. By the fact that today I vouch for what I did yesterday, that I vouch here for what I did elsewhere, I acquire not only my identity but through it I am also located in space and time; if on the contrary I lose my identity, space and time must perforce also collapse around me.[40]

Havel illustrated that collapse of space and time by his country's housing estates and industrialized farms: the resident of such a world, "ceasing to vouch for himself and for his life," necessarily loses all confidence and dignity, and resigns to life in a morass.[41] This predicament was by no means unique to socialism but indicative of a greater loss of sensitivity to the "absolute horizon" in modernity; the delight he took in reading Saul Bellow's novel *Herzog* in captivity arose in part from taking it as a reminder that even for someone living in complete freedom there is a danger that words can lose their weight if they are not "avouched by life."[42]

After prison, his first major essay, "Politics and Conscience," contrasted the horrors of modern living with an idealized (although not idyllic) pre-modern dwelling, a personally "avouched rootedness in the genius loci [*zaručovaná zakotvenost v povaze místa*]" in optimal proportion with the "natural order of things."[43] It would be a world for which we feel a direct responsibility, and as its central focus (*ohnisko*) would be the "distinct, integrated and dignified human 'I', vouching for itself [*svéprávné, integrální a důstojné lidské "já," ručící samo za sebe*]"[44] and resisting the evils of consumption, advertising, technology and formulaic speech by proceeding from "personally avouched [*zaručované*] and non-ideologically-censored experiences, measures, and imperatives."[45] In March 1985, in his

40 Havel, *Letters to Olga*, letter 109. See also letters 62, 95, and 138.
41 Havel, *Letters to Olga*, letter 118.
42 Havel, *Letters to Olga*, letter 123.
43 Václav Havel, "Politika a svědomí," in Havel, *Spisy* 4, 418–19.
44 Havel, "Politika a svědomí", 435.
45 Havel, "Politika a svědomí", 440.

reply to a *samizdat* questionnaire, Havel asserted that there was no single, universal guide to living life correctly, so each person must turn to his or her God and/or conscience, conduct an inner dialogue and then personally vouch (*ručit*) for the resultant standards of conduct. To avoid that process by relying instead on a ready-to-hand collection of maxims and commandments would only erode human integrity and make the world worse. Like Šafařík, Havel viewed Jesus as a "challenge" and "appeal" to produce something oneself for which one can vouch, not simply believe in.[46]

Havel's essays put the case for avouching truth and taking responsibility positively, while his plays did so mostly negatively, by showing the consequences of their absence.[47] (It is no coincidence that two rare examples of characters willing to avouch a truth are also the only characters in his plays who die: Filch in *The Beggar's Opera* and Plechanov in *Asanace*.) Havel's fourth full-length play, *Conspirators*, is the most graphic depiction of a world populated by hollow characters whose words are never "existentially avouched [*existenciálně zaručeny*]"—they speak in stilted, abstract formulas, even in private, leaving each other and the audience unsure whether they are ever sincere and authentic. No statement is pronounced that could not be just as easily renounced later, as it contains no truth that is "humanly avouched [*člověkem zaručované*]," backed by hard experience, and would still be defended if it were inconvenient or inexpedient. In the play's dance of intrigue, Havel commented, it is not a question of who among the conspirators is most perceptive in their grasp of the situation but of who can best use trite ideological conventions to pursue their goals and outmaneuver the others. The result, he said, is a crisis of identity that is also a crisis of truth.[48]

46   Václav Havel, "Odpověď do ankety Lenky Procházkové" in Havel, *Spisy* 4, 516 and 517.
47   James F. Pontuso, *Václav Havel: Civic Responsibility in the Postmodern Age* (Lanham, MD: Rowman & Littlefield, 2004), 114.
48   Václav Havel, "Komentář ke hře Spiklenci" in Havel, *Spisy* 4, 12-13 and 40.

The Absolute speaks

In other contexts, Havel did also demonstrate a belief in an absolute truth that reveals itself in snatches and glimpses, especially through art. Havel's grandfather Václav had been an avid practitioner of occult séances, the findings of which he presented as the underlying nature of the universe explained to him, via mediums, by spirits dwelling on astral planes. Those explorations were published and preserved in the family memory and Havel was reared by his deistic, masonic father not to be conventionally religious but to believe in an unseen cosmic order.[49] An early expression of this belief can be found in a letter Havel wrote at age 16 to an acquaintance, Radim Kopecký, in March 1953, just weeks after Stalin's death. As it has never appeared in English, I translate a revealing passage at length:

> You acknowledge an Absolute. So do I. I doubt, however, that our conceptions of it are at all similar. In my opinion it goes something like this: there is no dreamland in the clouds, strictly separated from this world, of whose existence a human worm has not even the right to receive any word, and that only in an extraordinary moment would reveal its presence to some mere worm on our little fleck of dust, etc. On the contrary. The most common everyday things, which you might hold in contempt, are the best evidence. I do not require miracles as proof, as Jews did in the time of Jesus, therefore no one attempts to parade any miracles before me. Is not a little nosegay, full of tiny little things that are so pretty and so cleverly arranged that a man with his clumsy fingers can only freeze in speechless delight, or the Universe with its distances millions of times greater than the largest expanse a person can imagine, or a snowflake, the structure of the atom, matter itself, sufficient proof of some higher, perfect force,

---

49 Václav Havel (Atom), *Kniha života* (Prague: Knihovna Václava Havla, 2011); Martin C. Putna, *Václav Havel: Duchovní portrét v rámu české kultury 20. století* (Prague: Knihovna Václava Havla, 2011), 27–42.

which is the essence of everything, guides everything, including the human body? That could be denied only by a blind man, who moves without seeing, who never reflects deeply on common things. But that higher substance will never appear as a person, let alone as a man (why not a woman?), in the way that Christians imagine. It cannot be a being as we would conceive of it, let alone a being with human attributes (longing for glory, the world created for the greater glory of God). [...] My conception of the Absolute is somewhat "Platonic-Aristotelian-Spinozan-Hegelian," that is, pantheistic. God is not beyond the world, it is not the case that he supplies the cause and then observes. On the contrary, God is everywhere all the time, in each action, in each phenomenon in each material. The world is in constant dialectical development. The old alternates with the new, but that would mean that even the dialectic will someday be replaced and the world become static, motionless. So there is something stationary (each dialectic presumes something static) that is the truth, the Absolute. The dialectic is the truth, because its principle will always apply. For example, the truth that Caesar was murdered in 44 BC today is no longer material but nevertheless is true. And it will be true in one hundred years, in one thousand, eternally, the truth does not change, it is not in development, it is absolute. Of course, if truth is what is beneficial to us, then the truth changes quickly, with people's needs. This is, however, a pragmatic (and actually Marxist as well) invention, the equation of benefit with truth. As if because it somehow suited me that Caesar died in year zero, then suddenly it becomes the truth that he died in year zero. My human, relative truth perhaps, but never the absolute truth. For me the truth is what I <u>believe</u> corresponds with obj[ective] reality. If all the people of the world believed something, it may be generally said to be true but is still not the absolute truth. We cannot encounter absolute truth because we are limited in time. We perceive only one moment, we do not know what will come next, we only remember what has been, which can therefore be erroneous (an idol). Thus truth is first of all the Absolute. [...] <u>The Absolute is everything, the Relative is how the human consciousness perceives everything, how things appear to it, how it judges.</u> The Relative here is the reflection of the Absolute, as in Plato's cave, where phenomena are reflections, shadows, ideas. We are three-dimensional, we understand three-dimensionally, etc. Our understanding and comprehension is imperfect in regard to the Absolute, but it is not something completely different, because we are a component of the Absolute. The Absolute is behind everything. It is timeless, so it is in every truth about the past (see above), so everything future is contained within it, hence determinism. I would apply a new term here: The Concrete, that is, what Marxists call "objective reality," but which is just a single moment. It is what is not in the past or the future, the point between them - the present. This concrete is a component of the Absolute, but the concrete changes constantly, and the human spirit changes constantly, the "now" me is ever so slightly different from the me of a minute ago, and noticeably from the me of a year ago and fundamentally from the me of 15 years ago. I am constantly different, contingent on time. That which changes is the concrete. What has been and will be is in the Absolute without concretization. Ideas are absolute, like for example the truth about the past. And as the concrete is always different in time and relatively, so is the Absolute always the same. And everywhere in everything. There will be truth, even if there will not be matter or man. Some say that the Absolute must have some sort of consciousness, in which it dwells. All reality is its consciousness. [...] The Absolute = Nature. And so on. It is somewhat similar to Spinoza's pantheism and Hegel's dialectic, which are related. [...]

I have strayed a bit into metaphysics (as it has been understood, of course, by everyone from Aristotle up to today, apart from Marx, Engels and their minions, thus not into methods opposed to the dialectic as Engels devised it in order to cause confusion, but as a branch of science occupied with the nature of existence, its causes, relations to human consciousness, etc., thus a part of philosophy), in part so that I could show you briefly my current opinion (and I admit that I do so in the secret hope that you will at least consent and it will lead to agreement), in part so that I can refer again to something from one of our old quarrels: namely, that I consider the higher branch of science the one that is occupied with the higher aspects of existence, the highest being the Absolute, the final substance and principle of everything, however the Absolute = Nature, therefore I have considered it to be evidence that the natural sciences are concerned with all things. You referred in a previous letter (from 19 February) to the fact that the social sciences are the product of human reason, they are therefore higher than mere nature (for example, your sentence that "They stand somehow above all nature" and such like, see the third paragraph of that letter). And this is my answer "for nature," which you for unknown reasons have not recognized and you denied your materialism, although if someone says that man is the highest being (there is no God, Absolute, nature is just at the bottom) he is clearly a materialist. Of course, I think that on your part it was just an oversight. For a person who is not blinded by the soulless technicism of the twentieth century and who is observant must object to the adulation of human creations: Is not the camera an imperfect imitation of the human eye, is not the atomic bomb an imperfect imitation of the sun, are not human creations imperfect compared to the Absolute in everything, in nature (and of course in man too)? But a definitive Amen to that.[50]

The adult Havel no longer described himself as an "avid devotee" of Platonic ideal forms,[51] but the fact that he once had is important; as he observed in one of his teenage poems, "nothing passes without a trace."[52] In adulthood, he subscribed to a metaphysics and ontology that rejected materialism and anthropomorphic monotheism alike. Eight years after writing the letter to Kopecký, he mocked the idea that truth was simply the product of social consensus in one of his first plays, a sketch about a disease, "motorism," that is turning people into cars:

50   Archive of the Václav Havel Library (AKVH), item 1783 (March 27, 1953); emphases in original.
51   Václav Havel to Jiří Paukert, November 22, 1953 (AKVH, item 1521).
52   Václav Havel, "Kamarádství," in Václav Havel, *Spisy* 1 (Prague: Torst, 1999), 170.

WOMAN: It's a disease?
LECTURER: Of course it's a disease! It is a clear deviation from all normal forms of biological activity in man.
BURSÍK: And how do you know what is normal?
LECTURER: The normal is everything that is commonplace under certain assumptions …
INAUGURATOR: And how do you know that you are right [*že máš pravdu*]?
LECTURER: There are centuries of empirical data, statistics…
WOMAN: Do you mean to say that the truth can approved by a vote [*pravda se dá odhlasovat*]?[53]

The notion that a truth exists and can find expression in many small ways underpinned the young Havel's conception of the role of the artist. Like the mediums his grandfather consulted, Havel's ideal artist was an outwardly ordinary person with an exceptional ability to channel something intrinsically truthful. Literature in the first half of the 1950s, Havel objected, had been only a feeble imitation of the strange world of Stalinism, and post-Stalinism needed writers who could express the experience of mankind in maximum wholeness and complexity.[54] To do this the poet must carry in him the "non-exclusive and unexceptional fate of the simple man," be employed somewhere, live somewhere, have a family, but live more intensely than the ordinary person, look more deeply into the world around him.[55] The poets in Group 42, including Jiří Kolář, and the short-story writer Bohumil Hrabal were producing exactly the sort of eyewitnessing, "substantial" art that Havel had in mind, one that maximized veracity (*pravdivost*), as did Western neo-realist film.[56]

53 Václav Havel, *Motomorfózy* (Prague: Galén, 2011), 27.
54 Václav Havel, "Pochyby o programu," in Havel, *Spisy* 3, 59.
55 Václav Havel, "Básník dnešní doby," in Havel, *Spisy* 3, 62 and 65.
56 Václav Havel, "Nové cesty," in Havel, *Spisy* 3, 126. See also Delia Popescu, *Political Action in Václav Havel's Thought* (Lanham, MD: Rowman & Littlefield, 2012), 4.

Later, in a more phenomenological (or spiritualist?) frame, he conceptualized the writer (and dissident) as a medium through whom the truth of Being expresses itself.[57] Theater since antiquity has been a place where, in a short space of time, the truth of a whole life might be exposed, perhaps the truth of the whole world, speaking through the author to a community.[58] But to do so theater must follow certain rules of its own:

> Let us imagine a situation in which a member of the audience in a theater must—for whatever reason—all of a sudden step out of the twilight of the auditorium and find himself on stage, in view of hundreds of people. Let us imagine that we were forced—by whatever means—to accept him in all that he did, that he did by himself and for himself, as a dramatic character—that spectator for a few minutes would suddenly, simply be playing himself. An interesting paradox would arise: on the one hand, we could not doubt the truthfulness, realism and contemporaneity of this character—it would be, after all, entirely authentic [*autentická*]— but on the other hand we could probably not avoid in most instances the feeling that this person does not belong on the stage, that there is something alien, false, non-theatrical and non-dramatic, in its own way untruthful [*nepravdivý*]. This simple example clearly supports the finding—in this context important—that even though truth is of course singular [*i když pravda je pochopitelně jedna*], nevertheless it expresses itself—as truth—in life entirely differently, and even differently on the stage.[59]

57 Václav Havel, "Odpovědnost jako osud" in Havel, *Spisy* 4, 408.
58 Václav Havel, "Dopis Milanu Uhdemu" in Havel, *Spisy* 4, 689.
59 Václav Havel, "Pravda života a pravda jeviště" in Havel, *Spisy* 3, 357-8. See also Václav Havel, "Zvláštnosti divadla" in Havel, *Spisy* 3, 821; and Havel, *Letters to Olga*, letter 114. For more on "theater," see Barbara Day's chapter in this volume.

It required not just the playwright but also a gifted director, such as Alfréd Radok, to elicit truthful performances from actors using methods Havel compared to those of a shaman or magician.[60]

To be truthful, however, art must sometimes disturb surface appearances, not reflect them; by the mid-1950s Havel already subscribed to Viktor Shklovsky's theory of literature as defamiliarization (*ostranenie*, in Czech *ozvláštnění*) and admired writers such as Hrabal who could use it effectively.[61] Defamiliarization induces a feeling of absurdity and meaninglessness not in order to cause despair in the reader or viewer, but quite the opposite: by disrupting conventions and stereotypes, he explained from prison in 1981, defamiliarizing art, especially theater, "opens the doors to a truly fresh, sharp and penetrating vision" that places us "face to face with truth."[62] Prison itself, as an unsettling and unusual experience, contained "far greater truth than the world outside," showing people and things "in their true form," like an x-ray that put that prior outside life in a defamiliarizing new light, creating a "moment of truth—the truth of my fellow inmates, my truth and the truth of the world in which it befalls us to live."[63]

Globe-trotting as president was also an unsettling, defamiliarizing experience, and he was prompted to prepare himself to encounter unfamiliar cultures in Asia and South America. In effect he was resuming the research he undertook after leaving prison in 1983, when writing a series of plays inspired by the Faust tradition; he felt that "something higher" spoke through the ancient myths in which

60 Václav Havel, "Radok dnes" in Havel, *Spisy* 4, 658.

61 Havel's notion of truth also resembles that espoused by Mikhail Bakhtin, but apart from a passing reference in the 1985 essay "Anatomy of a Reticence" Havel does not cite him.

62 Havel, *Letters to Olga*, Letter 73. See also Václav Havel, "Anatomie gagu," in Havel, *Spisy* 3, 591–95; Václav Havel, "Zvláštnosti divadla," in Havel, *Spisy* 3, 828–29; and Danaher, *Reading Václav Havel*, 23.

63 Havel, *Letters to Olga*, letter 5; Václav Havel, "Přítelkyně Evy Kantůrkové," in Havel, *Spisy* 4, 923.

he immersed himself.[64] As head of state, reading histories of human origins and religion, and the research of a Czech-American psychiatrist, Stanislav Grof, Havel came to assume the existence of a prehistoric, collective unconscious, expressed archetypically in virtually all religions but obscured by historic, local identities. Havel's major speeches in São Paulo, Hiroshima, Philadelphia, and at Harvard called for a "codex of human coexistence" using the "common roots of human spirituality and religiosity" to arrive at a spiritually-informed order (řád, a Fischer keyword) that—presumably—derived from a common underlying truth.[65]

Truth excites

Even when advocating agreement on certain principles, Havel staunchly opposed a forced, synthetic amalgamation of ideas that should otherwise be left standing in stark contrast. A lasting residue of his adolescent Hegelianism was his fondness for the juxtaposition of opposing views, not in order to blend them into an inoffensive mush—what he derided as the "dialectical metaphysics" of official discourse (and parodied in his early plays and typograms)—but to allow them to clash, for it is through that clash that a community arrives collectively at the truth. Here, too, Bohumil Hrabal's fiction of "total realism"[66] was an early exemplar: by confronting the perspectives of different characters, his stories provided "the most truthful image of the world, the most objective witness to it." Hrabal achieved this extraction of the full truth (of fate as well as reality) not through a linear, omniscient narrative, but through defamiliarization—using polyphony to make a story less obvious than it would

---

64   Václav Havel, "Thriller," in Havel, *Spisy* 4, 507.
65   Václav Havel, "Harvard University," 1995; "The Future of Hope Conference," 1995; "The Latin American Parliament," 1996.
66   "Paul Wilson on Bohumil Hrabal," *Asymptote*, https://www.asymptotejournal.com/special-feature/paul-wilson-on-bohumil-hrabal.

seem at first glance. Havel summed up Hrabal's method of "comparing truths" as if to say, "Behold, reader, such is the world in which you live, such are the people who surround you, I have informed you objectively, dispose of this information as you yourself are able."[67]

Hrabal's art served humanity by supplying truth without an authorial filter. He also did so in a way that Havel clearly found exciting, and excitation (*vzrušení*) was a telltale symptom of truthfulness. Excitement, it must be stressed, was not pleasure: on the contrary, Havel equated it with disturbance and added energy, as in physics. The wizardry of director Alfréd Radok's effect on actors so impressed Havel because it shocked them out of their familiar, comfortable mannerisms and agitated their personalities "into motion," with "excitement" being an "organic symptom of creativity."[68] Abstract modern art provokes and "hits us with its emotional truth and unnerves us with the elusiveness and indefinability of that truth."[69] The seminal 1964 essay "On dialectical metaphysics" opens with the proposition that we are secretly bored by statements with which we agree, suggesting that deep down they are less true than we would like to admit, whereas problematic, challenging statements excite and unsettle us, suggesting that deep down they contain more of the truth than we would like to admit.[70] This does not mean that we have to abandon the superficially more true-sounding statements just because they do not excite us; rather, the irritation of an opposing view is an appeal to engage in genuine dialectics, not evasive *akorátismus* (avoiding offence by cutting down the middle, taking

67 Václav Havel, "Nad prózami Bohumila Hrabala," in Havel, *Spisy* 3, 111-13. See also Václav Havel, "Příběh a totalita," in Havel, *Spisy* 4, 936, which asserts that every true story needs a pluralism of truths as well as characters, with a certain tension between them, the outcome of which is not clear in advance—there has to be an element of mystery. A story discloses to us the human world as the "exciting space of contacts [*vzrušující prostor styků*]" between many subjects.
68 Václav Havel, "Několik poznámek za Švédské zápalky," in Havel, *Spisy* 3, 439.
69 Václav Havel, "Text do katalogu Jiřího Janečka," in Havel, *Spisy* 3, 616. See also "O konvencích, informaci a kódu," in Havel, *Spisy* 3, 696-700.
70 Václav Havel, "O dialektické metafyzice," in Havel, *Spisy* 3, 619–29.

a bit from the chicken and a bit from the egg). A synthesis of sorts will take place, but it cannot be accomplished by one person, especially not one in an official capacity.[71] It is must take place by a social process, with all sorts of surprising twists and turns.

The truth of Spoon River

That sort of social process plays out in a work that the young Havel greatly admired, Edgar Lee Masters's *Spoon River Anthology*. A collection of short monologues as they might be spoken by more than 200 dead residents of a rural Illinois community, lying side-by-side in the town's cemetery, *Spoon River* exemplifies all the conceptions of truth that Havel had already worked out by the time he gave a public lecture on Masters in October 1957, shortly after his twenty-first birthday and shortly before he would depart for military service.[72] By giving us the voices of the dead, Havel told his audience, the collection has the defamiliarizing (*ozvláštňující*) effect of disrupting daily automatism, providing a new perspective on life as hitherto lived and a stronger sense of the true proportions of existence. It plays to our innate longing for a transcendent point of view that would behold the world in its most "real and unchangingly true [*pravdivé*] final form," a longing that Havel knew to be unattainable in life yet undeniably strong. The device of letting the dead speak from their unique vantage point—like the spirits communicating from the astral plane to Havel's grandfather through his mediums—allows the poem to strip away the trivialities and conventions of normal, everyday life, so

---

71 In June 1965 Havel denounced a speech by the poet and chairman of the writers' union, Jiří Šotola, for its dialectically-metaphysical "false contextualization" and "content-free verbal balancing act"; see "Projev na konferenci Svazu československých spisovatelů," in Havel, *Spisy* 3, 671. See also Veronika Tuckerová, "The Totalitarian Languages of Utopia and Dystopia: Fidelius and Havel," in *In Marx's Shadow: Knowledge, Power, and Intellectuals in Eastern Europe and Russia*, ed. Costica Bradatan and Sergei Oushakine (Lanham, MD: Rowman & Littlefield, 2010), 95–109 (at 98–99).
72 Václav Havel, "Spoonriverská antologie," in Havel, *Spisy* 3, 186–99.

that "a maximally truthful, undistorted view of that life is avouched [*zaručen*]." Only in death does everything in life achieve its "true resolution," only then can Masters's townsfolk tell the truth of what (they claim) happened to them.

The device of the graveyard also allows for the virtual death of the author: the narrator disappears after the brief, impersonal pro-em, "The Hill." The reader forgets that Masters is the creator of all these voices, and we have the sensation of an unbiased, unfiltered, "maximally truthful view of life and the world"—and truth, Havel said, "in the most general sense is of course the theme of every art form." In *Spoon River*, that truth emerges not from a single speaker, but from the confrontation of all the individual testimonies, often with excitingly divergent perspectives on the same event or circumstances; one attorney admits that another "drove through/The cardboard mask of my life with a spear of light [...]."[73] Havel said that the result is not relativism, but a truth that can only be arrived at by hearing all the witnesses (Masters himself was a lawyer by practice), spread across a great canvas like Michelangelo's "Last Judgement." The attraction of a polyphonic poem, which in its epilogue crosses into a drama in verse that reflects Masters's interest in *Faust*, shows that the young Havel was already on the path that would take him into playwriting.

Problems of Havel's truth: fanaticism and science

Spoon River, Havel reminded his audience, strove to present "a truthful image of real life in its social structure," offering the full spectrum of human experiences and outlooks, as if to say that each person's self-account is truthful only in the context of his or her neighbour's fates. Masters was doing so, in 1915, to protest the

---

73 Edgar Lee Masters, *Spoon River Anthology*, ed. John E. Hallwas (Urbana and Chicago: Univeristy of Illinois Press, 1992), 216.

growing anomie and partiality of his age, a time of deepening loss of spiritual and cultural unity, with the concomitant rise of scientific specialization and personal atomization. As the speakers give voice to lives of bitterness, resentment and spite, the circumstances of their deaths create an undercurrent of violence, danger and desperation: six of the characters were murdered, seven took their own lives, two were executed, one died after an abortion, and thirteen were killed in accidents.[74] Part of the backlash against the loss of harmony and community, Havel noted, had been the rise of intolerant fanaticisms promising a new form of belonging and salvation on earth for their adherents, at the expense of others.[75] Fanaticism remained something that Havel ardently opposed all his life, contrasting it (and utopianism) with his preferred expression of heartfelt belief, idealism (and the avouched truth lying behind it), as he expounded in prison letter 96 to Olga. In letter 141, part of his 16-installment ontological sequence, Havel set up fanaticism as a perverse other, in contrast to genuine faith; both stem from a sense of personal responsibility for the world, but fanaticism makes the "fatal error, unusually seductive to a lazy mind, a weak character" of concluding that "it is enough to 'think something up' and then blindly serve it—that is, create some intellectual project that permanently fixes and fulfils the original intention—and a person is thereby relieved of the duty of making the effort constantly to draw himself up toward Being: for it is conveniently replaced by the relatively undemanding duty of devoted service to the given project."[76] He returned to the matter in letter 163, from January 22, 1983 (and not in the published *Letters to Olga*):

---

74   Charles E. Burgess, "Edgar Lee Masters: The Lawyer as Writer," in *The Vision of This Land*, eds. John E. Hallwas and Dennis J. Reader (Macomb, IL: Western Illinois University Press, 1976), 55–73 (at 63).
75   Havel, "Spoonriverská antologie," 194.
76   Havel, *Letters to Olga*, letter 141.

Such a person [the fanatic] is wretched: he is, you see, permanently enthusiastic and at the same time permanently disappointed, he is a constantly naïve optimist and at the same time in constant danger of being plunged by any external chance event into the abyss of the deepest scepticism. He is a person capable of devoting himself to something very easily, very quickly, very impetuously, and without the slightest inner control or reservation (and of vigorously condemning anyone who does not devote himself to it with him), and capable with equal ease of turning away at first moment when things start to go wrong [skřípat] and just as quickly succumb to the pessimistic view that nothing has any worth (which lasts—in the best case—until there appears—or rather, until someone else discloses—something new with which it is possible to identify afresh and to which it is again possible to delegate entirely his reason, his conscience, his responsibility). Only he who relies on himself alone and does not depend on others has enough true persistence and stamina, has enough strength to always keep a sober spirit, his own wits, a healthy self-control and an always original, that is, unmediated view of the world. Which also applies in reverse: only he who can keep such a constant view truly believes – in the sense of belief as a state of mind, as an "orientation toward Being," and not belief as a blind identification with something that offers itself from without.[77]

But what distinguishes fanatical attachment from steadfast avouching of a truth? On what grounds can we deny membership in Šafařík's pantheon of slain avouchers to cult leaders such as Jim Jones, David Koresh, or Shoko Asahara? Or to those who would stake their reputations on conspiracy theories about the Kennedy assassination, the September 11 attacks or the masonic orders to which Havel's father belonged, and do so with the resolve of a Masaryk exposing forged manuscripts? Would we have to accord equal validity to

---

77   Havel, AKVH, item 2983.

Havel's prison letters and Hitler's *Mein Kampf*, written in captivity at Landsberg?[78]

Rádl, Šafařík and Havel all to some degree tried to distinguish their truths from the ravings of fanatics. Rádl drew a line between those who resort to violence and those who are willing to suffer it, with the former losing the right to recognition as bearers of truth. Šafařík similarly drew the line at fatal fanaticism—the conviction that justifies the killing of others—and any reliance on institutional back-up, such as a church or state-enforced moral codes, because they replace individual avouching with the suppressed conscience of the masses.[79] In prison letter 141, Havel rejected any campaign that opens the door to "all the horrors of bureaucracy, repression, arbitrariness, violence, terror, and terrorism."[80]

While the violence test provides a barrier to the claims of the most dangerous fanatics and their brainwashed followers, truth-as-avouching remains disarmed before the less coercive but still specious assertions in an age of "mobile truth," which "permits even fraudulent people to manufacture sincere belief in what they are doing".[81] As Aviezer Tucker put it:

Even after we eliminate forms of fanaticism as candidates for authenticity, there may still be competing and inconsistent forms of authenticity. Different people may claim to experience Being differently, claim to listen to different calls for responsibility for Being, and accordingly develop

78 Erich Fromm, who influenced Havel's thinking in the early 1970s, also worried that on a "subjectivist viewpoint" of ideals, "a Fascist, who is driven by the desire to subordinate himself to a higher power and at the same time to overpower other people, has an ideal just as much as the man who fights for human equality and freedom." Fromm's solution, as a psychologist, was to distinguish true from false ideals, the former being any that "furthers the growth, freedom, and happiness of the self." See Erich Fromm, *Escape from Freedom* (New York: Avon Books, 1941), 292 and 294.
79 Šafařík, *Sedm listů Melinovi*, 201.
80 Havel, *Letters to Olga*, letter 141; see also Aviezer Tucker, *The Philosophy and Politics of Czech Dissidence from Patočka to Havel* (Pittsburgh: University of Pittsburgh Press, 2000), 160.
81 Alan Harrington, *Life in the Crystal Palace* (New York: Knopf, 1959), 198.

different and conflicting systems of ethics of authenticity. Havel did not address this problem.[82]

Also problematic but more ambivalent for Havel was science, which in the modern age is extolled as the quintessence of truth. Under the influence of his early mentors Fischer and especially Šafařík, Havel accepted that science is important but that it could:

[…] never ensure [zaručí] a truly human life (in the scientific age it is possible to live in the most inhuman way), it will never give our lives meaning, it will never answer the most dramatic questions that we pose, it will never show us how we should truly—as people—live. And inclination to the so-called scientific interpretation of the world is an escape from truth rather than an inclination towards it (science, after all, does nothing but shift the basic riddles of reality from one level of reality to another); it is an escape from the obligation to avouch personally for one's truth, to be one's truth. […] Every modern system that wanted to serve mankind but in reality forced mankind to serve it has been connected—so it seems to me—to the myth of science: but science is not and never has been about mankind, it is at most about advanced mammals, psychological types, social examples, productive forces, consumers, etc., mankind for science is always just a special instance of something general, in which it sees only something generalized, thus what from the perspective of a personality [osobnost] is the least significant.[83]

Havel expressed these reservations in 1967 while writing his play *The Increased Difficulty of Concentration*, which parodied attempts to subject human identity to scientific analysis. He was also responding to the debates of the day on the necessity of "scientific-ness" (*vědeckost*) in management, which Havel feared was just a convenient

82 Tucker, *The Philosophy and Politics of Czech Dissidence*, 161.
83 Interview by Bohuslav Blažek, "Být svou pravdou," *Literární noviny* 25:16 (June 24, 1967), 4.

way of avoiding inconvenient questions, such as who was in charge, who should be in charge and who should decide who should be in charge.[84] In the 1980s Havel's attitude to science intensified in reaction to the hubris, folly, and reckless irresponsibility that produced the desolate landscape he depicts in essays like "Politics and Conscience" and "Stories and Totalitarianism." The older critique of "scientism" was reformulated by philosophers such as Zdeněk Neubauer (himself a biologist by profession) in ways that shaped Havel's views into the post-Communist period.[85] In his *Summer Meditations* (1991) he reiterated his 1960s reservations about science almost verbatim, adding that "science can lead people to discover atomic energy, but cannot ensure [*nemůže ale už zaručit*] that they will not destroy each other with the atom bomb. I can't help it: without the involvement of powers as little scientific as healthy human deliberation and human conscience, nothing can get done."[86]

While science in the service of industry, including industrialized farming, and harnessed to the impersonal power of the state[87] fully deserves Havel's rebuke, the "science" he has in mind is practically the opposite of the method advised in the philosophy of science. In Havel's telling, science is an arrogant set of claims to an empirically proven truth that reduces the mystery of the universe to cold laws and theorems. However, in the Central European phenomenological tradition, for which Havel had a marked affinity, science operates in the realm of contingent *probabilities*, in which even canonical mathematical expressions, such as Newton's law of gravitation, are acknowledged to be "idealizing fictions" and "approximations," an "ideal possibility" that does not exclude potential alternatives

---

84 Blažek, "Být svou pravdou," 5.
85 On Neubauer's influence, see Putna, *Václav Havel*, 206–35. Neubauer's writings on science are collected in *O počátku, cestě a znamení časů* (Prague: Malvern, 2007).
86 Havel, *Spisy* 6, 455.
87 Havel in the 1980s was very influenced by Václav Bělohradský's idea of modern power as impersonal discipline and technique; see Kieran Williams, *Václav Havel* (London: Reaktion Press, 2016), 142.

and thus cannot be taken as "absolutely valid."[88] When properly preached and practiced, the scientific method commands modesty, reflection, and relentless critical testing of falsifiable hypotheses, and major breakthroughs often entail a creative struggle to represent nature more akin to the poetic imagination Havel admired.[89]

The problem of science and truth would be academically marginal were it not for another issue of pressing concern to Havel, the fate of the global climate. He was one of the first heads of state to identify climate change as a threat, while also expressing alarm at humanity's peculiar inability to act:

It is truly fascinating how people today follow all kinds of catastrophic prognoses with such concern—books convincingly showing what calamities we are tumbling headlong into become bestsellers!—and how very little people take these into account in their everyday activities. For how many years now have most of these warning facts been taught in schools and yet how small is the influence of this knowledge on human behaviour! Does not every schoolchild know today that the resources of this planet are limited and that if we exhaust them faster than they can be renewed, it cannot turn out well for us? And yet we do it and, it seems, are not at all disquieted.[90]

The apparent failure of facts to speak for themselves compelled Havel to look for rescue in a spiritual turn toward greater responsibility in place of "the modern conception of the world as a set of phenomena controlled by certain scientifically identifiable laws, generated for God-knows-what purpose, that is, a conception which does not

88 Lee Hardy, *Nature's Suit: Husserl's Phenomenological Philosophy of the Physical Scienes* (Athens, OH: Ohio University Press, 2013), 34–35.
89 Fernand Hallyn, *The Poetic Structure of the World: Copernicus and Kepler*, trans. Donald M. Leslie (New York: Zone Books, 1993), and David Kaiser, *How the Hippies Saved Physics* (New York: W.W. Norton, 2011).
90 Václav Havel, "Address to FORUM 2000", 1997; see also, a decade later, his essay "Our Moral Footprint," *New York Times*, September 27, 2007, A33.

acknowledge the question of the meaning of Being and renounces any kind of metaphysics or any kind of metaphysical roots of its own."[91] But the danger of reliance on a spiritual awakening in a matter such as climate change is that decentering the science plays into the hands of powerful people who deny the threat's existence or its anthropogenic origin. Science may have been co-responsible for creating the calamity, but it is also essential to recognizing that the calamity is happening and to finding ways to mitigate its impact, especially on the powerless. To at least some extent, we have to rely on and protect what Hannah Arendt in her essay on "Truth and Politics" called "modest verities," simple facts that seem so basic yet so vulnerable to the "onslaught of power."[92]

91 Havel, "Address to FORUM 2000," 1997.
92 Hannah Arendt, *Between Past and Future* (New York: Penguin Books, 1977), 231.

HOME, HOMELAND: *DOMOV*
Irena Vaňková

Introduction

"I consider Hrádeček my existential home [*domov*]," Havel pronounced in November 2010 when the town of Trutnov made him
an honorary citizen.[1] He both said and wrote something similar
at different times in his life and in a variety of contexts, and if we
are familiar with Havel's biography, we know why. But what does
domov mean in the broader context of his thought? His writings
indicate that he considers it a foundational existential experience,
that is, a phenomenon that defines both individual and sociocultural
identity: *domov* is a concept in which values that are simultaneously
deeply personal and social—if not also political in the broad sense of
the word—coalesce. It is not just a place that we inhabit, rather the
very fact that we have a *domov*, in the proper sense of the word, constitutes what it means to be a human being (cf. "dwelling" in Martin
Heidegger's philosophical understanding). The essential point is that
Havel often examines *domov* in philosophical terms; he interrogates
the concept's ontical as well as its ontological dimensions, its relation to Being. In doing so, he draws on Jan Patočka's phenomenology and the work of other existentially oriented thinkers connected
with Patočka, which he then makes use of in his own original way.
Havel highlights *domov* as an experience that is inextricably bound
up with a sense of responsibility—for our own home, neighborhood,
city, country, and ultimately also the world as a whole. He relativizes
the boundary between closeness and distance, between what belongs

---

1   See https://www.idnes.cz/hradec-kralove/zpravy/hradecek-je-muj-existencialni-domov-rekl
-cerstvy-trutnovan-vaclav-havel.A101105_151305_hradec-zpravy_klu. Trutnov is the closest
town to Havel's country home, which is known as Hrádeček, or "Little Castle." Hrádeček is the
historic name of the hamlet that includes Havel's farmhouse and a few other cottages; it is an old
Sudeten German settlement near the ruins of a medieval castle, Bröckstein.

to us and what belongs to others. *Domov* thereby becomes associated with a number of paradoxes or reconceptualizations: it is our most personal space, but at the same time it has a global dimension; it is experientially concrete (it can refer to a specific home, even a "pseudo-home" like a prison cell) while simultaneously having transcendent dimensions.

It is evident, then, that *domov* occupies a place of some importance among Havel's keywords. Commenting on the translation of Havel's works into English, David S. Danaher has, however, pointed out that the Czech word itself is semantically much richer than its nearest English equivalents ("home" or "homeland"), and he has posed two largely related questions. Can *domov* be considered a cultural key word in the Czech context, and how exactly does Havel understand it?[2]

We have an answer, more or less, to the first question. The term *domov* has been subjected to comparative ethnolinguistic analysis, and its cultural significance has been confirmed.[3] While the general concept of "home" does have universal aspects shared across languages and cultures, *domov* is unique: its meaning points distinctively to the Czech cultural context. It is, after all, the Czechs and only the Czechs who chose a song with the rhetorical question *Kde domov můj?* as their national anthem.[4]

In this study, we will mostly attempt to answer the second question, which concerns the status of *domov* in Václav Havel's writings.[5]

---

2   David S. Danaher, "Translating Havel: Three Key Words," *Slovo a slovesnost* LXXI (2010), 250–259; see also David S. Danaher, *Reading Václav Havel* (University of Toronto Press, 2015), chapter 4. Paul Wilson, Havel's English translator, has a similar take; see Paul Wilson, *Bohemian Rhapsodies* (Prague: Torst, 2011), 100.
3   See Irena Vaňková, "Český pojem DOMOV ve světle jazykových, empirických a textových dat," in Jerzy Bartmiński et al (eds), *Leksykon aksjologiczny Słowian i ich sąsiadów. Tom 1 – DOM* (Lublin: Wydawnictwo Uniwersytetu M. Curie-Skłodowskiej, 2015), 123–148.
4   *Where Is My Homeland?* is the English title of the anthem. For more on this anthem, see below.
5   Texts considered here include Havel's essays from the 1970s and 1980s (including *Letters to Olga*), his presidential speeches and reflections (including *Summer Meditations*), and the books

We will delineate both the principal semantic domains that *domov* features in and also those aspects of *domov*'s semantic profile that Havel accentuates. We will focus on the role played by *domov* in our lived experience of the so-called natural world and also on how the meaning of this fundamentally spatial concept is informed, at least as Havel understands it, by the notion of the "absolute horizon." In actuality, these three concepts—*domov*, the natural world, the absolute horizon—serve collectively as the main coordinates in Havel's intellectual and spiritual universe. Their interconnectedness lies at the heart of Havel's thought, and only by reference to these three interrelated concepts are we able to clarify the meaning of other Havelian key words (e.g., "identity," "responsibility," "human," etc.).[6]

In examining the centrality of these three concepts, we will draw on principles articulated in cognitive-cultural linguistics and in the philosophical tradition of phenomenology. This is partly because Havel's thinking resonates with each of these traditions[7] and partly

---

Disturbing the Peace and *To the Castle and Back*. For methodological reasons, we will be leaving aside Havel's plays as well as texts from other genres.

6   For more on "responsibility," see the chapter in this volume. Danaher has previously analyzed the Havelian key words *lidský* ("human[e])") and *lidskost* ("human[e]ness"); see David S. Danaher, "An Ethnolinguistic Approach to Key Words in Literature: *lidskost* and *duchovnost* in the Writings of Václav Havel," in *Ročenka textů zahraničních profesorů 4* (Prague: Univerzita Karlova, 2010), 27–54 and David S. Danaher, "Revolution with a 'Human' Face: A Corpus Approach to the Semantics of Czech *lidskost*," in M. Fidler and V. Cvrček (eds), *Taming the Corpus: From Inflection and Lexis to Interpretation* (New York: Springer, 2018), 119–144.

7   For studies of the philosophical aspects of Havel's texts, see, for example, the following: Jindřich Chalupecký, "Potřeba bdělosti," *Paraf (Paralelní Akta Filozofie)* 4 (1986), 4-20; Zdeněk Neubauer, *Výzva k transcendenci: Consolatio philosophiae hodierna* (Prague: Václav Havel Library, 2010); Radim Palouš, "Filozofování s Havlem," in A. Freimanová (ed.), *Milý Václave… Tvůj. Přemyšlení o Václavu Havlovi* (Prague: Lidové noviny, 1997), 161–187; Martin C. Putna, *Spiritualita Václava Havla. České a americké kontexty* (Prague: Václav Havel Library, 2009); Martin C. Putna, *Václav Havel: Duchovní portrét v rámu české kultury 20 století* (Prague: Václav Havel Library, 2012); Aviezer Tucker, *Fenomenologie a politika. Od J. Patočky k V. Havlovi* (Olomouc: Votobia, 1997). The book Ivan Havel et al., *Dopisy od Olgy* (Prague: Václav Havel Library, 2011) documents Havel's philosophical influences during his years spent in prison and serves as a necessary complement to his *Letters to Olga*.

because the traditions prove intellectually complementary. Since the usefulness of the former tradition as applied to Havel has already been demonstrated,[8] we will focus on the second tradition, which we might also call "linguaphenomenology."[9]

Domov also figures prominently as a theme in the work of contemporary Czech phenomenologists (Patočka's disciples as well as their disciples).[10] This ongoing need to come to terms with *domov* as a philosophical phenomenon—as a foundational human value serving to anchor us in the (natural) world—itself testifies to Czechs' particular regard for the term.

Phenomenology (and not only the Czech kind) connects *domov* with lived experience in a space, with the body and bodily memory. In his approach to "poetics of space," Bachelard calls this "topoanalysis."[11] *Domov* represents both the starting point of our existence, which is then stored in our memories, as well as the main determinate of our identity. Our home (that is, our family home), which is the prototypical form of *domov* (see below), symbolizes primordial goodness and safety. It is a universe unto itself, both in corporeal and spiritual terms; we later return to this childhood *domov* in dreams.

8   In addition to Danaher's works cited above, other studies of Havel's texts from the perspective of cognitive-cultural linguistics include the following student theses from the Philosophical Faculty of Charles University, all of which were supervised by the author of the present chapter: Veronika Dajčová, "Pojem 'člověk' v textech Václava Havla" (under preparation); Michaela Stará, "Pojem 'naděje' v textech Václava Havla (2016); Ondřej Vinš, "Apel a absurdita v textech Václava Havla" (2017).

9   For more on this term, see Irena Vaňková, *Nádoba plná řeči. (Člověk, řeč a přirozený svět)* (Prague: Karolinum, 2007), 26–29.

10   See, for example, Anna Hogenová, *Fenomén domova* (Prague: Pedagogical Faculty of Charles University, 2013) as well as other texts by the same author and also Pavel Pavlovský, "Duševní nemoc a privace domova," *Paideia: Philosophical E-Journal of Charles University*, 12:1 (2015), 1–19. We could mention here Bohumil Janát's assertion that *domov* represents "a major theme of philosophy past, present, and probably also future"—see Janát, "Domov jako metafyzický horizont lidského života. Několik myšlenek k filosofii domova," *Filosofický časopis* XL:3 (1992), 382–393. In her thesis *Domov jako téma českých filosofických prací 20. a 21. století* (České Budějovice: Jihočeská univerzita, 2018), Pavlína Převrátilová provides a comprehensive survey of "*domov* philosophy" from Antiquity to Patočka.

11   Gaston Bachelard, *Poetika prostoru* (Prague: Malvern, 2009), 32.

Before we are, in the spirit of Heidegger, "cast into the world," we are "laid in the cradle of the house."

In the experience of every individual, *domov* plays a particular and always unique role. It is through generalizing this experience across many generations that we may arrive at an entrenched linguistic profile for the concept. The stable elements of its semantic structure are embellished and extended in particular discourse, and the original concept may come to acquire unconventional semantic features. This is the process we can observe in Havel's textual usage. But even there the bedrock of all his reflections—that which is always present in the author's pre-understanding—is the entrenched profile of the concept in his native language.

Domov in Czech: a linguacultural excursus

The linguistic surrogate in Czech for *domov* as a concept is the actual noun *domov* itself as well as the more frequent everyday adverbs *doma* ("at home") and *domů* ("homeward"). Conceptually, the meaning of *domov* overlaps with the meaning of "family" and "family home," but also with "home region" [*rodný kraj*], "native country" [*rodná země*], "homeland" [*vlast*] as well as with "living" in general. It is also related to core experiences of human existence: to our birth and infancy, to the place where we first enter the social realm. Everyone is from somewhere (as the Czechs are wont to say), and asking about where is something we usually do upon meeting someone for the first time. Havel himself attests to this: when he was in prison, the question "Where are you from?" was one of the first asked of a new arrival to a cell, and allegiance to this or that Prague district, for instance, would convey something essential about the newcomer.

The word *domov* is relatively new in Czech. Its meaning took shape in the first third of the 19th century during the National Revival when the modern Czech nation with its own sense of the world—the

Czech "semiosphere"—was coming into being.[12] The first dictionary that contains an entry for *domov* is the *Jungmannův slovník česko-německý* published in 1835. The song *Kde domov můj* was composed in 1834, and in 1918 it became the Czech part of the national anthem for the newly created state of Czechoslovakia; it remains the anthem for the Czech Republic today.[13]

According to dictionaries, *domov* is a "place where someone lives or was born, a place where someone feels a sense of belonging." This may pertain to a (childhood or current) apartment or house and to one's family home, but also to a street or neighborhood, town or city, region (province, state) or even to one's whole (native) country. In this respect, Havel writes, as we will see, of the concentric circles of one's *domov*. The notion that one feels a "sense of belonging" points to the connotational aspects of *domov*, which are emotive and strongly positive.

Etymologically speaking, *domov* is based on declensional forms of the noun *dům* ("residential house") in Old Czech (*dóm*, genitive *domovi*). It is a general Slavic word that has its origin in the Indo-European root *dem-* "to build." *Dům* (in the sense of a concrete "house" or "home") is in fact the prototype for *domov*: the former serves as the source domain for the metaphorical extensions associated with the latter. For example, the phrase "common house [*společný dům*]" also implies the idea of a "common home [*společný domov*]" in terms of our practical sense of responsibility toward it as individuals who place a high value on it. In this regard, we may speak of the "common house [*dům* or *domov*] of Europe," which

---

12 See Vladimír Macura, *Znamení zrodu a české sny* (Prague: Academia, 2015).
13 The song is from a play, *Fidlovačka*, written by Josef Kajetán Tyl, and the music was composed by František Škroupa. It has since acquired mythological status. Even today the song is subject to parody and has also been the subject of (both scholarly and naive) reflection. See Patrik Ouředník (ed.), *Kde domov můj. Varianty a parafráze* (Praha-Litomyšl: Paseka, 2004). It had great historical and cultural significance for Czech self-awareness at the time it was composed, and it remains a culturally distinctive and nationally self-identifying text for Czechs today.

is a phrase used not only in Czech discourse: the clear distinction between *dům* (as a specific house or building) and *domov* (as a kind of multidimensional superstructure) is elided.[14] In his presidential New Year's Address delivered on January 1, 1991, Havel himself invokes this same idea through a parable based on the image of a long-neglected house (*dům*) that has been inherited. It is house in ruins, which needs to be restored to a habitable condition. The country after 1989, Havel asserts, is that house, and it can be restored only if the citizens take collective responsibility for it and treat it as a common *domov*. He writes: "Please be aware that we have already gotten rid of the evil landlord [*domácí*]. And regardless of how badly the house [*dům*] was damaged during the long years of his rule, the house [*dům*] now belongs to us, and it is entirely up to us how we rebuild it."[15]

On the Czech internet one can find variations on a text with the words "Money can buy a *dům*, but not a *domov*," and this thematizes the distinction between the two concepts: the material "house" vs the non-material "home," which has a deeper value and is irreplaceable.[16] This speaks to the high regard for the concept of *domov* in Czech culture, which is also signaled in Czech phraseology where we note the high frequency of a proverb like *všude dobře, doma nejlíp* (literally, "everywhere good, at home the best" or just "home sweet

---

14 Note, in this connection, Lubomír Nový's 1994 essay titled "Evropský dům jako budova a jako domov (Od partikularismu k emergentnímu univerzalismu," which is available here: https://digilib.phil.muni.cz/bitstream/handle/11222.digilib/107085/B_Philosophica_41-1994-1_2.pdf?sequence=1 (last accessed on November 25, 2020).

15 There is an interesting allusion to Havel's speech in the 2019 song *Chátrám* (the title here means "I fall into ruins") by Tomáš Klus, which can be read as an allegory for the current state of Czech society. In the song, Klus refers to "Vaněk the caretaker [*domovník*]," which alludes to a character in several of Havel's more well-known plays who serves as an alter ego to Havel. The full song can be found here: https://www.youtube.com/watch?v=-7Ny897Jhng (last accessed on November 25, 2020).

16 Note analogous oppositions in "hours [*hodiny*], but not time [*čas*]" and "sex, but not love [*láska*]."

home") and the fixed phrases *teplo domova* ("warmth of home") and *pohoda domova* ("comfort of home").[17]

In the semantic structure of the concept *domov*, we can distinguish three profiled levels.[18] The meaning of the most basic level is spatial (i.e., "a place where..."), and at this level the subject's perspective is in focus. The other two levels of meaning—most notably the social level that profiles the subject's connection to others, that is, the move from the individual "I" to a broader understanding of "we"—are metonymically and metaphorically derived from the basic spatial sense. This most basic level of meaning highlights the topological sense of the concept—*domov* as one's place of birth and origin, as a place where one "dwells."[19]

The second level profiles the spatial nature of *domov* in broader terms, and here is where Havel can speak of the concept as implying "concentric circles." We move, in other words, from a prototypical home (a house or apartment), which is at center of the category, to related meanings that are more peripheral; thus the phrases "to be home [*být doma*]" and "to go home [*jet domů*]" may conceptualize

---

17 The meaning of Czech *domov* is, in fact, connected with the meaning of the culturally key word *pohoda*. For more on *pohoda*, see Irena Vaňková, "Buďte v pohodě! (Pohoda jako české klíčové slovo)," in I. Vaňková and J. Pacovská (eds.), *Obraz člověka v jazyce* (Prague: Philosophical Faculty of Charles University, 2010), 31–63. In his book *Udělej si ráj* (Prague: Dokořán, 2011), Mariusz Sczygieł has also written about *pohoda*, which he sees as a Czech cultural value that serves, at least to some extent, to make up for the absence of a strong religious tradition in Czech society. To somewhat overstate his point, Czechs seek to create a "paradise on earth," and the creation of this worldly "paradise" revolves around the concept of *domov*. We will later return to the idea of *domov* metaphorically understood as a kind of "paradise" in connection with Havel.
18 For further detail on this point, see Irena Vaňková, "Český pojem DOMOV ve světle jazykových, empirických a textových dat," in: J. Bartmiński et al (eds.), *Leksykon aksjologiczny Słowian i ich sąsiadów. Tom 1 – DOM* (Lublin: Wydawnictwo Uniwersytetu M. Curie-Skłodowskiej, 2015), 123–148.
19 The concept of *domov* plays a significant role in how we understand the culturally entrenched opposition WE–THEM; see Anna Pajdzińska, "Kategorie strukturující jazykový obraz světa: antropocentrismus a opozice vlastní – cizí, " in L. Saicová Římalová (ed.), *Čítanka textů z kognitivní lingvistiky II* (Prague: Philosophical Faculty of Charles University, 2007), 27–44. For more on the term "dwelling," borrowed from Heidegger, see below.

"home" as one's own house, a hometown, a home region (state, province), or even a home country (which can be one's native country, but also another country of permanent residence).

The third semantic level profiles aspects of meaning that are conceptually derived, via both metonymy and metaphor, from the basic spatial sense. These include: the material and practical side of *domov* (i.e., everything that is involved in having a shared household); the social side (one's family and, in the extended understanding of *domov* above, one's friends, neighbors, and fellow citizens at various levels of society); linguistic and cultural aspects of meaning (a shared language or languages as well as aspects of a shared culture: lifestyle, values, sense of humor); and also transcendent aspects of meaning (heaven in the sense of a place where one goes after death to be reunited with loved ones who have died, but also "home" as an imagined, idealized place).

In everyday language, we often use *domov* not in its denotational sense as a place where we were born and/or live, but by emphasizing certain connotations associated with it—and this is, as we will see, prominent in Havel's texts. The denotational meaning is the conceptual ground, the semantic core. This, however, does not mean that it is free of connotational associations; indeed, we can say that in terms of how the word is typically used, the connotational aspects of meaning often predominate.[20] The connotations serve to supplement the meaning of *domov* as a place where we are (or were) unconditionally accepted and loved, as a place we long (sometimes in vain) to return

---

20 In his book on phenomenology and politics (cited in note 7), Tucker argues differently, noting that "not every home is a permanent or fixed residence," that there is a "distinction between home and place of birth," and that "one's native place is not always home"; see Tucker, *Fenomenologie a politika. Od J. Patočky k V. Havlovi*, 225 with the English originals in Aviezer Tucker, T*he Philosophy and Politics of Czech Dissidence from Patočka to Havel* (Pittsburgh: University of Pittsburgh Press, 2001), 253. We can readily agree with these statements while also understanding that these are cases that do deviate in some way from the prototypical conceptualization. In a larger sense, this is the same paradox that we find in Havel's texts with *domov* as a theme: the semantic power of the concept lies in the fact that its denotational (or "dictionary") meaning enters into tension with its connotational (or "authentic") meaning.

to, as a place where we find our loved ones (the living and also the dead), where we feel fully ourselves, and where we are reminded of events from long ago with their cast of characters—as a place that symbolizes personal continuity and identity. It is, in short, a place of deeply felt belonging.[21] Denotational and connotational aspects of meaning ideally exist in harmony with one another, and the positive connotations of *domov* arise from its denotation as our birthplace and place of residence, both of which are typically held in high value (and often idealized). This does not mean that there are not "homes" where people feel neglected or where they are subject to domestic violence, etc. These are not, however, prototypical or ideal(ized) versions of "home," but rather ones that merely have the necessary and sufficient features to categorize them as such.

The connotational potential of the words *domov*, *doma*, and *domů* is positively marked (even if they are often used in a neutral sense in everyday speech). The semantics of derivational formations and phraseology are sometimes linked to the denotational sense (e.g., *Zítra nebudu doma* "Tomorrow I won't be home") while at other times they are linked to the connotational sense (*Buďte tu jako doma* "Make yourself at home").

Metaphorical conceptualizations and metonymical extensions related to *domov* emerge from the linguistic foundation as described above, and we find these in literary works and in philosophical treatments—and also in Havel's texts. Havel's statement about Hrádeček as his "existential *domov*" that was cited at the beginning of this study illustrates the polarity—or rather the complementarity—between the denotational and connotational meanings. Havel adds: "I am not a long-time resident, I wasn't born here, but after coming here for 33 years, I can safely say that I feel at least a little bit at

---

21   Note Havel's English-language translator on this point: "[Havel] often speaks of his 'concrete horizon' or his *domov* (the meaning of this Czech word comes close to what we mean when we say 'a sense of belonging')"; see Paul Wilson, *Bohemian Rhapsodies* (Prague: Torst, 2011), 100.

home in this city and this part of the country [*jsem trochu srostlý s tímto městem a krajem*]."[22]

Havel's words confirm the suggestion that for Czechs the denotational meaning of *domov* (i.e., "the place where someone was born") is at least as important as the connotational meaning (i.e., "the place where someone feels a sense of belonging or feels at home"). These two aspects of the meaning of a word typically work in harmony. Havel's statement illustrates how the concept functions both in terms of "concentric circles" (*domov* here includes the whole region, including the nearby town of Trutnov where he has his country house) and also in terms of the expressive link ("feeling at home" or Czech *srostlost*) with that part of the country, both of which allow him to label it his *domov* even if it is not his actual place of birth.[23]

The "human dimensions" of *domov*

"It seems to me unfortunate, symbolically speaking, that the most natural of questions—where is your home [*domov*]?—I have heard asked most often in prison," writes Havel. He further explains that he was asked this question whenever he arrived in a new cell and upon hearing that he was from Prague, his fellow prisoners would want to know where, specifically, in Prague he was from—and that this surprised him, at least at first. Later he understood that prison is a "world of individual stories" where such a thing "as old-fashioned as a city district" still plays a significant role. He became interested in the fact, not at all common in socialist Czechoslovakia, that some people still think of Dejvice, Holešovice, or Libeň as "not just addresses but a real home [*domov*]," which indicated to him that

---

22   See https://www.idnes.cz/hradec-kralove/zpravy/hradecek-je-muj-existencialni-domov -rekl-cerstvy-trutnovan-vaclav-havel.A101105_151305_hradec-zpravy_klu (last accessed on November 25, 2020).
23   Note also the adjective "existential," which further confirms that it is Havel's *domov* in a metaphorical sense, that is, in terms of its importance for his sense of self.

these were people "who have not capitulated to the standardizing and nihilizing pressure of the modern housing estate [*sídliště*]," that they "still cling to their streets, the pubs on the corners, the former grocery store across the road—and to the mysterious and secret meaning of the stories connected to these localities."[24] It is precisely this "mysterious and secret meaning" of stories that are uniquely tied to a place and shared by loved ones in that place (and then communicated to other people close to us) that substantially shapes our identity and our humanity [*lidství*].

For Havel, the connotational aspects of *domov* described above lead to the conclusion that the essence of *domov* lies in its human dimensions. It is incumbent upon us not just to acknowledge that these dimensions exist, but also—in everyday life as well as "philosophically" and where possible even politically— to cultivate them. He insists upon this with some frequency, both in his roles as dissident and later as president. (As we have already noted, "humanness" [*lidskost*] for Havel is a key word.)

Havel also frequently explains (most extensively in *Disturbing the Peace*) the reasons for this reduction of life to a collection of formalities and functions, which includes the loss of an authentic human link to the world that is part and parcel of a modern technocratic, consumerist, and institutionalized society (a kind of attitude that was not by any means manifested only under socialism). In a number of the contexts where Havel discusses this, he explicitly contrasts the notions of "home" [*domov*] and "residence" [*bydliště*], the latter of which lacks the connotational attributes of the former:

For example, it's important that man have a home [*domov*] on this earth, not just a residence or dwelling place [*bydliště*]; it's important that his world have an order, a culture, a style; it's important the landscape be respected and cultivated with sensitivity, even at the expense of growth

24 Václav Havel, "Příběh a totalita," in *Spisy* 4, 931–959.

in productivity; it's important that the secret inventiveness of nature, its infinite variety, the inscrutable complexity of its interconnections, be honored; it's important that cities and streets have their own face, their own atmosphere, their own style; it's important that human life not be reduced to stereotypes of production and consumption, but that it be open to all possibilities; it's important that people not be a herd, manipulated and standardized by the choice of consumer goods and consumer television culture, whether this culture is offered to them by three giant competing capitalist networks or a single giant noncompetitive socialist network. It is important, in short, that the superficial variety of one system, or the repulsive grayness of the other, not hide the same deep emptiness of life devoid of meaning.[25]

A similar treatment (mass housing that "guarantees accommoda-tion by denying a real home [*domov*]") appears in *Letters to Olga*, and here Havel inserts it into a Heideggerian passage that contrasts a life with concretely human dimensions that is ultimately oriented toward Being with a life "that has succumbed to its existence-in-the-world."[26] At stake here is a pivotal value-oriented opposition that Havel is constantly trying to elucidate: it is an opposition that we can find throughout his oeuvre and in all his various textual genres. Being is suffused with a sense of mystery and transcendence, respect for life and human authenticity—that is, with the very concept of *domov* in an existential and ontological sense; mere "existence-in-the-world," however, represents a "world of functions, purposes and functioning, a world focused on itself, enclosed within itself, bar-ren in its superficial variety, empty in its illusory richness, ignorant,

25 Václav Havel, "Dálkový výslech," in *Spisy* 4: 699-917, the English translation here is from Václav Havel, trans. Paul Wilson, *Disturbing the Peace* (New York: Vintage Books, 1990), 15–16.
26 Václav Havel, *Letters to Olga*, letter 136; the translations here (and all further translation from this book) are again by Wilson in Václav Havel, trans. Paul Wilson, *Letters to Olga* (New York: Henry Holt, 1989). The phrase Havel uses is *propadlost pobytu*, which echoes Heidegger's "fallenness" into the inauthenticity of "existence-in-the-world."

though awash in information, cold, alienated and ultimately absurd .”[27] For Havel, it is just such an un-human [*ne-lidský*] world that "is eloquently symbolized by high-rise housing, which guarantees accommodation by denying a real home: without a genius loci to transcend its function as a source of accommodation, it transforms the mystery of the city into something that merely complicates life.”[28] Simply put, it is only *domov* that serves as accommodation while also having a genius loci, that is, a uniqueness and specificity that testify to the human authenticity of its residents. *Domov* is, in other words, suffused with Being.

In *Summer Meditations*, Havel outlines a political and civic vision for Czechoslovakia (which soon after split into the Czech Republic and the Slovak Republic). Here also he speaks of the "human dimensions" of the most diverse spheres of life—and he does so in concrete terms with a view toward advancing an idealized model of what life in Czechoslovakia should be; in this connection, he also discusses *domov*. He writes: "Life in the towns and villages will have overcome the legacy of greyness, uniformity, anonymity, and ugliness inherited from the totalitarian era[, and i]t will have a genuinely human dimension [*vskutku lidská dimenze*]”; then he concretizes this: "Every main street will have at least two bakeries, two sweetshops, two pubs, and many other small shops, all privately owned and independent[; t]hus the streets and neighbourhoods will regain their unique face and atmosphere.”[29] And yes: without these "human dimensions" (variety, uniqueness, atmosphere) we can hardly speak of *domov*.

This is, however, conditional upon one thing: that people should live in a "natural world," and neither in Havel's time nor today do we actually live in such a world. An explicit account of what Havel

27 Havel, *Letters to Olga*, letter 136.
28 Havel, *Letters to Olga*, letter 136.
29 Václav Havel, "Letní přemítání," *Spisy* 6, 493; translation by Wilson in Václav Havel, *Summer Meditations* (New York: Vintage Books, 1993), 104.

means by the term "natural world" can be found in his essay "Politics and Conscience."[30] He begins the essay by describing a childhood memory of a sky darkened with thick smoke pouring from a factory smokestack; this memory evokes a sense of repulsion or even a specific sense of guilt that emerges from a feeling that the factory smoke has somehow violated the natural of order of things. The same situation would have been, Havel continues, unimaginable to Medieval people, who would have deemed the darkening sky the work of the Devil. Like pre-industrial humans, children have a tendency to see the world as having a natural arrangement, and this may include not only magical aspects but also ethical ones: the natural world has a perceived order and eternal laws.

As might be expected, Havel understands the concept of the "natural world" somewhat differently than Jan Patočka.[31] The latter emphasizes human experience in the world in terms of the bodily, the spatial, the sensory, and also intuition; the world as a whole becomes the central horizon of a human life (see below). Havel, however, develops only one aspect of Patočka's understanding. Just like Heidegger, he places the "natural world" in opposition to the world of Modernity with its unsettling technocratic mechanisms that complicate self-understanding. These mechanisms marginalize or are rather blind to essential aspects of what it means to be human—an awareness of the role that transcendence plays in each of our lives as well as an intimate bond with our immediate environment (our *domov*) that give us a strong sense of both humility toward and also responsibility for that part of the world entrusted to us (and this includes its natural attributes as well as people close to us who inhabit it). Modern civilization has disrupted this arrangement by subordinating the natural world to technology (nature has become

---

30 Václav Havel, "Politika a svědomí," *Spisy* 4, 418–445.
31 Phenomenologists tend to understand this concept in their own way; Husserl, Patočka, and Havel are cases in point.

something we exploit for our own benefit) and by institutionalizing and impersonalizing human relationships.

A sense of responsibility toward the world as a whole and a feeling that we are ourselves part of that whole means, in essence, treating the whole world as our *domov*.[32] This resonates with Heidegger's thought about a special kind of human ("poetic") dwelling "on the Earth and under the sky," that is, with regard to his so-called indivisible "fourfold" of "the earth and sky, divinities and mortals."[33] In a 1950 essay devoted to the opposition between closeness and distance, Heidegger points out that technologization changed the world irrevocably, disrupting previously existing cultural forms. While technology, according to Heidegger, has reduced a sense of distance, it has at the same time also eliminated a sense of true closeness because "everything gets lumped together into uniform distancelessness."[34] And it is closeness (as well as the opposition between closeness and distance) that makes a sense of *domov* possible. People living in the modern era (not to mention in the post-modern era) have ceased to dwell in "the world as world"[35]: they are no longer "at home" in it, but rather wander, homeless, through it.[36]

Life in a world that has been warped by technological impersonalization (in Havel's words, a world of the visually "uniform" and gray housing-estate) stands in opposition to the natural world of primordial, subjective human experience and an intuitively perceived order. Havel's "human dimensions" are those that turn an indifferent sense of place into a true *domov*: a colorful, diverse space that is full

---

32 Undoubtedly connected with this is the idea of "caring for one's *oikos*" with *oikos* as a word in Ancient Greek meaning "the family, the family's property, the house"; the *oikos* was the basic societal unit in most Greek city-states. In a certain sense, then, this would mean "caring for one's *domov*." The word *oikos* is the source of *eco-* in words like "ecology" and "economics."
33 Martin Heidegger, "Věc" in *Básnicky bydlí člověk* (Prague: Oikoymenh, 2006), 6–37.
34 Heidegger, "Věc."
35 Heidegger, "Věc."
36 Heidegger, "Hebel—domácí přítel" in *Básnicky bydlí člověk* (Prague: Oikoymenh, 2006), 147–175.

of life and shared with a community of family and friends. When Havel dreams of his country's future as its president in the early 1990s, he believes, among other things, that its citizens will once again know what it feels like to have a true *domov*. He imagines this possibility in far more concrete terms than Heidegger, although he shares the latter's inspirational source.

The concentric circles of *domov*

In the section of *Summer Meditations* that contains a lengthy discussion of *domov*, Havel makes direct reference to Jan Patočka. Patočka approaches the natural world (and, by extension, life) topologically, and he sees *domov* as the core and center of the human (natural) world, as that part of the world "with which we are most familiar, where we feel safe and there is no need for any discoveries, where every expectation has already been or can always be fulfilled in a typical way."[37] He writes of the "shading" of the home-world that runs "from family to locality, community, region, nation, state, etc." and "recedes into the indeterminate in a mixture of known and unknown, near and far."[38]

---

[37] Jan Patočka, *Přirozený svět jako filosofický problém* (Prague: Československý spisovatel, 1992), 85. On the same page, he continues: "Home is not merely our individual home; it includes community as well, with a variety of typical structures based on the various and variously intermeshed interests of the social groups that partake in it: the narrow family home with its life-functions of everyday close contact and order, the broader home of looser social relations which one feels more or less tied to and understands on the basis of traditions and of one's own personal interests. This more broadly conceived home is then differentiated into the domains or worlds of various professional occupations in which everyone is also, in various ways, 'at home,' and out of which he looks upon the others; yet, in a sense, all these human occupations, whose function we become accustomed to within our community, belong to our broader home." The English translations are taken from Jan Patočka *The Natural World as a Philosophical Problem*, I. Chvatík and Ľubica Učník (eds.), trans. Erika Abrams (Chicago: Northwestern University Press, 2016), 56.
[38] Patočka, *Přirozený svět jako filosofický problém*, 85; Patočka, *The Natural World as a Philosophical Problem*, 56. This "shading" corresponds to Havel's concentric circles of home. We have also already seen this aspect of the semantics of *domov* in our earlier analysis of its second profiled level.

To Patočka's philosophical analysis of *domov*, Havel adds the metaphor of "concentric circles [*soustředné kruhy domova*]"[39] at the center of which is the individual subject, and he speculates on the various aspects of belonging that *domov*, broadly speaking, may entail:

> My home is the house I live in, the village or town where I was born or where I spend most of my time. My home is my family, the world of my friends, my profession, my company, my workplace. My home, obviously, is also the country I live in, and its intellectual and spiritual climate, expressed in the language spoken there. The Czech language, the Czech way of perceiving the world, the Czech historical experience, the Czech modes of courage and cowardice, Czech humor—all of these are inseparable from that circle of my home. My home is therefore my Czechness, my nationality, and I see no reason at all why I shouldn't embrace it since it is as essential a part of me as, say, my masculinity, another stratum of my home. My home is not only my Czechness, of course; it is also my Czechoslovakness, which means my citizenship. Beyond that, my home is Europe and my Europeanness and —ultimately— it is this world and its present civilization and for that matter the universe. But that is not all: my home is also my education, my upbringing, my habits, my social milieu. And if I belonged to a political party, that would indisputably be my home as well.[40]

Havel, however, does not want merely to enumerate the various kinds of *domovy* that collectively comprise a person's life (or identity). This multilayered approach to *domov* leads him to consider

39 With regard to *domov*, Havel writes either of "circles" or "layers [*vrstvy*]," the latter of which he does not mean in a topological but rather metaphorical sense as aspects of our personality and self-identity in relation to our engagement in various experiential domains. These words evoke somewhat different, but complementary cognitive profiles. For a discussion of this point in relation to the translation of Havel's texts into English, see Danaher, *Reading Václav Havel*, 181ff.

40 Havel, *Letní přemítání*, 409; the English translation is Wilson's in Havel, *Summer Meditations*, 30–31.

implications in the political realm, and he states: "Every circle, every aspect of the human home, has to be given its due. It makes no sense to deny or forcibly exclude any one stratum for the sake of another; none should be regarded as less important or inferior" because all belong to our natural world and a "properly organized society has to respect them all and give them all the chance to play their roles." As always with Havel, the focus is on how to fully realize oneself as a human being—how, that is, to realize the full potential of one's self-identity. Identity must be given its due since "[a]ll the circles of our home, indeed our whole natural world, are an inalienable part of us, and an inseparable element of our human identity," and if we are deprived of all the aspects of our *domov*, we would be deprived of ourselves, of our very humanity [*lidství*].[41]

His approach to *domov* also helps him explain his views on the role played by national allegiances in the federative republic of Czechoslovakia. Czechoslovaks should not think of their *domov* primarily through the lens of nationality (as Czechs or as Slovaks), but should rather appreciate that a sense of *domov* emerges also from other experiential domains. He suggests that citizenship—that is, participation in a civil society—be the overarching principle underlying a sense of belonging because, on the one hand, it would certainly be less contentious and, on the other, it "represents the best way for individuals to realize themselves, to fulfill their identity in all their circles [*vrstvy*] of home." To establish the state on any other basis (nationality, ideology, religion) would mean "making a single stratum of our home superior to the others, and thus detracting from us as people, and detracting from our natural world."[42]

In a presidential address on October 28, 2002, which took place just after the Czech Republic had experienced devastating flooding,

---

41 Havel, *Letní přemítání*, 411; the English translation is Wilson's in Havel, *Summer Meditations*, 31.
42 Havel, *Letní přemítání*, 411; the English translation is Wilson's in Havel, *Summer Meditations*, 32.

Havel again interrogates the essential meaning of *domov*.[43] His answer is much the same as before but contains a new twist. As before, he emphasizes that *domov* "means simply that which is closer to us than whatever lies beyond." It is, however, less about the place itself than it is about the people who live there generation after generation, people who have a shared culture, language, and customs as well as shared archetypal ideas about the world. At the center of our individual home are family and friends, but if we expand our "concentric circles of *domov*" outward, then we should readily admit into our home—and treat as we do our loved ones—fellow Czech citizens we do not personally know as well as fellow Europeans.

Domov for Havel becomes once again a political matter, although this time in a context that extends beyond the confines of the Czech Republic. And if we ask where exactly closeness ends and distances begins (or where our sense of *domov* ends and a sense of foreignness begins), then the only reasonable response we can give is that everything is so interconnected in the contemporary world that we must naturally extend our sense of belonging—of closeness, of the limits of our *domov* [*domovskost*]—to the whole world. Here Havel metaphorizes the world as a single, encompassing organism that includes one's house and neighborhood, one's city and country, and ultimately also everything that extends beyond:

> Therefore, just as our house is firmly settled on our street and its occupants share the life of that street with its other inhabitants; and, just as our street constitutes an organic component part of our city, interconnected with its other parts through the same basic nervous system, the same veins enabling its blood circulation and the same metabolism, so is our state a component part of a broader human community. Even our entire continent no longer represents a world in itself or unto itself, because such closed worlds no longer exist. This was

43 Václav Havel, "Státní svátek České republiky," October 28, 2002.

not always the case in the past history of humankind; maybe it has not been that way ever before. But in the world of today, in which information, goods, achievements, ownership, money, habits, cultural values, and, of course, people travel far and wide through millions of channels, this planetary dimension of home must be recognized as well.[44]

What should above all else follow from an experience of *domov*'s "planetary dimension" is a sense of co-responsibility for the world as a whole.[45] Havel writes that "we cannot merely take pleasure in benefiting from all the advantages offered by the contemporary development of our civilization," but we must also "assume an increased measure of our co-responsibility for the overall state of affairs and boldly project this co-responsibility into our deeds." Recalling the international support received by the Czech Republic after the floods, Havel asserts that we should not see this as "merely an expression of somebody's compassion or good character, but as part of a greater process aspiring toward an all-embracing solidarity among human beings, which is the only course left for us in the contemporary world if it is not to end badly."[46] Havel thereby relativizes the concept of "otherness [*cizí*]," just as he does with the opposition between closeness and distance. Everything is close: closeness is a matter of grading. Each individual's *domov* has a different central locus, but we can also readily extend our sense of what is close (and what we care deeply about) to the world as a whole. This reconceptualization has political as well as philosophical dimensions.

When Patočka writes about the "growing reality in our consciousness" of the world as a phenomenon, he does not have in mind the world as planet. While he is thinking topologically, his target is different. The world—our context, our horizon—imparts meaning to

---

44 Havel, "Státní svátek České republiky," October 28, 2002.
45 For more on "(co-)responsibility" as a key Havelian word, see the appropriate chapter in this volume.
46 Havel, "Státní svátek České republiky," October 28, 2002.

everything, and it is only thanks to our awareness of the world as such that things make sense. Its opposite would be meaninglessness and chaos ("homelessness" in Heidegger's sense). We are, in Patoč-ka's words, "beings that have the world," and we are also beings that have a related sense of *domov*.[47]

Domov in philosophical thought

My family, friends, acquaintances, fellow prisoners, the unknown weatherwoman, my fellow passengers in the streetcar, the transport commission, those who go to see my plays, the public, my homeland and the state power-structure; countless relationships, tensions, loves, dependencies, confrontations, atmospheres, milieux, experiences, acts, predilections, aims and things with which I am loosely or closely connected—all of that forms the "concrete horizon" of my relating, because all of it is my world, the world as my home, the world in which I am rooted in a complex way, to which I ceaselessly relate, against the background of which I define myself, through which I simply am. It is the world of my existing, such as it presents and opens itself to me, as I make myself at home in it, as it constitutes itself for me through my experiences and as I—in one way or another—make it meaningful. Thus my "I" creates this world and this world creates my "I." And yet: my existence in this world and the way I relate to my "concrete horizon" cannot be explained... by some one-sided and unqualified clinging to them as such... It depends, rather, on something else: on the extent to which I direct my existence-in-the-world toward Being; not, of course, toward Being as something outside the world and which can be attained only by "leapfrogging" or ignoring the world, but on the contrary, toward Being as something that is "in the world" far more radically than anything the world declares and offers itself to be at first sight: that is, toward its own Being, i.e., to the

---

47 Patočka, *Přirozený svět jako filosofický problém*, 84; for English translations (which have been slightly altered here), see Patočka, *The Natural World as a Philosophical Problem*, 55.

very Being of this world. This can only mean that through my life, through the experiences and trials I undergo, I gradually penetrate beyond the different horizons of my "concrete horizon," I attempt to widen them, to step past them, to see beyond them, to get to what is on the other side of them—until ultimately I aspire toward a place beyond its ultimate, conceivable limit, the "horizon of all my horizons," to what I call the "absolute horizon" of my relating.[48]

Philosophers (and philosophically oriented psychotherapists[49]) have affirmed the connection between the experience of a specific, ontically understood *domov* and an ontological one. A significant role here is played by the experience of privation: either being deprived of one's *domov* or experiencing the absence of a place that has previously served as one. It is this absence (the experience of a "lost paradise") that triggers psychological recognition of both the value of what has been lost and also, more broadly speaking, the importance of anchoring one's life story in a *domov*. And this is the critical point: privation leads to a rediscovery and reaffirmation of the anchoring process every time it happens. As Hogenová has said (through an intellectual return to the philosophers of Ancient Greece as well as Heidegger), our *domov* is our "fire source [*ohňový střed*]," both the family hearth and also the sacred fire. If it is present within us, then it grounds our being: we can continually return to it for spiritual renewal throughout our lives, regardless of where we happen to be.[50]

According to Patočka, the experience of *domov* includes its very obviousness (or, as the case may be, its obscurity): this experience is usually not at the level of conscious awareness, but rather forms an

48 Havel, *Letters to Olga*, letter 140.
49 See, for example, Pavel Pavlovský, "Duševní nemoc a privace domova," *Paideia: Philosophical E-Journal of Charles University* 12:1 (2015), 1–19.
50 See Anna Hogenová, *Fenomén domova* (Prague: Pedagogical Faculty of Charles University, 2013).

unobtrusive background (a kind of screen) on which the events of our life are projected.[51] This, however, is not always the case, which is a fact attested to by those who have been involuntarily deprived of their *domov* or who have lost it altogether. A yearning for one's *domov* or the tragedy of losing it, whether it be because of war, emigration, or imprisonment—this is a deeply affecting experience. It is through privation, then, that *domov* can be best understood as an ontological phenomenon, that is, in terms of its relation to Being.[52]

Havel first formulated what *domov* meant for him in his letters from prison, that is, when he was suffering (for several years) from a lack of it. It was, then, an experience of privation that first prompted him to reflect ontologically on the meaning of the concept.

Havel's letters from prison are notable in how they develop certain themes, and the theme of *domov* is no exception. Havel's early letters betray his intense longing for home: they feature vivid recollections and imaginings related to home, but also his seeming need to continue to manage practical aspects of his home life from his prison cell. To the latter end, he gives his wife Olga detailed instructions and tasks to complete that relate to home maintenance, which allows him to be connected to his home environment at least in a certain way. Later letters then chart in some detail Havel's gradually changing attitude toward home as the opposition between his prison pseudo-home (the current home of the letter writer or his "here and now") and the inaccessible *domov* he left behind (his real home, his "there and then"). He begins to find it necessary to distinguish between (at least) these two homes: the home of his "concrete horizon" and a home linked to other horizons, which, in its most

---

51 According to Heidegger, that which is ontically closest is, at the same time, ontologically the most distant, which is why it is so difficult to apprehend one's own corporeality or language, that is, those aspects of our identity that are the most fundamental. By its very nature, then, *domov* is both obscured and covered over, even though it is a basic human experience and also the foundation of our identity.

52 According to Patočka, an idea can only be fully grasped through its negation; note the title of his book *Negativní platonismus* (Prague: Oikoymenh, 2007).

extreme and generalized form, is his "absolute horizon." He gradually transforms from a writer of letters who longingly recalls his absent *domov* into a writer of philosophical reflections about *domov* as a phenomenon.

At this point we would do well to recall, at least in passing, Jan Patočka's treatment of the three movements of human life.[53] The first movement, linked to childhood, is one of acceptance and "rooting" into the world: after we are born, we are "accepted" into the world and surrounded by love in our primary *domov*, which leads us to sink down roots in a specific human community. The second movement, the movement of self-sustenance or self-projection, occurs in adulthood: we "work and struggle," we take care of the needs of life. According to Patočka, both these movements are oriented toward the practical or "toward the Earth," which is our point of reference. Sometimes these movements may grow into a third movement, the most existentially important one—the movement of truth or self-transcendence. The third movement may be triggered by an existential shock or life upheaval: we lose our existential grounding by being deprived of certainties that we had come to take for granted, and this "absolute privation" leads to a complete change of perspective. The third movement no longer has Earth for its point of reference, but it is characterized rather by a turn toward the spiritual. It is a conversion of sorts, in which we begin to cultivate a philosophical attitude toward the world in its entirety.

It is obvious that Havel experienced an existential shock while in prison, which results in a shift of perspective that reminds us of Patočka's third movement. His prison letters testify to this shift in that they represent the beginning of purposeful reflection on philosophical topics. These letters are suffused with reflections on meaning both as a holistic phenomenon and with regard to his own particular

---

53 Patočka, *Přirozený svět jako filosofický problém*, 233–251.

situation; they interrogate the root sources of human identity. Simply put, they have as their primal focal point the "experience of Being."[54]

Havel's prison experience results in a more profound understanding of *domov* as a human phenomenon. The original *domov*—the one that consists of his "family, friends, acquaintances, fellow prisoners, the unknown weatherwoman," etc.—certainly remains, but in addition to this "concrete horizon" that situates each of us in the specific context of our own "home-world," there are other dimensions to *domov* to be taken into consideration. These other dimensions emerge given the extent to which, according to Havel, he "direct[s his] existence-in-the-world toward Being," how "through [his] life, through the experiences and trials that [he] undergo[es], [he] gradually penetrate[s] beyond the different horizons of [his] 'concrete horizon' and attempt[s] to widen them, to step past them, to see beyond them, to get to what is on the other side of them—until ultimately [he] aspire[s] toward a place beyond its ultimate, conceivable limit, the 'horizon of all [his] horizons,' to what [he] call[s] the 'absolute horizon' of [his] relating."[55]

This stratification of horizons (and *domovy*) is even more precisely described when the prisoner distinguishes the "horizon of [his] current environment, into which he has been thrown for the time being"—that is, his prison cell or the "small walled space" of his here and now (which is also a concrete *domov* or rather pseudo-*domov*)—from the *domov* that is currently inaccessible to him given his imprisonment, but is nonetheless concretely real and to which he is still emotionally and psychologically linked. But, as we understand, even this latter *domov* is still not the last and truly absolute

54   The philosopher and naturalist Zdeněk Neubauer, who was among Havel's friends and interlocutors who inspired the so-called "letters from Olga" (see Ivan Havel et al, *Dopisy od Olgy*), points to Havel's "philosophical conversion" as evidenced in his prison letters; see Neubauer, *Výzva k transcendenci: Consolatio philosophiae hodierna*.
55   Havel, *Letters to Olga*, letter 140.

horizon or "the metaphysical vanishing-point of life" that defines its full meaning and that many people experience as God.[56]

As cornerstones of Havel's key concepts, *domov* and the absolute horizon are correlative phenomena: they inform each other in intriguing ways. They also form the central axis of Havel's spiritual universe.

Domov, the absolute horizon, and the lost paradise of Being: from topology to existentiality

When we begin inquiring seriously after the meaning of life and Being, there usually begins to emerge, sooner or later, from the dimness of our unconsciousness the emotional assumption of this "absolute horizon," this "tablet" on which everything transitory is inscribed, this point of instability from which the entire order of Being grows and which makes that order an order in the first place.[57]

I would say that the meaning of any phenomenon lies in its being anchored in something outside itself, and thus in its belonging to some higher or wider context, in its illumination by a more universal perspective; in its being "hung," like a picture, within a higher order, placed against the background of a horizon.[58]

This inner echo of a home or a paradise forever lost to us—as a constitutive part of our "I"—defines the extent of what we are destined to lack and what we therefore cannot help but reach toward: for does not the hunger for meaning, for an answer to the question of what—in the process of becoming ourselves—we have become, derive from the recollection of a separated being for its state of primordial being in Being?[59]

56 Havel, *Letters to Olga*, letter 53.
57 Havel, *Letters to Olga*, letter 94.
58 Havel, *Letters to Olga*, letter 99.
59 Havel, *Letters to Olga*, letter 129.

Both *domov* and horizon (and also the world) are primarily spatial concepts, but both concepts can be metaphorically extended into intellectual and spiritual domains—and this is a general strategy in Havel's writing. Both concepts are also most definitely related to human identity. When Havel writes about *domov* from the perspective of different horizons of Being or in terms of concentric circles, he is invoking Patočkian philosophical principles. This is equally true when he attempts to articulate the connection between *domov* and identity and also when he considers the absolute horizon in correlation with the "I" and in terms of the multilayered nature of *domov*.

In Patočka, the "I" is always embodied.[60] Only through our embodiment in the world can we interact with things and cultivate relationships with both ourselves and others. Our bodies anchor us spatially and allow us access to the world as a whole. We become aware of our place in the world not only ontically, but also ontologically. Unlike animals, we "have" the world (a context)—or, as Havel would say, a horizon. The latter emerges from our personal spatiality,[61] in which *domov* occupies a paramount position. Patočka speaks about the structure of the natural world in terms of topological categories: for him, embodied spatiality is the ground for both thought and language, and this principle is shared in a cognitive approach to linguistics.[62]

We have already noted that the primarily spatial concepts of "world," "horizon," and *domov* become metaphorically projected into abstract domains. When we, along with Havel, speak of horizons that are less concretely manifested, including the "absolute" horizon, we are engaging in metaphorical extension of our physical

60   Jan Patočka, *Tělo, společenství, jazyk, svět* (Prague: Oikoymenh, 1995), 24.
61   Patočka, *Tělo, společenství, jazyk, svět*, 25.
62   See, for example, Ronald Langacker, *Grammar and* Conceptualization (Berlin: Mouton, 1999) or Mark Johnson, *The Body in the Mind. The Bodily Basis of Meaning, Imagination, and Reason* (Chicago: The University of Chicago Press, 1987).

embodiment via two experientially related source domains, spatiality and visuality (or rather the notion of visual orientation in space).

When Havel refers to the "specific horizon of his relating," he has in mind a complex of real-life contexts that represent everyday goings-on, whether they are taking place in prison (the locus of his writing) or took place before in his pre-prison life. It is not so much spatiality that is in focus here, but rather the general environment in which things happen—specific places with specific people along with certain kinds of situations, actions, discourse, relationships. Havel is invoking the overall psycho-social atmosphere of specific human communities in which he engages.[63] Havel's "concrete horizon" is, then, an individual complex of experiences representing a specifically construed world: a *domov*-world that shapes self-awareness and identity. Our "I" is correlative with this world—it is rooted specifically in it.[64]

In addition to this, however, there is something else that determines the nature of our existence in this world, and it is related to Being or rather, in Havel's words, to the extent to which we "direct [our] existence-in-the-world toward Being." During the course of our lives, various horizons of Being reveal themselves to us: some we may readily grasp while others will be more difficult to fathom, and the "absolute horizon" falls into the latter category. The absolute horizon invokes something "beyond this world" (see below), that is, something that lies outside normal spatial coordinates but that is still essentially linked to the physical world as such. Here we can agree with cognitive linguistics in claiming that we can access this extra-reality, at least to a certain extent, through language and specifically in metaphorical expressions that conceptually evoke it; note, for example, the phrases that Havel uses in certain passages:

---

63 Here he emphasizes the social dimension of *domov*. Note that for Havel theater represents a special kind of *domov* in this regard. See, for example, Havel, *Letters to Olga*, letter 107.
64 Havel, *Letters to Olga*, letter 140.

"orient ourselves to," "penetrate beyond," "see beyond," "aspire to."[65] While the semantic structure of the phrases that Havel uses is primarily spatial, at the same time they shift attention away from the purely topological toward the existential.

The absolute horizon is, then, associated with spatiality—the latter serves as the physical source domain for the metaphorical extension into the former's intellectual and spiritual domain—but the same could be said in regard to *domov*. *Domov* is, first and foremost, about closeness. But it is not concerned with physical or spatial closeness as much as it is with a kind of intimate familiarity that shapes our world and our identity as a lived experience in that world; it is this process that gradually leads us to an experience of the absolute horizon. In the broader context of Havel's reflections in *Letters to Olga*, then, *domov* (even in the sense of a "lost paradise") becomes identified with the absolute horizon.

Havel begins the first of his so-called sixteen philosophical letters with the following: "Birth from the maternal womb—as the moment one sets out on one's journey through life—presents a telling image of the initial condition of humanity: a state of separation."[66] The integrity of original being takes the form of a lost paradise, a lost primordial *domov*: we leave it behind at birth and we spend our whole lives longing to return to it (which would mean, of course, the demise of ourselves as individuals). Formulations such as this are attempts to express a vague memory that we were once also "at home" elsewhere than in the corporeal world.

The "voice of Being"—that primordial experience of a distant *domov* where we were once enmeshed in the totality of the universe— speaks to us when, for example, we become suddenly aware of another person's vulnerability. We can recall here Havel's narrative of sudden compassion for a television meteorologist who, on the screen

---

65 Havel, *Letters to Olga*, letter 140.
66 Havel, *Letters to Olga*, letter 129.

in front of millions of viewers, cannot handle the feeling of embarrassment that results from the accidental failure of her audio. In his story (which is also her story), he exemplifies his (and the French philosopher Emmanuel Levinas's) understanding of responsibility for another human being. We exist in union with everything and everyone: in a "prenatal state of being-in-Being," our *domov* once encompassed the totality of all. In certain life situations, we apparently feel that it still does.[67]

In other passages, Havel also equates, at least to some extent, the absolute horizon and Being, which makes it possible to assert the following: *domov*, the absolute horizon, and Being are all different aspects of the same phenomenon. In terms of the theory of conceptual metaphor as developed by George Lakoff and Mark Johnson, we can render the connections as *DOMOV* IS BEING, *DOMOV* IS ABSOLUTE HORIZON, and finally *DOMOV* IS WORLD (that is, it is my world).[68]

This seems to be a metaphorical conceptualization that we find in a more transparent form in the Czech (and not only the Czech) linguacultural context where it takes the form of a reciprocal metaphor, namely, *DOMOV* IS PARADISE / PARADISE IS *DOMOV*.[69] Both for philosophers and for ordinary people, *domov* serves as an ideal. It is a place where we feel a deep sense of belonging: we feel that we belong there more than anywhere else, and we yearn to experience that feeling. We would say that we are (or were) at our best in this place: among family and friends in an environment we know well where we feel both welcomed and expected. As Havel writes,

---

67 See Havel, *Letters to Olga*, letter 130.
68 See George Lakoff and Mark Johnson, *Metaphors We Live By* (Chicago: University of Chicago Press, 1980).
69 This conceptualization is related to our third profiled level in the semantic structure of *domov*, and it seems to occur only in certain kinds of textual sources—artistic literature, religious texts, memoirs, and, not surprisingly, philosophy. It stems from the belief that our second (maybe even our true) *domov* is situated beyond the material world. For more detail on this point, see Vaňková, "Český pojem DOMOV ve světle jazykových, empirických a textových dat."

it is a place characterized by a certain turn of humor, an intimately familiar life routine, a sense of shared values. Those people who also inhabit this place share with us a common history and a common culture in the broadest sense: everyone understands each other and feels good being together. Our *domov* is an idealized environment that we take as our whole world.

Conclusion: "I lived also here"

A theme I wanted to write about: what is home? A certain concrete horizon to which one relates... The hiddenness of that horizon. The more urgently one relates to it as a result. The outline of this horizon changes (sometimes it is created by mountains, at other times by an urban skyline); the arrangement of people, relationships, milieus, traditions, etc. changes, but the horizon "as such" remains. As something absolute.[70]

The first sentence of Patočka's book *The Natural World as a Philosophical Problem* reads: "The problem of philosophy is the world as a whole."[71] Havel's reflections in *Letters to Olga* are concerned precisely with the world as a whole—or rather with the most complex questions of human existence. In his own way and for his own benefit, he tries to come to terms with what his favorite philosophers often call the "existential situation," that is, with human being and human existence (the meaning of life, subjectivity, identity, responsibility, transcendence, etc.). At the core of all this lies the complex phenomenon of the absolute horizon, which Havel sees as associated—if not identical—with *domov*.

---

70   Havel, *Letters to Olga*, letter 52.
71   Patočka, *Přirozený svět jako filosofický problem*, 13; the English translation is from Patočka, *The Natural World as a Philosophical Problem*, 6.

As metaphor, *domov* extends its meaning from a topological source domain to an existential target domain, and the latter is understood in transcendent terms as one's belonging to the world as a whole. *Domov* is conceptualized as a supreme human value that is connected to the natural world: the emphasis here is on human identity and the uniqueness of humans as a species. Only humans are capable of having a *domov*. Neither humanity itself nor *domov* as a phenomenon can be "objectivized" in a simplistic and reductionist manner (that is, we cannot do this scientifically, within a certain ideological framework, or for technocratic-administrative reasons). The utilitarian and technocratic conception of a human being in a "living space" represents the most tragic failure of modern civilization. We need instead to reclaim responsibility for the world by living in it "humanly [*lidsky*]" and by treating as a true *domov*.

While in prison, Havel arrives at the stage of Patočka's third existential movement. The ontological fullness of *domov* reveals itself to him in privation—he deeply feels its absence. He writes philosophical reflections about this experience, in which *domov* figures as the most intimate space in the world as a whole and also as a launching point toward the absolute horizon as a phenomenon—and ultimately, more or less, as the absolute horizon itself.[72]

Domov is a place "where I belong more than anywhere else."[73] We have already noted that spatiality and the embodied experience of place form the basis of our human relationship to the world. Through the cognitive categories of closeness and distance, open-

---

72 This corresponds (*mutatis mutandis*) to the treatment of *domov* by certain Czech phllosophers, largely disciples of Patočka (see above), who work on *fil/sofie domova* ("*domov*-oriented philosophy"): "In its more profound sense, *domov* represents an injection of the vantage point of eternity into the finite temporality of human worldly existence" and "*Domov* is a conceptual space where human longing for eternal life resides"; see Janát, "Domov jako metafyzický horizont lidského života. Několik myšlenek k filosofii domova."
73 Patočka, *Přirozený svět jako filosofický problém*, 86.

ness and closedness, the path (as a transition from one space to another), viewpoint, etc., the subjective experience of spatial embodiment becomes the basis for conceptualizing essential human experiences of a non-physical nature. We conceptualize phenomena that are *trans*cendent and *meta*physical on the basis of cognitive strategies grounded in spatiality: they are understood as something that exists "beyond" physical space. This applies equally to *domov* as a privileged kind of space—and specifically to Havel's philosophical treatment of the concept.

Domov as our concrete place of residence is something that is both physically "here" and also, in some difficult-to-fathom sense, "elsewhere." In the excerpt below, Havel uses the words "here" and "somewhere here" to point simultaneously to both the *domov* of his "concrete horizon" and also to another space that is linked to the "absolute horizon" of Being. "Somewhere here" means not only "here," but also "elsewhere." From the vantage point of the absolute, space and time are integrated, and all that has been has also been deposited in the memory of Being, which is, its own way, another kind of *domov*. It is *domov* as the lost paradise that will perhaps once again be found.

All my life I have simply believed that what is once done can never be undone and that, in fact, everything remains forever. In short, Being has a memory. And thus even my insignificance—as a bourgeois child, a laboratory assistant, a soldier, a stagehand, a playwright, a dissident, a prisoner, a president, a pensioner, a public phenomenon, and a hermit, an alleged hero but secretly a bundle of nerves—will remain here forever, or rather not here, but somewhere. But not, however, elsewhere. Somewhere here.[74]

74   Havel, *Prosím stručně* (Prague: Gallery, 2006), 235; the translation is by Wilson in Václav Havel, *To the Castle and Back* (New York, Knopf, 2007), 330.

This fact, which is in all likelihood paradoxical, regarding the duality of human being—and likewise the ontical and ontological duality of *domov*—perhaps resonates well with the inscription on the memorial plaque at Havel's birthplace on Rašínovo nábřeží in Prague: I also lived here[75]

Václav Havel

---

75 The original Czech reads *zde jsem taky žil.*

PRISON: *VĚZENÍ*

Jiří Suk

Introduction

On Friday, January 14, 1977 after a week of intense interrogations brought on by the publishing of the Charter 77 declaration in Western media and also after a protracted bureaucratic proceeding accompanied by customary forms of police intimidation, Václav Havel was arrested and accused of subverting the republic. The cell doors in the Ruzyně prison closed on the youngest and most active of the Charter spokespeople. He didn't know when he would be freed—it could be a matter of a few weeks, or it could be months or even years. After four months and a week of a thorough investigation, they let him go and then attempted to discredit him publicly. Havel wrote a detailed report on each and every significant confrontation he had with the Communist authorities—and this confrontation was no exception; he chose, however, not to publish it given that it was too bound up with the personal trauma of an inexperienced political prisoner. Notebooks from his imprisonment and a part of the report that he wrote after his release were found in 2018.[1] These unique sources present a vivid picture of Havel's first imprisonment and its crucial influence on his "dissident" thought and public engagement. Few dissidents placed such emphasis on their prison experience as Havel did on his. For him, however, prison was not so much a source of thematic subject matter as it was an impetus, a mediating factor, a yardstick. This is what I will attempt to clarify in the pages that follow.

---

1 Václav Havel, *Zápisky obviněného: Diář Václava Havla* 1977, ed. David Dušek (Prague: Václav Havel Library, 2016) and the unpublished *Zápisky 77 (Z. Urbánkovi)*, which consists of approximately half of a typed manuscript (42 pages) found in 2018 in the estate of Zdeněk Urbánek and which is now in the archives of the Václav Havel Library.

A struggle for identity

After an initial feeling of "strange euphoria"[2] upon becoming a political prisoner, uncertainty prevailed: "I don't have the temperament for it, I'm too polite and anxious [*nervózní*]." Dark thoughts took hold of him: "There's no speedy return from here—they count everything against you." He didn't know what was happening with Charter, and he realized that if they also arrested Jan Patočka, a fellow spokesperson, then all would be lost—but he hoped that they "wouldn't dare" do so.[3] The Czech philosopher with a Socratic fate had become a guiding spirit, with whom Havel, in exceedingly difficult circumstances, had come to associate his thoughts about the new life he would lead after being released from custody. This association was only strengthened by Patočka's death on March 13. Havel read the daily newspapers (he had no other sources of information), and he knew that an anti-Charter campaign was already in full swing; he was both shocked by it and seized with "dread" at the mad frenzy that might still be to come. He was suffering through "great periods of hopelessness," and he was overcome with a "need to pound at the door."[4] The news brought to mind Stalinism's intensely charged atmosphere, and he noted that "they are writing about us as if we were a band of murderers."[5] When he looked at his reflection in the mirror, it seemed to him that he was looking at the face of a criminal.

This feeling of uncertainty was only strengthened by his experience with the interrogations that took place during his detention, which reimagined his past public engagement in terms of a sharply ideological way of perceiving reality; he understood that the Communist police knew everything about his life in detail. The police

2 Havel, *Zápisky 77*, 24.
3 Havel, *Zápisky obviněného*, 152.
4 Havel, *Zápisky obviněného*, 154.
5 Havel, *Zápisky obviněného*, 155.

protocols were filled with statements concerning his "subversive" activity, and the accused Havel engaged in these confrontations with a certain determination, so that days filled with interrogations paradoxically gave his prison life a kind of meaning. The isolated Havel even developed a bond of sorts with the lead investigator, Major Svoboda.

The investigation branched off in a number of directions: it touched on the "Ten Points" petition from the year 1969, memoirs of the persecuted democratic politician Prokop Drtina that had been sent abroad in manuscript form, Havel's open letter to General Secretary Husák, another letter written by Czechoslovak intellectuals to Western media in defense of the band The Plastic People of the Universe, Charter 77, and so on. To the prisoner, all this appeared to be a general reckoning, but the reality was that the investigators had no reasonable evidence against him. Their goal in this phase of the investigation was chiefly to back Havel into a corner and thereby deliver a keen blow to Charter 77. After instructions from high political circles, the Charter itself was removed from the indictment; Czechoslovak Communists were evidently not allowed to wreck the Soviet Union's policy of détente, and the investigators were forced to find other "means." Havel himself put all this together only much later after his release while at the time he remained uncertain, especially given that many of the interrogations concerned themselves with Charter; Havel gave detailed testimony about the organization and other matters. Eventually the original charge of subverting the republic gave way to the less weighty one of damaging the interests of the republic abroad in accordance with paragraph 112 of the legal code.[6]

Long days in a cell weighed heavily on the mind of the insecure prisoner. Havel experienced prison as a place that "destroyed the

6   See *Vyšetřovací a trestní spis proti obviněnému Václavu Havlovi* in the archives of the Secret Police of the Czech Republic (archival number V 32021 MV/7).

network of human relationships."[7] He repeatedly asked himself if the ordeal would somehow prove worth the cost, if he would ever be able to see it as good for him. At the time he couldn't be sure. He realized "what tenderness meant to him" and how he "yearned for a caress."[8] Under such circumstances, it is hardly surprising that a kind word, a faint smile, a decent human interaction were worth more than anything—even if these came from the Procurator General himself, whose "visit could not mean anything good"[9] (and, as was repeatedly made clear, never did). At the beginning of February, Havel wrote: "What are they trying to make me out to be? A spy? A profiteer [*spekulant*]?" He realized he was obsessing over the details and circumstances of his case: "I take every word very seriously—I think through everything—I try to decode it all."[10] He began to suffer from episodes of depression, particularly over the long weekends. "Here there is only the same ugliness—no flowers—no color…".[11] He was also obliged to share his cell with a fellow inmate who paid careful attention to everything that Havel did—in all likelihood in order to inform on him. The letters he received from relatives and friends were subjected to censorship and were therefore unable to provide more information about what was happening with Charter—from the daily news he learned only that Patočka had been received by the Foreign Minister of the Netherlands.

On Sunday, March 6 at a time when it was to be decided whether to release Havel or prolong his incarceration, he found himself in a mood similar to the one he had been in a month prior: "a heavy depression in the evening—it continued the next morning—what is this feeling that resists reason?" He was feeling hopeless: they would continue to accuse him of one thing or another and would extend his

---

7 Havel, *Zápisky obviněného*, 154.
8 Havel, *Zápisky obviněného*, 155.
9 Havel, *Zápisky obviněného*, 170.
10 Havel, *Zápisky obviněného*, 156.
11 Havel, *Zápisky obviněného*, 161.

incarceration. "You can't tell anyone here what you really think, you can't confess your doubts and insecurities"; you can only senselessly, time and again, think about your "case" and try to analyze it from all possible angles.[12] The pressure on him was building, and the regime was intensifying the class hatred toward the "renegade [*odpadlík*]" from a "family of millionaire moneybags": a calculated hit-piece titled "Who is Václav Havel?"[13] appeared in the trade-union daily *Práce* and was then picked up by other outlets in the state-controlled media. Two days afterwards on March 11, Havel noted: "I wasn't personally distressed by it—it's utter nonsense—what distresses me is that it's possible at all—what have we become—where is all this heading." This is followed by a note about the "shock" caused him by a proposal to prolong his incarceration, and this despite the fact that he had attempted to prepare himself mentally for just such a dire turn of events. His insecurity returned with full force: "Will I have a nervous breakdown? Will I be depressed on the weekend?"[14] Contrary to expectations, the weekend of March 12 and 13 was, however, a normal one: he focused on writing a response to the *Práce* article.[15]

From March 18 onward there are entries in his diary that mention frequent use of the anti-anxiety drug diazepam, which he had requested from the doctor. Around the same time he had begun an attempt to introduce a routine of sorts into his daily prison-life, and this involved diet, exercise, language study, and reading books from the prison library. Under the influence of an earlier reading of Solzhenitsyn's *One Day in the Life of Ivan Denisovich*, he intended to impose on himself a strict schedule that would anchor him to daily life in the prison as well as free him from overthinking. This was not, however, an easy thing to do as the investigation did not yet provide fixed landmarks around which he could arrange

12 Havel, *Zápisky obviněného*, 171.
13 Václav Havel, *Spisy* 4 (Prague: Torst, 1999), 1227–1236.
14 Havel, *Zápisky obviněného*, 174.
15 Havel, *Zápisky obviněného*, 175. See also Václav Havel, "Redakci *Práci*", in *Spisy* 4, 159–170.

his schedule and on top of that he received some tragic news. Jan Patočka, the 70-year-old philosopher and Charter 77 spokesperson, died on March 13 following exhausting questioning that he had undergone as an unindicted witness. Havel learned of his death four days after the fact, and he felt doubts about whether "[Patočka's] involvement" in the Charter had only made things worse for him. Havel processed his death in Socratic terms: "What wise words he still might have said"; "Such is the fate of those who know much of life and death"; "The world has lost some of its awareness [*Kus vědomí světa je pryč*]."[16] It was only on March 25 that Havel's wife Olga was able to visit him, and her presence naturally became for him the "most important event"[17] after two and a half months of isolation in the pernicious prison environment. They were allowed to talk only about family matters, and their half-hour conversation was recorded, transcribed, and analyzed for the assumed presence of coded messages.[18]

Already by early March the despondent prisoner, who had been stripped of all sense of security and certainty, had begun to contrive possible ways that he could get out of prison and still keep face. Along with this he had begun to develop far-reaching plans for his new post-prison life: "strike out on my own—belong nowhere," "seek out new circles."[19] On Sunday, March 27 he sketched out a grandiose plan for personal conversion: he would withdraw spiritually inward—to love, humility, poetry, philosophy, and other divine gifts.[20] He sketched ideas for this transformation on the empty pages of his diary. On the weekend of April 2 and 3, two entries stand side-by-side: "elaborate the idea of existential revolution" and "scrounged

---

16 Havel, *Zápisky obviněného*, 177.
17 Havel, *Zápisky obviněného*, 182.
18 Record from March 25, 1977 in *Vyšetřovací a trestní spis proti obviněnému Václavu Havlovi* (archival number V 32021 MV/7), scans 29–36.
19 Havel, *Zápisky obviněného*, 181.
20 Havel, *Zápisky obviněného*, 183.

3 dia[zepam pills]."[21] Psychiatric drugs helped him bear the stress caused by his situation and also supplied him with a distorted sense of "pride" as well as a longing to resist ("hunger-strike"),[22] which alternated with pressing doubts: "the situation is unclear—it's not at all certain that I'll go home on the 15th! What a blow!" On April 6, his desire for a quick resolution to the situation led him to take a step that would become, in the days and months and years that followed, the most sensitive and painful moment in his whole artistic and civic existence: "I wrote the procurator to ask for release—guarantees that I won't misbehave again [*záruky, že už nebudu zlobit*]."[23]

The investigators now had in hand something that they decided to use against, in an "operational" sense, both Havel and Charter. The essence of this was contained in one sentence in the letter, in which the accused promised the prosecutor that he would, upon release from custody, cease "to appear in public politically [*veřejně se politicky projevovat*]," especially insofar as the foreign media were concerned, and instead concentrate "only on his artistic work," which he considered his life's calling.[24] But this did not satisfy his investigators, and they decided to compel Havel—who evidently thought that the guarantee he was offering would suffice for release from prison on April 14—to profess even greater humility. They kept him in doubt until the very last minute, and on April 13 he noted: "A decision about me will apparently be made tomorrow—for three hours (really the whole day) there was a feeling that I would of course be going home—but at the last minute it was decided otherwise—shock."[25] With the clear intention of dispiriting the prisoner even more, his incarceration was, at the very last minute, prolonged until

21 Havel, *Zápisky obviněného*, 186.
22 Havel, *Zápisky obviněného*, 188.
23 Havel, *Zápisky obviněného*, 189.
24 "Dopis generálnímu prokurátorovi" from April 6, 1977 in *Vyšetřovací a trestní spis proti obviněnému Václavu Havlovi* (archival number V 32021 MV/7), scan 32.
25 Havel, *Zápisky obviněného*, 193.

May 15. This time, pills did not help stem the onslaught of depression. Havel knew that he had to pull himself together and once more mobilized his resolutions for a longer stay at Ruzyně—exercise, diet, English, writing in his diary. "Don't think about freedom and life outside of prison—stick to small goals in the here and now [upnout se ke zdejším mikrocílům]."

The investigation was nearing its end, and this gave the prisoner a somewhat different outlook. On Saturday, April 16 he spoke with an investigator: "some things were clarified—the matter is moving forward"; on Sunday he wrote his defense and his "feelings of depression ceased."[26] Two days later the accusations against him were read out and he presented his defense. In his diary he noted: "A change! Paragraph 112! I'm going home!"[27] The investigators were, however, interested less in the actual indictment, which had been reduced to contact that Havel had had with the emigrants Tigrid and Pelikán and which had a paltry evidential basis, than in the "operational" angle of the case, which they duly intended to make good use of: they knew that Havel "does not want to go to prison again [...] since the experience has a significantly depressive effect on him." Their intention was to use him operationally in two ways: during interrogations of other Charter signatories they would create "the impression that what we already know about them comes from statements made by Havel,"[28] which would destroy Havel's reputation in the Charter community, and they would also compel Havel to elaborate more systematically the guarantees he made in the letter to the Procurator General and to affirm them in a new statement—more precisely put, they wanted him to resign contritely as a spokesperson

26 Havel, Zápisky obviněného, 195.
27 Havel, Zápisky obviněného, 197.
28 Undated information (by Major Svoboda about the interrogation of Václav Havel on April 13, 1977 during the investigation of Charter 77) in Vyšetřovací spis Charty 77, V 33766 MV/10 in the archives of the Secret Police of the Czech Republic, scans 202–205.

for Charter 77 and, in doing so, to compromise himself publicly as a political failure.

The detailed "protocol of guarantees"[29] was compiled with an investigator on April 22, which marked the one-hundredth day of Havel's incarceration. Its contents were nothing more and nothing less than a point-by-point, thorough accounting of what Havel would refrain from doing if released and what he would do differently—everything, that is, that might be considered *political* activity. Havel did not say anything in this protocol that he would not stand by later: "… the decisions that I have arrived at emerge from my own reflections concerning my future position in society: I think of myself as a writer who has and can have opinions that differ from official ones, but that does not mean I think of myself as a 'dissident,' which means some kind of professional opponent of the regime."[30] These words that had been dictated into the protocol became, to a certain extent, Havel's calling card. On Thursday, April 28 he noted in his diary: "Familiarization with the case file—everything is in order—proposal for release."[31]

On the weekend, however, a new feeling of uncertainty seized him. "What will next week bring? Will I go home or will I again be let down by a false hope?"[32] The days that followed dragged by devoid of significant events. Once again the investigators postponed everything until the last day to decide whether to release him or to prolong his incarceration. They knew that the imprisoned writer was toying with the idea of a Faustian drama that would make use of his prison experience, and on May 12 they delivered a copy of Thomas Mann's *Doctor Faustus* to his cell. The following day (in

29 Havel, *Zápisky obviněného*, 198.
30 *Vyšetřovací a trestní spis proti obviněnému Václavu Havlovi* (archival number V 32021 MV/7), scans 167–177.
31 Havel, *Zápisky obviněného*, 201.
32 Havel, *Zápisky obviněného*, 203.

a way obviously designed to tempt Havel) a certain "Mr. Ř[íha]"[33] presented him with a statement that had been formulated on the basis of his own letter to the prosecutor, which would be published on the day of his release and which in all probability conveyed his penitent resignation as a Charter spokesperson. The official file for the investigation contains only Havel's disapproving response with the explanation that he was "ready—at the right time and in the appropriate way–to make public my stance [his declared intention to resign as a spokesperson], but only if it would not create the impression that I did so merely as an expression of my desire to be released from prison."[34]

Havel was satisfied with the refusal, but "Ř" immediately pressed him again on the thorny "issue of making public his stance upon his release." This caused Havel to feel "awful—I didn't sleep—thoughts of suicide [*myšlenky na mašli*]."[35] He knew then that they were intending to take advantage of his letter to the prosecutor (or other statements) in order to discredit him publicly, and it occurred to him that it might be better to stay in prison for the duration. They kept him in custody for another month. On Sunday, May 15 he wrote: "Since Friday, the worst days I've had here—I am in no position to judge whether I should do this given my particular situation. I am anxious [*úzko*] and unwell." He was apprehensive about how his friends and especially his wife Olga would react to this "complicated play"[36] of his, and he began to think through how he was going to explain it all to them after his release. He didn't know when he would be released, and he began to accept the possibility that it might be many more months or even years. He wrote a "new position statement," in which he categorically refused to sign any protocol

33 Havel, *Zápisky obviněného*, 210.
34 *Vyšetřovací a trestní spis proti obviněnému Václavu Havlovi* (archival number V 32021 MV/7), scans 103–105.
35 Havel, *Zápisky obviněného*, 210.
36 Havel, *Zápisky obviněného*, 212.

mentioning his release. On Monday, May 16 "Ř" informed him that it was too "late," and Havel realized that they would release him and subject him to public humiliation.

In his diary he wrote an account that would become part of his prison legend: "I'm not saying anything that I don't believe and that isn't true, but in this particular context the effect may prove terrible." This account undoubtedly refers to his statement that he thinks of himself as a writer, and not a dissident or professional opponent of the regime. Havel had divorced morality from politics, and he realized, given the context it would be placed in by the authorities, that it would seem like a defeat or withdrawal from the active community associated with Charter 77. The cited entry in his diary continues: "I'm utterly despondent. It's only *half* the truth!"[37] The addition to the entry confirms what was said. He had expressed to the investigator his readiness to resign the (political) function of a spokesperson, but not, however, to completely distance himself from Charter as a "focal point [*ohnisko*[38]] for moral and spiritual renewal," as a community of citizens who "have no intention of engaging in direct political confrontation."[39] His despair had to do with impugning the moral integrity of a Charter spokesperson, and not with the way he was distancing himself from politics as defined and controlled by the Communists.[40]

They released him on May 20. On the following day in *Rudé právo*, the article "Václav Havel's Letter to the Procurator General's Office" was published, in which excerpts from the letter were used as evidence to argue that Havel regretted the political misuse of Charter 77 in foreign press coverage and that he would in the

37 Havel, *Zápisky obviněného*, 211.
38 For more on *ohnisko* as a key word in Havel's thought, see Kieran Williams's analysis in this volume.
39 Havel, *Zápisky obviněného*, 229.
40 "Prohlášení Václava Havla z 21. 5. 1977 k souvislostem rezignace na funkci mluvčího Charty 77," in Blanka Císařovská, Vilém Prečan, eds., *Charta 77: Dokumenty I* (Prague: Institute for Contemporary History of the Academy of Sciences of the Czech Republic, 2007), 43–44.

future make use of the Czechoslovak legal code, which leaves ample room for the constructive expression of one's opinions. The article concluded with the falsehood that Havel had "resigned from the role of spokesperson for Charter 77."[41] In fact, only upon release from prison did Havel put this at the disposal of the signatories.[42] Havel's prison confrontation was met in Charter circles with various reactions, including harsh criticism for its failure of (political) responsibility.[43] The investigators' manipulation of him along with criticism from his friends, but most especially his own harsh self-condemnation, prompted him to exert considerable effort not only to defend his reputation but also to support other persecuted individuals. The authorities saw this as a continued attempt to subvert the republic and waited for a political signal to reopen the criminal case against him.[44]

Once released, Havel knew only too well that he could be arrested again at any time. In October 1977 he was given a fourteen-month sentence, suspended for three years, even though the charge leveled against him wasn't backed up with evidence of his guilt. He was *de jure* sentenced for sending a manuscript (Drtina's memoirs) abroad, but *de facto* for his role in Charter 77.[45] The trial had four defendants and was purely political in nature since the free exchange of information across the borders of Czechoslovakia was (at least

41 "Dopis Václava Havla Generální prokuratuře," *Rudé právo*, May 5, 1977, 2.
42 Charter 77 communiqué from May 26, 1977 in Císařovská, Prečan, *Charta 77: Dokumenty I*, 43.
43 "Zpráva pracovníků 1. odboru X. správy FMV o setkání signatářů na chalupě u Pavla Kohouta" (June 2, 1977), in Radek Schovánek, ed., *Svazek Dialog. StB versus Pavel Kohout. Dokumenty StB z operativních svazků Dialog a Kopa* (Prague-Litomyšl: Paseka, 2006), 75. See also Daniel Kaiser, *Disident: Václav Havel 1936–1989* (Prague- Litomyšl: Paseka, 2009), 138, and the author of this article's interview with Jaroslav Šabata in Brno on May 28, 2012, which is in the collection of the Center for Oral History of the Institute for Contemporary History of the Academy of Sciences of the Czech Republic, v.v.i.
44 *Vyšetřovací a trestní spis proti obviněnému Václavu Havlovi* (archival number V 32021 MV/7), scans 282–289.
45 Havel, "Závěrečné slovo," in *Spisy* 4, 177–181.

formally) guaranteed by the Helsinki Final Act's third basket, which was devoted to human rights. Havel was imprisoned for a second time at the end of January 1978 in connection with the unwanted attendance of certain Chartists at a dance for railway workers, and this time he spent six weeks in custody; this was not a serious attempt on the part of the authorities to convict Havel of a crime and imprison him, but rather another way to intimidate and warn him. Havel held up honorably during his second imprisonment; he dealt with the bullying he experienced there by rising above it and keeping his sense of humor.[46] From August 1978 to March 1979, he was forced to undergo yet another "dissident" rite of passage—around-the-clock police surveillance along with a seemingly inexhaustible variety of perfidious incursions against his personal freedom that were carried out by members of both the secret and regular police forces. He wrote two detailed reports concerning his "home imprisonment," and he concluded the reports with the affirmation that it was possible to tolerate even this unlawfully constrained life and that he would not emigrate.[47]

The philosophy of moral resistance

Let us return for a moment to Havel's first imprisonment as a crucible [ohnisko] for existential transformation. He sought to turn his prison experience into an artistic as well as political-philosophical question, thereby integrating it into his life and thought. He considered writing three or four one-act plays—so-called "dissi-tales"—in which he would, through the character of Ferdinand Vaněk, depict various aspects of a dissident's encounter with state authorities, and these were to be titled *Warning*, *Protest*, and *379* (the number of

---

46 Havel, "Zpráva o mé účasti na plese železničářů," in *Spisy* 4, 191–205.
47 "První zpráva o mém domácím vězení," and "Druhá zpráva o mém domácím vězení," in *Spisy* 4, 335–344 and 363–374.

his Ruzyně cell). These plans yielded only the one-act play *Protest*, which does not, however, take place in a prison.[48] He returned to the Faustian subject matter, which he considered a pivotal theme connected to his first imprisonment, only in 1985 when he wrote the full-length play *Temptation*, which also does not take place in a prison. The political-philosophical angle of his experience takes form in several crucial entries recorded in his prison diary, and in these it is easy to discern the essential characteristics of the ideas that he developed more fully in "The Power of the Powerless," which he finished in October 1978 at his country cottage of Hrádeček, encircled by the police, and which he dedicated to Jan Patočka.

As was already said, the imprisoned Havel did not know what was happening on the outside, how Charter was faring, how many signatories had been arrested; as a result he turned mentally inward—toward what Patočka called *caring for the soul*. Not that he had never considered this before, but rather that the stress of his confrontation with the authorities propelled him towards plans in which the active life yielded somewhat to a life of contemplation. He was going to read the gospels, Saint Augustine, Kierkegaard, Gabriel Marcel, and other existentialist thinkers as well as the poetry of Hölderlin and Novalis. He also planned to render account of the fruits of his intellectual immersion and of his attempts to transform his life (which would be "cut off from the dissi-world" as a political milieu) in systematically written diaries inspired by the Czech poet Jakub Deml. This prospective turn would have noticeably departed from the bohemian, adventuresome life of a banned Prague intellectual with international renown and financial means that he had lived up until this point—the life of a "protected species." Modeling himself after Michel de Montaigne, he intended to "construct and compose

48 Letter from Václav Havel to his literary agent Klaus Juncker, June 18, 1977. The Czechoslovak Documentation Center of the National Museum in Prague.

his own self"[49]—that is, both to create a life devoted to love and wisdom and also to document that life through written testimony.

What place did politics occupy in such introspection? Havel was an innate *zoon politikon*, and he could not expel politics from his thoughts; his inward turn, as a result, also projected back onto his thinking in general about living in a politically divided world and the role of Charter 77 in a "totalitarian system." These considerations were, moreover, not entirely new ones for Havel, but his profound prison experience had given them a new existential imprint. Havel rejected both Western "capitalism with its private ownership of the means of production" as well as "Soviet-style dictatorial socialism." In place of this "moronic antagonism of a divided world" he put "genuine socialism" with full economic and political democratization and the potential for a rich spiritual life. At the same time, he rejected the conservative "return to traditional religion" and its modern incarnations. He took inspiration for his "new conception of humanity" in Antiquity, early Christianity, and existentialism. The world's existential crisis, which has primarily a "moral and spiritual" character, would need to be overcome "through existential revolution." In this approach, political ideologies lost all their attractiveness: "It is not P[etr] U[hl]'s Trotsk[yite] opinions that have an impact on the world, but rather his personal convictions and courage to stand by them."[50]

This line of thinking ultimately led Havel, who knew perfectly well that prisoners have a "predisposition to utopianism,"[51] to the idea of creating a sort of Human Rights International that would work across the Iron Curtain against the established orders of both West and East. The bourgeois intellectual, whose plays had guaranteed him an income well above the average thanks to royalties from

49   Havel, *Zápisky obviněného*, 180, 181, 183, 191.
50   Havel, *Zápisky obviněného*, 186–187.
51   Havel, *Zápisky obviněného*, 186.

the prosperous West, was calling for a profound spiritual renewal of society as if he were a medieval flagellant. At the same time, he made a detailed list in his diary of luxuries and delicacies that he desired from Tuzex stores (under socialism only the most prominent had access to the stores, which offered Western goods) when he gained his freedom (a big bathtub, perfume, American cigarettes, lobster cocktail, Cinzano, a minute-steak with tartar sauce, fruit with whipped cream, special medications, etc.).[52] To what extent was Havel aware that the flip side of his dissident utopianism was bourgeois consumerism of the highest, post-industrial type that was generally associated with the quality of life available in developed Western-liberal democracies? He knew full well that this kind of consumerism was the life's goal of the average citizen of socialist Czechoslovakia; the real question is what would persuade the average citizen to choose "existential revolution" instead.

And what were his thoughts on the Charter? Of primary interest here is his comment that the initial signatories were expecting the regime to "tolerate [Charter's] existence by pretending it didn't exist [*tolerovat na jakémsi pomezí existence a neexistence*]," just as it had done with literary samizdat. Charter, then, should "gradually integrate itself into the life of soc[iety]." The assumption that "we will be a force that they'll deal with quietly" was demolished by the ferocious anti-Charter campaign in the regime-controlled media. "Everything has changed [...] What I initially supposed, given the situation, can't come true. The question is what will happen."[53] Even though Havel was isolated from events and didn't know what was actually happening with Charter, this comment was on target. Counting on the political influence of the Helsinki initiative in Czechoslovakia to gradually ease constraints on human rights

52 Havel, *Zápisky obviněného*, 179.
53 Havel, *Zápisky obviněného*, 228.

(freedom of speech, assembly, association, movement, etc.) now seemed unrealistic.

What then was to be done? Havel wrote: "Political change [is] out of the question and is not the goal—the goal is to defend specific cases—to rid people of fear in their own microcosms." The Charter is a "dissidence of conviction [*názorová disidence*]," a vehicle for "moral and spiritual renewal [*morální a duchovní renesance*]"; it produces "hotbeds of intellectual fermentation [*ohniska intelektuálního kvasu*]," and its tools are essays and analyses, magazines and projects, discussion circles and seminars. The dissident signatories of Charter are by no means professional opponents of the Communist dictatorship, but they have "become caught up, unwittingly and not through professional interest, in the 'dissi-situation'" and have taken upon themselves the accompanying "moral commitment"; they have subjected themselves to "inner monasticism [*vnitřní řeholí*]" and "moral order [*morální řád*]." They seek out contacts, find their way into new communities, form new friendships, and expand their networks of relationships. They are the above-mentioned flagellants (Havel spoke of "brothers " [*bratříci*] and it is not clear whether he realized that this word refers to Hussite warriors, but it is more probable that he had in mind the Czech brotherhood [*čeští bratři*] as followers of the pacifist religious thinker Petr Chelčický) who venture out into the world in order to raise it out of its ignoble, depraved state.[54] It was the late philosopher Jan Patočka who provided Havel with the connection between their present day and the medieval revivalist tradition. Havel was no longer able to talk with Patočka about responsibility[55]; he did, however, intend to assume Patočka's role of authority in the "dissi-world," which was understood "as an authentic manifestation of morality as such [*jako jeden z projevů mravnosti naprosté*]."[56]

---

54 Havel, *Zápisky obviněného*, 229.
55 For more on "responsibility" as a key word in Havel's thought, see Barbara J. Falk and Daniela Bouvier-Valenta's analysis in this volume.
56 Havel, *Zápisky obviněného*, 235.

Even given his insecurity and uncertainty while in prison and despite being enveloped in the investigators' ruses and intrigues, Havel aspired to supply Charter with a program of action. The sketch for just such a program that he made in his diary has the character of a thought-through, long-range strategy. The potential political effectiveness of these revivalist convictions, assuming they were meant to be put into practice vigorously, is not the point. Havel never yields the political ground, not while subject to the stresses and manipulations of prison life and not even when he has communicated an intention to "retreat to his private life and not engage publicly."[57] This is confirmed by the fact that Havel saw his guarantees to the prosecutor as only a "half-truth"; he will simply not give up being political, a fact which is born out in absolute terms by further activities that led to his long imprisonment from 1979 to 1983. From this point onward, he will, however, understand the "political" in different terms than other signatories of the Charter, whose thinking took shape within existing (radically democratic, liberal, or conservative) political traditions. In the years that followed, Havel would conduct friendly polemics with fellow signatories about the meaning of the Charter, and in 1989 his understanding of political opposition—and eventually of the role of Civic Forum—will come to clash with theirs.

Havel's "The Power of the Powerless" can be considered the masterpiece of dissident thinking, and we can also, in light of his prison notebooks, think of it as its own kind of distinctive and powerful political philosophy born from the "spirit" of imprisonment.[58] To this very day, Havel's text lends hope for shattering the seemingly invincible power of a system built on the "principle of social auto-totality,"[59] which requires the participation of both rulers and

57 Havel, *Zápisky obviněného*, 243.
58 See the collection Václav Havel et al., *O svobodě a moci I* (Kolín nad Rýnem: Index-Listy, 1980) and its English version Václav Havel et al., *The Power of the Powerless: Citizens against the State in Central-Eastern Europe*, ed. John Keane (Armonk, NY: M. E. Shape, 1985).
59 Václav Havel, "The Power of the Powerless," chapter VI.

ruled, in different measures, to function. Change is understood to take place over the long haul because it must mature slowly in the bowels of society; the dissident contribution to change takes place in the "hidden sphere" of societal consciousness and conscience. In demonstrating that "'living in truth' is a human and social alternative,"[60] dissidents indirectly shift the boundaries of the possible. As practice has shown, however, it was feasible to engage in the "pre-political"[61] arena through a variety of means, even those that are outright political—through broadcasts by the Czechoslovak section of Radio Free Europe, the Voice of America, and other such stations, by financing alternative culture with money from Western sources interested in promoting democracy, through interventions by Western governments in defense of human rights, by representatives of those governments who agreed to meet Charter signatories, etc. In its essence, the dissidence practiced by Charter 77 was a kind of political opposition, even though it could not operate normally as such[62]; from this inability to function normally as such, Havel managed to advance a theory of peaceful moral resistance with long-term scope and effectiveness.

A "new mastery" [*nová svrchovanost*]

A born dramaturge and playwright, Havel sought to incorporate both positive and negative events in his life into an overall plan and strategy, which gave these occurrences a proper place in the order of things and imbued them with meaning. Behind this determination lay an unusually strong will to lead a holistic and open life. He understood *theater* as political (as a "space for individual and societal self-discovering [*sebenalézání*]," as a "transcendent form of

---

60 Václav Havel, "The Power of the Powerless," chapter XIX.
61 Václav Havel, "The Power of the Powerless," chapter XVIII.
62 Cf. Petr Rezek, "Život disidentův jako 'život v pravdě'?," in *Filosofie a politika kýče* (Prague: Oikoymenh, 1991), 54–55, 68–59.

community," or even as a "crucible [*ohnisko*] for humanistic mobilization").[63] And when he became president, he turned competitive democratic parliamentary *politics* into a kind of theater. While his first and second imprisonment (along with his home imprisonment) left an imprint on "The Power of the Powerless" through its dissident exposition of oppositional (anti-)politics under extremely adverse conditions, his third and longest prison experience (1979–1983) is associated with *Letters to Olga*, in which he pressed into service the genre of existentialist introspection to affirm the orientation of his reflections in the conditions of Ruzyně, Heřmanice, and Plzeň-Bory.

In April 1978, after the founding of the Committee for the Defense of the Unjustly Persecuted (known by the Czech acronym VONS), leading Chartists found themselves on the verge of being arrested and jailed. The Communist regime naturally considered Charter 77 and VONS a "political platform" supported by the United States and aimed at destabilizing Communism.[64] The signatories understood well that sooner or later they would be jailed. The situation came to a dramatic head at the end of May 1979 with the arrest of ten VONS activists, five of whom—Petr Uhl, Václav Havel, Václav Benda, Jiří Dienstbier, and Otta Bednářová—were convicted in October of that same year. Their imprisonment involves a certain paradox: even though it meant a painful loss of freedom, they entered into it intending to find a kind of freedom and spiritual equilibrium. This applies perhaps more to Havel than to the others, which speaks to his efforts to atone for irresolution during his first imprisonment and also to the fact that his VONS-related activity, as compared with that of other co-defendants, was not as systematic.

63 Václav Havel, "Co dělá divadlo divadlem," in *Má to smysl! Výbor z rozhovorů 1964-1989*, Anna Freimanová, Tereza Johanidesová, eds., (Prague: Václav Havel Library, 2019), 164. For more on "theater" as a key word in Havel's thought, see Barbara Day's analysis in this volume.
64 "Zpráva o bezpečnostní situaci v ČSSR z 31. ledna 1980," in Petr Blažek, Tomáš Bursík, eds., *Pražský proces 1979. Vyšetřování soud a věznění členů Výboru na obranu nespravedlivě stíhaných* (Prague: Institute for Contemporary History of the Academy of Sciences of the Czech Republic, 2010), 220.

Havel was convicted *de facto* for co-founding VONS, advocating for it, and defending its legality. This time the investigation proceeded in an entirely different manner from the one in 1977 because Havel refused to give evidence about the details of the case, and he instead chose to take a principled stand: he defended his beliefs and actions by stating that he did not consider them crimes. He retracted the statements made in his already-mentioned letter to the procurator general from April 6, 1977, which the investigators offered as proof that he had violated the terms of his release. In doing so, he rid himself of the stains of the past.[65] He knew that he would go to prison, was reconciled to it, and refused to emigrate.

In a letter addressed to his wife Olga from Ruzyně prison shortly after the trial (letter 13 in *Letters to Olga*), Havel detailed his placid acceptance of the prison sentence. He would approach his imprisonment as the start of a process of "self-consolidation [*sebe-konsolidace*]," as a path leading to a "new mastery" [*nová svrchovanost*] over himself, which was not intended to result in transformative personal conversion but rather to his "be[ing] himself in a better way [*být lépe sám sebou*]."[66] This is an important moment in Havel's intellectual trajectory since the aspiration contained in the last statement would accompany him both as the oppositional (political) leader shortly before November 1989 and then also as president, in both cases *pace* Max Weber's view that it is necessary to exchange a stance grounded in (personal) conviction for a stance grounded in (political) responsibility.[67] One of the crucial motivations for forging this "new mastery" had its roots in the trauma of Havel's first imprisonment, in which he was threatened with the dissolution of his personal identity. The regime had cut him off from political

65 *Vyšetřovací spis Václava Havla z roku 1979*, archival number ZV 485 MV/5, scans 94–101.
66 Václav Havel, *Letters to Olga*, letter 13; see also letter 66.
67 For more on this, see the classic treatise by Max Weber, "Politika jako povolání [Politics as a Vocation]," in *Metodologie, sociologie a politika*, Miloš Havelka, ed. (Prague: Oikoymenh, 1998), 291.

engagement and he had accepted this, but at the same time he felt the need to justify this to himself and to integrate into his life the fact that his viewpoint (and the dissident viewpoint in general) lay in the moral power of resistance, which privileged *power of the powerless* and *anti-politics* over *politics* and *power*.[68] Prison letter 138, which reexamines at length his first imprisonment, is in my opinion a poignant testimony to his efforts to emerge from that political defeat as a moral victor.[69]

Once again, his long imprisonment did not so much provide him with thematic writing material (with the exception of the short play *Mistake*, which we can read as a parable for social "auto-totality [*samototalita*]" in a prison milieu, which is Havel's key metaphor[70]), but rather served as an impetus for reflecting on the identity and responsibility of the imprisoned *subject*. In the end, this ran parallel with Havel's intended undertaking to "self-consolidate." Havel's original authorial intent—to mine the uniqueness of his experience for the realistic portrayal of prison characters and scenes—came to naught. The notion that he could be both inmate and at the same time "detached observer"[71] of the goings-on around him quickly dissolved. Prison swallows a person whole, there is no possibility of detachment. Moreover, attempts to reflect on the experience were erased by the censor and were strictly punished by the fanatical prison warden. Later, after his release, this "deeply existential and deeply personal experience"[72] proved to be "ineffable [*nesdělitelná*],"[73] first and foremost because even after many years it was

68   For more on "power" as a key word in Havel's thought, see Delia Popescu's analysis in this volume.
69   Václav Havel, *Letters to Olga*, letter 138.
70   Václav Havel, *Spisy* 2 (Prague: Torst, 1999), 675–684.
71   Václav Havel's prison "Osobní spis," archival number A 63/83, Ministerstvo vnitra ČSR – Správa sboru nápravné výchovy, National Archives of the Czech Republic.
72   Václav Havel, "Dálkový výslech [Disturbing the Peace]," in *Spisy* 4: 851. In Disturbing the Peace, 146.
73   Havel, *Spisy* 4: 851.

too harrowing to recall in graphic detail with its "multiplicity of horrors" reminiscent of a "very distant nightmare."[74] Havel returns to this subject in his dialogic autobiographical texts *Disturbing the Peace* and *To the Castle and Back* in order to definitively refute the idea that he endured prison in a heroic manner—something that attests to his moral stature.[75] What, then, remained for him to do? Already subject in prison to frequent punishments, he further imposed strict personal discipline on himself, despite the conditions, in order to be able to write letters to his wife Olga (and through her to other friends) that served as meditations on Being and the meaning of life.

Constraints on the writing of these letters were strictly imposed: one four-page letter every week that was to be exclusively about family matters with nothing in it about his imprisonment (no references, allegories, or other forms of reflection). His fierce battle with the prison warden over the contents of certain letters is evident in both the subject matter and structure of *Letters to Olga*. Existential reflections on "Being," "responsibility," and philosophical "horizons" were repeatedly thwarted by the censor, and as a result he committed himself to writing, in the style of Michel de Montaigne and as he had resolved to do during his first imprisonment, about someone else, about home, about the possibilities and limitations of writing, about faith and hope and why losing them is wrong, about absurdity's hidden meaning, about the crisis of human identity and responsibility, about nothingness, about self-control and a determination to remain true to oneself, about his eight good moods and seven bad moods, about the murder of John Lennon as a shot in the face of existential revolution, about the challenges of growing up in a prominent family, about life continuity, about his passion for

---

74 Letter by Václav Havel to Paul Wilson, April 2, 1986. The Czechoslovak Documentation Centre of the National Museum in Prague.

75 In Václav Havel, *Spisy 4: Eseje a jiné texty z let 197–1989, Dálkový výslech*, 915–917 (*Disturbing the Peace*, 203–205), and *Prosím stručně* (Prague: Gallery, 2006), 240–241.

bringing people together, about the order of life and the order of the spirit, about the curse of evil and indifference [*lhostejnost*[76]], about death, about theater and its relationship to society and its era, about the mystery of collective consciousness, etc.

These reflections have an engaging, down-to-earth quality, but the better known and more cited reflections in the collection are written in Heideggerian jargon, a style which enabled Czechoslovak dissidents to adopt a language *different* from the heavily ideological political language of the time; this was a language that seemed better equipped to describe the deeper, "pre-political," moral foundations of the polis.[77] In an effort to establish himself as a subject (with a "new mastery" over himself in place), Havel fluctuated between use of the personal "I" and references to impersonal "Being," and this is particularly evident in the last *Sixteen Letters*, which are the most well-known and are sometimes published as a self-standing volume. In these letters he again appears as a champion of a deeply moored (anti-)politics based on noble human virtues; these virtues are listed one after another in the text, and they stand out somewhat against the larger background of existentialist jargon: "[l]ove, charity, sympathy, tolerance, understanding, self-control, solidarity, friendship" etc. He also cast himself in the role of a stern critic of the "traditional structures of contemporary society," a society that is epitomized by, among other things, "the rottenness [*prohnilost*] of establishments and the despair of the powerless masses."[78]

Who is capable of resolving a crisis as profound as this? Those who take proper responsibility for it and who are able to "devote their full efforts [*s plným nasazením*]" and act "with clear-sighted deliberation and humility that always goes with genuine faith

---

76 For more on *lhostejnost* as a key word in Havel's thought, see David S. Danaher's analysis in this volume.
77 See Theodor W. Adorno, *Žargon autenticity. K německé ideologii,* trans. Alena Bakešová (Prague: Academia, 2015).
78 Havel, *Letters to Olga,* letter 143.

[*s nezaslepeným rozmyslem a pokorou, provázející vždy skutečnou vírou*]."[79] In Havel's opinion, these characteristics are most present in modern resistance-oriented organizations: the youth movement, peace and liberation movements, ecological and human-rights organizations, and also groups oriented toward ecumenical religious revival. While these observations originated in a prison in Communist Czechoslovakia, Havel extended their scope well beyond the borders of the Eastern bloc; he suggested once again the need for a genuinely international movement to resist the "automatism [*samopohyb*] of global technological civilization."[80] He also again failed to ask the question of what type of politics an international movement of this kind would presuppose; he chose instead to remain free from ideologies and dogmas. He tried to carve out a space between the inexorable "absolute horizon" (*deus absconditus*) and the more welcoming concept of "Being," which is endowed with its own "infinite memory, an omnipresent mind, and an infinitely large heart" (the unnamed Christ).[81] *Letters to Olga* is consubstantial with "The Power of the Powerless." In his prison letters, Havel established himself as a *subject* in the context of a larger dissident community that was ostensibly advocating for global existential revolution. He became the voice of that community, and, after his release from prison, he would also become its (political) spokesperson.

Prison as a laboratory of totalitarianism

Letters to Olga was published in book form in January 1985 by the Toronto-based exile press Sixty-Eight Publishers (samizdat versions were circulating while Havel was still in prison); it came out with lightning speed in German translation—thanks to Havel's literary

---

79 Havel, *Letters to Olga*, letter 143.
80 Havel, "The Power of the Powerless," chapter XX.
81 Havel, *Letters to Olga*, letter 137.

agent Klaus Juncker and the translator Joachim Bruss—in 1984, and editions in other languages followed. The prison correspondence of Havel's fellow prisoners of conscience was published in Czech only after almost two decades had passed. It follows from this that after his release Havel had taken his place among the most well-known Central and Eastern European dissidents and enjoyed considerable international renown. Other released political prisoners did not receive nearly as much attention as Havel did. He became a living legend, and he was given awards, lionized, quoted; foreign journalists sought him out for interviews. Havel's intentions regarding his imprisonment are obvious given the efforts he made to control both his personality profile and his media image, which is something he continued to do in the years that followed, cultivating a myriad of contacts abroad through use of diplomatic post and by soliciting help from Czechoslovaks in exile.

It is understandable that in an oppressive society he would want to remain independent of political authority of any kind and he insisted that he was not by any means a "professional dissident or revolutionary or politician, but just a normal person who writes plays, at least to the extent that legitimate human, moral, and civic responsibilities don't interfere."[82] To what degree might this self-characterization have been a strategy linked to the traumatic experience of his first imprisonment? He must certainly have known that he was not a "normal person" in the everyday sense of that term; his opinions, when they were made public, had both immediate and also long-term import and effect. Prison, in which he had almost lost his life to pneumonia, became a crucial part of his life story as well as a key element in the legend that developed around him. The hardships he suffered surely entitled him to incorporate the singular, drastic experience of imprisonment into his own life narrative; at the same

82   Václav Havel, letter to Pavel Kohout, March 6, 1983. In Václav Havel and Vilém Prečan, *Korespondence 1983–1989* (Prague: Czechoslovak Documentation Center, 2011), 652.

time, however, there were pitfalls, in the form of too harsh an assessment of the state of the world and of ordinary life. The experience of prison proved too strict a standard.

Petr Rezek, an independent philosopher and critic of dissident thought, has pointed out that Havel spoke about prison more than other political prisoners and that he made it a conceptual starting point for how he thought about Czechoslovak society.[83] In his first comprehensive interview for the world press after his release, Havel claimed that a prison brims with uncommon human stories while a "housing project with thousands of residents [*mnohatisícové sídliště*]" is characterized merely by the mentality of a "docile herd that has long gotten used to indirect forms of manipulation."[84] Havel came to enjoy this very pointed dichotomy that disadvantaged individuals in the "totalitarian herd" (people who "tended not to end up in prison"), and he continued to use it.[85] In doing so, he realized that it carried a certain *moral* force and had a *political* effect. He wrote to exiled writer Pavel Kohout that the first interview after his release "was well received here (just about everyone knows about it, it is incredible how everyone is listening to broadcasts from abroad)."[86] In a series of other interviews for the world press, Havel employed this harsh "totalitarian" evaluation of the state of Czechoslovak society, even though it was not backed up by closer analysis of the situation. As a result, he sometimes sunk to using clichés about people who "substitute ideology for their own brains," succumb to the "fiction of objectivity," "believe in historical inevitability," and "sacrifice their common sense at the altar of ideology." The truth is, however, that life under totalitarianism was never so completely manipulated by

83   Petr Rezek, "Pohled na Václava Havla zdola," in *Filosofie a politika kýče*, 94.
84   Václav Havel, Interview with Antoine Spire for *Le Monde*, April 10–11, 1983. For the original Czech version, see Havel, "Na straně pravdy proti lži," in Freimanová, Johanidesová, eds., *Má to smysl! Výběr z rozhovorů 1964–1989*, 195.
85   Rezek, "Pohled na Václava Havla z dola," 94.
86   Václav Havel, letter to Pavel Kohout, May 2, 1983. The Czechoslovak Documentation Center of the National Museum.

the state that "everything [became] a matter of abstract, impersonal categories" and that normal people were turned into "mere robots."[87] In an interview with the political theorist John Keane[88], he provided an especially forceful characterization of how totalitarian conditions affected everyday life in Communist Czechoslovakia, which naturally excluded all possibility of social creativity on the part of the citizenry — even including devotees of the "cottage" or "cabin" culture [*chalupářství*], which Havel himself indulged in. The less frequently cited accounts by his dissident friends and critics (for example, Petr Pithart, Rudolf Battěk, Emanuel Mandler) did not avoid these topics.

As we know, Havel was a proponent of "non-political politics [*nepolitická politika*],"[89] which "operates on the moral plane of every individual's conscience." He himself epitomized a life lived with integrity and uncommon courage, which did not recoil when faced with prison. The question nonetheless remains how deeply he was able, and even whether he wanted, to impinge upon the sclerotic conscience of the typical "resident of the housing project [*sídlištní člověk*]." It can be assumed that his "attempt to reshape social relationships"[90] through moral action missed its target for a significant portion of the Czechoslovak population. Havel's influence unquestionably reached into certain parts of society, and this included, first and foremost, the cultural "gray zone" and the younger generation. He aptly captured the apolitical nature of the latter and was not mistaken in his claim that they were searching for authenticity in a space that lay "between truth and lies, between

---

87   Václav Havel, interview with Luigi Geninazzi for *Il Sabato*, September 1–7, 1984. For the Czech translation, see Havel, "Můj Bůh je mistr vyčkávání," in *Má to smysl!*, 222.
88   Václav Havel, interview with John Keane for The Times Literary Supplement, January 23, 1987. For the Czech translation, see Havel, "Lidská tvář Prahy," in *Má to smysl!*, 240–245.
89   We must leave aside here the terminological instability surrounding the use of "antipolitical" and "non-political," which may well be a consequence of translating from Czech to other languages and then back again.
90   Havel, "Můj Bůh je mistr vyčkávání," in *Má to smysl!*, 222.

living and not-living."[91] He was able to appeal to this segment of society more effectively—for example, with a thorough report on non-conformist popular music in Czechoslovakia, which came out as a Charter document.[92] In this he demonstrated both empathy and good political instinct: the younger generation would prove to be on his side from, at the very least, January 1989, and this primarily because he managed to appeal to them in non-political, moral, and generally cultural terms.

Havel's thinking about the state of Czechoslovak society after his release from prison involved an apparent division: on the one hand, there was cultural activity that was independent of state control, and he followed, welcomed, and supported its growth while, on the other hand, there was politics (meaning both the listless politics of "normalization" as well as the desire of Czechs and Slovaks to be active civic participants), which he considered to be in a deep stupor with no awakening in sight.[93] Since he knew the cultural domain best, he paid more attention to it; he took advantage of personal acquaintances and other contacts to cultivate it, and this is confirmed in, among other sources, his rich and still unstudied correspondence with exile figures.[94] At the same time, he thought about the cultural domain *politically*, with a view to its gradual breakthrough into the power monolith, which was something he had already experienced in 1968 and whose further development he had clearly foreseen in "Dear Dr. Husák" and "The Power of the Powerless." He spoke of the cultural "gray zone" (in this case in the theatrical context) as a phenomenon that "sucks up [*nasává*]" dissatisfaction and criticality [*kritičnost*]

---

91 Václav Havel, interview with Gabriele Nissim for *Il Giornale del Popolo*, July 7, 1986. For the Czech translation, see Havel, "Nepolitická politika," in *Má to smysl!*, 231.

92 Císařovská, Prečan, *Charta 77: Dokumenty I*, 540–552.

93 Havel, "Největším problémem je hluboká rezignace společnosti" and "Lidská tvář Prahy," in *Má to smysl!*, 211–212 and 270–271.

94 I will cite here only sources that have already been published in book form: Václav Havel, František Janouch, *Korespondence 1978-2001* (Prague: Akropolis, 2007) and Václav Havel, Vilém Prečan, *Korespondence 1983-1989* (Prague: Czechoslovak Documentation Center, 2011).

along with various longings from "society's subconscious,"[95] transforms them into a subject for public debate, and through this very work contributes to that breakthrough into the power structure. As I have already said, Havel was a *zoon politikon*. After his release from prison in 1983, he adopted a position that was, on the one hand, oriented toward global statesmanship, and this claim is supported by, among other forms of documentation, his 1986 address upon receipt of the Erasmus Prize with the queen of the Netherlands in attendance[96] as well as his correspondence with the West German president Richard von Weizsäcker shortly after the fall of Communism that looked toward a possible Czechoslovak-German reconciliation.[97] His position was, on the other hand, also political in a more local sense of the word, and here he made appeals to specific segments of Czechoslovak society—segments that he considered could be pushed in a productive direction. In July 1986 he told the Italian journalist Gabriele Nissim that his position was more "existential" in nature than "strategic."[98] As the crisis in the Soviet bloc showed in the years that followed, Havel's *position*, which the British journalist Mark Frankland described as a "philosophy of moral resistance,"[99] turned out to have long had a *strategic* place in the political field. His last imprisonment, which he spent in his own words as a "VIP" [*prominent*] in a special cell in Ruzyně from January to May 1989, amplified his international renown just as Communism was on the verge of collapsing and also laid bare the fact, which for various reasons had remained hidden until that very moment, that Charter 77 *was* the mother of a democratic opposition and that Havel *was* its (political) leader.

95 Havel, "Lidská tvář Prahy," in *Má to smysl!*, 256.
96 Havel, "Děkovná řeč," in *Spisy* 4, 613.
97 Havel, Prečan, *Korespondence 1983–1989*, 770–771.
98 Havel, "Nepolitická politika," in *Má to smysl!*, 231.
99 Václav Havel, interview with Mark Frankland for *The Observer*, July 30, 1989. For the Czech translation, see Havel, "Pokud chci žít, musím mít naději," in *Má to smysl!*, 324.

How did he act as a leader? The answer to that question lies in the drama of 1989. Until the very last moment he adhered to the principle of "half the truth" that he had, as we know, enunciated in May 1977: he was not and would never be a politician, he was a writer who was guided by his conscience and who said what he thought. Consequently and in accordance with his views on democracy that appear in "The Power of the Powerless," he was rejecting the notion of politics as a vocation that was being advanced by other oppositional groups and was associated with a certain radicalization in the public domain.[100] He took part in a competitive struggle for influence within the increasingly politicized dissident and tried to assert his idea of politics by co-authoring the civic appeal "A Few Sentences" and also attempting to establish contact with the Czechoslovak federal premier Adamec. He himself formally delimited his role in all this as one of a dramaturge, director, or mediator who does not belong to any one of the opposition groups but rather positions himself above them all as a shepherd to a flock. At stake, however, was nothing more and nothing less than who would have a deciding say in the composition, subject matter, and cast of the anticipated political negotiations that would take place "at the round table."[101]

As late as October, when the Eastern bloc was bursting at its seams, Havel was still asserting that oppositional groups overvalued their significance and wanted to decide for society what "in reality must and only can be decided by society as a whole."[102] It was as if the play's director refused to call the lead actors, who had been preparing to play their roles for a long while, onto stage and had

100 Emanuel Mandler, *Oba moji prezidenti: Václav Havel a Václav Klaus* (Prague: Libri, 2004), 64.
101 See entries from the political diary of the Charter 77 signatory, political prisoner, and politician Rudolf Battěk on the following dates in 1989: July 13, 14, and 19; August 18, 26, 27, and 30; September 2; October 2, 13, 16, 20, 21, 22, 23, 24, and 31; November 2, 7, 10, 11, 14, 15, and 16. The archives of Libri prohibiti in Prague.
102 Václav Havel, "Hodina mezi zkrachovancem a politikem," in *Spisy* 4, 1156.

instead relegated them to the status of extras in the production.[103] He himself naturally did not give up playing the role of a "political amateur"[104]: had he done so, his life story would suddenly have lost its *dramatic* coherence. What kind of play would it have been if its main hero had abdicated his role just before the final act? And what type of responsibility would he have been advocating if he didn't follow it through to its logical end and instead withdrew to the Theater on the Balustrade to be an "assistant dramaturge"?[105]

Havel knew that Czechoslovak society would be able "any day now" to take on a completely "different shape"[106] than it had for many decades, and he pinned on this dramatic moment his hope for a politics as a kind of collective emergence of civic virtue. After the student demonstration on November 17, he expressed affinity for the crowds who had gathered to await word of their liberation. He fully appreciated the demonstration's political potential, which had until then been seen as marginal. He had the striking students and artists on his side, and in no time managed to attract a decisive portion of the protesting public to it as well. He became, in three short weeks, the leader of a national movement for democratization of the country and also a presidential candidate! Prison played a central role in this astonishing metamorphosis because it endowed Havel's life story with a moral foundation and a certain dramatic contrast. "Truth and love must prevail over lies and hate!"[107]—this exclamation expressed the synergy of the moment when a recently released political prisoner became the head of state. Havel's conception of totalitarianism (confirmed by his own experience that saw prison

---

103 Václav Havel, interview with Ivan Lamper for the samizdat revue *Sport* in September 1989. See Havel, "Terén, na který nikdy nevstoupim," in *Má to smysl!*, 355–359.
104 Havel, "Terén, na který nikdy nevstoupim," 351.
105 Havel, "Terén, na který nikdy nevstoupim," 352.
106 Václav Havel, interview with Andrzej Jagodziński for *Gazeta Wyborcza*, October 9, 1989. For the Czech translation, see Havel, "Opatrně, ale s nadějí," in *Má to smysl!*, 362.
107 Havel, "Projev k demonstrantům na Václavském náměstí," in *Spisy* 4, 1176.

as totalitarianism's "futurological laboratory"[108]) rationalized the surprisingly rapid fall of the Communist regime in absolute moral terms. A system founded on lies could not withstand the truth! In the early hours of December 6, 1989 in the emergency headquarters of the Civic Forum, Havel cast doubt on his leading role in the "real-life drama" of the events that were unfolding, and he did so along already familiar lines: "I most certainly do not want to be president. But if the situation escalates to the point that my becoming president for a short time would prove to be in the interests of the country, then I am ready to do so. I have always tried to put the interests of the country above my own—if I hadn't done so, I would never have been in prison and so forth. But I do hope that the interests of the country will not be placed above my own personal ones and that I can sneak my way back into literature [*že budu moci vysublimovat do literatury*]."[109] How are we to understand this? As the misgivings of an intellectual on the verge of power? In part, yes. Havel knew what he wanted and consequently clung to the position of an "antipolitical politician,"[110] thereby opening a space that he would resolutely step into as an "extremely unconventional president."[111] At that moment, Havel himself became the focal point for political change in the role of a "revivalist [*buditel*]."[112] This moral guarantee was, however, only one side of the coin, and the other resided in the

108 Havel, "Na straně pravdy proti lži," in *Má to smysl!*, 194.

109 Documentary audio recordings from December 5–30, 1989 in the archives of Vladimír Hanzel, Prague. A relevant selection of these recordings was published in Jiří Suk, ed., *Občanské forum: listopad-prosinec 1989, 2. díl: Dokumenty* (Brno-Prague: Institute for Contemporary History of the Academy of Sciences of the Czech Republic, 1998), 87, 122, 179.

110 Recorded from a telephone call with František Janouch, October 4, 1989. Havel, Janouch, *Korespondence 1978-2001*, 529–530.

111 Václav Havel's address as presidential candidate at the first congress of the Civic Forum, December 23, 1989, in the archives of the Coordination Center of the Civic Forum, Institute for Contemporary History of the Academy of Sciences of the Czech Republic, Prague. Published in Suk, *Občanské forum: listopad-prosinec 1989, 2. díl: Dokumenty*, 281.

112 Michael Kocáb's characterization, uttered during a meeting of the emergency staff of Civic Forum's Coordination Center, December 5-6, 1989. Published in Suk, *Občanské forum: listopad-prosinec 1989, 2. díl: Dokumenty*, 86.

techniques of power itself. Given that Civic Forum as an organization oscillated between revolutionary and reformist political aims and was, as a result, institutionally incapacitated, Havel took up (the Communist) premier Čalfa's offer to compel the (Communist) parliament, through behind-the-scenes maneuvering, to unanimously elect the former dissident as president on December 29, 1989.

Havel had secured a position of power from that moment onward without needing to feel bound by "party" loyalty to either Civic Forum or its Slovak equivalent Public Against Violence, which had jointly nominated him to the country's highest office. He understood politics as theater and called it the "art of the impossible,"[113] which would consist of "morality in practice."[114] Since he considered "parliamentary democracy" to be, in the spirit of "The Power of the Powerless" and other pronouncements, merely a transitional phase to "something else, something new,"[115] he could suppose that the political and institutional framework for the newly revived parliamentary democracy would not be so important: the goal, after all, was a democratic society of a higher quality that would come into being through, first and foremost, existential renewal and only subsequently by making use of traditional political means.

Politics, which had for a short while capitulated to morality, nonetheless quickly returned in the form of conflicts and clashes. Moreover, it returned in an especially mobilized form, which began to obscure the discourse surrounding moral renewal and the creation of a moral society. The new president adapted himself to the situation and spoke of an unfinished revolution, the slow "disintegration of

---

113 Václav Havel, "New Year's Address," January 11, 1990. See also *Letní přemítání* (Prague: Torst, 1999), 15. Compare the title of one American collection of Havel's presidential speeches: *The Art of the Impossible: Politics as Morality in Practice* (New York: Knopf, 1997).
114 Havel, "Letní přemítání," in *Spisy* 6, 528, 531. Also see Havel, "Pokud chci žít, musím mít naději," in *Má to smysl!*, 327.
115 Václav Havel, interview with Karel Kašpárek for *Radio Free Europe*, July 15, 1989. Radio Free Europe, Czechoslovak Broadcasting Department, Panorama 174.

old totalitarian structures," the "tentacles of the invisible mafia,"[116] and he gave the green light to university economists who were advocating for a swift transition to capitalism under the so-called Washington consensus.[117] It was as if he had already forgotten about the hope he expressed during his first imprisonment for "real socialism," in which "workers... would decide about economic matters" and not "hidden economic mechanisms under political control" that would be dominated by "capitalism of the Western type."[118] Already by 1988 at the latest, Havel stopped implying that the socialist project had any future prospects, and he considered "socialism" a mere cover term for the totalitarian experience, that is, socialism in practice as the "bureaucratic apparatus of the Communist party"[119]; given this view, he could no longer impute to socialism any sort of positive content. He saw nothing resembling a social-welfare state in the totalitarian system, but rather understood it as its own kind of prison (and we can recall that he had described actual prison inversely as a "laboratory of totalitarianism"). That his own time in prison had a strong influence over this reversal of opinion seems undeniable. His profound experience as a (political) prisoner undoubtedly led him, as president, to declare an extensive prison amnesty on January 1, 1990[120], and in later years he often granted presidential pardons.[121] No subsequent head of state used the authority to grant pardons nearly as much as Havel did.

When the Czechoslovak state was being dissolved in the aftermath of the June 1992 elections and the last federal parliament repeatedly failed to elect him president, Havel reflected on his efforts to liken politics to morality in practice. He had lost in the political

---

116 Havel, "22. Výročí srpnové okupace," in *Spisy* 6, 243–248.
117 Gil Eyal, *The Origins of Postcommunist Elites: From Prague Spring to the Breakup of Czechoslovakia* (Minneapolis-London: University of Minnesota Press, 2003), 12, 30, 86.
118 Havel, *Zápisky obviněného*, 187.
119 Havel, "Šifra socialismus," in *Spisy* 4, 18.
120 Havel, "New Year's Address, January 1, 1990."
121 Lenka Marečková, *Milosti. Ohnisko lidství v trestním právu* (Prague: Academia, 2007).

arena, although he had emerged as a moral victor because he had tirelessly warned against "... political sectionalism, mindless party loyalty, lust for power, etc, etc." He consistently distanced his power potential from representation through a political party, and even though he was convinced that his own party would have received many votes, he never cared to found it—to do so would have meant ceasing to "be himself," that is, the self he had become in prison. He thought of his participation at the highest political levels as a kind of sacrifice, which he endured on behalf of the "significant portion of the public" who supported him: "There was an old woman in Trutnov who gave me a long lecture about how everything is just crap— she meant political parties, the parliament, etc.—and how I'm a real hero for slogging my way through it all..."[122] Seen from this angle, one paradox associated with Havel reaches its culminating point: while he went to prison in 1979 with the hope of finding freedom, he entered professional politics in 1989 and lost "a large piece" of it.[123]

122 Havel, "Letní přemítání no. 2," August 18, 1992. Unpublished reflection piece intended for Havel's staff, a photocopy of which was obtained by Havel's office in 2010 and is now in the possession of the author of this chapter.
123 Havel, *Prosím stručně*, 66 and *To the Castle and Back*, 89.

THEATER: *DIVADLO*

Barbara Day

Introduction

It was a beautiful September day in Prague, which was just as well, because the President of the Republic was giving an open-air party. It was to be held among the formal flower beds and stately trees of the Royal Garden on the northern side of the Castle, and preceded by a conference—or confrontation—in the renaissance *Míčovna*, the Ball Game Hall.[124] Václav Havel had invited representatives of global organizations and non-governmental initiatives to find common cause under the banner "Praga–dialogi locus."[125]

As one of the first to take my seat in the press gallery, I was able to look down on the final preparations. Professional stage manager that he was, Havel himself moved among the rows of chairs, checking sight lines and testing the levels of the microphones. More than anyone, he knew the importance of everyone being able to see and hear on such an occasion. This event–this dialogue–held many of the elements of *divadlo* in which even those who do not speak a word are participants.

Havel's theater studies were not academic hours spent at his desk or in a library. His training was practical, combining physical work with the honing of an acute sensitivity to the nuances of timing. Havel had demonstrated his ability to stage theater more than ten years earlier, at the time of the Velvet Revolution. This was not a revolution that took place behind closed doors, in private offices and council chambers. It was acted out in the biggest spaces available, first Wenceslas Square (45,000 square meters, plus surrounding windows, balconies,

---

[124] In fact, the original Ball Game Hall burned down at the end of World War II and was rebuilt by the architect Pavel Janák.
[125] This took place on September 23, 2000.

and roofs) and then the vast plain of Letná. Havel understood that everyone present was a participant, so they all had to be able to see and hear—sightlines and microphone levels again, set up by theater technicians. Moreover, it was essential for the show to be a comedy (in the Elizabethan sense of a play with a happy ending). He therefore used his experience as a dramaturge to structure the demonstration/performance: it must not be too long (the November temperatures were well below zero); the individual acts must be entertaining as well as brief, having the nature of a variety show (speeches interspersed with songs and interviews); and feature popular personalities (the controversial use of "normalization" stars, such as the singer Karel Gott); emotion must not be allowed to overcome rationality (no histrionics or rabble-rousing); the event should be inclusive (even Communists could join in). Indoor discussions with the current holders of power also had their dramaturgy—the photographer Jaroslav Krejčí[126] once told me that before the start of any negotiation Havel drafted scenarios of the different routes the discussion might take, and prepared alternative responses.

One of the phenomena most frequently remarked on during those November days was the way in which even the massive crowds behaved with a sense of responsibility, as though participating in a ritual in which they instinctively understood their role. How did Havel know how to do this? Where did his concept of how a revolution should conduct itself originate? How did he come to be equipped with the skills to manage one? Where did he learn not only how to put on a show, but also how to awaken the deep instincts of the public to a belief in themselves?

In this paper I shall trace, chronologically and thematically, the development of Havel's concept of theater, particularly from 1958

126 Krejčí's studio was on the island of Kampa in the center of Prague, its windows opening directly onto Čertovka. Full of artwork, books, and artefacts, in the 1970s it was the venue for lectures by Jan Patočka. In 2002, the 500-year floodwaters rose to the level of the story above the studio.

to 1968, with reflections on the four theater practitioners who influenced him. An early discovery was the transcendent power of theater; its ability to extend into the spiritual world. However, Havel learned by working backstage that this needed technical discipline behind it; it was not a solo journey but one that involved all those within that space. In its interaction, theater became a common activity, relevant and useful to all. The audience was to be treated with respect, and not dictated to or manipulated. He realized that the stirring up of superficial emotion was inadmissible; emotion was to come from within, as a personal response to the situation. Thus an element of distancing was involved, if the audience was to assess the truth of what was being presented; the creation of an arena of freedom in which the individual, a member of that community, could recognize his or her own responsibilities.

The theater was not Havel's intended profession, nor his chosen environment. It is probable that in less politically troubled times he would have found his fulfillment in the film world. Given his background, connections, and abilities, he could have made a career as a producer, director, or scriptwriter. Creatively, he inclined towards the skills of collage, juxtaposition, and cross-cutting. This, however, was the mid-1950s, and the Czechoslovak film industry, including Václav's uncle, was under suspicion of having collaborated with the Nazis while others were suffering in prisons and concentration camps. The Communist regime intended to keep culture firmly under its control.

In November 1980 Václav Havel wrote to Olga from prison: "If I could have freely chosen my education when I was young, I might well have become a film director instead of a writer; my longing to invent and create and thus to say something about the world and myself might have found a more appropriate outlet in the directing of films."[127] It is either ironic or appropriate (I tend to the latter)

---

[127] Václav Havel, *Letters to Olga*, letter 56.

that his last project before he died, the film of his final work *Leaving*, was his first direct experience of film-making and his first stab at being a director (even though Czech theater has a tradition of dramaturges who became theater directors—Jan Grossman is an example—there is no evidence that Havel, at least while at the Balustrade Theater, had any such ambition). Perhaps this frustration was partly behind an exceptionally sour diatribe in a letter of November 1981 against "the whole world of so-called professional theater, Czech theater in particular with its obsessive penchant for egghead theorizing and its everlasting personal conflicts and gossip" (though I can hardly imagine that the world of film would have been better in this respect).[128] He emphasizes in this letter that it was not the theater environment but the work he was doing that held him there, and the people he worked with—Jan Werich, Ivan Vyskočil, and Jan Grossman. With the addition of Alfréd Radok, I suggest that it was these contrasting theater practitioners who shaped Havel's concept of theater and how it applied in society.

Jan Werich: theater as an arena of freedom

The first influence, Jan Werich (1905–1980) was a legend from the inter-war period, when he and his partner Jiří Voskovec had performed in their accidentally named "Liberated Theater." The Liberated Theater was an offshoot of the Devětsil (1920–1930), an inter-disciplinary association of young artists, experimental and mainly left-wing. In 1934, however, its former members were hardly able to credit Andrei Zhdanov's declaration at the Soviet Writers' Congress that the task of art was to depict reality in its revolutionary development; a concept embodied in artworks that realistically portrayed turning points and heroic moments in the history of Socialism. The Czechs regarded their Soviet colleagues' commitment

---

128 Havel, *Letters to Olga*, letter 247.

to what came to be known as Socialist Realism as unbelievably reactionary, no more than the readoption of conventional and familiar forms. They themselves were analyzing their experiments in art by means of Structuralism and the technique of defamiliarization.[129] By this time the Liberated Theatre had become known for its political jazz revues, in which Werich and his partner Voskovec exposed Fascist aggression to ridicule in their partly prepared, partly improvised dialogues in the tradition of variety: "the artistic method really is liberated from any kind of constructive activity, [...] any maintenance of healthy respect and discipline," protested the German press.[130] By the time the Nazis reached Prague, Voskovec and Werich were in exile. Although they returned, a similar attitude prevailed in the totalitarian 1950s, when Voskovec went back to America and Werich was barely tolerated by the Communist regime but still admired by the public as a free spirit. When Werich died, Havel wrote:

He had one exceptionally important influence on me: he helped me realize, among other things, that theater can be something incomparably more than just a play, a director, actors, audience and an auditorium; it is a special focus of social and intellectual life, helping to create the 'spirit of the times' and embodying and manifesting its fantasy and humor; it is a living instrument of social self-awareness, one that is, in an unrepeatable way, lodged in its own time.[131]

In the introduction to Havel's collected theater writings, *O divadle*, the philosopher and diplomat Martin Palouš writes that it was Jan Werich who stimulated Havel's interest in the potency of theater "to make people who are not free feel free at least for a moment."[132]

129 In Czech, *ozvláštnění*: see below.
130 Jaromír Pelc, *Zpráva o Osvobozeném divadle* (Prague: Práce, 1982), 171.
131 Havel, *Letters to Olga*, letter 53.
132 Martin Palouš, "S Václavem Havlem o divadle a nejen o něm" in Václav Havel, *O divadle*, ed. Anna Freimanová (Prague; Knihovna Václava Havla, 2012), 8.

Palouš quotes Hannah Arendt on one of the sources of freedom being the human capacity to begin something new. According to Arendt, the Achilles' heel of totalitarianism is youthful defiance and this, writes Palouš, was likewise a natural starting point and major theme for Havel. Havel's employment by Werich came at a time when theater was—more dynamically than the other arts—disassociating itself from the ideology of Socialist Realism, so the concept of theater as an arena of freedom was implanted at the start of Havel's career. It fused with his belief that freedom is a task we carry out, rather than a gift to which we are entitled; that we have to create it by thinking and acting freely.

The interpretation of this became an issue for a discussion in November 1968[133] when, in the aftermath of the Soviet invasion, Czechoslovak citizens were flocking to revivals of patriotic plays which gave them the illusion of freedom. In Havel's view this was a surrogate program, pseudo-activity, even fraud. Jan Grossman saw it as a natural reaction in a land where the substitution of theater for political action had been historically significant. He was referring especially to the 19th-century National Awakening, when the response to the failure of the 1848 revolution was the creation of the Committee to Build a Czech National Theater, and when in 1868 the foundation stone of the National Theater was laid with the celebrations that were to have accompanied the coronation of Franz Josef as King of Bohemia (the unrealized Triple Monarchy). Under abnormal circumstances, substitution was bound to happen. To resist it at all had political outcomes, since it meant the pursuit of objective truth. In Grossman's words, "Every true art fights for freedom."[134]

133 "Ještě jednou obrození?" (discussion), *Divadlo* 1969/1 (January 1969), 26-37.
134 "Ještě jednou obrození?" (discussion), *Divadlo* 1969/1 (January 1969), 26-37.

Alfréd Radok and the suspension of disbelief

Writing to Olga in December 1981 Havel refers to "the ancient essence of theater as ritual."[135] Theater scholars generally concur that performance is rooted in ritual; in the human desire for a relationship with the supernatural. At the time Havel was beginning his theater career, the British director Tyrone Guthrie was comparing theater performance to the Christian church's Holy Communion: "Action on the stage is a stylized re-enactment of real action, which is then imagined by the audience."[136] His colleague Hugh Hunt wrote: "The ritual of the theater is [...] a meeting-place between our imagination and our reason."[137] Havel's colleague Petr Oslzlý (of Theater Goose on a String) wrote in 1992 of ritual as "a religious ceremony, played in what we call the 'sacred circle' [...] [T]he shaman or priest [...] led a dialogue with that supernatural being which the community sought, revered and worshipped. The whole community was enclosed in that sacred circle," affirming that the "great demonstrations of November 1989 were also theatre rituals invoking freedom, transferred now into the city squares, where the whole community could participate. It was reminiscent of the celebrations of the classical theatre, which also involved the whole community."[138]

It is a "meeting-place" in the sense that the performance of a ritual creates a link between the unknown and our understanding of it and provides the footing for our belief, or faith (the Czech word *víra* can be translated as either) in what we cannot experience directly.

---

135 Havel, *Letters to Olga*, letter 105.
136 Tyrone Guthrie, *A Life in the Theatre* (London: Hamish Hamilton, 1960), 313.
137 Hugh Hunt, *The Live Theatre* (London: OUP, 1962), 5.
138 Petr Oslzlý, "Theatre in a Sacred Circle," trans. Barbara Day, in Petr Oslzlý, *Divadlo za demokracii—Theatre for Democracy* (Brno: Janáčková akademie múzických umění, 2019). This text was originally given as a lecture in Richard Schechner's Performance Studies seminar at the Tisch School of Arts, New York University, on March 30, 1993.

Theater, like religion, requires belief—or at least the suspension of disbelief, sometimes wrongly interpreted as the abandonment of one's critical faculties. On the contrary, the suspension of disbelief requires the participation of all one's faculties. It is the process described by Arthur Koestler when he writes about the law of infolding.[139] Koestler explains "infolding" as the artist's sense of the techniques of selection, simplification (economy) and exaggeration (emphasis) to convey the truth of what they are presenting, whether it is a painting, poem, or performance. If the complexity and subtlety of the infolding corresponds to the receptiveness of the audience, then, by making connections (interpolations), following allusions (extrapolation), and interpreting what is seen and/or heard (transformation) they will experience that shiver of recognition, that moment of transcendent "here and now." This is the moment of understanding, of belief, of faith. It can range from the sublime realization of Christ's sacrifice down to grasping the meaning of a joke or gag.

It is possible, but unlikely, that Havel saw the 1986 production of Comenius's *Abrahamus Patriarcha* by Brno's *Ochotnický kroužek* (Amateur Circle). The script (which owes more to Kierkegaard than Comenius)[140] deals with the question of faith in an age of conformity and calculation, expressed through the story of Abraham, a man at odds with his time. The dramatic structure focuses attention on the "here and now" of theatrical performance—in this case Abraham's preparedness to sacrifice his son Isaac. An event can take place only once in history, but in the theater this "once" can be recreated in the presence of an audience. In Koestler's words, "[a]rt originates in sympathetic magic; in the illusions of stagecraft its origin is directly

---

139 Arthur Koestler, *The Act of Creation* (London: Pan Books, 1975). The terms "interpolate," "extrapolate," and "transform" are those used by Koestler on pages 84–85 and to which he returns on page 341.
140 Comenius was a cover; Luboš Malinovský, who created the script and co-directed with J. A. Pitínský, was exploring the ideas of Søren Kierkegaard (the philosopher Petr Osolsobě was also involved), but knew that Kierkegaard's name would not pass the censorship.

reflected."[141] The audience shares in the ritual—the act of (re)crea-tion—initiated by the performers and through that becomes aware of meaning.

Havel had explored the nature of faith (belief) in a letter to Olga in 1981 and concludes that "faith in meaning [*smysl*] transcends all relative utility" and that everything "has its own admittedly obscure meaning in relation to faith." Without this, he says, the experience of nonsense (*nesmyslnost*)—the absence of meaning (*absence smys-lu*)—would be unthinkable: "That is the case with so-called absurd art which, more than anything else—because it is a desperate cry against loss of meaning—contains faith."[142] Three months later he returns to the theme: "[T]he feeling of absurdity is never—at least not as I see it—the expression of a loss of faith in the meaning of life. Quite the opposite [...]."[143]

The "absurd" (absurdita, absurdnost) was a key theme of the avant-garde of the 1960s. Martin Esslin, author of the classic text The Theatre of the Absurd (in which a last-minute sub-section of a chapter is devoted to Václav Havel),[144] observed that although "it appeared as though the Theatre of the Absurd—introspective, oblivi-ous of social problems and their remedies—was the antithesis of the political theatre as preached by Brecht and his followers," under totalitarian regimes it actually turned into "an extremely vigorous and barbed kind of political theatre."[145] Havel saw the theater of the absurd as:

> [...] the most significant theatrical phenomenon of the twentieth century, because [...] it shows man as having lost his fundamental metaphysical

141 Koestler, The Act of Creation, 343.
142 Havel, *Letters to Olga*, letter 64.
143 Havel, *Letters to Olga*, letter 73.
144 Martin Esslin, *The Theatre of the Absurd* (Harmondsworth: Penguin Books, 1968). Havel didn't quite make it to the contents page, although he can be found on 314–316.
145 Esslin, *Theatre of the Absurd*, 306.

certainty, the experience of the absolute, his relationship to eternity, the sensation of meaning [*pocit smyslu*] [...]. This is a man for whom everything is coming apart, whose world is collapsing, who senses that he has irrevocably lost something but is unable to admit this to himself and therefore hides from it. He waits, unable to understand that he is waiting in vain [...] There is no philosophizing in these plays as there is in Sartre, for example. On the contrary, what is expressed tends to be banal. In their meaning, however, they are always philosophical. They cannot be taken literally; they illustrate nothing [...] They are not overblown, highly compassioned, or didactic. They tend, rather, to be decadently joking in tone.[146]

He found its authors, he wrote to Olga in 1981, "tremendously close to my own temperament and sensibility, and it was they who stimulated me to try to communicate everything I wanted to say through drama."[147]

In 1959, while working for Werich, Havel published an essay that resulted in an invitation to assist the director Alfréd Radok (1914–1976); an intense personality, half-Jewish, constantly under pressure from the Communist culture barons. Radok's brutal and hazardous rehearsal methods, intended to crack open the crust of techniques and mannerisms under which an actor sheltered, were a shock for Havel ("the chronic peacemaker" as he describes himself). Radok, wrote Havel, was instinctively aware of the inauthentic gesture and broke the actor down until the living personality was exposed for him to work with.[148] Havel recorded that Radok's "irrational procedures" included evocation, mood, feeling, and human contact. Rehearsals were not "building with children's bricks", but *theatre in*

---

146 Václav Havel, *Disturbing the Peace*, trans. Paul Wilson (New York: Vintage Books, 1990), 53–54.
147 Havel, *Letters to Olga*, letter 102.
148 Václav Havel, "Několik poznámek ze Švédské zápalky," in Havel, *O divadle*, 322–349; also in Václav Havel, *Spisy* 3 (Prague: Torst, 1999), 416–461.

action, dynamic, existential, pushing ahead, actual, living (Havel's italics).[149] It was through such arduous rehearsal that the theater director finds the moment of creation that unlocks a truth till then held in suspense; but it is a moment that the actor has to (re)create at every performance. With repetition comes the danger of falsification.

Alfréd Radok not only directed in Prague theaters, but was also (with the theater designer Josef Svoboda) the co-creator of the Laterna magika, a multi-media phenomenon merging film with live performance. Nowadays it is regarded as little more than a tourist entertainment, but mid-century it seemed to hold out opportunities to convey meaning through the juxtaposition of images. In its early days it employed many of the theater's young talents, including at one point Jan Grossman. Havel's 1959 essay (mentioned above), admired by Radok but at the time unpublished, was about the Laterna magika and probably betrays the twenty-three-year-old's ambitions to work in this multi-media genre.[150] After its triumph at the Brussels Expo 58, the Laterna magika was under political pressure to shun its origins as a variety show and become a respectable genre. Havel did not think that this necessarily caused a conflict: he regarded variety as a genuine art, an applied art rather than one of fine arts, but still a genre of its own that could also serve an educational purpose. It could however do much more; with its use of film combined with the live performer it had resources capable of reflecting, through contrast and conflict, the complexity of the modern world. At the same time Havel recognizes how easily this can slide into absurdity (he could have mentioned the Communists' disappointment that the show missed an opportunity to feature Sputnik), and that

---

149 Havel, "Několik poznámek ze Švédské zápalky," 247; also in Havel, *Spisy* 3, 427.

150 Václav Havel, "O laterně magice," in Havel, *O divadle,* 95–105; also in Havel, *Spisy* 3, 251–268. According to Grossman, he was co-author with Havel of the study (until 1999 unpublished), and borrowed some of its ideas for his article on the Laterna magika originally published in *Divadlo* in 1961: see Jan Grossman, "Výtvarné hledisko Laterny magiky a polyekranu," in Jan Grossman, *Mezi literaturou a divadlem II* (Prague: Torst, 2013), 1077 (note 1).

it needed to be anchored in a scenario, and the scenario in a philosophy. This complex (applied) art frees itself from the three classical unities of action, place and time, from slavish attention to external realism, and from ideological values.

As far as I know, Havel never was invited to join the Laterna magika. In May 1960, Radok was fired by the Communist culture mafia for his resistance to the excision of the centerpiece of the new program, Martinů's cantata *The Opening of the Wells*, and came close to a nervous breakdown. Havel venerated Radok above all other directors and continued to correspond with him even after he emigrated to Sweden in 1968. It was a correspondence he shared with Jan Grossman, a three-way discussion with Havel in the middle; although Havel's letters have survived, Radok's sadly are lost. It had always been Havel's ambition that Radok would direct one of his plays, and in 1976 this was about to be fulfilled when Radok flew from Stockholm to Vienna to direct Havel's *Audience* at the Burgtheater. But before rehearsals could start, Radok had a heart attack and died. In 2008 Radok's son, David, who had almost by accident followed his father's profession in exile, directed Havel's last play, *Leaving*, for the Archa Theater in Prague.

Ivan Vyskočil and the psychology of the audience

In the same year (1960) as Radok was fired from the Laterna magika, Ivan Vyskočil (born in 1929) invited Havel to join the recently founded Theater on the Balustrade. Vyskočil, who had studied at the Performing Arts Academy and the Psychology Department of Charles University, was interested primarily in the psychology of the audience. For Vyskočil the art of the theater lay in the relationship between the actor and audience, an encounter in an "empty space" that can be anywhere. Theater[151] does not require a formal

---

[151] Vyskočil later termed his genre of theatre *Nedivadlo* or "Non-theater."

173

building with a raised stage and technical equipment, but can take place in an improvised space which, without physical changes, can represent a palace or a pub, a forest or a city street. He trusted in the insecurity of the moment, a process described by Havel as "the desire to capture theatre in a state of birth."[152] Vyskočil had tested this with his "text-appeals [*text-apely*]"—a term he had coined in the tradition of Czech word play. The genre was really a form of literary cabaret, an expression he was reluctant to use. The resonances of American "sex appeal" gave the term a youthful, daring kick, but more important was the implication of "appeal," which expressed a relationship with the audience in which response was an essential element. Vyskočil's text-appeals were short, open-ended monologues, responding to the reactions of the audience in the informal surroundings of the Reduta jazz club, or after the scheduled performance at the Theater on the Balustrade—for in the 1960s the Balustrade foyer became a venue for late-night discussion of questions provoked by the performances. The writer Josef Škvorecký, at that time involved in fringe theater with his future wife Zdena Salivarová, recalled: "I liked the friendly atmosphere of the Textappeals [*sic*]—they had that atmosphere of conspiracy between the audience and the performers."[153] For a while Vyskočil formed a partnership with the multi-talented Jiří Suchý, whose songs interspersed the text-appeals (or vice-versa)—songs about the ordinary everyday things of life, about their usefulness and practicality, but also about their wonderful and inspiring qualities.

Earlier that year Havel, writing "on the fringe of the young Prague stages" (the Balustrade, Semafor and Rokoko), noted the "variety" format of their programs, held together by a loosely conceived theme and by a humor that worked through abbreviation and allusion (Koestler's interpolation and extrapolation). It makes greater

---

152 Havel, *Disturbing the Peace*, 46.
153 Josef Škvorecký, letter to the author, September 30, 1984, author's archive.

demands on the audience: "[I]nsofar as its principle is concerned, it can be defined as *absurd humor*, which means that, unlike satirical humor growing out of a mere deformation of the real theme, it grows out of somehow turning the real theme on its head, i.e., the reversal of reality into the absurd."[154]

Havel quotes Vyskočil:

> Authors want their characters to be true to life [...] They are driven by the logic of ordinary reality. And alongside such plays I would like sometime to see or hear one that is completely different—different in its approach to reality. One that has a real, substantial relationship as the basis of its story. And to elaborate and update this central relationship in new situations, in unexpected reversals and antitheses. For example, taking a particular discussion *ad absurdum* so that through its inconsistency the significance of a particular attitude can be demonstrated and emphasised more clearly.[155]

The philosopher Jan Patočka later wrote about Ivan Vyskočil's performances:

> That which has no sense [*smysl*] is not necessarily senseless [*nesmyslný*], absurd; absurdity is not a lack of sense, but rather a special kind of sense, it is the negation of sense, which takes place in the context of meaningful [*smysluplný*] action, of that which has sense and meaning [*význam*] as its aim. Lack of sense is the starting point of the human world, absurdity or nonsense [*nesmysl*] is its constant threat.[156]

Patočka's essay on "The World of Ivan Vyskočil" was published in an issue of the magazine *Divadlo* devoted to the theme of nonsense

---

154 Havel, "Na okraji malých pražských scén" in Havel, *O divadle*, 122; also in Havel, *Spisy* 3, 305–306.
155 Havel, "Na okraji malých pražských scén", 121; see also Havel, *Spisy* 3, 308–309.
156 Jan Patočka, "Svět Ivana Vyskočila," *Divadlo* 1963/10 (December 1963), 72.

and the absurd. Havel's essay on "The Anatomy of the Gag" appeared in the same issue.[157] In this, Havel analyzes gags from silent film, noting that they are created where two conventionally acceptable activities are juxtaposed in a way that disrupts our expectations. In writing about silent film Havel was following the tradition of the Devětsil's interest in the 1920s, and the Prague Structuralists, among them Bogatyrev and Mukařovský, whose essays on Chaplin appeared in the 1930s.[158] Like them, he adopts Viktor Shklovsky's term "defamiliarization" (in Czech, *ozvláštnění*), a concept once current in the avant-garde but now outlawed in favor of Socialist Realism (which worked on the opposite principle of familiarizing, or conventionalizing, the work of art). It is defamiliarizing, says Havel, that drags reality out of automatism: "A gag is neither nonsense [*nesmysl*] nor the absence of logic, but the process of one logic rendering another one nonsensical [*nesmyslnění*]; its surprising quality stems not from the revelation of the unknown, but from the unexpected look at the known. It does not deny reality, but thinks it through; it does not contradict conventions, but rests on them and works with them."[159]

Havel concludes his essay on the gag with the rather surprising claim that absurd humor can lead to the state of *catharsis* or cleansing. *Catharsis*, if we remember our Aristotle correctly, occurs when our emotions of pity and fear are purged by "an action that is serious, complete, and of a certain magnitude."[160] There is hardly any magnitude to a gag, so what is Havel talking about? Three paragraphs earlier he analyzed "the complexity of our time" and noted that "some natural human need to resist and oppose all of these

157 Havel, "Anatomie gagu" in Havel, *O divadle*, 170–182; see also Havel, *Spisy* 3, 589–609.
158 Petr Bogatyrev, "Chaplin, The Fake Count" and Jan Mukařovský, "An Attempt at a Structural Analysis of an Actor's Figure (Chaplin in *City Lights*)" in David Drozd, Tomáš Kačer, Donald Sparling (eds.), *Theatre Theory Reader: Prague School Writings* (Prague: Karolinum, 2016).
159 Václav Havel, "The Anatomy of the Gag", trans. Michael Schoenberg, *Modern Drama* XXIII:1 (1980), 13–24.
160 *Aristotle's Poetics*, trans S. H. Butcher (New York: Hill and Wang 1961).

pressures" led to absurd humor as possibly the only way of cleansing contemporary man "adequate to the world in which he lives." A similar shock to the system was provided by Vyskočil's text-appeals; in Jiří Suchý's words, "Little by little a shiver went down your back, even if every now and then you unexpectedly had to burst out laughing."[161] What else is this but pity and fear? Socialist Realist art could not do this; maybe it could provoke (the wrong kind of) laughter, but hardly a shiver. Whatever the magnitude of its themes, it was incapable of bringing the *catharsis* that Havel claims for the humble gag.

In his early essays Havel is exuberantly aware of being carried on a rising tide of energy and experiment in the arts. His setbacks, such as when Vyskočil rejects his contribution to the supposedly co-authored *Hitchhike*, or Grossman locks him in a hotel room to finish writing his script, are trivial (even absurd) compared with those past and still to come. A photograph from this period shows Havel, dapper in a short haircut and smartly pressed suit, nonchalantly relaxing alongside a distraught Radok.[162] However, although the Theater on the Balustrade became a second home to him, Havel was not a performer or a technician (though he took on these roles when required); and in spite of the daydream of being a film director, he never seems to have considered directing in the theater. Theater was, however, a place where he could write in a particular, creative way. Grossman later noted: "Havel functions as a dramatist not when he is invited or when there are plays to be written, but at the moment he senses the latent dramatic quality of his theme, when he realises that dramatic expression is the *only* and *necessary* expression of his material."[163]

161 Jiří Suchý, typescript memoirs, quoted in Barbara Day, *Trial by Theatre* (Prague: Karolinum, 2019), 125.
162 Zdeněk Hedbávný, *Alfréd Radok: Zpráva o jednom osudu* (Prague: Národní divadlo / Divadelní ústav, 1994), 290.
163 Jan Grossman, "Václav Havel, Protokoly" in Grossman, *Mezi literaturou a divadlem II*, 1159.

Havel writes of the period from 1962–1968 that "what the Theater on the Balustrade was for those few years can neither be represented nor explained [*se nedá ani zpřítomnit ani vysvětlit*]; that whole phenomenon was an integral part of its time and that time is over."[164] For Havel, each theater had its particular atmosphere depending partly on the physical environment and partly on the "community," made up of the company and the regular theater-goers. His respect for what he termed "conventions" formed a part of this; his relationship to them, however, was a little ambiguous. Writing at the end of 1981, he emphasizes their importance and complexity before anticipating "the rich world of their potential destruction."[165] Where the proscenium arch stage is concerned, he remains conventional; neither Havel nor Jan Grossman were in favor of "experimental" staging, with the audience sitting on more than one side of the action or even moving among the performers.[166] In his experience, this violated the suspension of disbelief and prevented the formation of the "collective spirit" that unified the audience. In spite of—or maybe because of—his sense of being an outsider, Havel appreciated the social value of theater:

The first embryonic appearance of genuine socialness happens the moment those participating in the theater ceases to be a mere group of people and become a community. It is that special moment when their mutual presence becomes mutual participation; when their encounter in a single space and time becomes an existential encounter; when their common existence in this world is suddenly enveloped by a very specific and unrepeatable atmosphere, when a shared experience, mutually understood, evokes the wonderful elation that makes all the sacrifices worthwhile.[167]

164 Havel, *Letters to Olga*, letter 102.
165 Havel, *Letters to Olga*, letter 106.
166 Although his experience of the work of the Brno Theatre Goose on a String must surely have changed his mind in this respect.
167 Havel, *Letters to Olga*, letter 103.

Jan Grossman and the power of understatement

It was the pursuance of a writing career that drew Havel to Jan Grossman (1925–1993), a writer and editor who later became his colleague and neighbor on the Vltava quay. They first met in a literary context when Grossman was (briefly) an influential editor and Havel an aspiring young writer. Grossman was Havel's fourth and final mentor in the theater: "He was for me an authority," Havel wrote in the preface to the first collection of Grossman's writings, *Analýzy* (*Analyses*), "I liked his special kind of humor; his sense for irony and self-irony."[168] To the end of Grossman's life they addressed each other as *vy*, the formal second person. I am devoting some space to Grossman in this essay, not only because of his influence on Havel, but because, while researching this paper, I found out that they had worked together even more closely than I realized, not only in shaping the profile of the Theater on the Balustrade, but also by contributing to each other's writing.

Grossman is also an important figure in his own right, as someone for whom intellectual study and theater practice became inseparable; unfortunately, little of his writing has been translated into English.[169] In the 1930s he attended the Prague English Grammar School where he learned a gentle, humorous English that was not as inadequate as he pretended. He was still a schoolboy when he fought in the resistance against the Nazis; after the war he studied aesthetics and comparative literature while working as an editor for *Mladá fronta*. Grossman did not take up an anti-Communist

---

168 Vaclav Havel, "Předmluva k sborníku Grossmanových textů Analýzy" in Havel, *O divadle*, 400.
169 As far as I know, the only essays by Jan Grossman translated into English are a shortened version of "Kafkova divadelnost?" in *Theatre Czech and Slovak* (5/93 and 6/93) and "O výkladu jednoho textu" in *Visegrad Drama I Weddings*.. Grossman merely shares a short chapter with Miroslav Macháček and Evald Schorm in Jarka M. Burian's *Leading Creators of Twentieth-Century Czech Theatre*, but my *Trial by Theatre* includes some substantial summaries, and David Whitton of Lancaster University provides an analysis of his production of *Don Juan* ("An absurdist *Don Juan* in Prague" in *Molière: Don Juan*, Cambridge: CUP, 1995).

position automatically; it was simply that any kind of ideology was alien to him. He approached literature from the point of view of objective analysis and, unable to compromise in his arguments with basically uneducated Communist critics, was expelled from the university and unable to publish.[170] Instead of taking refuge in an archive and writing for posterity, Grossman realized that there was another career open to those who worked with words—the theater. Nevertheless, it was not until 1954 that he found his way to the theater expression he was searching for—work in progress, rough and immediate, incomplete until confronted by the audience.

Václav Havel had read and admired Grossman's articles in *Listy*[171] immediately after the war. When, in the brief thaw of 1956, Grossman was allowed to return to *Československý spisovatel* as editor, they came to know each other personally through discussions in the Café Slavia about Havel's first literary efforts. By 1958 Grossman had been thrown out of the literary world for good, but in 1962 he took over from Ivan Vyskočil as head of the drama company at the Balustrade Theater where, by coincidence, Havel was already working. The next six years were intensely productive on the Czech stage as a whole. However, the Prague Spring of 1968 brought not only outside interest but also internal tensions to the Balustrade Theater. With international success came political accountability. Relationships between management and artists became tense, and by the time of the Soviet invasion in August, Grossman and Havel had already left the company. Invitations to direct abroad initially kept Grossman in work, but after his passport had been confiscated (as a consequence of his presence at the clandestine performance of Havel's *Beggar's Opera*) he could direct only as an occasional guest in provincial Czech theaters. He returned to the Balustrade Theater

---

170 One of Grossman's most virulent critics was the drama critic Jiří Hájek, father of Petr Hájek, who wrote *Smrt v sametu* (2012) in which Havel is depicted as the servant of Satan.
171 *Listy* (1946–1948) was a quarterly for art and philosophy edited by Jindřich Chalupecký.

in 1988; his work was as compelling as ever, but his health was broken and he died in 1993.

"We did everything together," Havel wrote later, "we chose the actors, the plays, the directors, we sorted out the everyday working problems of the theatre."[172] In an interview in 1968, Grossman maintained that "Václav Havel [...] was not only the main author [of the Theater on the Balustrade], he was the main co-creator of the drama company."[173] But it would be wrong to see Grossman and Havel as the perfect working partnership. Havel admits in his preface to *Analýzy* that their time together at the Balustrade Theater was marked by disputes over Grossman's approach to specific productions, and that for a long time he admired Grossman more as a writer than a man of the theater; later, he said, he came to realize that Grossman was a theater director above all else. Grossman and Havel differed in much, including their attitudes towards their own writing; whereas Havel found satisfaction in the publication in 1999 of the plump green volumes of his collected works, Grossman was always moving on with new ideas, and notorious for extensive rewriting at proof stage.[174] And whereas Havel was to become a figurehead of the opposition movement, spokesman for Charter 77, and President of the Republic, Grossman, according to the theater scholar Jindřich Černý:

> [...] never wanted to be either an engineer of human souls or the conscience of the nation. He never demonstrated for anything, he was never spokesman for anything, he always only just worked [...] After all, that was the only thing for whose authenticity [*pravost*] he could vouch

---

172 Havel, *Disturbing the Peace*, 48.
173 Jan Grossman, "Proč odešel Jan Grossman?", interview with Grossman in *Mezi literaturou a divadlem*, 1258.
174 Although I remember his pleasure in June 1989 when he was presented with the samizdat edition of *Analýzy*. I also remember my surprise that this could be done in the relatively public surroundings of the Balustrade foyer (a sign of the times).

[*ručit*]; with that Anglo-Saxon understatement [*věcnost*] of his, which never had aspirations above its station [...].[175]

The word *věcnost* is usually translated as "objectivity" or "matter-of-factness." However, in one of his longest and most complex essays, *Síla věcnosti*,[176] Grossman repeatedly used the English word "understatement" to explain what he meant by *věcnost*; this has led me to translate the title as "The Power of Understatement." Grossman published the essay in the autumn of 1961, the year he joined the Balustrade Theater as dramaturge. It was prepared as a response to a paper by the critic and dramaturge Jan Kopecký,[177] "A Transformation of Acting?", itself an attack on Grossman's "A Transformation of Acting."[178] Kopecký identifies "understatement" (translating it rather oddly as *pod míru pravdy*) as a resurgence of pre-war Civilism and condemns it as being "in conflict with the basic developmental tendencies of society." "What the Socialist world needs and requires from theatre," he affirms, "is for a work of art to transform randomness into order. To illuminate that which is unclear and leaves an impression of chaos; to overcome nature by understanding developmental necessity."

Grossman begins by referring to Kopecký's paper and cautions him against generalization. Then he comes to *věcnost*, listing its

175 Jindřich Černý, "Váňové" in *Jan Grossman: Svědectví současníků*, eds. Marie Boková and Miloslav Klíma (Prague: DU, DAMU, DLA Elekta and Pražská scéna 1996), 91.
176 Jan Grossman, "Síla věcnosti" in Grossman, *Mezi literaturou a divadlem II*, 913-928. Anna Freimanová chose the same title (I do not know whether consciously or unconsciously) for a collection of tributes to Olga Havlová shortly after her death. .
177 Jan Kopecký (1919–1992) had a complex history. After making a considerable contribution to the Bolshevization of the theater in the 1950s, he redeemed himself in the 1960s with adaptations of folk plays. After 1968 he suffered the fate of other reform Communists.
178 Jan Kopecký, "Proměna herectví?" in Jan Kopecký, *Nedokončené zápasy* (Prague: Československý spisovatel 1961), 158–197 and Jan Grossman, "Proměna herectví" in Grossman, *Mezi literaturou a divadlem II*, 906–912. Both papers were contributions to the 1958 Conference of Drama Critics; see Terezie Pokorná, "Neodpovídat na falešně položené otázky", *Bubínek Revolveru*, 7. 1. 2019: http://www.bubinekrevolveru.cz/neodpovidat-na-falesne-polozene-otazky-jan-grossman-na-konferenci-o-cinoherni-kritice-1958.

positive values, above all its practical and social functions; *věcnost* is the world as we see it around us. He analyzes the changes he observes in a society that (following betrayal, occupation and revolution–my note) has lost faith in man and now believes only in the evidence of what is material, of what can be seen and handled. The essay is essentially a challenge to Grossman's ideologically-minded critics to come out of their splendid isolation and face the reality of everyday life, to leave behind the heroic gestures of Socialist Realism that are inappropriate when the actor is seen in the more intimate context of contemporary theater, illuminated by modern technology. To the modern audience, suppressed emotion is more intense than over-acting and self-control more impressive than histrionics. A terrible event becomes more terrible when the participants are wearing their everyday clothes.

Grossman returned to these ideas two years later at a conference held to discuss the growth of the small stages. In his paper, "The World of Small Theater",[179] he notes that conventional theater, by modelling its work on the ideology of Socialist Realism, had turned its back on the real world in which each individual's relationship to society is based on a continuous process of confrontation between one's private world and the "whole world." Now, however, new theater creators—young, energetic, and flexible—were entering the theater without traditional techniques and were finding their own ways of communicating. Their inexperience was, by definition, transitional. Whereas Vyskočil had wanted theater to remain "in a state of birth," Grossman compared its development to that of young writers who must set themselves tasks, solve problems and understand their limitations (drawing an analogy with Chaplin's development of the gag in film). He defined his dramaturgical principles as the analysis of the problems that lead to today's conflicts and the choice of the

---

179 Jan Grossman, "Svět malého divadla", in Grossman, *Mezi literaturou a divadlem II*, 1095-1113.

material and means to express them. Individuals, involved in a practical way in the increasingly complex pressures of the contemporary world–a world of interpretations, of conventions, illusions, ideas, hopes, and fears–can come to terms with them through theater. Art can help man to disentangle these impressions. It cannot solve problems, but it can expose them. This was, in a sense, Grossman's manifesto for the Balustrade Theater, and certainly Havel must have been involved in its preparation.

In his analysis of his own 1964 production of *Ubu roi*, Grossman wrote:

> The exceptional monstrousness, relying on hundreds and thousands of ordinary people, who by their normality in fact legalise and normalize it, and thus de facto rid it of exceptionality—that is essentially absurdity: on the one side a phenomenon we "naturally" consider to be unnatural; on the other side the rational system, custom, and convention which justifies this "unnaturalness" and makes it natural and ordinary.[180]

"Absurdity is tragedy in the field of banality," he continues. Although he does not mention Hannah Arendt, in the context the allusion to the camps is clear. It is the *věcnost* of *absurdnost*—the matter-of-factness of absurdity—that exposes the horror in full. It is a reminder of the horror of totalitarianism manifested not only in the Holocaust but in the very recent reign of Stalinist terror, or in any society at any time where this process of distortion is implemented. Nearly two decades later, when Grossman's life and career had been further twisted from his control by malicious bureaucrats, he described:

> [...] the inexorable march of an order which is not fatal, but which deforms a person into becoming not only a victim but also an agent in the

---

180 Admired by Peter Brook in his book *The Empty Space* (London: Penguin Books, 1990), 78.

deformation of others, into becoming the upholder of that order. The order consolidates itself not by its victory over the victim but through the victim. The hangman does not turn the condemned man into a corpse but into another hangman. And the living organism, incapable of defending itself against the infection by not accepting or rejecting it, must swallow it as a foreign body, assimilate it, absorb it, and go on living with it and through it. A person fights with pettiness for so long that he himself becomes petty, and he can suppress cruelty only by crude means—which then cease to be the means and become the aim.[181]

Grossman was writing about the heroine of the 19th-century theater classic *Maryša*. In his interpretation, she becomes a perpetrator of the social system that has abused her. It was an interpretation for the era of "normalization" and a challenge to the audience, accustomed to see Maryša as an innocent victim. The recreation onstage of an absurd or bygone world and making it present "here and now" was intended to provoke a response in the audience, and with the response, a sense of responsibility. Grossman termed this effect *apelativnost*, a word he coined with a nod in the direction of Vyskočil's text-appeal. *Apelativnost* is the quality inherent in a theater production that, instead of "transforming randomness into order,"[182] invites a response from the audience to the questions it has raised. Grossman did believe in man, not as an abstraction but as an individual human being, involved in practical ways in the complex pressures of the contemporary world. Theater can help him/her to disentangle this world of conventions, illusions, ideas, hopes, and fears. It cannot solve problems, but it can expose them: "Theater, like art in general, should not only describe life but

181 Jan Grossman, "Interpreting Maryša," in *Visegrad Drama I Weddings* (Bratislava: The Theatre Institute / Divadelný ústav 2002), 75.
182 See the earlier discussion of this citation from Jan Kopecký. For a complementary discussion of *apelativnost*, see Danaher in this volume.

help to change it."[183] Grossman saw this quality in revolutionary theaters, theaters of action, such as those of Piscator or Meyerhold. *Věcnost* and *apelativnost* together form a Möbius strip. The withholding of emotion is met by a response that channels emotion into action. The power of this *věcnost* was demonstrated in a production that Grossman and Havel worked on together for several years, Kafka's *Trial* (1966); Havel hoped that Radok would direct the production, but for unknown reasons—maybe some instinct in Radok—this did not happen. Havel, when writing about the theater of the absurd, had described its impact on him as being only a little less than that of Kafka. Grossman, in his production notes, wrote:

> The first striking feature of a Kafka novel is the inexorable matter-of-factness [*věcnost*], its sobriety and thoroughness of style [...] From the point of view of style the trick is clear. It is founded on provocative tension: the character and exciting event is seen through the eyes of an impersonal, non-participating, disinterested chronicler. It is presented seemingly without any evaluation of any kind; however, for that very fact it is indirectly evaluated as a common and banal fact [...] The chronicler distances himself from the story, but, by doing so, he enters it.[184]

Grossman related this "distancing" to the Alienation-effect[185] advocated by the playwright and theorist Bertolt Brecht (1898-1956); not Brecht the ideologue, but Brecht the man of the theater, whom Grossman always admired and on whose work he was an authority. Havel, however, always found it difficult to accept Brecht's status—writing from prison in February 1982, he made one of his rare comments on the Socialist playwright: "I respect Brecht, but

183 Grossman, "Svět malého divadla,", 1107.
184 Jan Grossman, "The Dramatic Quality of Kafka?", *Theatre Czech and Slovak* 6 (November 1993), 36.
185 Martin Esslin, *Brecht: A Choice of Evils* (London: Heinemann Educational Books 1965), 106–129.

it's a cool and polite respect; frankly, I only like his non-Brechtian moments."[186] (All the same, according to his agent Klaus Juncker, books by Brecht were to be found in Havel's "den".)[187] Interviewed by Karel Hvížd'ala, Havel evokes that distancing in his recall of early feelings of being an outsider looking on, and how that influenced him in the writing of his plays: "What else but a profound feeling of being excluded can enable a person better to see the absurdity of the world and his own existence?"[188]

In spite of Havel's deep involvement in the history of his age, he saw himself as an observer. It is appropriate that one of the last projects he worked on with Jan Grossman was the story of a trial—a trial that never reaches the courtroom. One could recall John van Druten's play *I Am a Camera*,[189] in which the character identified as Christopher Isherwood is "quite passive, not thinking, recording." This is most evident in the so-called Vaněk plays that Havel wrote when, in the 1970s, he was without a theater or professional actors and relied on friends and relations performing in a garden or living room. Ferdinand Vaněk, like Josef K in *The Trial*, says very little, although the action is seen through his eyes (or rather heard through his ears). As Havel says, Vaněk is not himself, the author, any more than "Isherwood" in *I Am a Camera* is Isherwood. But without Vaněk's presence, there would be no drama, so he is both the trigger for the behavior of others and the witness of it. He is a dramatic device constructed by Havel, witness of the real world, to enable us to focus on a particular detail of our world. In this respect, Havel's later play, *Largo Desolato* (1985), is a Vaněk play in multiple, focusing on a sequence of characters rather than on one (or on one couple). In conversation with Hvížd'ala, Havel uses the image of

---

186 Havel, *Letters to Olga*, letter 115.
187 Carol Rocamora, *Acts of Courage* (Hanover, NH: Smith and Kraus, 2004), 55.
188 Havel, *Disturbing the Peace*, 6.
189 Adapted from Christopher Isherwood's *Goodbye to Berlin* and better known as the musical *Cabaret*.

a probe, which leads him to thoughts about the theater as revealing "the hidden logic of things":

> This kind of theater neither instructs us, nor attempts to acquaint us with theories or interpretations of the world, but by 'probing' beneath the surface, it somehow inspires us to participate in an adventurous journey toward a deeper understanding, or rather to a new and deeper questioning, of ourselves and the world.[190]

Conclusion

Havel set out on this adventurous journey thirty years earlier; we can follow him in his relatively simple and exuberant essays about the contemporary theater in the 1950s and 1960s as he constantly shifts around the concept of *divadlo*, looking at it from different angles, modifying his opinions. In the 1980s, no longer directly involved in the theater (or even keeping up with it, since he knew his attendance at a public performance could cause problems for others), he reflects on what theater has meant to him (first from prison and then again before his fiftieth birthday). In his last two decades he had little time to spend on the theater; for the period after 1989 the published collection of his theater writings can only produce three speeches and a few brief contributions in the form of forewords, memorials, and occasional notes. Even at the end of the 1980s, when he attended performances more often and could write for the samizdat *O divadle*,[191] he scarcely used the opportunity. An excerpt from his program note for the Vienna Burgtheater's production of *Temptation* in the first issue of *O divadle* explains the reason: "A dramatist without a theater is like a bird without a nest; he is deprived of his

---

190 Havel, *Letters to Olga*, letter 104.
191 This should not be confused with the 2012 published collection of Havel's writings with the same title.

very own home, the life-giving ground of that specific social 'here and now' from which and for which he writes."[192]

And yet towards the end of his life, with no specific theater or company in mind, he wrote the play *Leaving*. It is well recorded that the role of Irena was written for his second wife, the actress Dagmar Veškrnová, as it occasioned a scandal when the National Theater refused to cast her and Havel withdrew the play.[193] We are probably right to presume, since he played the role in the film, that Havel wrote the part of the "Voice" for himself. That, however, does not necessarily mean that it *is* the author's voice, any more than Irena *is* Dagmar. (In the Czech script, it is simply *Hlas*, not "The Author's Voice" as in the English translation.) The Voice is a character like Vaněk, whom the audience will, erroneously, tend to identify with Havel. (I think Havel has an "alter ago" in every play: Hugo, Pludek, Mr. Gross. Foustka.) However, just as Havel expects the audience to question the affirmations and intentions of the other characters, so the Voice is also to be questioned—aren't some of the things it says a little trite, a little obvious? Or somewhat overblown? Or, on the other hand, too self-deprecating? Havel is again exercising his theater technique—putting the audience in an objective state of mind. And he is again writing for a case of friends and family—for a "living-room theater."

He himself said he was returning to his beginnings as a playwright, while at the same time: "The play's called Leaving, and by that I mean 'leaving' in the most general sense of the word. Time passes, everything that happens never happens again, yet at the same time everything that's happened cannot 'unhappen.' So all these moments pass us by in our lives, things 'leave,' yet at the same time new things 'arrive,' and of course some things 'return.'"[194]

---

192 Václav Havel, "Daleko od divadla", *O divadle* I, (Prague: samizdat edition, July 1986), 132.
193 As it turned out, Veškrnová withdrew during rehearsals because of illness.
194 Quoted by Rob Cameron in "Václav Havel, 'Leaving' but also returning," *Radio Prague*, May 22, 2008. Accessed at https://www.radio.cz/en/section/arts/vaclav-havel-leaving-but-also-returning.

For Havel, theater had to belong: to a place, a time, and a people (relevance, topicality). At the same time it had to distance itself. It had to bring people together (community, collective spirit). It had to be useful (an applied art). It had to be properly prepared (intellectually, emotionally, and practically). It had to be truthful (see suspension of disbelief), and it had to be free. Even when on a large scale, it had to be intimate and familiar. It had to be open-ended and interactive, offering questions rather than answers. It had to have meaning, meaning that could be grasped both intellectually and emotionally. Above all, it had to be a positive force for change.

That, however, is not to say that Havel put the concept of theater behind him. As a politician, he was always aware he was on the public stage. He was conscious of the audience, not as a passive Kafkaesque presence, but as a gathering of rational individuals. Havel respected his audience (who could change the world) and never tried to dazzle them by stagecraft.[195] He was concerned about the reception of his appearances because he believed that the performance could only be judged by its outcome—by the action taken by the theater-goers (diváci) who, individually and collectively, were participants as much as he.

I opened this essay with a scene where, unobserved, I watched Havel from the balcony as he set the stage, demonstrating that as President he remained a theater professional. In 1996, receiving an honorary doctorate from the Academy of Performing Arts, he reflects on a critic who claims that a serious matter like politics should have nothing to do with the frivolity of theater.[196] What a misunderstanding of the origin and meaning of theater and drama, he tells

---

195 The world-famous stage designer Josef Svoboda created an elaborate mirror staging for the first production of Havel's *The Garden Party*. The story of how Havel and Grossman deliberately destroyed it is alluded to in Rocamora's *Acts of Courage* and told in detail on the DVD *Theatre Svoboda* made by Svoboda's grandson in 2011.
196 Václav Havel, "Čestný doktorát Akademie múzických umění," in Havel, *O divadle*, 611–617 and Havel, *Spisy* 7, 642–652.

the students, of an art that has its roots in a spirituality fundamental to man's interpretation of the world. As though already preparing for *Leaving*, he muses on how some things come earlier and some later, how they repeat themselves and make connections, following the logic of space and time from exposition through to catharsis. What is politics but taking care of man in the world in which he/she lives? It too is a collective art with beginning, middle, and an end. Theater is a system of signs in time and space; politics too has its signs and symbols, its ceremonials and its diplomatic rituals. They help to address human existence, to connect one to the secret order of the world.

He reminds the students, however, of one important difference between theater as an artistic genre and theater of political dimensions. A crazy performance by a bunch of fanatics is part of the plurality of culture and even contributes to the space of freedom. A crazy performance by a bunch of fanatical politicians can end in disaster for millions.

HOTSPOT: *OHNISKO*
Kieran Williams

Introduction

Here is the dissident's dilemma. If she engages in openly subversive activity, she invites persecution and prosecution, and so has every reason to restrict her discourse to constructive, lawyerly appeals for the regime to honor its constitutional and international obligations. This was, to the bitter end, the line taken by Václav Havel, Charter 77, and other human-rights groups in Czechoslovakia in the 1970s and 1980s. Havel's *travaux préparatoires* for Charter 77 insisted that the emerging citizens' initiative "does not want to struggle against state power, but on the contrary to operate in its area of interest as [the state's] assistant and partner [...] so that problems be solved before they erupt into conflicts."[1] Even when sentenced to prison one last time in February 1989, Havel explained to the court, "As a citizen who cares that our country develop in peace and quiet, I firmly believe that state power will at last draw the correct conclusions [...] and open a dignified dialogue with all segments of society and bar no one from that dialogue by labeling him an anti-socialist."[2] But that line invites derision from those who see no point to engaging the state in dialogue, or from historians such as Mirek Vodrážka, who lambast Havel and other dissidents for their "pro-system" petitioning and for thinking in terms of power and powerlessness.[3] By contrast, the cultural underground associated with Ivan Martin Jirous, Egon Bondy, and the Plastic People of the

---

1 Quoted in Jiří Suk, *Politika jako absurdní drama: Václav Havel v letech 1975-1989* (Prague: Paseka, 2013), 61. All translations are mine unless otherwise noted.
2 Václav Havel, *Spisy* 4 (Prague: Torst, 1999), 1117.
3 Mirek Vodrážka, "Antisystémová queer politika undergroundu a prosystémová politika Charty 77," *Paměť a dějiny* 6:1 (2012), 121–130 (at 125). See also Suk, *Politika jako absurdní drama*, 233, on the "paradox" of Charter 77.

Universe is said to have stood for the truly radical erasure of power altogether and with it all Western notions of domination (*ovlád-nutí*) and representation.[4]

Even if we accept Vodrážka's critique of the Charter's outwardly non-subversive methods and of the better-known side of Havel's political writing, we need not accept it as applying to the whole. Here I want to argue for the subversiveness of an aspect of Havel's thought that has received little attention, namely, his assumptions of how change happens and events are set in motion. The telltale marker is his use of the key word *ohnisko*.

Ohnisko (plural, *ohniska*) can refer to the heart of a fire (*oheň*) or more figuratively to a hotspot, hotbed, flashpoint, center (of a storm), epicenter (of earthquakes), outbreak (of a disease), or focal point (of a camera).[5] In general usage, as recorded in the Czech National Corpus, the word is most commonly collocated with epidemiological terms (relating to infection, flu, ticks) and wildfires, and to a secondary degree with human conflict or unrest.[6] Havel applied it to places in which people band together in intense but momentary solidarity, and do something creative, meaningful, and potentially unsettling. In his reminiscences, *ohnisko* referred to episodes in the life of an institution—a theater, a journal, a jazz club—but was not synonymous with the institution itself; the fire could go out but the institution carry on, lacking what had once animated it by no particular design. Potent examples from his youth include Jan Werich's ABC Theater in the late 1950s, where Havel worked as a stage-hand and learned, he later claimed, that "theater does not have to be just

4   Without denying the indisputable philosophical differences, we should remember that Jirous also signed Charter 77, joined the Committee to Defend the Unjustly Prosecuted (VONS), and made the very "pro-system" move of petitioning in 1988 to protest the death in custody of Pavel Wonka; see Petr Blažek, "Akce 'Ivan-2'," *Paměť a dějiny* 6:1 (2012), 103–113 (at 104).
5   I have derived these translations from the Treq database of the Czech National Corpus, accessed June 25, 2019, http://treq.korpus.cz/index.php.
6   According to the KonText (SYN version 7) database of the Czech National Corpus, accessed June 25, 2019, https://kontext.korpus.cz/.

a collection of plays and actors, coat-checkers and spectators, but can become a center [*ohnisko*] of, I would say, some spiritual-social vibrating of its time, a mirror of the sensibility of the time."[7] Likewise the theater Na zábradlí (On the Balustrade), where he staged his first hit plays in the mid-1960s, was a "center of societal self-reflection of that time [*ohnisko sociální sebereflexe té doby*], a center of that time's sensibility" and also "probably the happiest period in my life."[8]

While theaters were the place where Havel most often felt the presence of an *ohnisko*, not all theaters had that quality. Havel was drawn only to small, intimate houses, ranging in their repertory beyond the canon but still observing conventions of stagecraft:

> It was a question of theater that was [...] something other and something more than just an enterprise for conducting plays: For me it was—and theater for me to this day still is—a sort of center [*ohnisko*] of spiritual life, one of the cells of society becoming self-aware, the intersection of the spiritual, moral and emotional powerlines of the time.[9]

He put it in similar terms in the long, mid-1980s interview with Karel Hvížďala translated into English as *Disturbing the Peace*: "a living spiritual center [*ohnisko*], a place of society becoming self-aware, an intersection of the powerlines of the time and its seismograph, a place of freedom and an instrument for human liberation."[10]

A letter to his wife Olga from prison in 1981 similarly praised the potential "second sphere of sociality" of a theater, transcending

---

7   Richard Erml and Jan Kerbr, "Krásná doba mého života I," *Divadelní noviny* 13:1 (January 16, 2004),16. See also Václav Havel, *Spisy* 4 (Prague: Torst, 1999), 738, and Václav Havel, *Letters to Olga*, letter 53. For more on Havel's views on theater, see the chapter on *divadlo* in this volume.
8   Jana Bendová and Viliam Buchert, "Největší absurdita? Že jsem byl prezidentem," *Mladá fronta Dnes,* September 30, 2006 (*Víkend* supplement), 1–3.
9   Havel, *Spisy* 4, 636.
10   Havel, *Spisy* 4, 738.

the bare fact that any performance brings persons into a shared space, when it also becomes:

> [...] something more than just an institution: It is a focus [*ohnisko*] (more accurately, one of the foci) of social life and social thought, an irreplaceable component of the "soul of the nation," a small organism, bound by thousands of threads to the great organism of society and playing within it an irreplaceable and relevant social role. It has its own community, which is not just the mechanical sum of its regular and occasional theater-goers but again, something more: a special kind of community.[11]

Havel, it should be noted, used two different words for community in that last sentence: in the former instance *obec*, then *pospolitost*. *Obec* is a more neutral administrative designation, often in the immediate physical sense of one's place of residence and its local authorities; if expanded as *obecenstvo* it can be a synonym for theater audience. *Pospolitost* connotes more intense bonds of camaraderie, togetherness, affect—what an *ohnisko* should strive to bring about. It could also acquire a mildly clandestine quality: another of Havel's most fondly remembered places, the Reduta Akord jazz club in the early 1960s, housed a "conspiratorial community" (*spiklenecká pospolitost*).[12]

These moments were important not just because they emotionally and creatively enriched the persons passing through them, but also for their wider eventual impact; as Havel saw it in hindsight, these enclaves were safe locations to explore ideas that later would be let loose on the whole country:

> [...] the small theaters at that time were centers [*ohniska*] for society's becoming self-aware, which was a very important phenomenon. The

11   Havel, *Letters to Olga*, letter 107.
12   Havel, *Spisy* 4, 742.

political changes known as the "Prague Spring" [of 1968-69] were preceded by long years of this becoming-self-aware of society, of its self-emancipation, its growing courage to be free.[13]

Later, Havel would vest the same power in the dissident networks such as Charter 77, writing to a Canadian political scientist in April 1986:

It could be said that the Charter is a sort of small center [ohnisko] of relative independence, a center [ohnisko] from which, of course, independence continually radiates well beyond its boundaries. It is hard to know what effect this radiating has or will have on the irradiated area, what kind of ripening or fermenting it will assist (even if just as a catalyst) and what share this radiating will have in eventual social movement, should any arise. The recent Polish developments are a classic example of this: For a long time it seemed that the Workers' Defense Committee (KOR) and its activists could not in any way visibly budge the general social situation or influence it, and then suddenly, when there occurred another outbreak of societal dissatisfaction, the work of KOR was reevaluated virtually overnight in an entirely unexpected way: It is hard to imagine that the multimillion-strong Solidarity could have arisen without KOR's preparatory analytical and conceptual work.[14]

The extension of the *ohnisko* concept to the Charter confirms that theaters were not the only places from which meaningful change could emanate; in June 1969, in perhaps his earliest public application of the word, Havel had denounced the banning of the weekly periodical of the Czech writers' union for depriving society of an

13 Marta Švagrová, "Zatím jsem se nemusel omlouvat," *Lidové noviny*, December 8, 2007 (*Kulturní revue* supplement), 13–14.
14 Havel, *Spisy* 4, 648. The radiation imagery of Havel's reply is striking, given its composition in the month of the Chernobyl disaster, but it is probably also coincidental: the accident occurred on April 26, and Czechs did not learn of it until early May.

"important center of self-reflection [*důležité ohnisko své sebereflex-e*]."[15] Nearly twenty years later, he would advocate the underground revival of the newspaper *Lidové noviny* as a "school or crystallizing hotbed [*ohnisko*]" for free journalism.[16] In the mid-1980s he welcomed signs that society was starting to "revive again in various centres [*ohniska*] and cells [*buňky*] of relatively independent life,"[17] and saw all of Central Europe, in particular Prague, as the "complicated (ethnically, culturally and historically), structured *ohnisko* of European events."[18] In February 1988 he detected a new *ohnisko* of politics not in the machinations and maneuvers of the Communist élite, but in "the visible and hidden levels of [society's] activity, feeling and thinking."[19] In the letters he wrote to his wife Olga from prison in 1979–83, Havel fantasized about their country retreat, the farmhouse at Hrádeček in eastern Bohemia, urging her to convene gatherings there of "various friends," because "I was always happy when people came to visit us and Hrádeček was an oasis of calm and a sort of spiritual center [*ohnisko*]—that should continue, even though I am not there."[20]

Narrowing down still further, we find that even an individual, if sufficiently charismatic and original, could be an *ohnisko*. One such person was Zdeněk Neubauer, a microbiologist by training and theologian-philosopher by calling, who was identified in the chapter in this volume on "truth" as an influence on Havel's thinking about science. Havel described Neubauer as "always at the center of a certain important spiritual action, was always—if it can be expressed this way—the spiritual crossroads of the age or at least the inspirational focus [*ohnisko*] of its spiritual life, was always the center of

15 Havel, *Spisy* 3, 909.
16 Havel, *Spisy* 4, 991.
17 Havel, *Spisy* 4, 720.
18 Havel, *Spisy* 4, 447.
19 Havel, *Spisy* 4, 1039–1043.
20 Václav Havel, *Letters to Olga*, letter 36.

attention in certain circles and a central authority [...]"[21] One such circle was the unsanctioned Kampademy seminar. Seeking to bridge the two cultures of science and religion, the Kampademy held midsummer workshops at Havel's Hrádeček cottage that juxtaposed sessions on traditional philosophical questions of ontology with ones on astrology, alchemy and Tarot symbolism.[22] Capping off the days with a yoga workout, VCR viewings of *Amadeus*, *The Lord of the Rings*, or *Rambo*, or a trip into the "fourth dimension" courtesy of psychotropic mushrooms, the Hrádeček seminars remind us that the *ohnisko* can be at once ludic and deadly earnest.[23]

Proceeding from Neubauer the man to the questions he pressed Havel to think about, we find that *ohnisko* can even suggest a providential ordering force, rather as the Presocratics meant by "γνώμην, ὁτέη ἐκυβέρνησε πάντα διὰ πάντων" (that is, "the will that steers all things through all," in Heraclitus) or "δαίμονα κυβερνητιν" ("governing divinity," in Parmenides).[24] Here it serves as still another of the various terms Havel preferred as alternatives to a deity, such as "absolute horizon" or "Being."[25] While not a practicing member

21 Václav Havel, "Cena Nadace Vize 97 Zdeňku Neubauerovi", in Václav Havel, *Spisy 8: Projevy a jiné texty 1999-2006. Prosím stručně. Odcházení* (Prague: Torst, 2007), 139.

22 Daniel Kroupa, *Dějiny Kampademie* (Prague: Knihovna Václava Havla, 2010).

23 Zdeněk Neubauer, *Consolatio philosophiae hodierna: k Šestnácti dopisům Václava Havla* (Prague: Knihovna Václava Havla, 2010), 40. Kroupa reports that when Jan Patočka heard about the creation of the Kampademy, "at first he just waved his hand and said, 'It's probably just some game.' Then he checked himself and added, 'But it could turn into a very serious game [*moc vážná hra*]" (quoted in Martin C. Putna, *Václav Havel. Duchovní portrét v rámu české kultury 20. století* [Prague: Knihovna Václava Havla, 2011], 197).

24 Daniel W. Graham, ed., *The Texts of Early Greek Philosophy. Part 1* (Cambridge: Cambridge University Press, 2010), 148 and 222. For an alternative translation of *gnōmē* as "plan" or "pattern," see Patricia Kenig Kurd, "Knowledge and Unity in Heraclitus," *The Monist* 74:4 (1991), 538 and note 42 on 547.

25 In prison letter 159, which was not included in the collection smuggled abroad and published in Canada, Havel explained his preference for "Being" over "God," in that the latter too precisely concretizes the feeling most people have of another, unseen layer to their existence, making of it a single entity (*bytost*). Havel, at least at that time (in December 1982), preferred something capturing his feeling that something *is*, in a very general, unclear, and multifaceted way, that exists within everything and lies behind everything; in middle age he

of any church, Havel professed to believe in something "mysterious above me," which he defined as the "center of all meaningfulness and the highest authority [*ohnisko veškeré smysluplnosti a nejvyšší autorita*] that gives the world its "deeper order and meaning.."[26] In prison letter 129, the beginning of a cycle of meditations inspired by Emmanuel Levinas, Havel reflected on the fundamental human condition: to be a subject aware of his separate, individuated existence, unable to understand it but equally unable not to want to understand it. This subject thus becomes the "focus [*ohnisko*] of the transformation of Being-in-the-world, which hides itself from him and only him, so that at the same time, speaking through the world, it can summon him to his search; the subject as the focus [*ohnisko*] of this search."[27] In prison letter 71 he explained that his 1976 play *Horský hotel* (Mountain Hotel) had tried to depict in miniature this world, "shaken, incoherent, turned upside-down" owing to a "fateful lack of focus [*ohnisko*] or perspective":

We are for the most part people who do not find in this "hotel" or outside it a firm point, to which they might relate unambiguously, constantly and without problems, which in their eyes would impart a central meaning to everything, above all to their stay in this "hotel" [...].

Whereas the small theaters in *ohnisko* mode tapped into the "powerlines" of the age, and were connected by "thousands of threads" to the wider society, the metaphysical *ohnisko*—if it could be found—would be the center from which streamed "the rays of all connections and meanings."[28]

---

apparently retained something of the pantheism he professed as a youth. He also presumed an unattainability with Being that was at odds with the Christian blissful merging with the divine. See Putna, *Václav Havel*, 216.

26   Havel, *Spisy* 4, 897.
27   Havel, *Letters to Olga*, letter 129.
28   Havel, *Letters to Olga*, letter 71.

So what was all this—the *ohnisko* below, above, and around—to lead to? One of his finest essays, "Politics and Conscience" (1984), suggested that it was a matter of finding an answer to the truly important existential question:

Whether it will be possible in some way to reconstitute the natural world as the proper terrain of politics, rehabilitate man's personal responsibility as the initial measure of things, put morals before politics and responsibility before purpose, restore meaning to human community [*pospolitost*] and content to human speech, make the focus [*ohnisko*] of social action the autonomous, integral and dignified human "I," vouching for itself because drawn to something greater than itself and capable of sacrificing something or, in an extreme case, everything of its quotidian, prosperous private life—that "domination by the everyday," as Jan Patočka would say—or the sake of that which gives life meaning.[29]

But *ohnisko* by its nature is fleeting, a victim of its authentic spontaneity; precisely because it is indicative of so much else taking place around in it, a "spiritual-social *ohnisko*" such as the small theaters of the 1960s was linked to the "social (and ultimately the power) structure of the time" and its success, even if controversial, shows that it bears "some kind of witness to the social structure" while subtly changing it.[30] That success condemns it to fairly early demise; as letter 107 to Olga rued: "Sooner or later, a theater loses the identity it has had hitherto, its atmosphere passes away, the sense of community [*pospolitost*] among its audience [*obec*] dissipates and that entire 'spiritual home' irrevocably vanishes into the mists of time [...]."[31] Its impact on society or cosmic Being is indelible, and may

29 Havel, *Spisy* 4, 435.
30 Havel, *Letters to Olga*, letter 112.
31 Havel, *Letters to Olga*, letter 107.

have incalculable, revolutionary consequences, but there is nothing more forlorn than a hotspot whose heyday has passed.

And herein lies the problem of Havel's ideal: it was the *ohnisko* episodes in his life that he remembered most fondly, and through those passionate recollections encouraged us to make our own as the most meaningful form of the small-scale work that would improve the world, yet by their very nature they cannot simply be conjured up or decreed. It was in his years of greatest formal power—as head of state from 1989 to 2003—that he least often experienced *ohnisko* moments. Toward the end of his presidency he sponsored Forum 2000, envisioned as an annual gathering of—in the spirit of the Kampademy—people of faith and science, and did so in Prague, "a city that at various times in its long history has been a significant cultural crossroads, a center [*ohnisko*] of spiritual and cultural life and a place where thinkers, religious philosophers could meet scientists, astronomers and astrologists."[32] Likewise, on leaving office he and his second wife Dáša set up a presidential library, to serve as not just an archive and monument to his career, but a "thoroughly independent center [*ohnisko*] of understanding" and a "center [*ohnisko*] of critical thought," one that by making available "authentic" materials from the past would make identity possible, for "without memory and continuity there is no identity," no being ourselves unless "we know today what we did yesterday, and we take responsibility for it."[33]

As Havel used *ohnisko* frequently but not systematically, it helps to distinguish it from several concepts to which it may bear a facial resemblance but is not reducible (friendship, civil society, a "public mafia"), and then compare it to concepts with which there is a stronger affinity but still not identity (deterritorialized milieu, the butterfly effect).

---

32 Havel, "Projev prezidenta republiky Václava Havla na slavnostním zahájení konference Forum 2000," 1999.
33 Havel, *Spisy* 8, 297–298.

Ohnisko and friendship

Is the *ohnisko* not simply a new take on an old Aristotelian category such as political or civic friendship (ἡ φιλία πολιτική), or that arising from the mutual enjoyment of each other's company (διὰ τὸ ἡδύ) or the primary friendship (ἡ πρώτη φιλία) based on virtue (δι' ἀρετήν)? Going by the moments recalled by Havel, the *ohnisko* is at once less and more than any of the kinds of affection found in the *Nicomachean* or *Eudemian Ethics*. It would not be enumerated in the set of conditions for living well as a human being,[34] or be connected to the purpose of government, which Aristotle says is to bring about amity as a matter of justice.[35] This is the justice that makes society possible, first at the immediate household level, then expanding to underpin the polity.[36] An *ohnisko*, by contrast, is not constitutive of society or the state but presupposes them, taking advantage of opportunities arising in existing settings and institutions, and indifferent to societal concord.

Aristotle's civic or political friendship rests on a footing of equality and has elements of mutual utility; equal shares of benefit and burden is the "ruling principle," and it can be likened to a mutually beneficial transaction and "definite agreement."[37] Owing to that equality, Aristotle associates civic friendship with the democratic form of state, because there men are most equal and have the most in common; they have the least under tyrants, so there one will

---

34 Such as "good health, adequate material resources, and good luck"; Stephen Salkever, "Taking Friendship Seriously: Aristotle on the Place(s) of *Philia* in Human Life," in John von Heyking and Richard Avramenko (edss), *Friendship & Politics: Essays in Political Thought* (Notre Dame, IN: University of Notre Dame Press, 2008), 67.

35 Aristotle, *Eudemian Ethics*, trans. H. Rackham (Cambridge, MA: Harvard University Press, 1935), 416.

36 As Salkever observes ("Taking Friendship Seriously", 68), Aristotelian friendship is entangled in two orders of causality, being both necessary for something but also constitutive of it.

37 In contrast to virtue friendship, civic friendship has a contractual understanding that is "profitable" (Aristotle, *Eudemian Ethics*, 426). See also Aristotle, *Nicomachean Ethics*, 504, in which amity between citizens is motivated by pursuit of "the useful."

find the least friendship. *Ohniska*, however, can flourish under severe political conditions, as Havel's own examples show; perhaps it flourishes most in the absence of democracy, so long as the state tolerates a modicum of free play within official structures (as in 1960s Czechoslovakia). And judging by Havel's accounts, there is no requirement of equality or even the good will (εὐνοία) and like-mindedness (ὁμόνοια) that Aristotle presupposed for civic friendship.

Aristotle observed that small associations often form purely for enjoyment, so the *ohnisko* might have a closer resemblance to friendship from pleasure. Such friendships, Aristotle observes, are easily dissolved when the feelings of enjoyment fade, and there is little of the bitterness that accompanies the failure of a more utilitarian friendship.[38] The delights of *ohnisko*, however, go beyond the bonhomie of a drinking party, the gymnasium or the agora; there is a creative element, some work of collaboration, that draws in the participants, who may vary considerably in their ability to contribute and may bear grudges years later.[39] And the work they do may, if Havel is right, have repercussions well beyond and long after the *ohnisko* has dissolved, which would not normally be credited to friendship from pleasure.

The *ohnisko* bears the least resemblance of all to "primary" or "first" friendship, for Aristotle the only true friendship because arising as the reciprocal, deliberate choice of each other's company owing to each other's virtue as a self-contained, stand-alone attraction, and not because that virtue will remedy a defect or deficit in one of the parties to the friendship.[40] True friendship requires extensive testing over time to ensure that someone is a proper partner for

---

38 Aristotle, *Nicomachean Ethics*, 460.
39 Consider the lasting rancor between Havel and other members of the *Tvář* editorial board in the 1960s, and the friction that developed between Havel and Ivan Vyskočil after their period of fruitful collaboration at the Theater on the Balustrade, yet both places could be considered *ohniska*.
40 David K. O'Connor, "Two Ideals of Friendship," *History of Philosophy Quarterly* 7:2 (1990), 109–122.

discourse, and thus does not arise casually; in Derrida's terms: "For the reliability of the stable [*bébaios*], that on which virtue depends—therefore of liberty, decision and reflection—can no longer be only natural. [...] In the history of the concept of nature—and already in its Greek history—the virtue of friendship will have dug a trench of an opposition."[41] Combined with the pronounced equality and absence of quarrel, the deliberateness of true friendship is at odds with the spontaneous, unplanned organicity of an authentic *ohnisko*, which emerges rapidly from interactions that have not been put to any test.

A final reason not to reduce *ohnisko* to a form of friendship is that Havel discussed friends and friendship at length but in a different context, outside politics and without reference to the potential ramifications of *ohnisko* activity.[42] The young Havel yearned for meaningful friendship as a way to transcend the acute class sensitivity of his childhood and the isolation imposed in adolescence under Stalinism.[43] He took as his model the idealized friendship between the poets Konstantin Biebl and Jiří Wolker; as he wrote to a fellow member of the Thirty-Sixer literary circle in autumn 1953: "Friendship, the collective, the gang, those are the most sacred concepts."[44]

Also already revealing in the young Havel's idealized friendship is how far it ranged beyond the immediate proximity that Aristotle assumed essential. Evoking not just the folksy Wolker and Biebl but also the demotic pantheism of Walt Whitman, Havel's early poetry dreamed of a connection to his surroundings uncomplicated by class and status. In doing so, however, he was wandering far from Aristotelian primary friendship, which is possible only by restricting

---

41 Jacques Derrida, *The Politics of Friendship*, trans. George Collins (London: Verso, 1997), 23.

42 For example, he told a philosopher in 1993 that "I don't think that friendship should be a political program, that would truly be difficult" (Václav Bělohradský, *Mezi světy a mezisvěty: Filosofické dialogy* [Prague: Votobia, 1997], 167).

43 See Havel, *Letters to Olga*, letters 74 and 75.

44 Pavel Kosatík, *"Ústně více": Šestatřicátníci* (Brno: Host, 2006), 44.

oneself to a few close acquaintances, whose bond to oneself can be properly tested over time. While he who lives best will have the fewest friends, and they will become steadily fewer, "one who has many friends has no friend."[45]

Indeed, Havel was guilty of this very polyphilia—the acquiring of too many acquaintances. This is not to demean the role of the people Havel considered a friend and who considered him their friend in turn, and to whom he often paid moving tribute, starting in 1969 with an obituary for the artist Jiří Balcar that acknowledged the consolation of friendship generally.[46] But the list of people gaining the rank of *přítel* (friend) or *kamarád* (mate, buddy) in Havel's reminiscences seems endless, to the point, as is often the case with statesmen, where it was bestowed so freely as to be emptied of substance. Was Havel, a self-described "Czech bumpkin [*balík*],"[47] really friends with the non-Czech-speaking Richard von Weizsäcker, François Mitterrand, Queen Beatrix, King Juan Carlos, Mário Soares, Árpád Göncz, the elder George Bush, Hillary and Bill Clinton?[48] Can one truly be friends with the Pope, even if language was not a barrier for John Paul II?[49] Did Havel spend enough time with Joan Baez, Robert Redford, Mikhail Gorbachev, Sergei Kovalev, and Elena Bonner to claim them all as "friends"?[50] Was this not

45   Aristotle, *Eudemian Ethics*, 444. See also Derrida, *The Politics of Friendship*, 21: "There is no belonging or friendly community that is *present*, and first present *to itself, in act*, without election and without selection."

46   Havel, *Spisy* 3, 898–899. See also his tributes to the actor Pavel Landovský ("Úvodem k holandskému vydání hry Pavla Landovského Objížďka," in Havel, *Spisy* 4, 397–398 and "Pavel z Teplic," *Spisy* 4, 926–930) and the writer-translator Zdeněk Urbánek ("Svět bez Zdeňka,, *Mladá fronta DNES*, April 23, 2010, 12). When asked which of his friends Havel most missed in later years, Havel singled out Landovský, Urbánek, and actor Jan Tříska (Václav Havel, *Prosím stručně* [Prague: Gallery, 2006], 183).

47   Havel, *Letters to Olga*, letter 18.

48   As he leads us to believe in Havel, *Prosím stručně*, 224–225.

49   On friendship with the Pope, see Havel, *Prosím stručne*, 19.

50   Havel, *Prosím stručně*, 177, 153, and 166; Petruška Šustrová, "Můj vězeňský syndrome," *Lidové noviny*, November 15, 2003, 13–14. In Havel, *Letters to Olga*, letter 60 (December 21,

Havel dressing up his confessed weakness for celebrities, the obverse of his self-consciousness about class status?[51]

Ohnisko and civil society

As will be seen in Aspen Brinton's chapter in this volume, Havel is remembered for his advocacy of civil society as an intermediate supplement to the neoliberal catallaxy of individuals, parties, firms and the state favored by rival political figures such as Václav Klaus. But Havel himself cautioned against making too great a distinction between his views and those of Klaus, whose economic policies Havel endorsed at the outset.[52] Conversely, many on the Czech Right were perfectly receptive to the idea of an active civil society.[53] Instead, a pronounced difference lies between what Havel understood as civil society and his *ohnisko*.

Havel's civil society, like that advocated by many since the 1970s, is a meliorative, not an alternative to the West's political economy. "Despite its emancipatory and oppositional aura," writes Jon Beasley-Murray, "the concept of civil society becomes part of the toolbox of governmentality" and "plays into the hands of technocratic neoliberalism."[54] As a response to the legitimation crises of the welfare state and emergence of new social movements, civil society took on some of the burdens of governance and in so doing reduced pressure

1980), he expresses confidence that physical proximity is not necessary to be able to "experience very intensively" someone's personality.

51 Putna, *Václav Havel*, 325.

52 For a scathing view of the two Václavs as a perverse tandem, see Petr Schnur, "Nesvatí Václavové, dali jste nám zhynout! Politická nepolitika druhé normalizace," in Pavel Barša et al, *Kritika depolitizovaného rozumu: Úvahy (nejen) o nové normalizaci* (Všeň: Grimmus, 2010), 163–172.

53 Seán Hanley, *The New Right in the New Europe: Czech transformation and right-wing politics, 1989–2006* (Abingdon: Routledge, 2008), 123, 138, and 143.

54 Jon Beasley-Murray, *Posthegemony: Political Theory and Latin America* (Minneapolis, MN: University of Minnesota Press, 2010), 75. See also Gideon Baker, "Civil Society and Democracy: The Gap Between Theory and Possibility," *Politics* 18:2 (1998), 81–87.

for revolutionary change. So, as Havel himself admitted in his 1994 New Year's speech, "Talk about civil society is of course also talk about the character of the state."[55]

Havel's remarks on civil society grew out of mid-1990s debates in Czech politics, such as whether to use corporatist mediation in making public policy and whether to take seriously the constitution's requirement of a regional tier of government.[56] Staying above the gritty detail, Havel began to set out a general vision of state and society that by the twentieth anniversary of the fall of the Communist Party had reached this distillation:

[Civil society is] the most varied types of self-structuring of society from below, thus the creation and work of institutions that are to some degree independent, not fully dependent on the state. It is the life of societies, academic life, nonprofit organizations, churches, unions, but in a certain sense also local and regional government. Man is a social creature and civil society allows him to associate freely with others and thus live more creatively or authentically. At the same time, it contributes significantly to the stability of the state. It is thus, among other things, the best defense against every attempt to usurp power.[57]

Unpacking this, we find Havel arguing for decentralization of the state so that it could open itself up to assistance by outside groups, and thereby become more efficient and efficacious; as he had put it in 1994: "A well-founded local government—as one of the instruments of civic co-responsibility for public affairs—is not a complication for

55   Havel, *Spisy* 7, 180.
56   Martin Myant, "Klaus, Havel and the Debate Over Civil Society in the Czech Republic," *Journal of Communist Studies and Transition Politics* 21:2 (2005), 248–267; James F. Pontuso, "Transformation Politics: The Debate between Vaclav Havel and Vaclav Klaus on the Free Market and Civil Society," *Studies in East European Thought* 54:3 (2002), 153–177; and John Keane, *Václav Havel: A Political Tragedy in Six Acts* (London: Bloomsbury, 1999), 446–447.
57   Václav Havel, "Jednou budem dál," Česká televize, November 14, 2009 (Archive of the Václav Havel Library, item 3890).

central power, but on the contrary a relief, removing it from the forced pretense of omniscience."[58] The state may remain the guarantor of certain rights, duties, and entitlements, but need not be the provider of the services that realize them in daily life.[59] To an American audience, he put it in stark cost-benefit terms: "I think a person need not be a great economist or arithmetician to realize that civil society pays off [*se vyplácí*]."[60]

Havel's civil society was thus the delegation by the state of certain functions to non-state groups; it was also a vision of society and human nature following a line that could be traced back to his 1953 essay on "optimalism."[61] Devolution brings out the prosocial side of people, by unfolding "a colorful fan of possibilities to become involved not just privately but publicly as well, and to develop the most varied forms of civic co-existence, solidarity, and participation," which in turn fosters a law-abiding "responsibility for the whole, and thereby indirectly a good attitude to our country."[62]

Havel's fear of septic discontent—a revision of his frequent warnings to the socialist regime that it ignored or persecuted dissidents at its peril—perfectly illustrates the uneasy relationship of civil society to fundamentalism or fanaticism. To cite Beasley-Murray again: "The truth of civil society theory is that it imposes a series of boundaries, drawing on the force of social movements to legitimate political order, but restraining that force at the point at which it might challenge the state. Tendencies that might overspill or dissolve those boundaries are ostracized as fundamentalist. [...W]henever the concept of civil society is invoked, it always depends

58 Havel, *Spisy* 7, 177. For a more extended definition from ten years earlier, see "Symposium 'Myšlenky Václava Havla a koncept občanské společnosti'," in Havel, *Spisy* 7, 849–858.
59 Havel, *Spisy* 7, 851.
60 Havel, *Spisy* 7, 856.
61 Putna and Hron, *Rozhovory 36 a Stříbrný vítr*, 18–25.
62 Havel, *Spisy* 7, 178 and 179; see also 857. For compliance as bodily habit (temporal and spatial) rather than mindful consent, see Beasley-Murray, *Posthegemony*, 174–198.

upon the demarcation of a fanaticism that is its other."[63] For Havel, whose longstanding abhorrence of fanaticism was noted in the chapter on truth, the antidote to the "strange brotherhood"[64] of collective hatred, was glocalization—the sandwiching of the filleted nation-state between a densely participatory local government and international organizations (see also the chapter in this collection by Falk and Bouvier-Valenta on "responsibility"). The residual states will go from "the mystical embodiment of national ambitions and cult object"[65] to "far simpler and more civil, less powerful and above all more rational administrative units, comprising just one of the levels of a complex and multilayered planetary social self-organization."[66]

The *ohnisko*, by contrast, has none of civil society's mission to lighten the state's load, provide services more efficiently, or ward off fanatics. It is affective with no ambition of being effective. While embedded in society and revealing (or anticipating) vital developments, an *ohnisko* displays nothing of the organization that a civil-society group would, with officers, boards, fundraisers, by-laws, and dues-paying members; the *ohnisko* is thus a better expression of Havel's preference for *ad hoc* formations, declared in "The Power of the Powerless," than is any nonprofit.[67] It also is not necessarily bounded by the need to register itself with the state (either through incorporation, tax exemption or subsidy), or be in tune with the political economy of the state, whether neoliberal or social-democratic. Above all, the *ohnisko* is not representational—no one attends in order to speak on behalf of an interest.

---

63 Beasley-Murray, *Posthegemony*, 95.

64 Václav Havel, "Konference o nenávisti," 1990 and Pontuso, "Transformation Politics," 165.

65 Havel, *Spisy* 7, 857.

66 Václav Havel, "Společné zasedání obou komor kanadského parlamentu", in Havel, *Spisy* 7, 860. See also Pontuso, "Transformation Politics," 167.

67 Václav Havel, "The Power of the Powerless," chapter XXI.

Ohnisko and the public mafia

In many respects, in cheerleading for civil society and courting celebrities, Havel was following the example set by his father, Václav Maria (V.M.) Havel, in interwar Czechoslovakia. The older Havel, a property developer renowned for the Barrandov terraces and villas overlooking Prague, was active not just in the kinds of organizations his son would have liked to see work with local authorities, but also in more secretive associations, such as masonic lodges. More secretive, however, does not mean subversive; V.M. Havel's causes aimed to improve souls and the quality of existing institutions, through a mix of individual moral overhaul and group concertation.

The kickstarting moment for V.M. Havel came in March 1920, when, at the age of 22, he was in the audience as the first president of Czechoslovakia appealed for the formation of a "public mafia." Reflecting on the recent world war and revolution that had ended the Austro-Hungarian empire, Tomáš Masaryk came to the long-term challenge of changing norms and outlooks:

> During the war I observed people from all lands, from all walks of life, I observe them here at home, and I see how difficult it is to overcome old opinions and habits, and how hard it is for them to rise to the challenges that they themselves proclaim and accept. We all call for "de-Austrianization". It's not just a matter of removing the dynasty and constitutional forms, it's a matter of transforming our entire moral habitus. [...] I should like us to have many men in all sectors (*oborech*) who know how to observe and think, and only the cooperation of what I would call a "public mafia" could ensure our successful development.[68]

---

[68] T.G. Masaryk, *Cesta demokracie I. Projevy - články - rozhovory 1918-1920* (Prague: Masarykův ústav, 2003), 233. Masaryk was invoking the legacy of the wartime "Czech mafia," the network of his supporters who stayed behind when he went into exile and agitated for the independence of Czechoslovakia.

The call inspired V.M. to organize a student "renewal movement" for self-improvement that was also profoundly democratic, anti-violent, and open to socialism "if it serves the raising of all humanity, and not just one class."[69] (V.M.'s son at first followed his father's affinity for a socialism of small-scale, employee-managed enterprises, but in the late 1980s abandoned the word as too compromised and overextended.[70])

The public mafia led by example, starting with a residential "colony" constructed and financed by students tired of waiting for places in university halls. There soon followed affiliation with the World Student Christian Association and the creation of a Czechoslovak YMCA in 1921.[71] In 1925, on the initiative of Masaryk's son Jan, came the formation of a Prague Rotary Club, in which V.M. represented the real-estate sector (and chaired club meetings in 1937).[72] Less public but overlapping in membership was the October Twenty-Eighth masonic lodge, which V.M. was invited to join in 1923 by the writer Karel Čapek.[73] Four years later, a group involving Havel quit to set up their own lodge, named in honor of philosopher Bernard Bolzano; by the mid-1930s, V.M. was its leader.[74]

In late 1932, as Europe was troubled by economic slump and the specter of fascism, V.M. began to assemble on the pavilion at Barrandov around 40 peers, well connected to yet frustrated by Czechoslovakia's political and economic elites.[75] Wanting a "quality" (*kvalitní*) democracy instead of the entrenched party cartel, the group recast the Masarykian public mafia as a "cultural elite,"

69 V.M. Havel, *Mé vzpomínky* (Prague: Lidové noviny, 1993), 158.
70 Havel, *Spisy* 4, 1062–1065.
71 Havel, *Mé vzpomínky*, 122–144 and 173–176. He describes his role in setting up the student colony in his contribution to the *Almanach studentské kolonie na Letné 1920–1930* (Nymburk: Jaroslav Plaček, 1931), 42–45.
72 Havel, *Mé vzpomínky*, 197.
73 Havel, *Mé vzpomínky*, 153.
74 Jana Čehurová, *Čeští svobodní zednáři ve XX. století* (Prague: Libri, 2002), 118.
75 Havel, *Mé vzpomínky*, 210. There was an inner set of 16, of whom ten were freemasons, that met at the Havel country estate in May 1933 to refine the group's principles.

understood as an informal, unorganized "fellowship of creative minds" that would represent society's "cultural authority" and "intellectual [*duchovní*] government," to whose level the rest of society would be drawn through an education system fostering self-motivation, character, and work discipline.[76]

Before I contrast the interwar public mafia with Václav Havel's *ohnisko*, we should pause to appreciate the ways in which the son did follow the father. The culture-engineers of the public mafia rendered Masarykian discourse into terms that anticipated Václav Havel's catchphrases; the student renewal movement announced: "We are convinced that the purpose of human life is conscientious work for the spiritual and material ennobling of humanity, the struggle for the government of truth, good and love in the world. [...] Proceeding from respect for the personality and life of one's neighbor, we strive for the creation of people who would be in the service of the highest human ideals and be aware of their personal responsibility for their deeds."[77] The Barrandov group's program, which converted that spiritual principle into a political ideal (the words "responsible" and "responsibility" appear 12 times in the brief statement), avoided affiliation to left or right and to any existing party, preferring instead a "front" to bring new people into politics.[78]

While famously opposed to violence, like his father, Havel was also no pacifist (which he equated with fanaticism[79]), and at times his drive for moral and cultural improvement could take an assertive, even aggressive form and a desire to shock that belied his reputation for diffidence. He saw the very purpose of culture as a catalyst for movement: "Isn't perhaps precisely this 'putting things into motion

---

76 Havel, *Mé vzpomínky*, 259.
77 Havel, *Mé vzpomínky*, 157.
78 Havel, *Mé vzpomínky*, 248.
79 See also his comments on the West European peace movement in the 1980s (Havel, *Spisy* 4, 523–561) and advocacy of intervention in Kosovo (Havel, *Spisy* 7, 867).

[*do pohybu*]'—again, in the deeper, existential sense—the primor-dial intention of everything truly cultural?"[80] Come the events of November 1989, Havel showed himself capable of managing direct political action even while ambivalent about his place in it. On the one hand are the images and accounts of Havel and his entourage on the go, fueled by slivovice and protected by bodyguards as they weave through tunnels and backstairs into and out of secret meetings and onto balconies of tall buildings.[81] Those balcony moments, however, were not to whip up the crowd into a populist embrace but to put limits on the multitude; as Havel later advised Cuban dissidents:

> Because when it did fall apart, someone with power had to act on behalf of the public. Someone had to speak from the balconies and organize those balconies. Documents could not be written by random passers-by, who could also not be put in charge of the whole popular resistance. The whole outcome had its prehistory in the hopeless resistance of those apparent troublemakers [dissidents]. [...] And it is necessary to prepare representatives of the opposition so that they can also become politicians and stand at the head of the state. And that they have to prepare for this alternative.[82]

Yet with the shift from socialism to capitalism and from dissent to political office, Havel lost the ability to shock things and people into the desired motion. In 1994 he implored fellow artists at the PEN Club's World Congress to

---

80   Havel, *Spisy* 4, 490–491. "Motion" is a multifaceted concept in Jan Patočka's philosophy of history, but Havel is using it in just the second of Patočka's three ways, to refer to involvement in the world; see Petr Rezek, *Filozofie a politika kýče* (Prague: Jan Placák – Ztichlá klika, 2007), 65–71 and 90–105, and Petr Rezek, *Jan Patočka a věc fenomenologie* (Prague: Oikoymenh, 1993), 68–93.
81   Miroslav Vaněk and Pavel Urbášek (eds.), *Vítězové? Poraženi? Životopisná interview. I. díl. Disent v období tzv. Normalizace* (Prague: Prostor, 2005), 125.
82   Šustrová, "Můj vězeňský syndrome," 13–14. See also Havel's exchange with Oswaldo Payá in *Journal of Democracy* 15:2 (2004), 160–169.

[…] slowly start to create some kind of worldwide lobby, a special fraternity or, if I may use the word, a somewhat conspiratorial mafia, which would adopt for its goal not just to write splendid books or occasional manifestos, but have a coordinated, solidaristic and purposeful effect on politics today and its human perception—if need be, with the kind of personal dedication that Susan Sontag showed in Sarajevo—and open its eyes by all sorts of interventions, seen and unseen, into it.[83]

His rebuke to the Czech political elite in 1997, during a joint session of the legislature after the collapse of the scandal-ridden Klaus government and onset of recession, generated an equally strong reaction, in the form of a cross-party attempt to reduce the power of his office.[84] Harder still did he find it to put things in motion (*do pohybu*) when up against a globalized civilization that, as Havel acknowledged, ensnares people in "automatism" (*samopohyb*); this, at least, was one way he tried to explain why, when he lectured a gathering of corporate executives in Paris on big business as "part of a trend in contemporary civilization towards uniformity and depersonalization, [which] certainly has a pernicious effect on the entire sphere of human morals," his audience responded not with boos or a walkout but a standing ovation.[85]

And it is this unwanted applause from the sorts of men his father kept company with at the Rotary Club and the Bolzano Lodge that brings us back to the *ohnisko* and the public mafia's major difference: unlike the public mafia, the *ohnisko* has no manifesto,

83 Václav Havel, "Projev prezidenta republiky Václava Havla na zahájení Světového kongresu PEN klubu", in Havel, *Spisy 7*, 318-319. Havel was referring to Sontag's staging of Beckett's *Waiting for Godot* in July 1993, as recounted in her essay, "Godot Comes to Sarajevo," *New York Review of Books*, October 21, 1993.
84 Andrew Roberts, "Demythologising the Czech Opposition Agreement," *Europe-Asia Studies* 55:8 (2003), 1273–1303 (at 1291).
85 Václav Havel, "Konference firmy UPS Longitudes 04", in Havel, *Spisy 8*, 273-283; for Havel's fear/hope that the crowd would be outraged, and his mortification on being cheered, see Havel, *Prosím stručně*, 29.

even if writing emanates from it, and no pretense to be any sort of highbrow vanguard. The public mafia, in its masonic-Barrandov aspect, aspired to non-fascist concertation, as elaborated in Josef Ludvík Fischer's *Krise demokracie* (Crisis of democracy, 1933), in order to reconcile individuals and groups "rid of the slag of crowd affect [*strůsek davových afektů*] and purified into a cultured form."[86] As rising, restive backbenchers, the public mafia had no subversive quality, which would require a mix of the unexpected and unintended; perhaps least subversive even while most secretive, a masonic lodge is bound by its own rules to respect the government of the country in which it is located, and if it cannot, then the lodge must dissolve itself.[87] Being non-representational, an *ohnisko* would never fit into a democratic corporatism (although it might lurk within one of the components). And unlike an *ohnisko*, the public mafia were do-gooding killjoys: "We want to live healthily, in accordance with moral ideals, and therefore consider it our duty to attend to physical fitness and struggle against injurants to life (alcoholism, prostitution, epicurism, etc.)."[88]

Ohnisko and deterritorialized milieu

"Living lightly," "leading a very fun life," and "making merry in general" may not have been the public mafia's priority, but according to Alexei Yurchak they are the fond memory of the last Soviet generation as a side-effect of the state's promotion of education, high culture and urbanization.[89] By enabling people to engage in intellectual pursuits and providing weakly supervised places in which to do so, the state created "deterritorialized milieus" of unsanctioned,

86   Havel, *Mé vzpomínky*, 258.
87   Čehurová, *Čestí svobodní zednáři ve XX. století*, 74.
88   Havel, *Mé vzpomínky*, 157.
89   Alexi Yurchak, *Everything Was Forever, Until It Was No More: The Last Soviet Generation* (Princeton: Princeton University Press, 2006), 132.

spirited discourse—known in Russian as *obshchenie,* an intense process of interaction and also "a sociality that emerges in that process, and both an exchange of ideas and information as well as a space of affect and togetherness."[90] The illustrative examples include after-school clubs and circles that took on lives of their own, historical and archeological societies, scientific institutes, and city cafés. Yurchak takes pains to stress that none of these opportunities had to be carved out, since the state readily made them available in the belief they would serve the official ends of modernization.

Here we are certainly moving closer to Havel's *ohnisko,* but differences remain. An *ohnisko* may arise in a state-enabled location (such as a permitted club), but it may occur in a private setting (such as Hrádeček or, Havel hoped, his presidential library); it may be one person (Neubauer) or a network (the newspaper *Lidové noviny* in its clandestine phase). The deterritorialized milieu of late Soviet socialism was more directly parasitical on the state, even if the occupants were indifferent to it. Sidestepping easy binary divisions into official and alternative cultures, Yurchak underscores that "the very existence of creative, dynamic, and relatively independent milieus of theoretical scientists and other cultural producers was an indivisible, if somewhat paradoxical, element of the Soviet state's cultural project, not its opposite [...] Indeed, outside of the Soviet state project, this milieu would have made no sense and would have failed to thrive."[91] Even hang-outs (*tusovki*) such as the Leningrad cafés of the 1960s and 1970s, which more closely resemble the *ohnisko* in their lesser reliance on state sponsorship, still illustrate "how the state enabled such milieus": they were allowed to stay in business because the KGB found them useful for the purposes of surveillance.[92]

90 Yurchak, *Everything Was Forever,* 148.
91 Yurchak, *Everything Was Forever,* 140–141.
92 Yurchak, *Everything Was Forever,* 144.

Obshchenie, on Yurchak's telling, was a pervasive practice in late-socialist daily life, which made that existence more bearable, but it more closely resembles the Aristotelian friendships discussed above.[93] Furthermore, when engaging in this intense interaction, the participants adopted a perspective of abject indifference to current affairs (being *vnye*), neither subscribing to official values nor resisting them. By contrast, Havel's *ohnisko*, as quoted above, stands at "the intersection of the spiritual, moral and emotional powerlines of the time"[94]—by being tapped into those lines, the *ohnisko* has a potential for subversive feedback.[95]

Finally, "the intersection of the spiritual, moral and emotional powerlines of the time" can mean of *any* time, not just a particular couple of decades under a defunct regime in a country that no longer exists, whereas Yurchak's description of living *vnye* as "fun" has been critiqued as specific to a relatively (and briefly) low-stress phase in Soviet history.[96] Not only would it not have been possible or as enjoyable in more austere decades, but under capitalism the state and market would be far stricter in patrolling the use of the facilities they provide (under the guise of accurate accounting, transparency, fairness and efficiency); compare Yurchak's depiction of the "Saigon" café in 1960s Leningrad with the McCafé around the corner in today's Saint Petersburg, and history speaks for itself.

---

93 Yurchak, *Everything Was Forever*, 149, quotes one source that "Friendship—the emotion that occupied the 1960s—became the source of independent social opinion." Yurchak prefers to put it beyond friendship, into "kinship-like intimacy" (151).
94 Havel *Spisy* 4, 636.
95 Havel had used the similar-sounding idea of being "outside" (*vně*) to describe Charter 77's position as neither left nor right on the conventional political spectrum, concerned only with "truth" (Havel, *Spisy* 4, 628). This truth, however, was the "clear truths" (opposed to lies) that Yurchak distinguishes from the "deep truths" (ones opposed by an equally deep truth) discussed in deterritorialized milieus (*Everything Was Forever*, 126–127).
96 Kevin M. F. Platt and Benjamin Nathans, "Socialist in Form, Indeterminate in Content: The Ins and Outs of Late Soviet Culture," *Ab Imperio* 12:2 (2011), 301–324.

Ohnisko and the butterfly effect

That history, however, should not be treated as linear: it can be shunted onto different tracks by imperceptibly minor changes. Yurchak's critics are also more open than he was to the idea that the little actions of these various deterritorialized milieux could have, over the long run, major political consequences, despite their consciously apolitical stances: "Although we have no desire to dismiss or invalidate individuals' sense that they were beyond politics, constructing their own alternative social realities, nonetheless individuals do not always determine the social or political resonance of their language or behavior."[97] While in prison, Havel struggled with the interplay between the smallest human acts (such as theater in *ohnisko* mode) and the fabric of the cosmos, working always from the assumption that there had to be a connection for life to have meaning. As that connection would consist of billions of small acts, the cosmos (Being) defies any single interpretation or representation, and thus requires pluralism against the single face of fanaticism.[98] Pluralism does not mean a universe of chaos, but its own forms of order.[99] That order of Being or "higher structure," however, was fluid and unfixed: "its blurriness, 'softness' and ambiguity suit me."[100]

Into these prison meditations came a letter from Havel's brother Ivan using eddies to illustrate the challenge of scientific observation. An eddy (*vír*) is not a separate or bounded thing, but belongs to the whole river, and the river to it. "If an eddy appears in one place, it must be connected with the disappearance of an eddy somewhere far

---

97 Platt and Nathans, "Socialist in Form, Indeterminate in Content," 321.
98 Much of this was set out in Havel, *Letters to Olga*, letter 78 on pluralism of views of the world and Havel, *Letters to Olga*, letter 141 on rejecting fanaticism.
99 Havel, Letters to Olga, letter 80.
100 Havel, *Letters to Olga*, letter 140. Havel's metaphysics are summed up in Radim Palouš, *Hovory s Havly: Dálkové rozhovory s Václavem Havlem a s Ivanem Havlem* (Středokluky: Zdeněk Susa, 1999), 8–10.

away from it (but are these not two occurrences of the same eddy?)." Eddies may appear as a result of natural fluid dynamics or of an observer sticking a hand into the flow to cause one, thus becoming a part of what is being observed.[101] Havel seized on this, comparing eddies to the theater-as-*ohnisko* in letter 112 to Olga:

It is a bit like with Ivan's eddies: theater is an eddy in the river; it is we who make it, of course, but through it we also confirm that the river is a river; we make it, and then we observe the swirling surface, which of course is now irrevocably different from what it was before our intervention. After Samuel Beckett, we live in a different world than we did before him. The eddy he caused will, of course, subside and eventually vanish altogether—the river will again be calm or spin in entirely different eddies. But even if to all appearances it may seem that everything is as before and that nothing has actually happened—it's not true: that eddy will swirl on forever in the memory of the spirit as an imperceptible part of that great and preposterous activity by which the order of the spirit fulfills its mission in the order of Being. And just as the river is what it is only because that eddy was in it, so by this work the order of the spirit tries to fight its way through to its secret super-identity.[102]

In his presidential speeches, talk of eddies, the order of spirit, and Being yielded to more accessible pop theories, such as James Lovelock's Gaia hypothesis of the Earth as an integrated, self-regulating life-support system.[103] At the Davos World Economic Forum in 1992, Havel invoked Edward Lorenz's idea of meteorological non-linearity in the bastardized version delivered by a character played by Havel's "friend," Robert Redford, in a recent film:

101 Ivan Havel et al, *Dopisy od Olgy* (Prague: Knihovna Václava Havla, 2010), 127.
102 Havel, *Letters to Olga*, letter 112.
103 Václav Havel, "Medaile svobody," 1994. On Lovelock, see John Gribbin, *Deep Simplicity: Chaos, Complexity and the Emergence of Life* (London: Penguin, 2005), 200–217.

Certainly you know of the "butterfly effect." It is the conviction that everything in the world is so mysteriously and complexly mutually linked that the imperceptible and seemingly entirely insignificant flap of a butterfly's wings in one place on the planet can cause a typhoon somewhere thousands of kilometers away. I think that in politics it is necessary to believe in this effect. We must not think that our admittedly microscopic yet truly unique daily acts have no meaning because they do not solve the gigantic problems of today's world. Such an *a priori* nihilistic certainty is a display of precisely that proud modern reason that thinks it understands how the world works.[104]

Leaving aside the facts that the butterfly effect was uncovered by a professor at the Massachusetts Institute of Technology by applying "proud modern reason" (a twelve-equation computer simulation) and that it led him in true scientific fashion to be more, not less, modest in his claims to understand how the world works, it fit Havel's long-standing attraction to natural metaphors for change, such as his forecast in 1975 that someday Czechoslovakia would be hit by a sudden "tornado" of political upheaval.[105] Because all the "subtle processes" in a society are indivisible, he wrote then, "We never know when an inconspicuous little fire [*ohýnek*] of insight, kindled within a few cells somehow specialized for the organism's self-awareness, will suddenly illuminate the path of all society, without it ever knowing how it came to see that path."[106] And it is for that reason that Havel remained hopeful during the long years of "normalization" even when there was no grounds for optimism, as

104 Václav Havel, "Projev prezidenta ČSFR Václava Havla na Světovém ekonomickém fóru," 1992. In *Havana* (1990), Redford's character says: "A butterfly can flutter its wings over a flower in China and cause a hurricane in the Caribbean." Lorenz's 1972 paper had speculated whether a butterfly in Brazil could set off a tornado in Texas; the butterfly image was suggested by meteorologist Philip Merilees, in place of Lorenz's original seagull. See Peter Dizikes, "When the Butterfly Effect Took Flight," *Technology Review* 114:2 (2011),M12–M15 (at M15).
105 Havel, *Spisy* 4, 101–102.
106 Havel, *Spisy* 4, 91.

he expressed in his objection to Milan Kundera's scorn for sign-ing petitions under socialism: "It has meaning [*to má smysl*] even despite the fact that a person seems or may seem ridiculous while doing it."[107]

One question that metaphors from nature do little to answer is just how radical Havel's idea of change was. His pre-presidential corpus includes rousing calls for an "existential revolution," such as in prison letter 143 (August 28, 1982). A four-page document of just over 1,000 words that contains almost all the key words covered in this book, this letter to Olga snuck past the censors a vision of a new community (*pospolitost*) based on a "renaissance of elementary hu-man relations"—love, goodness, compassion, tolerance, solidarity, friendship and "concrete responsibility" for one another—and re-lying on a certain "turbulence" to avoid regression into bureaucra-cy, rotten "establishments," and the hopelessness of the powerless masses.[108] That turbulence would entail an unrelenting examination of society's workings and of "what is truth and what is a lie, what is genuine [*opravdové*] and what is false, what is moral and what is immoral, what is living and what is deadening."[109]

What remained of the "existential revolution" after the Velvet Revolution, besides promotion of civil society, protection of liber-ties, and individual responsibility for the world? Metaphors from nature and science, such as the butterfly effect, can just as easily be enlisted to work within, and not transcend, a bounded system. Hav-el's speech in Davos—at a gathering of the politically and econom-ically powerful—imagined marvelous things emanating from their rarefied Alpine retreat:

---

107 Havel, *Spisy* 4, 884. See also Patrick J. Deneen, "The Politics of Hope and Optimism: Rorty, Havel, and the Democratic Faith of John Dewey," *Social Research* 66:2 (1999), 577–609 (at 580–581 and 587–588).
108 Havel, *Letters to Olga*, letter 143.
109 Havel, *Letters to Olga*, letter 143.

What do we know of whether a chance conversation of two bankers with the Prince of Wales over dinner tonight in Davos will not be the seed from which will grow a beautiful flower, at which the whole world will be amazed? In a world of global civilization, only someone who seeks a technical gimmick for its global salvation can despair. He, however, who modestly believes in the mysterious force of his own human being, which mediates his contact with the mysterious force of the world's being, has no reason to despair.[110]

That Davos is unlikely to be a subversive *ohnisko* is exemplified by that same Prince of Wales's own way of looking at the river eddies that enchanted the Havel brothers: far from disruptive, Charles saw them as evidence of a natural equilibrium, because "for a water vortex to spiral as it does, a similar movement of water or air must be on the move in the opposite direction."[111] It is just a blip in a self-cancelling, organic harmony rather than the source of unpredictable downstream disruption. And Havel also admitted, as one of his many paradoxes, to yearning for a world in harmony, for which there is a Czech intellectual tradition going back to Jan Amos Komenský in the seventeenth century, a time as out of kilter as our own.[112] This tension between a hankering for naturally arising order and for jolts of existential chaos could already be found in the adolescent Havel's pantheism, oscillating between Spinoza and Hegel, between the static and the becoming.[113]

Perhaps, in the end, the only resolution is a poetic one, as the 19-year-old Havel expressed in "Saturday":

110 Havel, "Projev prezidenta ČSFR Václava Havla na Světovém ekonomickém fóru," 1992.
111 The Prince of Wales with Tony Juniper and Ian Skelly, *Harmony: A New Way of Looking at Our World* (New York: Harper Collins, 2010), 110–111.
112 Věra Schifferová, et al (eds.), *Idea harmonie v díle Jana Amose Komenského* (Pardubice: Pavel Mervart, 2014). This collection of essays opens with a short tribute by Havel. See also Martin Bermeiser, *Václav Havels Reden: Aspekte einer holistichen Rhetorik* (Stuttgart: Ibidem, 2017), 22–25 and 193–195.
113 Kieran Williams, *Václav Havel* (London: Reaktion Books, 2016), 49.

I'm going out for Saturday.
A tie, pleated pants, nails, hair, a final
Glance in my wallet. But my thoughts

Are elsewhere.
And here, in the bathroom, bit by bit I realize,
How horrible is the thought that history
And God live only in the present,
The former its judge, the latter its meaning.

And suddenly my future son is standing beside me,
inquisitively examining every gesture of his father.
He knows full well that everything I do
I contribute unavoidably to his fate

and thus to the future of humanity.
For where is it written, that my son will not be
a new Hitler or new Einstein?
And where is it written, that it was they who decided the fate of the world?

And that a random degree of historical causality
Should also be the measure of responsibility for deeds?

I light a cigarette and go out.[114]

114 Havel, *Spisy* 1, 146–147.

POWER: *MOC*

Delia Popescu

Introduction

In Havel's writings, power and powerlessness are a conceptual pair. There is a transformative path between them, an ebb and flow of power-powerlessness, and much of Havel's work is dedicated to plotting the dynamic of power between self and others, and within the self and others. In essential ways, power for Havel is a mechanism of individual and social engagement that is grounded in both individual and collective agency. Power is interchange, and through that lens, empowerment is interchange grounded in truth and responsibility, both of which start with self-awareness.[1] I will spend the following pages fleshing out the concept of a lived experience of power and powerlessness, and the way in which I understand Havel's work to appeal to us and our sense of understanding experience. I start at the broad level, with the system that Havel calls post-totalitarianism, and then connect the strands of power-disempowerment-empowerment by pulling together Havel's views of fear, consciousness, ideology and their performative interplay.

The difficulty with defining Havel's view of power is that it is all-encompassing. All strands of his thought converge to animate his view of power. Power operates at the individual level as will-power, self-empowerment, and exemplary action. Power is also a collective manifestation of an official script, sometimes more-sometimes less countermanded by the "hidden transcript" of collective empowerment (to use James Scott's phrase).[2] Power finds expression in

---

1   For more on "responsibility" as a key word and in relation to "truth" and "power," see Falk and Bouvier-Valenta in this volume.

2   James C. Scott, *Domination and the Arts of Resistance: Hidden Transcripts* (New Haven: Yale University Press, 1990).

its lived ideological form, in the Newspeak narrative of "official truth," which as Havel shows in his plays, can cause the individual to be overpowered by the cognitive demands of the Weberian "iron cage." Power is also performing authenticity, shaking the veil of lies through everyday acts of "living in truth." And power is also power to the people, defined as a self-aware attempt to collectively live the complicated life of post-democracy—a society in which political organizations ebb and flow according to need.

Havel's examination of power leads him to define a new type of political system: post-totalitarianism. The prefix "post" is meant to emphasize a metamorphosis, rather than to suggest that totalitarianism is a thing of the past. Havel's conceptual contribution is two-fold: he points to this new type of power arrangement and at the same time grounds it in Modernity, which in turn links post-totalitarianism with liberal democratic power practices in the West. Havel is explicit about this connection, and cautions a Western audience that many of the stultifying devices of post-totalitarianism can be found, albeit in altered forms, at the heart of liberal democratic systems. Lies, fear, consumerism, environmental destruction, and a nagging existential dread all buttress political constructions throughout the modern world. As I have written elsewhere, Havel's view of post-totalitarianism amounts to a Dorian Gray motif, in which post-totalitarianism is the grotesque illustration to the hollow bimbofication of the Western exterior.[3] In his seminal essay "The Power of the Powerless," Havel writes: "And in the end, is not the greyness and the emptiness of life in the post-totalitarian system only an inflated caricature of modern life in general? And do we not in fact stand (although in the external measures of civilization we are far behind) as a kind of warning to the West, revealing to it its own latent tendencies?"[4] Havel's forebod-

---

3 Delia Popescu, *Václav Havel's Political Thought: The Responsibility of Resistance* (Lanham: Lexington Books, 2011).

4 Václav Havel, "The Power of the Powerless," chapter VI.

ing tone is just as poignant today as it was in 1978, the year he wrote "The Power of the Powerless."

This exploration is, by necessity, episodic: I briefly dwell on the markers of power in Havel's work, and suggest the connections. I am also mindful that, from a Havelian perspective, power and powerlessness are human experiences, and as such, their content can be transmitted to us through a variety of gnoseological means, aesthetic and performative forms included. Havel's plays are an important counterpart to his essays: while the essays lay out his view of repression under Communism, many of his descriptions rely on metaphors or vignettes that find a much more elaborate expression in his plays. The plays perform aesthetic meaning, which is meant to appeal to both reason and to what feeds into our reason by way of a hermeneutic unsettling that prompts us to reconsider reality. In the same vein discussed by David S. Danaher,[5] I generally consider Havel's work a mosaic of styles that speak to a central theme, which is the construction of power, both under East-European Communism and in its conceptual counterpart, namely Western liberal politics.

Post-totalitarian power: the environment of fear

One of Havel's seminal contributions to political thinking is to lay out the power mechanism of late Communism in Eastern Europe, or what he calls *post-totalitarianism*. The prefix "post" here signals an evolution in coercive sophistication over "classical dictatorship."[6] Post-totalitarianism is an "evolved" variant of oppression that combines fear with modern manipulatory devices like consumerism, careerism, and ideological Newspeak. Thus, post-totalitarianism is a sort of mid-way point on a power continuum. At one end stands the brute force of dictatorship, and at the other, the hypnotizing force

---

5 David S. Danaher, *Reading Václav Havel* (Toronto: University of Toronto Press, 2015).
6 Havel, "The Power of the Powerless," chapter II.

of consumer capitalism. Havel unambiguously connects post-totalitarian expressions of control with power mechanisms within liberal democracy, and undercuts the East-West conceptual antagonism. Post-totalitarianism is, ultimately, "a convex mirror of all modern civilization,"[7] and its power arrangement is made possible by structural deceptions familiar in the West. Havel's work reflects an evolutionary movement of power that reveal its protean character.

On one side of the theoretical scale, the distinction between "dictatorship" and "post-totalitarianism" is predicated on the degree of ideological fervor and personal conviction that imbues the power apparatus. "Our system is most frequently characterized as a dictatorship," Havel remarks, but "I am afraid that the term 'dictatorship,' regardless of how intelligible it may otherwise be, tends to obscure rather than clarify the real nature of power in this system."[8] The totalitarian dictatorship of old is "bound up with the lives of those who established it,"[9] the charismatic leaders followed by political converts, and it is buttressed by military might and the punitive reach of a gulag. We picture totalitarian dictatorship[10] as the work of "a small group of people who take over the government of a given country by force; their power is wielded openly, using the direct instruments of power at their disposal, and they are easily distinguished socially from the majority over whom they rule."[11] The precursor of post-totalitarianism divides society in "us versus them," and grants political power accordingly. The dramatic life of

---

7   Václav Havel, "Politics and Conscience," trans. Erazim Kohák and Roger Scruton, in *Open Letters: Selected Writings 1965-1990* (New York: Vintage, 1992), 259.
8   Havel, "The Power of the Powerless," chapter II.
9   Havel, "The Power of the Powerless," chapter II.
10   Havel ("The Power of the Powerless," chapter II) explains that Eastern European totalitarianism "is totalitarian in a way that is fundamentally different from classical dictatorship, different from totalitarianism as we usually understand it." While Havel claims to pit post-totalitarianism against "classical" dictatorship, it is clear that he is referring here not only to Czarist absolutism but also to what Arendt calls *totalitarian dictatorship*, which includes Stalin's and Hitler's regimes. See Arendt, *The Origins of Totalitarianism* (London: Harcourt, 1985).
11   Havel, "The Power of the Powerless," chapter II.

Stalinism capitalizes on the classical hallmarks of power: awe, state terrorism, and secular worship, and Havel describes its magnitude:

> In the fifties there were enormous concentration camps in Czechoslovakia filled with tens of thousands of innocent people. At the same time, building sites were swarming with tens of thousands of young enthusiasts of the new faith singing songs of socialist construction. There were tortures and executions, dramatic flights across borders, conspiracies, and at the same time, panegyrics were being written to the chief dictator.[12]

Post-totalitarianism alters this power dynamic to adapt to a post-Stalinist historical reality, in which the cult of personality and ideological zeal no longer have the same political traction. The new order avoids the political costs of volatility and replaces the massive state effort dedicated to ideological adulation with the realm of the putatively pragmatic bureaucrat intent on securing the public acquiescence of a quick signature or an automatic vote. As Vladimir Tismaneanu remarks, "in the post-totalitarian order, the dominant structures seem to be exhausted,"[13] and the burden of political self-perpetuation is shifted elsewhere, to the fabric of society itself. Post-totalitarianism recasts "existential fear" through "manipulatory devices so refined, complex, and powerful that it no longer needs murderers and victims."[14] What it needs instead is apathy, disengagement, and a demoralized society trapped in the "shapeless fog"[15] of "gray, everyday totalitarian consumerism."[16]

"Existential fear" is the first hallmark of post-totalitarian power, and Havel emphasizes how the system normalizes its presence

---

12 Václav Havel, "Stories and Totalitarianism," trans. Paul Wilson, in *Open Letters: Selected Prose 1965–1990* (London: Faber and Faber, 1991), 331.
13 Vladimir Tismaneanu, *Reinventing Politics* (New York: The Free Press, 1992), 153.
14 Havel, "Stories and Totalitarianism," 332.
15 Václav Havel, *Disturbing the Peace*, trans. Paul Wilson (New York: Vintage Books, 1990), 120.
16 Havel, *Disturbing the Peace*, 120–121.

in everyday concerns. In a centralized system in which all jobs are given by the state, and everything from housing to food is state distributed in the "public interest," the recipe of "Real Socialism" involves a broad scheme of state control over livelihood, social dignity, and any professional standing. The power of the system rests in the ability to unplug the source of income, deprive of career or schooling, and publicly slander anyone. It is a pervasive fear that touches on every aspect of life and that can reach anyone within the system, young or old. It is useful quoting Havel at length here:

> For fear of losing his job, the schoolteacher teaches things he does not believe in; fearing for his future, the pupil repeats them after him; for fear of not being able to continue his studies, the young man joins the Youth League and participates in whatever activities are necessary; fear that, under the monstrous system of political credits, his son or daughter will not acquire the necessary total of points for enrollment at a school leads a father to take on all manner of responsibilities and to 'voluntarily' do everything required. Fear of the consequences of refusal leads people to take part in elections, to vote for the proposed candidates, and to pretend that they regard such ceremonies as genuine elections; out of fear for their livelihood, position, or prospects, they go to meetings, vote for every resolution they have to, or at least keep silent […] Fear of being prevented from continuing their work leads many scientists and artists to give allegiance to ideas they do not in fact accept, to write things they do not agree with or know to be false, to join official organizations or to take part in work of whose value they have the lowest opinion, or to distort and mutilate their own works.[17]

Havel clarifies that this is substantially different from the deportations, tortures, and executions of the previous systems of oppression.

---

17 Havel, "Dear Dr. Husák," in *Open Letters: Selected Prose 1965–1990* (London: Faber and Faber, 1991), 52-53.

Existential fear is systemic and works effectively as a social under-current: not in an "ordinary psychological sense as a definite, precise emotion," but rather as an ethical context that determines every other emotion and reaction. The insidious pressure of "ethical fear" unites society into an "auto-totality" of both conscious and unconscious compliance. The conformity generated by ubiquitous angst becomes a "substantive part of the actual world"[18] and of the shared mental universe of its inhabitants. Power is precisely that environment of fear.

Fear in Havel's account has a panoptical effect. The individual trapped in the post-totalitarian environment develops a sense of himself as the subject of latent transgressions. "External adaptation" becomes second nature and "the only method of self-defense," because "everyone has something to lose," from those that occupy a putatively privileged place in the hierarchy and enjoy "undisturbed work, advancement and earning power," all the way "down to the mere possibility of living in that limited degree of legal certainty available to other citizens."[19] Existential fear is the consistent threat of extreme alienation in a system that relies on it.

Havel, Bettelheim, and Arendt: on existential fear

Although they draw on different conditions, there are significant similarities between Havel's account of disempowerment through fear, and those related by thinkers like Bruno Bettelheim and Hannah Arendt. Like Bettelheim and Arendt, Havel is concerned with the disintegration of the psyche under the pressure of mass dissimulation. Bettelheim remarks that "in the modern totalitarian state it is not possible to retain self-respect and live in inner opposition

---

18 Václav Havel, "Dear Dr. Husák," 53.
19 Václav Havel, "Dear Dr. Husák," 54.

to the system."[20] Lack of conformity invites an existential dilemma: to reveal inner beliefs and risk persecution, or to publicly play by the rules, which requires the totalitarian subject to "trick himself, to look for excuses and subterfuges." Bettelheim notes that public capitulation causes the individual to lose "exactly that self-respect which he is trying to maintain, a self-respect he needs desperately in order to retain his feeling of autonomy."[21] The Hitler salute is, in Bettelheim's view, the daily test of that surrender. Havel exemplifies a similar mechanism of submission with the parable of the greengrocer who puts the officially issued sign "Workers of the world unite!" in the shop window, despite his lack of Marxist convictions.

The similarity between Havel and Bettelheim's accounts is limited by the context. Bettelheim's reasoning is predicated on a direct and brutal confrontation with repression, in a system that demands personal devotion. The choices of life "facing the extreme"[22] are limited: submit or be broken. The "advanced" world of Havel's greengrocer has done away with the risky confrontation between self and overt power; instead, the new order rests on two "subtle and selective forms": existential pressure couched in ritualistic ideology coupled with what Havel calls a system of public bribery. The greengrocer in Havel's vignette is rescued, as it were, from the stark duality of Bettelheim's choice—accept or surrender—through a sophisticated mechanism of self-exculpatory means. The system's success hinges on its ability to allow the greengrocer to say "What's wrong with the workers of the world uniting?"[23] For this hermeneutic conversion to work, and for the greengrocer to repress the conscious side of anxiety and acquiesce, fear must be couched in something different; it

20 Bruno Bettelheim, "Remarks on the Psychological Appeal of Totalitarianism," in *Surviving and Other Essays*, ed. B. Bettelheim (New York: Knopf, 1979), 318.
21 Bettelheim, "Remarks on the Psychological Appeal of Totalitarianism," 318.
22 See Tzvetan Todorov, *Facing the Extreme: Moral Life in the Concentration Camps* (New York: Holt, 1997).
23 Havel, "The Power of the Powerless," chapter III.

must be veiled by the possibility that there is something compensatory to cling to. The post-totalitarian individual is encouraged to shift attention, and embrace consumer culture, thereby paving the way for "an escape from the public sphere," and Havel adds:

> Rightly divining that such surplus energy, if directed outward, must sooner or later turn against them—that is, against the particular form of power they obstinately cling to—they do not hesitate to represent as human life what is really a desperate substitute for living. In the interest of the smooth management of society, then, society's attention is deliberately diverted from itself, that is, from social concerns. By fixing a person's concern on his mere *consumer interests*, it is hoped to render him incapable of realizing the increasing extent to which he has been spiritually, politically, and morally violated. Reducing him to a simple vessel for the ideals of a primitive consumer society is intended to turn him into pliable material for complex manipulation.[24]

The "hypnotic charm" of material possessions prompts an inward turn. "Most people are loath to spend their days in ceaseless conflict with authority,"[25] especially since the persistence appears to be futile, and the only price is paid by the recalcitrant individual and his family. The space created by public disengagement is then filled with the system's ideological script. In need of a signaling method, post-totalitarianism deploys what Havel calls "the bridge of excuses." In the absence of personal dedication, ideological fervor is hollowed out and transformed into a bureaucratically inspired meta-language in which words no longer denote their own meaning, but rather they signal the assent of the subject uttering them.

Post-totalitarianism provides a way to save face through a vocabulary of submission filled with ostensible truisms, generalities,

---

24 Havel, "Dear Dr. Husák," 12, emphasis added.
25 Havel, "Dear Dr. Husák," 58.

and stock phrases. This narrative form-without-essence builds the "dominant transcript" of ideological performativity, and everyone is part of it. Obedience is measured through the use of the code. The greengrocer hangs the slogan in the window, because he can claim to himself that the message is meaningless, and the alternative is a direct confrontation with the system. Faced with the prospect of absurd punishment, the greengrocer is likely to project the ideological script and say "everything seems fine to me, we have popular government, everyone has a job, everyone can benefit from free education, nobody starves!"[26] Eventually, the logic of self-preservation becomes unassailable, and the gesture—automatic. The greengrocer turns inward and allows the lingo to stand in for him, thereby effectively surrendering his voice.

The generic and generalized script engages all state institutions which are devoted to coining Newspeak. Fundamentally, the transmogrification of meaning into mere language requires a key ingredient: lies. In post-totalitarianism, lies are a political force: they serve as the performative in-between of social and political interaction. The post-totalitarian web of lies does not require belief but mere public performance. "We are no longer governed by fanatics, revolutionaries, or ideological zealots," Havel argues, and concludes that "the country is administered by faceless bureaucrats who profess adherence to a revolutionary ideology, but look out only for themselves, and no longer believe in anything."[27] The proliferation of disengagement buttresses a legal and political system that uses ideology as a justification for any action it takes. Ideology is pliable because its meaning is set by the system at will, and it serves as political alibi for any abuse. The power to control society is relegated to this "bridge of excuses."

In *Eichmann in Jerusalem*, Arendt similarly describes the effect of bureaucratic embeddedness on what she calls the unthinking

---

26 Havel, "The Power of the Powerless," chapter III.
27 Havel, "Stories and Totalitarianism," 334.

individual. Observing Adolf Eichmann, a high-level bureaucrat who facilitated the logistics of the extermination of the Jews, Arendt was surprised at his apparent ability to suspend thinking and use the automatic obedience to the *Furhrerprinzip* as his guiding framework. While in *The Origins of Totalitarianism*, Arendt depicts the savage self-abnegation of totalitarian zeal, in *Eichmann* she catches a glimpse of an ideological disengagement which does not resemble either stupidity or the radical evil of the *Einsatztrupps*. Arendt concludes that evil does not require a personal ideological grounding, and coins the term "the banality of evil" to reflect this perspective.

Arendt's view of Eichmann's "curious, quite authentic inability to think"[28] reflects Havel's description of the "bureaucratic pedant whose reliable lack of idea makes him an ideal guardian of late totalitarianism's vacuous continuity."[29] Both Havel and Arendt's portrayals emphasize a suspension of thinking, of the kind of reflective, other-directed thinking that Arendt calls judgement. "His inability to speak," Arendt writes about Eichmann, "was closely connected with his inability to think, namely, to think from the standpoint of somebody else."[30] She emphasizes that "no communication was possible with him not because he lied, but because he was surrounded by the most reliable of all safeguards against the words and presence of others, and hence against reality as such."[31] Arendt identifies "officialese" as this best of safeguards, and points out that it "became his language, because he was genuinely incapable of uttering a single sentence that was not a cliché."[32]

The collapse of ethical bearings is the core of Havel's theory of disempowerment. "Living within a lie" dulls the thinking mind and

---

28   Hannah Arendt, *Eichmann in Jerusalem* (New York: Viking Press, 1969), 417. See also Hannah Arendt, *The Life of the Mind* (New York: Harcourt Brace Jovanovich, 1978), volume I.
29   Havel, "Stories and Totalitarianism," 335.
30   Arendt, *Eichmann in Jerusalem*, 48.
31   Arendt, *Eichmann in Jerusalem*, 48.
32   Arendt, *Eichmann in Jerusalem*, 48.

leads to the "breakdown of all criteria of decency," the destruction of meaning and values like truth, honesty, and altruism, and plunges life to a "vegetable level."[33] Like Eichmann, who "had not the slightest difficulty in accepting an entirely new set of rules," the post-totalitarian individual projects the formulaic answers of the system, suspending his ability to tell right from wrong. This cognitive surrender pushes a sense of responsibility away from its personal locus, and makes possible the pervasive banality of evil. In a bid to seek the path of least resistance and highest personal reward, both Eichmann and the post-totalitarian individual prop the system's brutality.

As in Bettelheim's case, the rich parallel between Eichmann and the post-totalitarian individual has its limits.[34] Arendt's unique portrayal of Eichmann is the first glimpse at a new totalitarianism, in which a legion of Eichmanns would eventually replace the death commando veterans. In this "mature" version of a degenerate totalitarianism, "the fanatic whose unpredictable zeal for the 'higher cause' might threaten this automatic process has been replaced by the bureaucratic pedant."[35] Havel's view of power is extensively Eichmannized.

Havel hones in on acts of everyday indifference that "democratize" the banality of evil beyond the top career echelons. Fear and the resulting environment of threat have a relative and generalizable effect in post-totalitarianism:

[I]t is not so much what someone objectively loses, as the subjective importance it has for him [...] Thus, if a person today is afraid, say, of losing the chance of working in his own field, this may be a fear equally strong, and productive of the same reactions, as if—in another

33 Havel, "Dear Dr. Husák," 62.
34 For a longer discussion about Havel in comparison with Arendt see Popescu, *Political Action in Václav Havel's Thought.*
35 Havel, "Stories and Totalitarianism," 335.

historical context—he had been threatened with the confiscation of his property. Indeed, the technique of existential pressure is, in a sense, more universal.[36]

The wide-ranging alienation of living with existential fear results in a power mechanism dependent on ideology as a means of social interchange. Both Havel and Arendt contend that meaning and its expressive nuance are co-created through human interchange. The meaning of language reflects "a human dimension" that bonds the self and others in an imaginative exchange. Ideology undercuts that creative potential by delivering fixed official signifiers meant to project the locus of power and obedience to it. "Individuals can be alienated from themselves only because there is something in them to alienate,"[37] Havel writes, and ideological language is the necessary sedative for alienation.

To understand the inner workings of ideological power over the individual, I briefly turn to Havel's plays. The descriptive analysis in Havel's essays is complemented in his dramaturgical work through an evocative set of aesthetic emotions, which conjure up what could be called a dramatic tableau of disempowerment. The thrust of the absurdist interplay between person and system is not to evoke tragic resignation, but rather to awaken a sense of discontinuity between self and the world. The plays are tools intended to disrupt the mindset of an audience trapped in an environment of power seemingly beyond its control. In this sense, Havel's dramaturgical point is to project the disempowerment of his characters in order to prompt an act of active witnessing and self-empowerment.

---

36 Havel, "Dear Dr. Husák," 54.
37 Havel, "The Power of the Powerless," chapter VIII.

Entrapment, uprootedness, and power

What surprises about some of Havel's plays is the almost disarming powerlessness of the characters. Many times, the plays show a protagonist bewildered and trapped by a self-replicating plot. The Vaněk plays (*Audience* 1975, *Unveiling* 1975, *Protest* 1978),[38] broadly portrayed as auto-biographical, show a humble individual perplexed by the unwillingness of his friends and acquaintances to acknowledge or live up to reality, or rather, to responsibly accept and respond to what happens to them. *Audience* is a dialogue between a brewmaster and Vaněk, a writer of banned material who is forced to work in a brewery. The brewmaster who is supposed to covertly keep an eye on Vaněk, spends the play trying to convince the writer to pen the weekly secret reports on himself. Vaněk consistently refuses, but the play ends in a "reset": Vaněk walks back in and restarts the conversation with the brewmaster.

The play is a double entrapment: the brewmaster, who is supposedly in charge and entrusted with the job of controlling Vaněk, pleads that he is ultimately forced to do this and thereby powerless. Compelled by existential threat to look beyond making good beer, the brewmaster resents both his spying and its subject—the writer who is important enough to attract the attention of the system. Although Vaněk holds on to his principles, he is also trapped in the cycle of resentment and powerlessness, and destined to repeat the interaction ad nauseam. Neither seem to break free.

The same cyclicity is reflected in *Unveiling*, a play about Vaněk's visit to the swanky apartment of yuppie friends Michael and Vera. Proud of their indulgent lifestyle populated by superfluous objects like an almond peeler acquired abroad, Michael and Vera "entertain" Vaněk by cataloguing their "niche" finds. Their self-importance is peppered with paternalistic advice about what "respectable"

---

[38] Václav Havel, *The Garden Party and Other Plays,* (New York: Grove Press, 1993).

job to get, decorating, cooking, and having children, which are all meant to correct Vaněk's life. Eventually, Vaněk attempts to leave, but their reaction is extreme. With an identity dependent on an audience to impress, Michael and Vera are social succubi who trap the decent Vaněk in their consumer desperation. Faced with shaming rebuke for abandoning them, Vaněk sits back down, and the play is again "reset" when the characters slip back into normal dialogue.

The leitmotif of "resetting" is significant: it accentuates the absurdity of the situation and it is meant to jar. One feels the tragic-comical tension projected by Vaněk's inability to leave, his surrender to their neediness. Putatively the positive character in the play, Vaněk cannot escape the dialectic of the situation. He too is trapped by the microenvironment's self-replicating force, and by the need of those surrounding him to use him as an excuse. In a sense, the brewmaster, Vera, and Michael represent an inner fight, and Vaněk is the external projection of a moral arbiter, and they need his approval. Vaněk's role as moral paragon is emphasized in *Protest*, a dialogue with Staněk, a writer whose daughter is pregnant while her musician fiancé is in jail on a trumped-up charge. Staněk asks Vaněk to protest the arrest, but when Vaněk shows him a letter to that effect, Staněk declines to sign citing a myriad of "subjective" and "objective" pretexts. Staněk points out that Vaněk is the one he turns to whenever he thinks of doing something "for the sake of ordinary human decency," simply because Vaněk is his standard on "moral matters."[39] Vaněk's standing in the plays is accentuated by his mild demeanor. He never responds in kind to accusations, and his silence and humility further frustrate and incite his interlocutors. His quizzical acquiescence is the vehicle for the heightened absurdity of these interactions.

---

[39] The weight of serving as moral arbiter is further explored in Havel's *Largo Desolato* (New York: Grove Weidenfeld, 1987); for a broader discussion see Phyllis Carey, "Living in Lies: Václav Havel's Drama," in *CrossCurrents* 42, no. 2 (summer 1992): 200-211.

Auto-replicating absurdity is the main dramaturgical drive in two of Havel's best-known plays, *The Memorandum*[40] and *The Garden Party*.[41] *The Memorandum* opens with the Director of an unknown institution, Joseph Gross, reading apparent gibberish from an official document, and absurd hilarity ensues. The plot reveals that it, the memorandum, was written in a newfangled bureaucratic language, Ptydepe, meant to programmatically enhance the precision of office communication. Gross sits through Ptydepe language classes in which no one seems able to learn it, and frantically searches around the institution for a way to translate the piece. The red tape sets him on a circular path and, eventually, he can only secure a translation by calling in a personal favor that requires his secretary, Maria, to break institutional rules. The parallel between scientific Socialism and Ptydepe is hard to miss, and the crux of the play is a clever juxtaposition between the commentary on language and the human damage it inflicts. As is the case in other Havelian plays, the good receive no reward for their decency, and Maria is fired by Gross when he regains his post. In the play's coup of Havelian cyclicity, the memorandum orders the purging of Ptydepe which is then promptly replaced by its antithesis, Chorukor, an idiom dedicated to utmost nuance. Ideology resets itself in a new form thereby preserving its raison d'etre: to control and organize the human interaction in the institution.

Language and its mesmerizing effect on consciousness is also the core of *The Garden Party*. The play is a sort of absurd linguistic race engaging the young Hugo Pludek who tries to catch up with the "officialese" of his interlocutors. Attending a garden party of the ominously named Office of Liquidation and Inauguration, Hugo slides into a discussion with the staff and adopts their increasingly

---

40 Václav Havel, "The Memorandum," in *The Garden Party and Other Plays* (New York: Grove Press, 1993).
41 Václav Havel, "The Garden Party," in *The Garden Party and Other Plays* (New York: Grove Press, 1993).

formulaic language. By the end of the play Hugo exchanges bureaucratic lingo so fluently that he outshines even the Director in sloganeering and replaces him as head of the Central Committee. The toll of mastering officialese is immense: at the end of the play, Hugo no longer knows who he is and doesn't recognize his parents. The Havelian "reset" here casts Hugo as the architect of a new institution to replace the old one.

There is much to say about language and ideology in Havel's plays.[42] Importantly, Havel emphasizes language as a mechanism of shaping and controlling a sense of the self. As Jan Grossman remarks, "the chief actor in *The Garden Party* and *The Memorandum* is the mechanism governing the human being,"[43] and language is the vehicle for her disempowerment. Immersion in the hollow ideological language of post-totalitarianism results in separation from both self and from reality. The officialese is devoid of intrinsic meaning, but it still occupies the mind thereby robbing it of an opportunity for Arendtian introspection and a chance to relate with self and others. Havel calls this colonization of the mind pseudo-ideological thinking:

> The essence of it is that certain established ideological patterns are deformed and fetishized and thus become an immobile system of intellectual and phraseological schemata which, when applied to different kinds of reality, seem at first to have achieved, admirably, a heightened ideological view of reality when in fact they have, without our noticing it, separated thought from its immediate contact with reality...[44]

42 See Popescu, *Political Action in Václav Havel's Thought*; Danaher, *Reading Václav Havel*; Carey, "Living in Lies: Václav Havel's Drama"; and Robert Pirro, "Václav Havel and the Political Uses of Tragedy," *Political Theory* 30:2 (2002): 228-258.

43 Jan Grossman, "Protokoly," in Michael Špirit, ed., *Čtení o Václavu Havlovi: Autor ve světě literární kritiky* (Prague: Institut pro studium literatury, 2013), 31.

44 Václav Havel, "On Evasive Thinking," in *Open Letters: Selected Writings 1965–1990*, (New York: Vintage Books, 1992), 11.

The double disconnect from self and reality paves the way to disempowerment. Havel uses theater to highlight this uprootedness, and he wants us to take note of its unsettling effect.[45] Characters appear trapped in a tragi-comical cycle of powerlessness, but Havel wants us to see and feel something different here; his intention is demonstrative. The performative value of powerlessness in Havel's plays is the ability to transform the perspective of the audience.[46] By watching Vaněk or Gross trapped in a situation they cannot seem to control, we are given a chance to empathetically reflect on our own situation. To identify with their powerlessness is to see the world "from below" and shake away certain "illusions and mystifications."[47] Havel calls on us to recognize in his plays the symbolic fight between ourselves and the tools of our alienation. Vaněk is vulnerable because he is self-aware: he is our perspective from below, and his "powerlessness provides the best vantage point for getting a true view of society."[48] In one of his best formulations, Havel explains: "There are times when we must sink to the bottom of our misery to understand truth, just as we must descend to the bottom of a well to see the stars in broad daylight."[49] As Milan Šimečka writes, "powerlessness was elevated by Havel into a virtue,"[50] because it lays the groundwork for that cathartic experience that allows one to see the world as it really is. The unsettling experience of vulnerability is the core of Havel's theater of (cathartic) appeal

---

45   As Pirro remarks, Havel speaks frequently of catharsis as a vehicle for self-recognition. Pirro, "Václav Havel and the Political Uses of Tragedy." For more on "theater" as a key word, see Day in this volume.

46   James Pontuso calls "embeddedness" this connection with an audience that is supposed to act as witness and reflect on their role; see his *Václav Havel: Civic Responsibility in the Postmodern Age* (Lanham, MD: Rowman & Littlefield, 2004), 75.

47   Václav Havel, "Second Wind," trans. Paul Wilson, in *Open Letters: Selected Prose 1965– 1990* (London: Faber and Faber, 1991), 5.

48   Havel, "Power of the Powerless," chapter XVI.

49   Havel, "Power of the Powerless," chapter XVI.

50   Milan Šimečka, "The Sorrowful Satisfaction of the Powerless," in *Living in Truth*, (Boston: Faber and Faber, 1990), 269.

(*divadlo apelu*).[51] The performance of powerlessness is meant to awaken the reality of empowerment.

Self-empowerment and the polis

The question at the core of Havel's work is quintessentially political: "how is the condition of being free as a philosophical subject involved in solitary reflection related to the condition of being free as a political subject involved in collective action?"[52] Drawing on the theme of Greek tragedy, Pirro argues that the unsettling renewal of catharsis is central to Havel's perspective.[53] Havel's theater performs multiple functions: it is Havel's own cathartic effort to "live in truth," to reflect the world as he sees it, and it is also an artistic work meant to expose the system and appeal to our own understanding. Neither entirely private, nor exclusively collective, the fabric of consciousness in Havel's writing feeds into individual behaviors, which in aggregate result in the environment of power. And much of this environment is performative. As Karfíková remarks, Havel "recognizes some kind of 'ritual' of life in falsehood, which 'dissolves' human beings as individuals and unbinds them from responsibility, and in doing so makes anonymous the power thus maintained."[54] The power of the plays stands in their ability to transmit the existential nature of the everyday rituals of an oppressive system.

Havel's concept of the political has something in common with that of the ancient Greeks: politics is the life of the polis, the stuff of everyday interaction in a subscribed community in which we are immersed, and which, as Socrates remarked, is our mother and father.

---

51 See Pirro, "Václav Havel and the Political Uses of Tragedy," and Danaher, *Reading Václav Havel*. For more on "appeal" as a key word, see also Danaher in this volume.
52 Pirro, "Václav Havel and the Political Uses of Tragedy," 252.
53 Pirro, "Václav Havel and the Political Uses of Tragedy," 231.
54 Lenka Karfíková, "'The Intentions of life': Philosophical Points of Departure in The Power of the Powerless," *East European Politics, Societies and Cultures*, 32:2 (2018), 272.

The polis raises us as it were, and Socrates thought that we owe it for that constructive embeddedness that results in who we are. Havel is a modern thinker, with a modern appreciation of the self: he shifts the focus to a dual track of self and society which are dialectically co-created, yet also insists that there is that certain something of humanity and individuality that has the potential of showing us right from wrong independent of outside forces. As Petrusek and Cassling remark, Havel is hardly a "radical individualistic liberal" but "he does place exceptional emphasis on personal responsibility for oneself and for others (and in this he resembles Zygmunt Bauman)."[55] But Havel does not require sacrifice, nor heroic gestures; instead he expects the environment of power to push us toward the kind of cognitive dissonance that we can no longer bear in our everyday lives. "Something in our greengrocer snaps,"[56] Havel says, and the offenses of everyday oppression are actuated in the greengrocer's mind because "in actual fact, then, nothing remains forgotten," including "all the fear that one has endured, the dissimulation that one has been forced into, all the painful and degrading buffoonery, and, worst of all, perhaps, the feeling of having displayed one's cowardice."[57]

Once the greengrocer stops "living within a lie," he consciously refuses to attend the party meetings, to vote automatically, and to display the slogan in his window. He is punished for his political transgressions, because "by breaking the rules of the game, he has disrupted the game as such. He has exposed it as a mere game."[58] The exemplary act of reclaiming reality loosens the power grip of pseudo-ideological control,[59] "and because the emperor is in fact naked, something extremely dangerous has happened: by his

---

55 Miloslav Petrusek and Robin Cassling, "Václav Havel (1936-2011): Remarks on Havel's 'Lay Sociology,'" *Czech Sociological Review* 48:3 (2012), 570-571.
56 Havel, "The Power of the Powerless," chapter VII.
57 Havel, "Dear Dr. Husák," 79.
58 Havel, "The Power of the Powerless," chapter VII.
59 Pirro, "Václav Havel and the Political Uses of Tragedy," 245.

action (he) has addressed the world."[60] Pirro argues that Havel's view of the power of example is to be understood through Havel's experience with theater. Havel draws a parallel between the cathartic experience of the spectator watching a tragedy and the effect of "living within Truth" over the individuals in the post-totalitarian world. Consequently, Havel grounds his view on what Pirro calls the "human sense of dramatic order." Pirro argues that the role of the dramaturgical tragic "as providing an occasion for becoming reconciled to existential burdens constitutes a (third) distinctive aspect of Havel's tragic thought."[61]

There is a certain tension in Havel's writing between the degree to which he expects an individual to be overpowered by a system of institutionalized lies and existential pressure, and the degree to which he expects that same individual to overcome the pressure. It is not clear what critical mass of abuse one can take before reaching the bottom of that well and becoming receptive to exemplary acts of resistance. Perhaps, for some, the bottom of the well is deeper, although Havel clarifies that post-totalitarianism labors to keep us not from reaching the bottom of the well, but from *thinking* we reached it. Careerism and consumerism are just two of the modern, systemic tools of self-deception, and post-totalitarianism exploits the human ambition for public self-actualization. Havel acknowledges the complexity of manipulative devices and our different vulnerabilities, but he is ultimately hopeful that at least some people would suffer the cathartic renewal of their conscience. While "individuals can be alienated from themselves because there is something in them to alienate," by the same token, individuals can reclaim their agency because there is something in them that allows them to do just that.[62] An inner call for matching self and reality results in "living

60 Havel, "The Power of the Powerless," chapter VII.
61 Pirro, "Václav Havel and the Political Uses of Tragedy," 245.
62 I read Havel to say that every human being has this potentiality, because it is fundamentally the ability to love, empathize, and act in solidarity with others; I disagree with commentators who

in truth," opening up as many potentialities as there are avenues for expression: a letter, a strike, a concert, a demonstration, a play, a refusal to vote, "(or, for that matter) any free expression of life...including forms of expression to which in other social systems no one would attribute any potential political significance, not to mention explosive power."[63] From this perspective, "living in truth" is an eminently political act, which challenges the very structure of "outward adaptation." This potential for change is spread throughout society and it can be activated like a viral outbreak, by the act of any one person "who may be struck at any moment (in theory, at least) by the force of truth (or who, out of an instinctive desire to protect their position, may at least adapt to that force)."[64] Perhaps this is where Havel is at his most optimistic: in his belief in the exemplary power of everyday human action, which calls not for pitchforks and torches, but for consistent acts of inner belief that are meant to be witnessed and shared through the fabric of social consciousness. By taking the sign out of his shop widow, the greengrocer alone has disrupted the imposed version of the pseudo-mundane. The greengrocer has empowered himself and also initiated the potential empowerment of others. Havel thinks that such an act always has some reverberations, and they are potentially world-shattering.

Power universals and the West

In 1982, Samuel Becket dedicated the political play *Catastrophe* to Havel who was then imprisoned for "subversive activities."[65] In response to Beckett, a famous Western playwright he admired,

consider Havel's recipe of "awakening" to be mostly limited to intellectuals (the so-called thinkers and "dissidents" visible in the West). I find that Havel explicitly rejected the notion of a particular type of dissidence or dissident.

63 Havel, "The Power of the Powerless," chapter VIII.
64 Havel, "The Power of the Powerless," chapter VIII.
65 Samuel Beckett, "Catastrophe," in *Living in Truth*, (Boston: Faber and Faber, 1990).

Havel wrote *Mistake*.[66] The play focuses on a group of inmates who pressure a newcomer into following the self-imposed rituals of prison life. XIBOY, the new inmate, does not respond throughout the play, frustrating his indoctrination. Angered by his silence, the group of organized inmates decide on a death sentence for the "bloody foreigner." The play focuses on the factional need to invent and follow rules that predictably trade in inhumanity. Commenting on the play, Havel points out that it is a warning "against the omnipresent danger of *self-styled totalitarianism*, present today in every society in the world, large or small."[67] In the auto-biographical essay "Second Wind," Havel reinforces the notion that even his older plays have appeal beyond their context because of "the charge of energy given to them by their maternal environment," which was "obviously capable of being discharged elsewhere."[68] When Havel exposes the mechanism of power in post-totalitarianism, he means to reflect on power everywhere, because power has to contend everywhere with the universals of modern human existence. Temptation is ubiquitous and modern institutions facilitate the dispensation of superficial rewards. So, Havel argues, "instead of a free share in economic decision making, free political participation in political life, and free intellectual advancement, all people are actually offered is a chance freely to choose which washing machine or refrigerator they want to buy."[69]

Havel is a modernity "knocker," to use Charles Taylor's term.[70] Modernity for Havel acts as the underground stream feeding political expressions everywhere. There is a dialectical interplay between modernity, a certain pathology of the modern individual, and the

---

66 Václav Havel, "Mistake," in *Index on Censorship* 13 (February 1984), 13-14.
67 Václav Havel and Frantisek Janouch, *Korespondence 1978-2001* (Prague, Akropolis, 2007), 477, emphasis added.
68 Václav Havel, "Second Wind," 8.
69 Havel, "Dear Dr. Husák," 60.
70 Charles Taylor, *A Secular Age* (Cambridge: Belknap Press, 2007).

means that exacerbate this pathology. Like Marx and other modern thinkers, Havel recognizes alienation as the essential manifestation of the modern self. The impersonal structures of bureaucratic life, the anonymity of offices and regulations, the formulaic language of law and policy all contribute to distance individuals from their own human needs and from the needs of others. Pseudo-ideological thinking tears apart the logic of connectedness and fuels solipsism. Consumerism and careerism act as the new, artificial bonds of society. In this context, power over the individual is measured by the degree of her alienation. Havel's view is reminiscent of Rousseau's archetypal modern thinker who upon hearing a man being murdered under his window "has nothing to do but clasp his hands to his ears, argue a little with himself to hinder nature, that startles within him, from identifying him with the unhappy sufferer."[71] Distance is the marker of modern power.

Havel's writing consistently reflects the central idea that "totalitarianism, taken as a concept of liberal consciousness, provides the latter with its other" and that "to understand a form of self-consciousness is therefore to understand it in relation to its other."[72] The ritual of power has similar markers in the West: careerism, consumerism, and a lack of existential anchoring. While both Havel and Arendt identify careerism as a foil for turning away from conscious critique, Havel emphasizes the role of consumerism in facilitating this regression. "[T]he post-totalitarian system," Havel argues, "[...] has been built on foundations laid by the historical encounter between dictatorship and consumer society."[73] Post-totalitarianism is the next wrung on the ladder of oppression, one that

---

71   J.J. Rousseau, "The Second Discourse: Discourse on the Origin and Foundations of Inequality Among Mankind," in Susan Dunn, ed., *The Social Contract and The First and Second Discourses*, (Yale: Yale University Press, 2002), 107.
72   Michael Halberstam, *Totalitarianism and the Modern Conception of Politics*, (Yale: Yale University Press, 1999), 4.
73   Havel, "The Power of the Powerless," chapter VI.

for Havel finds a natural continuation through the heart of modern, consumer society, the kind we readily recognize in the capitalist West. Capitalism and its technological drive undercut the liberal project by trumping one set of humanistic values with the values of economic exchange and self-benefit. "The hierarchy of values existing in the developed countries of the West has, in essence, appeared in our society," Havel laments, and his diagnostic is unambiguous: "what we have here is simply another form of the consumer and industrial society with all its concomitant social, intellectual, and psychological consequences."[74]

The capillaries of modern power subversively run through every political system feeding its ideological pretense. The temptation to turn away from public concerns and build life around limited, private interests creates the distance necessary to allow for systemic forms of domination. Havel frequently mentions environmental exploitation as the direct result of the "inward orientation" fostered by a consumer-industrial system. Surprisingly perhaps, he does not talk much about sexism or racism (although he showed some worry regarding rising nationalism and the fate of the Romani population in Eastern Europe), but his theory certainly illuminates the systematic "turning away" from the concerns of others that motivate the construction of gender and race across both East and West. For Havel, the inward orientation is not some simple return to privacy, but rather a refusal to recognize the common project of political life. In the West, politics has been relegated to the professional few, while the many cling to "their own business" as the sole source of legitimate interest. The distance between politics and

---

74   Havel, "The Power of the Powerless," chapter II. In "Politics and Conscience," Havel puts a finer point on it: "Let me repeat: totalitarian power is a great reminder to contemporary civilization. Perhaps somewhere there may be some generals who think it would be best to dispatch such systems from the face of the earth and then all would be well. But that is no different from an ugly woman trying to get rid of her ugliness by smashing the mirror that reminds her of it," in Havel, *Open Letters*, 260-261.

individual pursuits denies a basic Havelian truth: that "the fundamental lines of conflict run through each person," and while our
ability to act is a matter of degree, "everyone is in his own way both
a victim and a supporter of the system."[75] Havel speaks to every
individual's role in the structural sexism and racism that buttress
inequality and oppression. When XIBOY is called a "bloody foreigner," one recognizes the knee-jerk othering that builds the power scaffolding of a totalitarian tool that can be deployed anywhere.
Recent attitudes and policies in both Europe and the US illustrate
this dynamic. The auto-totality of othering challenges all modern
political systems.

Ultimately, Havel calls for a politics of human need, understood
as the true and complete need of a human life based on self-worth
and social solidarity. Power in this context is agonistic and based
on constant renewal, with an eye to human integrity, decency, and
happiness. The life of the polis is hard work, and the ossification of
power has a single antidote: change, driven by the capacity of human beings to follow their life goals.

To the Castle

It would be fair to say that in 1989 Havel was reluctant to take on
lengthy political office.[76] Prague Castle represented the challenge of
facing head on the ossification of power that Havel always dread-
ed. At the same time, Havel believed in the possibility of a political
practice that was redemptive, dignified, and humble. To be a dissident was to reclaim the politics of human concerns, and to be a politician in an era of rebirth was to be equally able to recast politics
in its proper human terms.[77] Humanizing politics required mak-

---

75 Havel, "The Power of the Powerless," chapter VI.
76 Havel, *Summer Meditations*, trans. Paul Wilson (New York: Vintage Books, 1992), xv.
77 Havel, *Summer Meditations*, 1 and 18. See also Kieran Williams, *Critical Lives: Václav Havel*,
(London: Reaktion Books, 2016), 164.

ing way for a healthy dose of the unconventional and even defiant "shakedness" of creativity. Yet the Presidency, a role-dependent office with legal responsibilities and limitations augmented by post-89 party politics, presented particular difficulties for Havel's spontaneous take on political agency. Havel's view of the appropriate presidential role downplayed direct decision-making and focused on the moral stature of the person in office as a "watchman of political culture" who imprints "a certain guarantee"[78] of legitimacy and guides constitutional developments.[79]

As Andělová and Suk argue, paradoxes were built into Havel's presidential practice but these tensions did not necessarily betray an inconsistent *view* of politics.[80] Havel was unwilling to march along with a political party, even the one that propelled him into power, Civic Forum, but he showed moments of pragmatism regarding the necessity of parliamentary democracy in a transitional period and in relation to joining NATO, and he reversed some of his dissident stances on particular policies. Havel's responses must be filtered through his otherwise steady message of an authoritative discharge of moral mandates as the source of legitimate power. As Williams points out, his presidential terms can be charted along an arc of coping with the political work of the office while at the same time building on his view of "moral renewal" in both politics and global life.[81] If his first term was dedicated to restoring the legitimate basis of government through truthfulness, his second term required Havel to address the palpable frustrations following the revolutionary high. Havel made constant references to the need for a political ideal built on dignity, and the higher ground of responsibility, while

78 Havel, *Spisy 7: Projevy a jine texty z let 1992-1999*, quoted in Williams, *Václav Havel*, 167.
79 Havel, *Summer Meditations*, 23-24.
80 Jiří Suk and Kristina Andělová, "The Power of the Powerless and Further Paradoxes in the Stream of Time," in *East European Politics and Societies and Cultures*, 32:2 (2018), 214-231.
81 Williams, *Václav Havel*, 170.

cautioning against rampant consumerism and a slavish imitation of Western capitalism.[82]

The point of broader political responsibility was key to his third term, which was marked by the split of the Czech and Slovak republics, the Yugoslav crisis, and the drive to join NATO. Havel's third term grounded the idea of "moral renewal" in a more developed and proactive notion of political authority, not only as rightful legal or governmental power, but as the legitimate source of human responsibility broadly understood.[83] Havel spoke frequently of the authoritative appeals made on humanity by the very real needs of the universe, combining human and environmental concerns. During his fourth term in office, Havel insisted on decentralized institutions that might elevate local concerns and undercut top-heavy power. His political ideal pushed against a uniform, modern, and Western-centric notion of the human condition. He intertwined his plea to the West to create a web of common concerns with an appeal to open Western thinking to other traditions of thought and dig deeper for essential human interests that can co-create a "codex of human coexistence."[84]

Over the course of his presidential terms, Havel's penchant for larger, moral and global conceptual themes was understood by some as a sign of aloofness, or as a mismatch between the persona of the dissident and that of the pragmatic politician.[85] Both views underplay Havel's moral intent not to represent the political office as a cog in the institutional apparatus, but rather to embody his presidential authority as the "quiet constant" of aspirational ideals.[86] Havel resisted an understanding of power as the duty of the office and

82 Havel, *Summer Meditations*, 124.
83 Williams, *Václav Havel*, 170.
84 Havel, *Spisy 7: Projevy a jine texty z let 1992-1999*, quoted in Williams, *Critical Lives: Václav Havel*, 178.
85 See Andělová and Suk, "The Power of the Powerless and Further Paradoxes in the Stream of Time," 216-217, 221, 224.
86 Williams, *Václav Havel*, 167.

insisted on what he considered the quintessential political charge of a person in any office: individual decency, and what he saw as a sense of appropriateness or having tact in politics.[87]

Political decency in Havel's view requires the unobtrusive and consistent agency of a vigilant moral observer who foregoes political dictates and grand gestures. The result of political decency across institutional offices is collective: a solidarity of the political rightly understood as the realm where human needs meet human aspirations. Fundamentally, Havel never let go of the idea of an environment of power which is co-created by responsible individuals who have the agency to represent both themselves and human dignity, no matter the office. As a result, there is a tension between Havel's view of power which starts with the individual responsibility of everyday acts, and the modern view of the presidency as a position of responsibility detached from the person that fills the post. In this light, Havel appears too inner-oriented for a public service position that is supposed to rely on compromise and decisive leadership. Even Havel's speeches about the environment could sound like calls to join a personal global crusade at a time dominated by anxiety with domestic economic pressures. It is not that Havel did not understand these concerns, but he saw his role as less technocratic and non-partisan, and generally guided by a wider view of human ideals and foundational concerns. Not everyone agreed.

The question whether or not Havel's view of power is consistent with his presidency is largely dependent on what we are judging: Havel's responsibility to stay true to his own representation of basic human decency or his exercise of power in relation to the public policy goals described by the political system. Havel pegged his political aspirations to essential concerns like changing the definition of "politician" to include "one who does not lie." In taking this perspective, Havel divested himself of much of the power in modern

87 Havel, *Summer Meditations*, 11-12.

politics. This stance is hardly consistent with a picture of the pragmatic modern politician, and influenced the extent to which Havel used his presidential powers. As Williams argues, President Havel did not press to increase the powers of his office and, like Masaryk, used his veto sparingly (only 27 times in ten years), mostly to send a message about political aspirations.[88] Grounded in a view of politics that relied more on persuasion than institutional power, Havel considered himself a political mediator whose job was to provide the tools for healthy debate and consensual outcomes that would eventually provide a platform for political transformation beyond parliamentary democracy and toward the spontaneous political life he called "post-democratic" in "The Power of the Powerless."[89] This view advanced a very different type of political system then the one he took over, and different than the one that was ultimately institutionalized after 1989.

The revolutionary value of Havel's insistence on power as individual responsibility in everyday life may lead to the conclusion that the presidential office was never going to be a palatable platform for Havelian agency, and Havel himself had questions about the tantalizing hold of power over him. His consistent aim was never to forget the human foundations of his drives and motivations. If the stuff of everyday life is the stuff of politics, then Havel advanced a transformational view of the political that registered as tedious and perhaps even boring in its insistence on dignified political tact, but it is unclear if this perspective registers as failure on Havel's part or as the system ultimately failing him and his vision.

88 Williams, *Václav Havel*, 168.
89 Havel, "Power of the Powerless," chapters XXI and XXII.

RESPONSIBILITY: *ODPOVĚDNOST*

Barbara J. Falk and Daniela Bouvier-Valenta

> Responsibility is our obligation which is, to a certain extent,
> a metaphysical one. It is a commitment to a special partner,
> to the memory of being, to a certain complexity of the world.
> It is our commitment to what gives meaning
> to everything that exists.
>
> — Václav Havel, 2007[1]

Introduction

This chapter analyzes the concept and multiple meanings of responsibility and shared or co-responsibility (*odpovědnost* and *spoluodpovědnost* respectively) as elaborated in the feuilletons, longer essays, and political speeches of Václav Havel. Our arguments are based on a number of interrelated assumptions. First, Havel's work on responsibility is situated in late-20th century philosophical discussions as well as the Czech tradition of phenomenology (the work of Jan Patočka). Second, *all* Havel's works should be interrogated—after all, they were written by the same person. Indeed, Havel often "tested out" the same ideas he skillfully elaborated in essays in his plays, both through the development of his characters and the trajectories of the plots in which they found themselves, although in this chapter we limit ourselves to the former.[2] Third, Havel's views on responsibility are intrinsically connected to his formulations of both power and truth, which are examined elsewhere in this volume. After an overall analysis of the numerical incidence of responsibil-

---

1   Václav Havel, "Gala Opening of the Forum 2000 International Conference," 2007.
2   On reading Havel in a manner that "does not fragment but rather integrates the diversity of his writings and political contributions," see especially David S. Danaher, *Reading Václav Havel*, 5-7 and chapter 1.

ity in the Havelian canon, the specific words used, and how they are translated, we discuss Havel's original contribution to the philosophical examination of responsibility, after which we elaborate our "trinitarian" view of power, truth, and responsibility. Havel's differentiation of individual and shared responsibility (or co-responsibility) is also analyzed. Because Havel wrote about responsibility concretely, we discuss specific examples—responsibility for the past and the work of commemoration and recognition of historical wrongdoing; forms of global responsibility across borders; and responsibility to and for the environment. Throughout the chapter, we provide concrete textual examples to support our analysis. Finally, we conclude that not only does Havel's concept of responsibility matter, but that his elaboration matters especially now.

A search in the archival documentation center of the Václav Havel Library reveals that the number of documents in which Havel discusses responsibility is quite comparable to the number of documents in which he discusses power and truth. The search turns up 1286 Czech-language and 211 English-language documents on "responsibility," 2159 Czech-language and 183 English-language documents on "power," and 1353 Czech-language documents and 82 English-language documents on "truth." The documents translated into English are mostly public speeches given by Havel, with a handful of interviews as well as a few articles and written statements. The Czech-language search also includes a considerable amount of scanned personal correspondence; Havel's plays and poetry and other published texts, such as his letters to Olga, that also exist elsewhere in English translation; audio of Havel's radio appearances; some of Havel's older texts from the 1950s and 1960s; and a handful of other materials. Because the archival documents translated into English are largely from Havel's most public discussions of his views and beliefs, they are a logical place to begin our analysis of his understanding of the concept of responsibility. In a textual analysis of the Havelian oeuvre, a comparison of the

English-language translations of Havel's references to responsibility with their Czech counterparts indicates that there is little discrepancy in translation practices.

It is almost always the Czech word *odpovědnost* that is translated as "responsibility" in the English-language versions of documents. Throughout, Havel interprets responsibility as a deeply personal, individual, spiritual concept that underlies much of his overall philosophy and especially his thinking on the concept of power and on individuals in positions of power. In 1995, speaking at Harvard University, he states: "Regardless of where I begin my thinking about the problems facing our civilization, I always return to the theme of human responsibility, which seems incapable of keeping pace with civilization and preventing it from turning against the human race."[3] He repeats many times that the greatest task for the coming era was "a radical renewal of our sense of responsibility."[4]

However, Havel also frequently uses the word *spoluodpovědnost*, which is generally translated as "co-responsibility" or "shared responsibility." Decidedly, Havel does not mean "collective responsibility" when he discusses *spoluodpovědnost*; in fact, he very explicitly warns against the potential dangers of collective responsibility in its traditional sense, which he believed allows individuals to absolve themselves of responsibility and complicity under the assumption that someone else will take on the work of taking care of the collective good.[5] Speaking at the Oslo Conference on "The Anatomy of Hate" in August 1990, he goes so far as to say that such a society deprived of individual responsibilities is "a wonderful starting point for collective hatred," especially in its propensity to subscribe to the idea of collective "otherness."[6]

3   Václav Havel, "Harvard University," June 1995.
4   Václav Havel, "Harvard University," June 1995.
5   See for example, Václav Havel, "The Visit of German President Richard von Weizsäcker," March 1990, and Václav Havel, "Vilnius University," April 1996.
6   Václav Havel, "The Oslo Conference on 'The Anatomy of Hate'," August 1990.

Rather, Havel's idea of co-responsibility derives from individuals who realize their own full responsibility to their communities and their world. As Aviezer Tucker points out, this burden of co-responsibility—often expressed as responsibility to the transcendental order of Being, or to the world as a whole, is based on his own synthesis of Heidegger, Patočka and Levinas.[7] Individual and co-responsibility exist at various levels, which one can imagine as ever larger concentric circles emanating from each individual.[8] Havel discusses the responsibility of citizens to their local community and state, of political rulers to their citizens, of states to the world system, of people to their place in history and to future generations, and generally of humanity to the health and well-being of the planet. All these types of responsibility are still very personal and active; individual senses of responsibility make up the sense of shared responsibility.

Responsibility in philosophy: Havel's engagement

Havel's views on responsibility require contextualization. In terms of personal formation, Havel grew up in a prosperous First Republic home; his patrician father Václav expanded the family construction and property business while his uncle founded the Barrandov film studios. Václav and his brother Ivan were steeped in "the intellectual atmosphere of Masarykian humanism"—surrounded by good books, with parents devoted to their sons' well-being who were themselves involved in their communities through civil society engagement.[9] However, while Havel was indeed privileged, he was also painfully aware of his status—during his younger years as bourgeois in

---

7   See for example, Václav Havel, "A Joint Session to Congress," February 1990; Aviezer Tucker, *The Philosophy and Politics of Czech Dissidence from Patočka to Havel* (Pittsburgh: University of Pittsburgh Press), 176-177.

8   This formulation is indebted to David S. Danaher's use of frame analysis and his formulation of Havel's "circles of home"; see Danaher, *Reading Václav Havel*, especially 181-187.

9   Václav Havel, *Disturbing the Peace*, trans. Paul Wilson (New York: Vintage, 1990), 7. See also Michael Žantovský, *Havel: A Life* (New York: Grove, 2014), especially 15-24.

a village context, later as teenaged "class enemy" who was deemed unworthy of an academic education. In analyzing himself, Havel surmised that early experiences of exclusion and instability fostered a sense of absurdity, as well as antagonism toward undeserved advantage, social humiliation, and any form of indignity. Havel's own self-awareness, desire to bear witness, speak truth, and develop personal responsibility beyond oneself toward the world reflects his upbringing. Indeed, he acknowledged that "no one ever develops and achieves self-awareness in a vacuum, beyond all eras and systems. The period you grow up in and mature in always influences your thinking."[10] However, Havel was not alone in his resuscitation of responsibility as a theoretical concept and essential axiom.

In terms of later intellectual formation, Havel's deliberations can be situated within a late-20th century philosophical treatment of responsibility that includes Hans Jonas, Paul Ricoeur, Jan Patočka, and Emmanuel Levinas.[11] In turn Havel's work has influenced his interpreters, including, *inter alia*, Jean Bethke Elshtain, Martin Beck Matuštík, and Aviezer Tucker. Hans Jonas generated a renewed continental discussion of responsibility with his 1984 text *The Imperative of Responsibility: In Search of Ethics for the Technological Age*.[12] Jonas developed what might be called a demanding and environmentally sustainable categorical imperative of responsibility, which requires human action to be "compatible with the permanence of genuine human life," or to *not* act in such a manner that destroys the future possibility of life.[13] This extensive view of inter-generational responsibility aligns with Havel's views about responsibility for the environment.

---

10 Havel, *Disturbing the Peace*, 8.
11 Both Heidegger and Husserl loom large in the background of Havel's thought, but are largely mediated through the work of Levinas (especially Heidegger) and Patočka (especially Husserl).
12 Hans Jonas, *The Imperative of Responsibility: In Search of Ethics for the Technological Age* (Chicago: University of Chicago Press, 1984).
13 Hans Jonas, *Le principe responsabilité* (Paris: Cerf, 1995).

There are two lines of reasoning regarding responsibility in Paul Ricoeur's thought, one legal and one anthropological, and the latter is consonant with the predominant view in the Havelian canon. In contract law, responsibility is a legal obligation, requiring the parties to be fully competent in terms of ability (age, cognition) and also action (not under duress). Ignoring one's responsibility leads to a breach of legal obligation and liability. Anthropologically, and in moral philosophy, responsibility begins with immediate family, especially via the assumption of parental responsibility and providing physical and emotional sustenance for children. This responsibility does not require the bonds of social solidarity, trust, law, or expectations of reciprocity; it just *is*. Yet parental responsibility points to an inherent conceptual and social tension, the contradiction of both autonomous (free) action and the limitation of another's autonomy.[14] Both freedom and responsibility in this sense are fragile and limited. In Matuštík's view, Havel's approach to responsibility echoes both Fyodor Dostoevsky and Emmanuel Levinas in *Letters to Olga*: "responsibility establishes an asymmetrical ethical situation" that cannot "be preached, but merely borne."[15] There is no expectation of reciprocity. This conception, we submit, is similar to Ricoeur's anthropological responsibility but also, as Matuštík elaborates, to Patočka's sense of responsibility as an ethical response to existence and truth.

Havel's view of responsibility is also deeply influenced, as are many of his philosophical reflections, by Jan Patočka, especially Patočka's elaboration of the "care for the soul" and the "solidarity of the shaken"—both of which are undergirded by a thick notion of responsibility. For both Patočka and Havel, philosophy is not only an introspective activity, but a *vita activa* requiring courage and risk.

---

14 For an analysis of Jonas and Ricoeur on responsibility specifically on this point, see Yvon Pesqueux, "On the topic of responsibility," *Journal of Global Responsibility* 3:1 (2012), 25.
15 Václav Havel, *Letters to Olga*, letter 122; Martin Beck Matuštík, "'More than All the Others': Meditation on Responsibility," *Critical Horizons: A Journal of Philosophy and Social Theory* 8:1 (2007), 50.

"Care for the soul" demands personal responsibility and commitment and eschews nihilism and decadence. Moreover, care for the soul is beyond philosophizing or reflection, and implies "praxis" and a "specific target"—truth.[16] For Patočka, Socrates as an ideal and a prototype personifies care for the soul; for Havel, the individual citizen reclaiming responsibility and living in truth is paramount.[17] Both Havel and Patočka are acutely aware of both the historical and philosophical traumas of the preceding centuries—rapid industrialization, the two world wars, the political laboratory made of *Mitteleuropa* by the twin ideologies of fascism and authoritarian communism, the collapse of metaphysical certainty, the death of God. Yet the survival of culture, common humanity, authenticity, and decency depends upon recognizing and addressing these traumas head on, developing what Patočka calls the "solidarity of the shaken." Again, taking responsibility is paramount.

In *Letters to Olga*, Havel focuses on the importance of responsibility as a driving first principle, both in politics and philosophy. In one letter, he states that:

[...] the importance of the notion of human responsibility has grown in my meditations. It has begun to appear, with increasing clarity, as that fundamental point from which all identity grows and by which it stands or falls, it is the foundation, the root, the center of gravity, the constructional principle of the axis of identity, something like the "idea" that determines its degree and type.[18]

16 Arpád Szakolczai, "Thinking Beyond the East-West Divide Foucault, Patočka and the Care of the Self," *Social Research* 61:2 (1994), 07.
17 See especially Jan Patočka, *Plato and Europe*, trans. P. Lom (Stanford: Stanford University Press, 2002); Jan Patočka, *Heretical Essays in the Philosophy of History*, ed. J. Dodd, trans. E. Kohák (Chicago and LaSalle: Open Court, 1996). On responsibility and the connection to "care for the soul" and "solidarity of the shaken," see Ivan Chvatík, "The Responsibility of the 'Shaken': Jan Patočka and his 'Care for the Soul' in the 'Post-European' World," in "Jan Patočka and the Heritage of Phenomenology: Centenary Papers," eds. I. Chavtík and E. Abrams, *Phenomenology* 61 (2011), 263-279.
18 Havel, *Letters to Olga*, letter 62.

And later in the same letter:

[H]uman responsibility is precisely the agent by which one defines oneself as a person vis-à-vis the universe, that is, as the miracle of Being that one is [...] I would say that responsibility for oneself is a knife we use to carve our own inimitable features in the panorama of Being; it is the pen with which we write into the history of Being that story of the fresh creation of the world that each new human existence always is.[19]

Havel's elaboration is similar to philosopher Hannah Arendt's statement in *The Human Condition*, which in turn has later echoes in Paul Ricoeur's view of human birth as ontologically engendering responsibility:

The miracle that saves the world, the realm of human affairs, from its normal, "natural" ruin is ultimately the fact of natality, in which the faculty of action is ontologically rooted. It is, in other words, the birth of new men [*sic*] and the new beginning, the action they are capable of by virtue of being born. Only the full experience of this capacity can bestow upon human affairs faith and hope, those two essential characteristics of human existence which Greek antiquity ignored altogether, discounting the keeping of faith as a very uncommon and not too important virtue and counting hope among the evils of illusion in Pandora's box.[20]

To bring Arendt to Havel, the *action* she describes, the *vita activa* she prescribes, reclaiming agency and exercising power in the sense of acting together in concert, is exactly what we call the "thick" notion of responsibility and co-responsibility that Havel suggests. Havel requires we take action and assume responsibility. But he also argues

---

19 Havel, *Letters to Olga*, letter 62.
20 Hannah Arendt, *The Human Condition* (Chicago and London: University of Chicago Press, 1974), 247.

this sense of responsibility is something we *deserve* by virtue of our humanity—necessary for our well-being so we are not reduced to a set of skills that can be replaced via robots or artificial intelligence.[21]

In Tucker's reading, Havel parts with Heidegger on morality and with Kant on the absolutism of categorical imperatives. "Responsibility for Being is the basis of absolute, nonsituational, deontological, non-anthropomorphic morality," Tucker writes, effectively the opposite of a philosophical consequentialism.[22] As with Matuštík, Tucker credits Havel's inspiration to Levinas, especially his "ethics of responsibility to Being"—as is evident here:

> [E]ither the primordial, "irresponsible" "responsible for everything" gradually takes on—through its existence-in-the-world, space and time— the dimensions of the responsibility of the "I" for itself and responsibility "toward" (in other words, becomes "the responsibility of man for his own responsibility") and thus leads man to a permanent, and permanently deepening, relation with the integrity of Being—or else man devalues such Responsibility, retreats from it, renounces it (with the help of various self-deceptions) and replaces it with a utilitarianism that is completely tied to the demand of his existence-in-the-world. His morality is then the morality of the "hypothetical imperative" (for instance, he cares for— including those who have yet to come—only to the extent that is useful and practical within the terms of his own existence-in-the-world).[23]

Already we see Havel's critique of consequentialism—when responsibility is reduced to a utilitarian calculus, we are on a slippery moral slope.

In a different vein, Jean Bethke Elshtain reflects on Havel to resolve the age-old philosophical contradiction between theory and

---

21 Havel, *Disturbing the Peace*, 15.
22 Tucker, *The Philosophy and Politics of Czech Dissidence from Patočka to Havel*, 155.
23 Havel, *Letters to Olga*, letter 135.

practice, *theoria* and *praxis*. For Elshtain, Havel's approach to theory and practice offer an alternative to the anti-foundationalism of Richard Rorty. Havel is concerned with immediacy—both enacting and performing political thought, but also (ironically and seriously) re-enacting by taking responsibility for the past cognizant of the dangers of repeating it.[24] And here we begin to see the connection between not only theory and practice, but politics and theater. In Elshtain's reading of Havel, "politics is the sphere of concrete responsibility; just as theater is the concrete institution in which characters enact positions."[25] Rejecting the binary of intentionality and consequentialism, Havel offers narrative and character development. Not unsurprisingly, Havel's most famous essay offers a parable about, not a philosophical entrée to, power. In "The Power of the Powerless," Havel is silent on the greengrocer's deliberation to remove the sign from his shop window (something simply "snaps") and his injunction to "life in truth" is maddeningly vague as well. Still, the story resonates, and responsibility is the necessary corollary if any actions toward living in truth result.

Responsibility: Havel's evolution before 1989

Havel was never a "professional" philosopher in the vein of Kant, Patočka, or Ricoeur. He was in a different tradition, in keeping with Marx and Machiavelli, a *spectateur-engagé*, neither solely witness nor activist but both. He was a philosopher as a side hustle to his day job, and that day job kept shifting from theater to politics, and often included both. Particularly after assuming public office in 1990, his philosophical reflections on responsibility are often embedded in

---

24   Jean Bethke Elshtain, "A Performer of Political Thought: Václav Havel on Freedom and Responsibility," in *Theory and Practice*, eds. I. Shapiro and J. Wagner DeCew (New York: New York University Press, 1995), 468.
25   Elshtain, "A Performer of Political Thought: Václav Havel on Freedom and Responsibility," 470. For more on "theater" as a key word, see Day in this volume.

his commentary on national and global affairs. And if Havel is well known for his elaboration of two important philosophical concepts, however, it is usually not responsibility but his discussion of truth and power. Indeed, power and truth are the subjects, respectively, of his most famous essay, "The Power of the Powerless," and his personal motto—"truth and love must prevail over lies and hatred." Yet without understanding responsibility, you cannot really fully understand either truth or power, nor Havel's contribution to all three. These three concepts are a kind of holy trinity in the Havelian oeuvre. Much like thesis, antithesis, and synthesis are to a discussion of Hegel's dialectic; and emotion, chance, and reason are to Clausewitz's formulation of war as politics by other means; or land, labor, and capital are to the work of Karl Marx.

Throughout his collected works, Havel weaves together power, truth, and responsibility.

Already in the archive's earliest translated document referring specifically to responsibility, Havel's 1975 letter to Gustáv Husák, the connection between power and responsibility in Havel's thinking is evident, and this theme continues throughout the documents. Havel emphasizes in this letter that political leaders have both the power and responsibility to determine the climate and conditions of their countries, but that this responsibility must never be absolute. It must be shared with the public; citizens must feel that they, individually, have responsibility for their communities through their daily actions. He warns that by suppressing the vibrancy of ordinary civil society and protecting the absolute power of the leadership, Husák and his government were effectively destroying the spirit of society, and that they should have more carefully considered their historic responsibility to the long-term well-being of their country.[26] Of course,

---

26 Václav Havel, "Dear Dr. Husák," trans. unidentified, in *Open Letters: Selected Prose 1965–1990* (London: Faber and Faber, 1991). For more on "civil society" as a key term, see Brinton in this volume.

Havel elaborates further on the concept of power and especially the power of ordinary people in "The Power of the Powerless," in which responsibility and its relation to power also explicitly appear approximately 30 times. In these earlier works, Havel's thinking on responsibility is very clearly tied to his experiences living in what he called a late totalitarian system. In his 1987 essay, "Stories and Totalitarianism," he laments how advanced totalitarianism spurs the rapid decline of individuality and how its blandness and uniformity lead to rampant irresponsibility. When the centralized system wields all the power, individuals feel helpless, and the concept of individual responsibility vanishes, because ordinary people feel that they have no power to effect change and shape their societies.[27]

To the extent there is a dissident "program" outlined by Havel—and here we do not constrain dissidence or dissent to Central and Eastern Europe in the 1970s and 1980s but very much as an ongoing phenomenon—it cannot be encapsulated only as "living in truth" or the "power of the powerless" but must include "responsibility to and for the world."[28] This requires indefatigable commitment and is morally and physically exhausting. The bar is high—and this is one of the deepest criticisms of Havel—that not everyone has the necessary human capital or personal resources to "live in truth," take responsibility, as well as both challenge and assume power directly. This kind of responsibility is purposefully discomforting. This is at the heart of David Ost's condemnation of Havel—for the resource-weak, living in truth is too tall a price to pay.[29] But here is

---

27   Václav Havel, "Stories and Totalitarianism," trans. Paul Wilson, in *Open Letters: Selected Prose 1965–1990* (London: Faber and Faber, 1991).
28   Václav Havel, "On Evasive Thinking," trans. Paul Wilson, in *Open Letters: Selected Prose* (London and Boston: Faber and Faber, 1991), 194; quoted in James Krapfl and Barbara J. Falk (eds.), "The Power of the Powerless Today," special issue of *East European Politics and Societies and Cultures* 32:2 (2018).
29   David Ost, "The Sham, and the Damage, of 'Living in Truth'," in "The Power of the Powerless Today," James Krapfl and Barbara J. Falk (eds.), special issue of *East European Politics and Societies and Cultures* 32:2 (2018), 301-309.

where we disagree with Ost—Havel never suggests that we all need to live in truth or take responsibility in exactly the same way. Again, the greengrocer is a parable, not a recipe. Resistance and dissent are a continuum, static in neither time nor space. A local struggle to improve working conditions or wrest some respect on the job can result in meaningful change without calling out the boss or demanding regime change—acting "as if" those in power cared and could respond and developing a strategy around piecemeal amelioration. In the Czechoslovak context this is akin to Masarykian *drobná práce*, the small-scale work of building the political community.[30] However, acting "as if" is decidedly not about "state capture" or the grandiose assumption that sweeping political and even institutional reform can fix challenges that are within the realm of political culture, society, or external in nature—as the Soviet model was propped up by force or the threat thereof before 1989. Havel's approach to the powerless, obtaining some measure of power, is bottom-up and happens in and through what Václav Benda, his Chartist contemporary and prison mate, called the *parallel polis*.[31]

In the same way, ideology obscures power; it allows us a convenient "out" in terms of taking responsibility, not simply responsibility for living in truth, but also for living a lie. Ideology, or just lazy ignorance, makes us more comfortable in our unquestioning obedience and functions pragmatically as a legitimizing principle, even offering the illusion of "identity, dignity, and morality."[32] In living a lie, you don't need to *actually accept* the lie as a lie—just your life

---

30 Masaryk believed the moral, metaphysical, and practical work was critical to building (literally) a democracy; small-scale work required participation and functioned as an instrument of social levelling. See H. Gordon Skilling, *T.G. Masaryk: Against the Current, 1882-1914* (University Park: Pennsylvania State University Press, 1994).
31 See both Václav Benda, the original text of "The Parallel *Polis*," as well as his responses to an *anketa* forwarded by H. Gordon Skilling in H. Gordon Skilling and Paul Wilson (eds.), *Civic Freedom in Central Europe: Voices from Czechoslovakia* (Houndmills, Basingstoke, Hampshire and London: Macmillan, 1991), 35-41 and 48-56.
32 Václav Havel, "The Power of the Powerless," chapter III.

as it is. Thus, Havel famously states: "individuals confirm the system, fulfill the system, make the system, *are* the system."[33] In Havel's play *The Memorandum*, managing director Gross engages in exactly this behaviour—by accepting the logic of his slick underling Ballas and the imposition of the obfuscatory "new" and "rational" language Ptydepe, by wanting to "salvage this and that"—he actually confirms the system and, intentionally or not, promotes the lie.[34] Even when later exonerated, he cannot take responsibility or act courageously. This is also effectively Havel's criticism of Alexander Dubček upon signing the Moscow Protocols—hoping to recapture some gains, but in reality, because "[t]he leadership made concession after concession in the hopes of salvaging something [...] all it did was saw off the very limb it was sitting on."[35]

In his essay, "On Evasive Thinking," Havel discusses how false contextualization, constant equivocation, what he calls "vacuous verbal balancing acts"—which today we might call media efforts to include "balance" in reporting where none exists—contributes simultaneously to the effectiveness of ideology and indolence, robbing an individual of agency or even the basis for evidence-based analysis and reflection. For how can there be balance when one side is unhinged from any connection to rationality, fact, or truth, however defined? In Havel's words: "When we lose touch with reality, we inevitably lose the ability to influence reality effectively."[36] For Havel, if there is no agency, there is no responsibility.

33 Havel, "The Power of the Powerless," chapter IV.
34 Václav Havel, *The Memorandum*, trans. Vera Blackwell (New York: Grove Weidenfeld, 1980), 35.
35 Havel, *Disturbing the Peace*, 110.
36 Havel, "On Evasive Thinking," 14.

Responsibility: Havel's evolution after 1989

After the collapse of Communism in 1989, Havel's speeches turn more concretely to the politics of the here and now, and how responsibility is inextricably interlinked with freedom and democracy. In his "New Year's Address to the Nation" on January 1, 1990, Havel discusses the legacies of the communist period, including a weakened community and moral atmosphere. He argues that everyone must accept some measure of responsibility for the world in which they lived under Communism, and therefore for reviving a vibrant civil society moving forward. He especially emphasizes that governments cannot achieve much on their own and that "freedom and democracy include participation and therefore responsibility from us all."[37] Later that same month, in an address to the Polish Sejm and Senate in Warsaw, he further discusses, now liberated from the dark repression of totalitarian rule, an ambitious new presidential program:

[T]o bring into politics a sense of culture, of moral responsibility, of humanity, of humility and respect for the fact that there is something higher above us, that our behavior is not lost in the black hole of time but is written down and evaluated somewhere, that we have neither the right nor the reason to think that we understand everything and have license to do anything we wish.[38]

From this passage we see Havel believed not only that leaders are responsible to their citizens and communities in the immediate sense,

---

37 Václav Havel, "New Year's Address to the Nation," January 1990. Havel returned to the same theme on the tenth anniversary of November 17, 1989, linking the fall of communism not only to "liberation of millions of oppressed and humiliated human beings" but also to the resurrection of "a sense of responsibility"; see Václav Havel, "Address on the Day of Students' Fight for Freedom and Democracy," November 1999.
38 Václav Havel, "The Polish Sejm and Senate," January 1990.

but also that the responsibility of all people to the global community of the present and the future is equally as important.

In his 1994 "New Year's Address to the Nation," he further elaborates that "democracy is a system based on trust in the human sense of responsibility," and that politicians should "think less about making their mark and belittling others and more about the common good."[39] Having the power of leadership places a particular individual burden due to that person's ability to affect so many people's lives far into the future. Thus, Havel is adamant that "politics should principally be the domain of people with a heightened sense of responsibility."[40]

By the end of his presidency, Havel confidently describes how his political activity was rooted in the concepts of humility and common human decency, growing from the tradition of Czech leaders and thinkers such as Jan Amos Komenský (Comenius) and Tomáš Garrigue Masaryk. His philosophy and approach to leadership crisply focus on responsibility or "politics as the practice of responsibility toward the world, not merely as a technique of power; politics as true service to one's fellow citizens and their descendants."[41] Havel's thinking on responsibility throughout these documents is extremely conscious of the long term, of how the past affects the present and the present the future, and of how people can never know the impact their words and actions will have once they are no longer alive themselves.

Havel's speeches also display a deep commitment to learning from the past and understanding how it affects the present. In particular, Havel references the traumatic impact of two historical catastrophes repeatedly as key turning points and lessons: the 1938 Munich Agreement that resulted in the dismemberment of Czechoslovakia,

---

39 Václav Havel, "New Year's Address to the Nation," January 1994.
40 Václav Havel, "Asahi Hall," 1992.
41 Václav Havel, "The National Prize of Germany," 2003.

and the Holocaust and the destruction of European Jewry. With respect to Munich, Havel seeks to demonstrate, more broadly, the irresponsibility and short-sightedness of appeasement policies, as well as potential devastating long-term consequences. He warns against repeating a historical inability "to recognize emerging evil in time," which he believes grew out of an "absence of a wider sense of responsibility for the world."[42] Regarding the Holocaust, Havel also emphasizes how an evasion and erasure of personal responsibility made the Nazi *Endlösung* possible. He describes the Holocaust as an event so horribly devastating that he believes it "compels us to perceive the true weight of our responsibility for this world" in a way few other historical events have the ability to do.[43] In a speech given at a memorial concert for Czechoslovak Holocaust victims, Havel brings particular attention once again to the individual and to how "thousands of anonymous, non-homicidal anti-Semites helped send their fellow citizens to the gas chambers" through all sorts of daily, seemingly minor actions that collectively created the environment in which such atrocities could occur with impunity. He finishes this speech with an appeal for people *not* to instinctively avoid what shocks them but to face it head on and repeatedly in an effort to maintain a consciousness of the "universal nature of [...] responsibility."[44]

More generally, Havel often speaks about how central Europeans have been geographically and historically at the centre of conflicts spurred by deeply rooted prejudices, national and otherwise. Only by remembering these tragic events, facing them head-on, and working to overcome their root causes, can Europeans set themselves on a new path leading into the twenty-first century, founded in "mutual understanding and genuine trust."[45] At a dinner in honour of German chancellor Helmut Kohl in 1992, he waxes poetically on

42 Václav Havel, "The George Washington University," 1993.
43 Václav Havel, "A Concert in Memory of Czechoslovak Holocaust Victims," 1991.
44 Havel, "A Concert in Memory of Czechoslovak Holocaust Victims," 1991.
45 Václav Havel, "Dinner in Honor of German Chancellor Helmut Kohl," 1992.

"a historical chance to make the ancient dream of Europe come true," one which rejects "alienating ideologies, nationalism, intolerance and a sense of superiority, a Europe unified in its differences."[46] He expresses his belief that "an aspect of our common sense of responsibility for Europe" is to make this dream come true.[47] He puts these arguments into specific practice throughout the 1990s in the context of the Yugoslav wars, calling on the Council of Europe in June 1995 to condemn the violence in the Balkans and play its part in bringing an end to the conflict that went against all the values upon which the Council was founded.[48] Later that year, speaking in Prague, he repeats that the cult of collectivism at the root of the Yugoslav wars could not co-exist with a society based on a strong sense of individual human responsibility, essential to a healthy and free democracy.[49] During the first NATO summit that the Czech Republic joined as a new member of the alliance in 1999, Havel again spoke of combatting ethnic hatred and fanaticism—and in so doing defended the bombing campaign in Kosovo, a divisive topic within the country at the time.[50]

Throughout his political career, Havel remained a staunch supporter of the European Union (EU), partially as an antidote to dangerous particularism and nationalism. He expressed concern regarding the potential slide from patriotism to dangerous nationalism, which he saw as a form of personal and collective irresponsibility. In 1999 Havel points out that, while the Czechs were celebrating their victory in the world ice hockey championship, in "an outburst

46 Havel, "Dinner in Honor of German Chancellor Helmut Kohl," 1992.
47 Havel, "Dinner in Honor of German Chancellor Helmut Kohl," 1992.
48 Havel, "Inauguration of the Human Rights Building," 1995.
49 Havel, "Conclusion of the Month of Bosnia and Herzegovina in Prague," 1995.
50 NATO's Operation Allied Force consisted of air strikes against Serbia to halt the campaign of ethnic cleansing in Kosovo and lasted from March 24, 1999 to June 10, 1999. Havel's most notable speech defending NATO's actions and pledging Czech support was his address before the US Congress on April 23, 1999. Again, Havel contextualized his defense of NATO within the larger context of "responsible conduct.".

of a darkly archetypal love of our own tribe" a "few people of a different colour of skin" were beaten up.[51] Indeed, responsibility for Europe and its past is interwoven in Havel's oeuvre with avoiding narrow patriotism, a form of "self-love [and] rejection of all that is different" while embracing "wise and responsible engagement."[52] He also understood the paradoxes inherent in European "civilization"—which once irresponsibly and aggressively imposed its values on the planet, but in the postwar era sought to mend fences and repair the neighbourhood—effectively eliminating violence as a means of political action. In a 2000 speech to the European Parliament, Havel states:

> The technical civilisation which now extends all over our planet has its earliest origins on European soil, and was decisively influenced by the Euro-Atlantic sphere of civilisation. Europe thus has a special *responsibility* for the condition of this civilisation. But this *responsibility* must never again take the form of a forcible exportation of our own values, ideas or properties into the rest of the world.[53]

Unlike some leaders who engage in double discourse, with contradictory messages for foreign versus domestic audiences, Havel is consistent. In his advice to the Czech Chamber of Deputies the same year, he acknowledges Europe's "forcible exportation of its culture, its religion, its civilizational values to the rest of the world" was an "erroneous path" while highlighting European responsibility for external threats and challenges.[54] He was certainly no advocate of "Fortress Europe." Later he would call for "reinforced

---

51 Václav Havel, "Address in acceptance of Open Society Prize," 1999.
52 Havel, "The National Day of the Czech Republic," 1999.
53 Václav Havel, "Address before the Members of the European Parliament," 2000, emphasis in the original.
54 Václav Havel, "Address to the Chamber of Deputies of the Parliament of the Czech Republic," 2000.

responsibility"—for "unifying, rich and advanced Europe" as a whole but especially for newer EU states to recall not only advantages of membership but also their full share of responsibility as well.[55] His statements form a sharp rebuke to contemporary Central European illiberal Euroskeptics such as Viktor Orbán who bash Brussels but happily accept EU development funds.[56]

While president, Havel also repeatedly discussed responsibility with reference to global politics; his speeches keep pace with debates from the mid-1990s regarding the scale and rapidity of technological, social, cultural, economic and political globalization. Havel was not anti-globalization but advocated an all-encompassing global responsibility on the part of citizens, states, and regions for increased global cooperation, reform of the United Nations, as well as participation in multilateral fora, transnational trade, and treaty regimes. Yet Havel's warning regarding speed and depth of globalization surpassing human capacity and humility to morally cope with the consequences is prescient: "Globalization in the fields of information and business is not accompanied by a growing sense of global responsibility. Conscience appears to be limping behind science, research and technology."[57]

Co-responsibility: *spoluodpovědnost*

Spoluodpovědnost, the shared burden of responsibility, is invoked time and again with respect to membership in the North Atlantic

---

55 Václav Havel, "Opening of the Conference 'Enlarged Europe—Reinforced Responsibility'," 2004. The same sentiment, for a growing rather than a diminished European responsibility, is expressed in Václav Havel, "European *Responsibility*, a Common Project (Voice)," *Project Voice*, October 10, 2005.
56 See *inter alia* Paul Lendvai, "The Transformer: Orbán's Evolution and Hungary's Demise," *Foreign Affairs* 98:5 (September/October 2019), 44-54 and Ivan Krastev, "Eastern Europe's Illiberal Revolution: The Long Road to Democratic Decline," *Foreign Affairs* 97:3 (May/June 2018), 49-56.
57 Havel, "New Year's Address," 2000.

Treaty Organization (NATO).[58] Speaking to the Czech Chamber of Deputies in 1993 about seeking NATO membership, Havel emphasizes that the position of the Czech Republic in the center of Europe on the border of West and East created "a particularly acute awareness of [Czech] co-responsibility for European security."[59] He stresses throughout his years as the leader of the country, as well as afterwards, that joining NATO and other organizations would bring greater safety and possibilities for peace to the Czech Republic, but also prove the country's willingness to assume its share of responsibility for the state of the continent and the world as a whole, essential in an increasingly globalizing and insecure world.

One arena stands out in the Havelian canon regarding his frequent invocations of global responsibility: the Forum 2000 initiative founded by Havel together with Japanese philanthropist Yohei Sasakawa and Nobel Peace Prize Laureate and Holocaust survivor Elie Wiesel. From 1997 onward, annual conferences organized by the Forum 2000 Foundation have attracted global "norm entrepreneurs" and participants "whose common denominative is experience with bearing responsibility."[60] As Havel states in the 1999 opening ceremony of Forum 2000: "[A]ll the Forums have had one thing in common, that is, our concern for the world of today; the search for the sources of new responsibility for the world,

---

58   Havel, "Address at the Congress of the United States of America," 1999. At the time of the signing of the North Atlantic Treaty, Havel emphasized the importance of the Czech Republic meeting "our share of responsibility [*odpovědnost*] for the freedom of nations, human rights, democratic values and peace on our continent" ("Message of Václav Havel, the President of the Czech Republic, on the Occasion of the Signing the Instrument of Accession of the Czech Republic to the North Atlantic Treaty," 1999). However, the theme of co-responsibility [*spoluodpovědnost*] is reiterated as undergirding the principle of collective defence (Article V of the Washington Treaty), including in his address to the meeting of the North Atlantic Council in Prague in November 2002.
59   Václav Havel, "Address to the Chamber of Deputies of the Parliament of the Czech Republic," 1993.
60   "Background," Forum 2000 Foundation, accessed August 2, 2019, https://www.forum2000.cz/en/about.

and the responsibility that could protect our world from the threats that are looming over us."[61] One year later, Havel reiterates the "responsibility-mission" of Forum 2000: "[I]n this era of Globalization it is most important to foster a global *responsibility* of man for this world, of awareness of belonging to humanity, of caring for the world on which we live [emphasis in original]." For Havel this "elementary *responsibility* for the world" is a "moral minimum," a critical undertaking for common humanity.[62] By linking responsibility to humanity, Havel provides the basis for rights and obligations we have by virtue of being human—the conceptual foundation for understanding and enacting human rights. However, Forum 2000 conferences have not simply resulted in hortatory platitudes regarding greater responsibility but include concrete projects and initiatives. In 2017, under the auspices of Forum 2000, the International Coalition for Democratic Renewal (ICDR), a "group of intellectuals, activists, and politicians, concerned with the expansion of power and influence of authoritarian regimes and the simultaneous weakening of democratic systems from within" issued the Prague Appeal, addressing declining living standards, anti-immigration sentiment, "post-truth" politics, and the erosion of support for liberal democracy.[63]

Havel's focus on the shared global responsibility for the world and the well-being of future generations quite logically translates into genuine and deep concern for the health of the environment, well before a global consensus emerged on the impact of climate change.[64] As early as 1984, in his essay "Politics and Conscience," Havel extends his concept of responsibility to the environment and

---

61 Václav Havel, "Gala Opening of the International Forum 2000 Conference," 1999.
62 Václav Havel, "Opening of the Working Sessions of the Forum 2000 Conference," 2000.
63 "International Coalition for Democratic Renewal," Forum 2000 Foundation, accessed August 2, 2019, https://www.forum2000.cz/en/projects/coalition-for-democratic-renewal.
64 Minimally, this global consensus solidified with the 2007 report of the Intergovernmental Panel on Climate Change. See https://www.ipcc.ch/report/ar4/syr/; accessed August 2, 2019.

the ecosphere as a whole.[65] Later in his political career, as well as afterwards as a private citizen, Havel focused increasingly explicitly on climate change and other ecological concerns. In 1997, speaking at Taras Shevchenko National University in Kyiv, he cites the nuclear disaster in Chernobyl as a major warning of human innovation exposing humanity to "unprecedented dangers unless we somehow try to deepen our responsibility for this world," lamenting the arrogance and political interests that led to this disaster with such enormous ecological and human costs.[66] In 2002, in the wake of major flooding in Prague and elsewhere in the country, he writes forcefully in an article for the *Financial Times* about the importance of humans accepting responsibility for their actions, specifically for "the often over-extravagant development of our civilisation" and "long-term attacks on the natural fabric of the landscape."[67] In this article, he pleads for us to be cognizant of the damage we have done and continue to do to the world in which we live, as well as to "learn about the impact of our activities on the environment and to draw the right lessons from what we learn," lest we allow ourselves to live through avoidable and increasingly extreme natural disasters. In his 2003 "New Year's Address," he hopes that the lesson learned from the floods would be that "we are not the masters of the world, the universe, our planet and nature, but are only a part of them," and that it is imperative to always consider the long-term impacts of human development on the well-being of the planet and future generations.[68]

While accepting the Mahatma Gandhi Peace Prize in India, Havel continued this plea to consider humanity's long-term responsibility to our planet, emphasizing that, while large corporations may

65 Václav Havel, "Politics and Conscience," trans. Erazim Kohák and Roger Scruton, in *Open Letters: Selected Writings 1965-1990* (New York: Vintage, 1992).
66 Václav Havel, "Taras Shevchenko National University," 1997.
67 Václav Havel, "Lessons from Prague," *The Financial Times*, August 21, 2002.
68 Havel, "New Year's Address," 2003.

have the most damaging effects on the environment, it is the behaviour of ordinary citizens that allows these impersonal giants to
continue their destructive activity. In 2007, he wrote about climate
change for the *International Herald Tribune*, calling for increased
"education, ecological training and ethics," for people to take climate change more seriously, and to consider the responsibility of
current generations to take care of the planet for the prosperity of
future generations.[69] Here is where he echoes the multigenerational
environmental responsibility of Hans Jonas. Even when discussing
such a global and all-encompassing issue, his focus is constantly on
individual responsibility, and on how the collective actions of individuals have the ability to effect great change.

One of the last areas addressed by Havel, now acting as a global
statesman and norm entrepreneur rather than a political officehold-
er, is the UN's commitment to the Responsibility to Protect (R2P).
Given his previous positions and commitments, R2P was a natural
fit for Havel. The underlying principle of R2P is that, while retain-
ing sovereignty, when a state fails to protect its own citizens from
genocide, war crimes, ethnic cleansing and crimes against humanity, the international community has a responsibility to step in, first
to prevent such mass atrocity violence, to assist states in meeting
these obligations and finally, and only as a last resort, to intervene
to protect civilians when a state manifestly fails to provide such
protection.[70] Havel was heartened by the "clear and unequivocal"
commitment made by the United Nations 2005 World Summit to
R2P, and together with Archbishop Desmond Tutu he co-authored
an introduction to an edited collection by Jared Genser and Irwin

---

69   Václav Havel, "The Planet is not at risk. We are," *International Herald Tribune*, September 25,
2007.
70   For more information, see United Nations Office on Genocide Prevention and the
Responsibility to Protect, "Background," available at https://www.un.org/en/genocideprevention
/about-responsibility-to-protect.shtml, last accessed August 28, 2019.

Cotler on the topic.[71] Yet Havel was not always discerning in his enthusiasm for humanitarian intervention. He backed the US-led coalition in 2003 War in Iraq and in 2011 supported Western military action in Libya. He did not live long enough to weigh in on the much-criticized "mission creep" that attended NATO's Operation Unified Protector in Libya or how the invasion of Iraq facilitated the growth of *Daesh* or ISIS.[72] We can only surmise that Havel would have continued to both follow and intervene in these debates and would not have shied away from the challenges of mixed motives for intervention, or hypocrisy of decisive intervention in some cases (Libya) but not others (Darfur, Syria).

Conclusion

Havel's views on responsibility continue to matter because his work resonates with relevance to contemporary political and social life, both globally and locally. In addressing the dehumanizing and omnipresent power of communist regimes and generally all forms of what he calls "anonymous, impersonal and inhuman power—the power of ideologies, systems, apparat, bureaucracy, artificial languages and political languages"—Havel suggests in "Politics and Conscience" that we each take responsibility to live in truth.[73] Responsibility implied resistance and dissent then, and it does so now, and must

---

71 Václav Havel and Desmond M. Tutu, "Preface," in *The Responsibility to Protect: The Promise of Stopping Mass Atrocities in Our Time*, eds. Jared Genser and Irwin Cotler (Oxford and New York: Oxford University Press, 2012). There is a burgeoning literature on R2P, beginning with the 2001 report of the International Commission on Intervention and State Sovereignty that "birthed" the concept. For an excellent overview, see Aidan Hehir, *Humanitarian Intervention: An Introduction* (Basingstoke: Palgrave Macmillan, 2013). On recent literature and the debates involved, see Barbara J. Falk and Sara Skinner, "The Responsibility to Protect: A Normative Shift from Words to Action?" *International Peacekeeping* 23:3 (2016), 1-13.
72 See Aidan Hehir and Robert Murray, eds., *Libya: The Responsibility to Protect and the Future of Humanitarian Intervention* (Houndmills, Basingstoke: Macmillan, 2013), Jessica Stern and J.M. Berger, *ISIS: The State of Terror* (New York: HarperCollins, 2015).
73 Havel, "Politics and Conscience," 267.

include among its targets "consumption, advertising, technology, or cliché"—the extent to which these modes and methods deny the limits of the natural world.[74] In a passage outlining what he means by "antipolitics," Havel echoes again a Kantian commitment to deontological rather than utilitarian ethics, as well as the Aristotelian ideal of practical morality (which he echoed again later by inverting Aristotle with his speech and later book of the same name, *The Art of the Impossible*). His "responsible politics" (our phraseology) is based on "practical morality, service to the truth, as essentially human and humanly measured care for our fellow humans."[75]

By focusing on building a civic culture based on human rights, economic justice, and stewardship of the environment, Havel exhorts the EU to "revive the tradition of responsibility for the world that its culture once helped to articulate."[76] These are not quaint or empty words—the European project was birthed as a result of two catastrophic world wars and is worth defending. It remains the great example of pooled sovereignty, neither a post-national state nor simply a compendium of treaties, that allows for multiple *and* shared identities, as well as collective economic and social action. In a speech delivered to George Washington University on April 22, 1993, soon after the Velvet Divorce, Havel's words resonate profoundly as a warning for our current moment:

In a situation where one thing has collapsed and something new does not yet exist, many people feel hollow and frustrated. The state is a fertile ground for phenomena such as scapegoat-hunting, radicalism of all kinds, and the need to hide behind the anonymity of a group, whether socially or ethnically based. It encourages hatred of the world, self-affirmation at all costs, the feeling that everything is now permitted, and the unparalleled

74 Havel, "Politics and Conscience," 267
75 Havel, "Politics and Conscience," 269.
76 Václav Havel, *To the Castle and Back*, trans. Paul Wilson (New York and Toronto: Alfred A. Knopf, 2007), 307.

flourishing of selfishness that goes along with this. It gives rise to the search for a common and identifiable enemy, to political extremism, to the most primitive cult of consumerism, to a carpetbagging morality, stimulated by the historically unprecedented restructuring of property relations, and so on and on.[77]

In the destabilizing aftermath of the 2009 global financial crisis; the widening gap between the very wealthy and the rest of humanity; an increasing rise in xenophobia, anti-Semitism, and Islamophobia; cultural narcissism and casual cruelty fostered by reality television, social media and polarizing political leaders, these words still matter. Havel was keenly aware of the potential for violence stoked by hatred at times of political instability and transition.

While advocating globalization involving both integration and decentralization to a local and human scale, Havel continued to warn about "various nationalisms, fundamentalisms, or fanaticisms, be they ethnic, religious or ideological."[78] From the same 2001 speech, entitled "Europe's New Democracies: Leadership and *Responsibility*," Havel spoke about how the "information revolution enhances our global interconnection and eliminates all censorship; at the same time, however, it opens up a vast expanse of human *irresponsibility*."[79] Irresponsibility, for Havel, involved "pandering to the masses," and "politics that opportunistically adapts to the broad

---

77 Havel, "George Washington University," 1993.
78 Havel does not use the term "glocalization" but his attention to the simultaneity of universal and particular, as well as global social processes and practices, adapted locally and attentive to local diversity, are in keeping with the discussions of glocalization in sociology in the 1990s. See Roland Robertson, *Globalization: Social Theory and Global Culture* (London: Sage, 1992) and Barry Wellman and Keith Hampton, "Living Networked On and Offline," *Contemporary Sociology* 28:6 (November 1999), 648-654.
79 Havel, "Address at the Conference 'Europe's New Democracies: Leadership and Responsibility'," 2001. In his "Message to the Representatives of World's Religions" at Prague's St. Vitus's Cathedral on October 16, 2001, he called his version of globalization a "globalization of good" uniting "people who feel responsibility for the future of humankind on this planet" linking responsibility, globalization, and environmental sustainability.

and colourful spectrum of prejudices held by the majority."[80] Havel did not live to see the rise of populist illiberalism, but he certainly foresaw *how* such a narrowing of attitudes given so *much* accessible information could be possible. To extend Havel's analysis, the internet and social media (and their underlying algorithms) have destabilized existing democratic structures, weakened truth, and diluted our collective capacity for deliberative discourse and responsible action.

Returning to our argument that power, truth, and responsibility form a holy trinity in the Havelian canon, the powerless many can have power *only if* political action is infused with conscience, morality, and even a modicum of "living in truth." However, "living in truth" only works if the ongoing *living* happens, and that is the process of claiming and reclaiming political agency and the absolute necessity of taking responsibility for ourselves, our political systems, and our planet. It is the *only* solution possible for 21st-century responsible politics.

---

80 Havel, "The National Prize of Germany," 2003.

INDIFFERENCE: *APATIE, LHOSTEJNOST*
David S. Danaher

> Paradoxically, though, this indifference [*lhostejnost*] has become
> an active social force. Is it not plain indifference [*lhostejnost*],
> rather than fear, that brings many to the voting booth, to meetings,
> to membership in official organizations? Is not the political support
> enjoyed by the regime to a large degree simply a matter of routine,
> of habit, of automatism, of laziness behind which lies nothing
> but total resignation? Participation in political rituals in which
> no one believes is pointless, but it does ensure a quiet life—and
> would it be any less pointless not to participate? One would gain
> nothing, and lose the quiet life in the bargain.
>
> — Václav Havel, "Dear Dr. Husák"[1]

Introduction

In this chapter, I treat the concept of "indifference" as a key word in
Havel's thought from two perspectives. The first involves tracing the
features of Havelian indifference in texts where the concept is lexically represented (in his essays, speeches, letters, and his memoir)
and also in those texts where the concept plays a central role without being lexically present (his plays). The second perspective raises
the necessary question of translation equivalency with regard to the
first set of texts: how are the Czech terms that Havel uses rendered
into English by professional translators, and do these translations
communicate a meaning equivalent to the meaning of the original
Czech words?[2] I will argue that these two perspectives are related

---

1   Václav Havel, "Dear Dr. Husák," trans. unidentified, in *Open Letters: Selected Writings
1965–1990* (New York: Vintage, 1992), 58.
2   To be clear, I will not be suggesting that the translator is at fault for not rendering the Czech
term properly into English, but instead will consider the question through the lens of cultural
linguistics.

to each other, and I will tease out subtle differences in meaning between Czech *lhostejnost* and the English path-of-least-resistance translation "indifference"—differences that impact Havel's extension of the term from the everyday and interpersonal to the sociopolitical and philosophical.

Indeed, we see an indirect hint of the different emphases carried by, on the one hand, English "indifference" and, on the other, Czech *lhostejnost* in the distinct etymology of each. The English term emerges from Latin *in-* "not" + *different* "differing, deferring" with the word in late Middle English meaning "being neither good nor bad" while the Czech term comes from *lho-* < *lehko* "easy, light" + *stej-* (related to Proto-Slavic *stojati* "to stand"), yielding a surprising source meaning of something like "being (standing) at ease."[3] In the English, the emphasis falls on an implied act of will on the part of the observer-subject: given a choice, the subject is not moved to choose and remains "indifferent," an adjective that the OED defines, implicitly privileging the subject, as "without difference of inclination; not inclined to prefer one person or thing to another" and secondarily as "not inclined to one thing or course more than to another; having no inclination or feeling for or against a thing." The Czech etymology directs us elsewhere with decidedly less emphasis on the subject's will to choose and more on the resulting state that an attitude of *lhostejnost* leaves the subject in: the subject stands lightly and freely, undisturbed by a need to favor one entity over another. Indeed, the meaning of the noun in Old Czech was, again quite surprisingly, something like "enjoyment [*potěšení*]" or even "extravagant merriment [*rozmařilé veselí*]" and it tended to occur alongside the word *rozkoš* ("pleasure, delight"); the semantic shift to contemporary "unconcern, indifference" seems to have emerged

---

3   Each word also has a common suffix for abstract nouns: *-nost* in Czech and *-ce* (*-cy* in other English words; cf. Latin *-cia* and *-tia*). Note also the etymology of "apathy," which is from Greek *apatheia*, meaning the absence of sensation (pain, suffering) and is related to English "impassive."

through the kind of *bezstarostnost* ("carefreeness, lightheartedness") that usually accompanies merriment and delight.[4] While etymologies are not determinative for later meanings, they can leave a trace. For the English case, we might detect a trace in the OED's focus on the "inclination" (presumably of the subject-observer), a definitional element lacking in Czech lexicographic explications of *lhostejnost*. For the Czech word, we can detect an etymological trace in the epigraph to this chapter, in which Havel describes *lhostejnost* under Husákian normalization somewhat oddly as "an active social force" that requires conformity to the (meaningless) rituals of public life in exchange for being left alone by state authorities—that is, left to enjoy a private "quiet life [*klidný život*]," which represents a subdued variant of the older Czech carefree merry-making.[5]

To explore this more systematically and see why Havel might view *lhostejnost* as an "active social force" requires us both to examine the general features of Havelian "indifference" beyond this one passage and also to sketch, with the help of the Czech National Corpus (CNC) (https://korpus.cz), a contemporary semantic-discourse portrait of *lhostejnost* (and related forms). To what extent is Havelian *lhostejnost* grounded in the baseline Czech understanding of the term (as supplied by CNC data) and how might Havel deviate from—embellish and extend—that baseline definition? And, related to this, do Czech *lhostejnost* and English "indifference" function as translation equivalents?

---

4   For Czech etymological data, see Václav Machek, *Etymologický slovník jazyka českého a slovenského* (Prague: Československá akademie věd, 1968), 330 and Jaromír Bělič (et al), *Malý staročeský slovník* (Prague: Státní pedagogické nakladatelství, 1978), 123. English eytmological information is courtesy of Google.

5   The word *klid* ("peace and quiet, serenity") with its related forms is at the center of key motif in "Dear Dr. Husák" and is arguably a keyword in Havel's oeuvre as a whole, and it lacks a stable translation pathway into English; see David S. Danaher, *Reading Václav Havel* (Toronto: University of Toronto Press, 2015), pp. 65–67, 119–120, 127, and 179ff.

For the purposes of this analysis, I examined 26 texts by Havel written from 1956 to 2006.[6] I identified 102 contexts containing "indifference"-oriented vocabulary with the following distribution of terms:

Word	Instances	Total frequency
lhostejnost (noun)	38	37.3%
(ne)lhostejný (adjective)	28	27.5%
apatie (noun)	20	19.6%
apatický (adjective)	10	9.8%
zlhostejnělý (adjective)	3	2.9%
zlhostejnět (verb)	1	1%
apaticky (adverb)	1	1%
lhostejně (adverb)	1	1%

As we can see from the chart, Havel uses forms of both Czech *lhostejnost* and its international doublet *apatie* ("apathy") with the former predominating over the latter (about 70% to 30%). Usage of these words cuts across both times periods (pre- and post-1989) and genres (essays, open letters, addresses and speeches, prison letters, a long interview in the form of a collaborative book, a memoir). This vocabulary is particularly evident in three major texts, *Letters to Olga* with 35 examples and both "Dear Dr. Husák" and "The Power of the Powerless" with 12 examples each; it is evident to a lesser degree also in one book-length text written after 1989, his memoir *To the Castle and Back*, with eight.

In what follows, I first examine the general features of Havelian indifference in texts where the concept is lexically represented as well as those where it is not. Then, relying on data from the CNC,

---

6 For a list of texts in my sample, see the appendix to this chapter. Most of these texts are available in their original Czech in Havel's collected works (*Spisy*, Prague: Torst, 1999) with speeches available online. I have cited Czech titles where English translations are not, to my knowledge, extant.

I look at translation equivalents for the terms and also at collocational data from contexts in the CNC as compared to Havel's usage.[7] In doing so, I demonstrate that Havel's understanding of "indifference" as a key word emerges more from the meaning of Czech *lhostejnost* than English "indifference," and that his account is arguably as relevant for us in the post-1989 globalized world as it was for Czechoslovaks (and other East Central Europeans) prior to 1989.

Features of Havelian indifference

In summarizing Havel's understanding of the term, I will proceed chronologically and focus mainly on the texts mentioned above, which will serve to illustrate the development of Havel's thought. The first major text in which "indifference" plays a central role is his 1975 open letter "Dear Dr. Husák," the text which contains this chapter's epigraph.

Havel addressed this letter to Gustáv Husák, who was at the time the general secretary of the Czechoslovak Communist Party, and his intention was to describe "normalized" and "consolidated" Czechoslovak society after the 1968 Soviet invasion. As the epigraph makes clear, Havel saw the "indifference" of the general public, cultivated by the regime that Husák led, as one of this society's driving forces. As Havel makes clear in the letter, the post-invasion regime encouraged an attitude of civic indifference, which was preferable, from the regime's perspective at least, to the unrest (*neklid*) of the 1960s and which would enable the regime to keep its hold on power. In the section immediately preceding the epigraph, Havel asserts that

---

7 Collocates are words that typically co-occur with a given word-form in discourse. According to Paul Baker, analysis of this kind "elucidates semantic preference" (*Using Corpora in Discourse Analysis,* London: Continuum, 2007, 86), which means that it indicates a possible relationship between a given word and a set of semantically related words. Baker goes on to note that when two words frequently collocate, then there "is evidence that the discourses surrounding them are particularly powerful" (114), and he gives the example of the word "rising" in the British National Corpus, which co-occurs with "incomes, prices, wages, earnings" (86).

the invasion, followed soon after by a policy of Husákian "normalization," led Czechoslovaks to turn inward and seek ways of escape from a public sphere in which they felt powerless. Czechoslovaks succumbed "to apathy [*apatie*], to indifference [*nezájem*][8] toward suprapersonal values and their fellow men, to spiritual passivity and depression."[9] Normalization introduced a "system of existential pressure"[10] that encouraged "external adaptation"[11] to the new circumstances as "the only effective method of self-defense" for citizens.[12] Citizens were encouraged to be indifferent to public life while nonetheless participating in civic rituals that symbolically affirmed their allegiance to the regime. Havel called this "public bribery"[13]: by adapting to conditions according to these rules, citizens were allowed to focus on their private lives without interference from the authorities. Most people, the regime reasoned, did not want to "spend their days in ceaseless conflict with authority... So why not do what is required of you? It costs you nothing, and in time you cease to bother about it."[14] Those who did try to resist became viewed by ever more "indifferent neighbors [*zlhostejnělé okolí*]" as eccentrics, fools, Don Quixotes, and those "indifferent neighbors [*zlhostejnělá komunita*] may expel such a person from their midst or shun him as required, for appearances' sake, while sympathizing with him in secret or in private, hoping to still their conscience by clandestine approval of someone who acts as they themselves should, but cannot."[15]

To encourage a shift from outward to inward concerns, the regime partially refocused the economy on the consumer sector:

---

8 Note here that the Czech word *nezájem*, literally "disinterest," has been translated into English as "indifference".
9 Havel, "Dear Dr. Husák," 57.
10 Havel, "Dear Dr. Husák," 54.
11 Havel, "Dear Dr. Husák," 53.
12 Havel, "Dear Dr. Husák," 53.
13 Havel, "Dear Dr. Husák," 56.
14 Havel, "Dear Dr. Husák," 58.
15 Havel, "Dear Dr. Husák," 57–58.

outward-looking citizens could thereby become inward-focused consumers, and the authorities "welcome[d] and support[ed] this spillover of energy into the private sphere."[16] Havel writes that by "fixing a person's whole attention on his mere consumer interests, it is hoped to render him incapable of realizing the increasing extent to which he has been spiritually, politically, and morally violated."[17] The deal the regime cut with the public came with a reward, but the moral costs of accepting it were, in Havel's estimate, high.

Havel concludes the letter by reiterating that indifference was officially encouraged and adding that this strategy activated a certain historical tendency in Czechs and Slovaks to "succumb to total apathy [*lhostejnost*], to take no interest in anything but our bellies, and to spend our time tripping one another up."[18] More generally speaking, Husák's normalized society amplified the worst human qualities: "egotism, hypocrisy, indifference [*lhostejnost*], cowardice, fear, resignation, and the desire to escape every personal responsibility, regardless of the general consequences."[19]

In his 1978 master essay, "The Power of the Powerless," Havel develops his analysis of "indifference" in several ways.[20] Indifference as an "active social force" is understood to be a cornerstone of leading a "life in lies," and in the parable of the greengrocer Havel gives us a skeletal account of a Czechoslovak who one day decides to no longer play by the rules. The grocer stops placing the sign "Workers of the world, unite!" in his shop window—he ceases

---

16 Havel, "Dear Dr. Husák," 59. See also Paulina Bren, *The Greengrocer and His TV: The Culture of Communism after the 1968 Prague Spring* (Ithaca: Cornell University Press, 2010) for an examination of the regime's calculated cultivation of the entertainment industry as another way to promote a shift in energy from public to private life.
17 Havel, "Dear Dr. Husák," 59.
18 Havel, "Dear Dr. Husák," 82.
19 Havel, "Dear Dr. Husák," 82.
20 For contemporary views on this essay, see the special edition of *East European Politics and Societies* (volume 32: 2, 2018) devoted to this topic. See also Jiří Suk and Kristina Andělová (eds.), *Eseje o Moci bezmocných* (Prague: Institute for Contemporary History of the Academy of Sciences of the Czech Republic, 2016).

being "indifferent" to ideological manipulation—and Havel posits that he will come into conflict with the authorities as a result. In this essay, Havel also extends his analysis in another significant direction: he sees "indifference" as an active force not only in the East, but also in the West. The East thereby comes to be understood as a "grotesque caricature"[21] of the West, a fun-house mirror version of it, which led Delia Popescu to provocatively assert that, for Havel, the West is Dorian Gray and the East is Dorian's portrait.[22] If "Dear Dr. Husák" establishes "indifference" as an active force in the sociopolitical realm in the East, by 1978 Havel argues that this is merely a localized version of it, and he begins to conceive of it much more broadly as a force that shapes human identity in the modern world writ large. Here Havel previews, at least from one particular angle, Václav Bělohradský's argument in his 1979 text *Krize eschatologie neosobnosti* [*The Eschatology of the Impersonal in Crisis*].[23] Bělohradský makes the case that modern society is characterized by bureaucratic impersonalization, which emerges directly from the European philosophical tradition of rationalism, and that this underlies a crisis of human identity. Involvement in civic life may indeed prove to be particularly challenging against a background of technocratic impersonalization across society as a whole, and thus "indifference" to civic engagement in favor of pursuing one's

21 I borrow this phrase from a later essay: see Václav Havel, "Politics and Conscience," trans. Erazim Kohák and Roger Scruton, in *Open Letters: Selected Writings 1965–1990* (New York: Vintage, 1992), 260.
22 Delia Popescu, *Political Action in Václav Havel's Thought: The Responsibility of Resistance* (Lanham: Lexington Books, 2012), 135ff. See also chapter 3 in Danaher, *Reading Václav Havel* for an account of Havel's East-West hypothesis.
23 Bělohradský's text first saw the light of day in Rome in 1979, but it made its way back to Czechoslovakia as tamizdat. It was eventually published abroad in Czech by an exile press in 1982 (London: Rozmluvy). Havel himself did not read it until after his release from prison in 1983. Havel's samizdat press Edice Expedice issued it in 1984, and he mentions the work for the first time in his 1985 essay "Politics and Conscience." To my knowledge, no published English translation exists. The underlying connection between Havel's "The Power of the Powerless" and Bělohradský's work is likely Jan Patočka's *Heretical Essays* (New York: Open Court, 1999).

personal interests becomes an easier path to follow. In "The Power of the Powerless," then, the concept of indifference begins to have broader philosophical implications.

Havel continues the theme of extending the scope of indifference beyond the borders of the totalitarian East in his letters from prison, which were written from 1979 to 1983 and published in a volume titled *Letters to Olga*.[24] Again previewing Bělohradský, he notes that the very structure of the modern world encourages an attitude of indifference:

> The world modern man creates is an image of his own condition, and in turn, it deepens that condition. It is a world that, as they say, has got out of hand. It is driven by forces that utterly betray particular horizons and particular responsibilities. At the same time, the stronger these forces are, the stronger their momentum becomes and the harder they are to control and thus, the stronger the magnetic field dragging man deeper and deeper into his own helplessness, alienation, depersonalization and ultimately—something that may represent the bottom itself—into a state of apathetic [*lhostejný*] contentment with his condition.[25]

Havel also raises "indifference" quite explicitly to the level of a philosophical category: it is the opposite of faith in Being and becomes for Havel the worst kind of "unbelief" (*nevíra*). He argues that human life is a constant spiritual struggle that is "waged by the powers of faith [*víra*] and the experience of nothingness [*zážitek nicoty*]," and if the latter wins out, then the "dramatic tension vanishes, man

---

24 In order to conform to the limitations placed on him as a (political) prisoner, the letters were written ostensibly to his first wife, Olga, but we know now that Havel was also addressing a group of Czechoslovak intellectuals who engaged with him in a philosophical back-and-forth. See Václav Havel, *Letters to Olga*, trans. Paul Wilson (New York: Henry Holt, 1983); see also Daniel Kroupa, *Dějiny Kampademie* (Prague: Václav Havel Library, 2010) and Martin C. Putna and Ivan Havel, *Dopisy od Olgy* (Prague: Václav Havel Library, 2010). See Danaher, *Reading Václav Havel*, 47ff for a discussion of *Letters to Olga* as *explications du texte* for the rest of Havel's writings.
25 Havel, *Letters to Olga*, letter 118.

surrenders to apathy [*lhostejnost*], and faith and meaning exist only as a backdrop against which others become aware of his fall."[26] Genuine absence of meaning and unbelief manifest themselves for Havel as "indifference [*lhostejnost*], apathy [*apatie*], resignation, and the decline of existence to the vegetative level."[27] One more thing we might highlight in *Letters to Olga* is that Havel's discussion of "indifference" spans the domains of the personal and the sociopolitical[28]: he devotes a number of passages to how his own personal apathy plagues him while in prison (it is one of his "bad moods" that he describes at length)[29] but then he also, as we have just seen, applies the idea to modern society as a whole.

In later texts, Havel continues to analyze "indifference" as a sociopolitical force. In his presidential memoir, for example, he suggests that general apathy in difficult times is for Czechs a regrettable historical tendency:

In modern Czech history, a situation repeatedly comes up in which society rises to some great occasion but then its top leaders execute a retreating maneuver, a side step, a compromise; here they capitulate, there they give something up or sacrifice something, and they do it all, naturally, to save the nation's very existence. And society, traumatized at first, quickly backs down, 'understands' its leaders, and ultimately sinks into apathy [*apatie*] or goes straight into a coma. Then a tide of mud inundates public life, the media is taken over by the dregs of society, and only a handful of dissenters or resisters struggle to maintain the continuity of the free spirit and human dignity, and for their pains they

---

26   Havel, *Letters to Olga*, letter 64; see also letter 96.
27   Havel, *Letters to Olga*, letter 73.
28   The meaning of many of Havel's key words span personal and political domains. See the chapter in this volume on the concept of the "appeal" and also Danaher, *Reading Václav Havel*, chapter 4.
29   See Havel, *Letters to Olga*, letters 13, 48, 58, and 69.

are perceived by the majority of the population as provocateurs who are pointlessly dragging the rest of them into danger.[30]

He drives home this point by linking it up with Czech small-mindedness: "Look after Number One, don't get mixed up in other people's business, keep your head down, don't look up."[31] He then recounts an anecdote about a friend of his, the literary critic Jan Lopatka, who had a chronic illness, and:

[...] collapsed one afternoon on a busy Prague square. He apparently lay there for two hours before someone helped him and called an ambulance. Indifference [*lhostejnost*] to others is frequently offered to us as a national program, and many people subscribe to it. Not everyone, of course, and not always; even in the darkest times there have been honorable expressions of solidarity.[32]

The idea that indifference represents a kind of "national program" certainly evokes Husákian normalization, but undoubtedly not only.

In the memoir Havel also holds out some hope that "indifference" as a social force can be eradicated. In discussing American views of the war in Iraq (and more generally a policy of judicious intervention in the world to combat human-rights abuses), he writes:

I am often asked my opinion, and I always say the same thing. It's not possible—and particularly in today's interconnected world—for us to remain entirely and permanently indifferent [*lhostejný*] when massive and cruel crimes are committed against people somewhere. You can't forever tiptoe around a regime that wipes out its own citizens or throws them

30 Václav Havel, *Prosím stručně* (Prague: Gallery, 2006), 60 and Václav Havel, *To the Castle and Back*, trans. Paul Wilson (New York: Knopf, 2007), 118.
31 Havel, *Prosím stručně*, 60 and Havel, *To the Castle and Back*, 117.
32 Havel, *Prosím stručně*, 60 and Havel, *To the Castle and Back*, 117.

into swimming pools filled with acid, the way people walked around Jan Lopatka lying helpless on the sidewalk.[33]

He also sees hope for the political future of the Czech Republic, particularly given that younger generations are:

[...] no longer deformed by communism. They have not grown up in circumstances that demand hypocrisy and spinelessness, conditions that support selfishness, indifference [*lhostejnost*] to others, and xenophobia, under a regime that was always talking about the working class, which was meant to be in charge, while in reality cultivating the basest forms of petit bourgeois values in its citizens.[34]

Over a dozen years after he wrote the memoir and eight years after his death, however, these expressions of hope ring somewhat hollow. We have, alas, become quite adept at the kind of careful tiptoeing-around that Havel laments in the first passage. The second passage raises the additional question of whether the indifference Havel describes was a feature only of pre-1989 East Central Europe: indeed, his analysis of "indifference" in texts prior to 1989 strongly suggests otherwise, and this is a point I will return to shortly.[35]

Non-lexical representations of "indifference": Havel's plays

In analyzing "indifference" as a key word in Havel's thought, I would be grossly negligent to omit discussion of his plays. Even though the concept is not lexically represented in the plays, it is a strong motif in most of his plays in one way or another. We could summarize this

---

33 Havel, *Prosím stručně*, 86 and Havel, *To the Castle and Back*, 187.
34 Havel, *Prosím stručně*, 176 and Havel, *To the Castle and Back*, 341.
35 The Czechs' (and Slovaks') intense resistance to accepting any refugees during the 2015 crisis would be a case in point.

motif in general terms in the following way: characters in a given play exist in a theatrical world that is absurdly dysfunctional, but few of them seem to care or even notice, and they focus instead on personal matters, like the characters in *The Memo(randum)* who are obsessively concerned with what the lunch special of the day is in the office cafeteria. In depicting absurd but recognizable worlds that are populated by characters indifferent to the really important goings-on around them, Havel seeks to activate the audience's conscience: we bear frustrating witness to the consequences of living in a world that has been rendered grotesquely absurd—perhaps largely because of the general apathy of those who inhabit it. While each play realizes this process in its own way through specifics of setting and character, the overall thrust of Havel's theatrical message is to provoke the audience to extrapolate the frustration they experience with the absurdity of the on-stage world to the real world outside of the theater.[36] In terms specifically related to "indifference," the plays ask the audience: to what extent might we focus on our own personal lives to the exclusion of other concerns and how, then, does our disregard for civic matters—our lack of a sense of co-responsibility for our community—help to shape that world in which we live?[37]

I would argue that this is especially true of the Vaněk trilogy of one-act plays, each of which offers a psychological portrait of how living in a totalitarian society deforms identity.[38] The character (or rather dramatic principle) of Ferdinand Vaněk acts a foil to his interlocutors: instead of speaking, he remains largely silent and lets his interlocutors—a brewery foreman in *Audience*, a married couple

---

36 A similar view has been expressed by James Pontuso, who considers Havel's plays to be "Heideggeran thought experiments" that are "intended to show the unreality of an amoral world"; see his *Václav Havel: Civic Responsibility in the Post-Modern Age* (Lanham, MD: Rowman & Littlefield Publishers, 2004), 111ff.

37 For more on "co-responsibility" as a key word, see the corresponding chapter in this volume.

38 Much has been written about these plays: see, for example, Danaher, *Reading Václav Havel*, 33ff for one perspective along with a summary of other views.

with a young child in *Unveiling*, and a fellow intellectual in *Protest*—"confess" to him.[39] The audience takes on the implied role of witness to each confession (if not also jury and judge at the implied "trial" of each of Vaněk's interlocutors). In each of these plays, we see an attempt by Havel to come to terms with the various characters' "indifference" to the society in which they live: for the brewery foreman, it is grounded in a feeling of powerlessness in the face of his circumstances; for Michal and Věra, there is a semi-conscious realization that they have chosen the wrong life path and they berate Vaněk for his engaged (i.e., "dissident") life in an increasingly desperate attempt to justify their own lack of engagement, for which they have been allowed a materially comfortable, if spiritually distressing, life; in the last play, Staněk's indifference to civic matters is arguably the most nuanced, given that he does seek Vaněk's help with a political matter, but he does so only for very selfish reasons and he is unwilling, when all is said and done, to put his career at risk by committing an act of public dissent.

All these theatrical scenarios, each in its own way, embody the etymological association with *lhostejnost* that we noted at the start of this chapter: the characters' "indifference" is grounded in their desire to be left alone to live their lives and pursue their own interests. None of Vaněk's interlocutors is, however, satisfied with this state of affairs, and their discomfort—along with how their circumstances have distorted their human dignity—is forcefully conveyed to the audience. In his prose, Havel seems to strongly condemn "indifference" as a moral lapse; in the plays, he complicates this picture by giving the audience a glimpse of the characters' personal circumstances, which may serve to justify, depending on your reading of the play, their indifferent stances. In other words, he acknowledges

---

39 Indeed, in *Unveiling*, one of the curated pieces of decor in Michal and Věra's newly redesigned apartment is a confessional that they have rescued from a church, one that was presumably shuttered by the officially atheistic regime.

that "indifference" is not only a personal but also a structural matter at the level of society as a whole; at the same time, however, he also refuses to let individual characters off the moral hook. The plays provoke the members of the audience to think through the complexities of this scenario for themselves and ideally in reference to their own lives.

A final point that I would make about the plays is that they suggest, like some of the prose works, that "indifference" is a force operative not only in the pre-1989 East. I have taught a monograph course on Havel's writings at a university in the American Midwest for well over a decade, and my students have had no difficulty extrapolating from the indifference implicit in Havel's play-worlds to their own lives in contemporary America. The complex existential scenario that Havel depicts in his theatrical worlds in an attempt to activate the audience's collective conscience with regard to their own real-life situations has clear ongoing relevance for the post-1989 globalized world.

Translation equivalents for *lhostejnost* and *lhostejný*

Given that "indifference" is a key concept in Havel's oeuvre, we are confronted with the question of his lexical starting point, that is, Czech *lhostejnost*, and whether it is indeed equivalent in meaning to English "indifference." We have seen two distinct etymological sources and hinted that there is a trace of the Czech etymology in Havel's characterization of *lhostejnost* as an "active social force" under normalization (and beyond). In this section and the next, I examine the question of translation equivalency in an effort to go beyond etymology and paint a coherent semantic-discourse portrait of Havel's understanding of *lhostejnost*.[40]

---

40 I will mostly limit myself to the noun *lhostejnost* and the adjective *lhostejný*, if only because these comprise the great majority of instances in Havel's works.

For a baseline reading of translation equivalency, we can rely on data provided by the CNC's Treq tool.[41] A Treq query for *lhostejnost* yields 374 examples with the great majority (77%) rendered into English as "indifference". "Disregard" is the second most frequent translation (6.4%) with "apathy" in third place (4.3%). Other less well-represented translation pathways, which are nonetheless suggestive for a semantic-discourse portrait of *lhostejnost*, include "inertia," "casualness," "indolence," "carelessness," "unconcern," "detachment," "callousness," "ignorance," "insensitivity," "neglect," "lack of initiative," "nonchalance," and "complacency."

The adjective *lhostejný* yields 528 examples in Treq, and translation pathways are more varied, although "indifferent" still predominates with 54.7% of the English contexts. The phrase "not care" is second at 8.9%, and other possible pathways include "not matter," "casual," "insensitive," "careless," "impassive," "oblivious," "disregard," "unconcerned," "lackadaisical," "apathetic," "blank (face, mind, expression)," "negligent," "listless," "immaterial," "lethargic," "unheeding," "stolid," "bored," "inattentive," "complacent," "slack," "lukewarm," "imperturbed," "heedless," "nonchalant," "phlegmatic," "impartial," "blasé."

Some examples of the less-frequent translation pathways will suffice to sketch a discourse portrait that I flesh out below:

(1) *Talíř přistál s nádhernou lhostejností ke všemu, co bylo dole, a zničil rozsáhlou oblast jedněch z nejdražších nemovitostí na světě, včetně značné části obchodního domu Harrods.* "[The flying saucer] had come down with a wonderful disregard for anything beneath it and crushed

41   Treq makes use of the InterCorp corpus, a parallel corpus containing over 30 languages and almost 1.5 billion words. For more on Treq, see M. Vavřín and A. Rosen, *Treq* (Prague: FF UK, 2015) at http://treq.korpus.cz as well as M. Škrabal and M. Vavřín, "Databáze překladových ekvivalentů Treq", *Časopis pro moderní filologii* 99:2 (2017), 245-260; for InterCorp, see https://intercorp.korpus.cz. Note that all searches in this study are based on lemmas, an approach that generates all possible grammatical forms of the given word.

a large area of some of the most expensive real estate in the world, including much of Harrods."[42]

(2) *Toto srovnání ukazuje cynickou lhostejnost vůči obětem porušování lidských práv ve světě.* "This comparison shows a cynical disregard for the victims of human rights violations throughout the world."[43]

(3) *Korupce a nevýkonnost státního aparátu a neschopnost a lhostejnost vlády neponechávají mnoho nadějí na opravdové zlepšení životní úrovně.* "The corruption and inefficiency of the state apparatus and the government's incompetence and inertia leave no hope for a real improvement in living standards."[44]

(4) *Bohužel jsme viděli na izraelské straně značnou míru lhostejnosti.* "Unfortunately we have seen a large degree of carelessness by the Israelis."[45]

(5) *Mají dost tvé lhostejnosti.* "They've had it with your insensitivity."[46]

(6) *Ospravedlňoval snad fakt, že matka přisla o jednu dceru, její lhostejnost ke druhé?* "Did the fact her mother had lost one daughter justify her neglect of the other?"[47]

(7) *To ukazuje lhostejnost, aroganci a nevědemost federalistů ve vztahu k voličům.* "This demonstrates the nonchalance, arrogance and ignorance of the federalists towards voters."[48]

(8) *Dlouho předtím, než otázku položil, si jeho nevinné modré oči vybraly zubící se, lhostejnou postavu kapitána místní policie.* "Long before he asked the question his innocent blue eyes had singled out the grinning, lethargic figure of the local police captain."[49]

---

42   This text is originally English and comes from the fourth book in the science-fiction humorist Douglas Adams' *Hitchhiker's Guide to the Galaxy* series.
43   From proceedings of Europarliament.
44   From a journalistic source.
45   From proceedings of Europarliament.
46   From film subtitles for an English-language film.
47   The source here is an English novel translated into Czech.
48   From proceedings of Europarliament.
49   The source here is a novel by John Le Carré.

(9) *Avšak nepodkopávejme schopnost tohoto průmyslu zotavit se tím,*
že budeme nevšímaví a lhostejní. "However, let us not undermine this
industry's capacity for recovery by being lax and negligent."[50]

Although the data set is limited, I would point out one strong tendency that comes through particularly in the contexts above that
feature less common translation pathways. They all imply condemnation of the "indifference" in the given passage. For example, in
(1), the "disregard" is valued negatively (if humorously) in the given
text, and in (2) it is a "cynical" stance; all the other examples here,
each in its own way, point in the same general direction. The focus,
then, is not so much on a person's stance toward something, which
would be oriented toward the subject's will, as it is on the (sometimes
feigned) absence of caring, which is understood in many contexts as
a mistake or even a character flaw. The data suggest, in other words,
that our "indifference" is inappropriate, if not unethical, and the
uncommon translation pathways highlight, sometimes subtly and
sometimes quite blatantly, this value judgement.[51] Needless to say,
these are aspects of the meaning of "indifference" that Havel sought
to highlight in his own work.

Leaving the Treq results behind us and looking at Havel's texts
in my sample that have been professionally translated into English,
there is a strong tendency to conform to the path-of-least-resistance
renderings via "indifference" and "indifferent" (with some examples of "apathy" and "apathetic"): these comprise 88% of the translated contexts. As the Treq data set above suggests, however, this
does not mean that *lhostejnost* is necessarily semantically equivalent
to "indifference," and this becomes clearer when we expand our investigation to collocates.

---

50 From proceedings of Europarliament.
51 Without wading into the details, this analysis is supported also by Treq data for *apatie* and
apatický as well as for most contexts that feature the path-of-least-resistance translation via
English "indifference."

Collocational data from the CNC and Havel's texts

For collocational data, I limited the scope of analysis to the noun *lhostejnost* in both the CNC and in Havel's writings. In examining each of these sources, I relied on manual analysis of the discourse contexts. For data in the CNC, I searched *lhostejnost* as a lemma using the concordance tool KonText with a specification of plus or minus five places, and this yielded over 750 contexts; my analysis focuses on a randomly generated sample of 500 of these contexts. In examining my subset of Havel's texts, I looked at all contexts with *lhostejnost* and also focused on which words co-occurred five places before and after. For the CNC data, I divided collocates into groups largely by part of speech and noted the most frequently co-occurring words in each group. Given the large amount of data present in the CNC, I will eschew lengthy exemplification and present instead a summary of the overall picture that emerges, and then compare this to Havel's usage. The picture that emerges largely reinforces, with some additional emphases, the Treq data that I have discussed above.

I summarize collocational data from the CNC in the three tables below: nominal, verbal, and adjectival collocates that occur in at least two (different) sources. After the tables, I analyze the data set by highlighting a number of clear elements to add to our semantic-discourse portrait and then compare the CNC usage to Havel's.

Table 1: noun collocates with *lhostejnost*[52]
krutost "cruelty" (6)
apatie "apathy" (5)
únava "fatigue" (5)
sobectví "selfishness" (3)

---

[52] Numbers in parentheses indicate the raw number of occurrences of the collocate in the data set.

nezájem "disinterest" (3)
klid "serenity, calm" (3)
chlad "cold(ness)" (3)
pohrdání "contempt" (3)
maska "mask" (3)
zoufalství "despair" (2)
nenávist "hatred" (2)
pasivita "passivity" (2)
pokrytectví "hypocrisy" (2)
úsměv "grin, smirk" (2)
neznalost "ignorance" (2)
rezignace "resignation" (2)
strach "fear" (2)
odpor "defiance" (2)
smutek "sadness" (2)
lítost "pity" (2)

Table 2: verb collocates with *lhostejnost*[53]
předstírat "to pretend, feign" (17)
propadat/propadnout "fall into, surrender to" (4)
dávat najevo "to show, demonstrate" (4)
vytrhnout se z "to break free of" (4)
skrývat se "to lurk, skulk" (3)
vládnout "to be in control" (3)
vybavovat/vybavit "to outfit, furnish" (2)
přepadnout "to attack, seize" (2)
zmocnit se "to seize hold of" (2)
zmizet v "disappear into" (2)
obrnit se "to arm oneself with" (2)
upadat/upadnout do "to sink into" (2)

[53] The verb *cítit* ("to feel") also co-occurs many times.

Table 3: adjectival collocates with *lhostejnost*[54]

předstíraná "feigned" (14)

naprostá "absolute, total" (13)

hraná "pretend, feigned" (6)

pohrdavá "contemptuous" (5)

chladná "cold" (3)

tupá "dull, obtuse" (3)

zdvořilá "polite" (3)

ledová "ice-cold" (3)

vzájemná "mutual" (3)

rostoucí "increasing" (3)

současná "contemporary" (3)

podivná "strange" (2)

náboženská "religious" (2)

absolutní "absolute" (2)

falešná "false" (2)

lehká "light" (2)

pouhá "mere" (2)

First and foremost, the collocates and the contexts in which they occur suggest, not surprisingly, that *lhostejnost* is a negative, undesirable state: it is associated with cruelty, selfishness, contempt, despair, hatred, passivity, hypocrisy, ignorance. It tends to be considered the opposite of a normal human response to a given situation: it is cold, unemotional, dead, cut off.[55] It is sometimes associated with superiority—that is, the viewpoint of a powerful, wealthy, or (supposedly) sophisticated person who does not need to be concerned with

---

54 Also represented to a significant degree are personal modifiers ("my," "your," "his," "her"…). Note that I have listed adjectives in their nominative feminine form because *lhostejnost* is grammatically feminine.

55 Some one-off collocates in the data that reinforce this point are: *studené srdce* ("frigid heart"), *bezcitnost* ("hardheartedness") and *necitelnost* ("callousness"), and *emoční chlad* ("emotional coldness").

a given matter because they are above it (cf. the original Czech sense of *lhostejnost* as "merry-making"). That sense of superiority may be feigned, and indeed feigned *lhostejnost* (or *lhostejnost* that is perceived by someone as feigned) is strongly represented—and equally strongly condemned—in the CNC data for both verbs and adjectives.

Another element evident in the data, again perhaps not surprisingly, is that *lhostejnost* spans domains of human experience from the personal to the sociocultural and political. There are contexts that discuss *lhostejnost* in terms of interpersonal relationships (family and friends) as well as contexts that expand the scope outward to ever broader circles of home. We see this in adjectival collocates where personal modifiers are prominent but also adjectives that depict *lhostejnost* in societal terms ("contemporary" with three occurrences as well as "Czech" and "civic" and other modifiers with one occurrence each). Collocations that function as nominal modifiers in the genitive case (i.e., "indifference" of what or whom) tend to point to the concept's broad scope: the "indifference" of "society" and "of the public" with two occurrences each as well as "of the community," "of the universe," "of people," and others with one occurrence each. Collocations with the preposition *k* "to" (i.e., "indifference" toward what or whom) highlight both the personal and the sociocultural: we have a wide range of contexts, mostly with only one occurrence each, such as *k dětem* ("to children"), *k dceři* ("to [one's] daughter"), *ke svým bližním* ("to [one's] neighbors"), *k polibku* ("to the kiss"), *k budoucnosti* ("to the future"), *ke všemu* ("to everything"), *k náboženským tradicím* ("to religious traditions"), *k tomuto světu* ("to this world"). The spanning of domains of experience is an element associated with many of Havel's key words: he seems to rely on common human experience of a concept's meaning as a way to ground the extension of that meaning to the sociopolitical sphere.

One more point is that we see a number of metaphorical conceptualizations in the CNC data. One metaphorical motif implies that *lhostejnost* is a real force with real power: it can "attack" or "seize hold" of us, and we have to try to "break free" of it or, if unsuccessful, we "surrender" to it.[56] A related metaphor here, but from a different perspective, is that *lhostejnost* may function as a kind of armor (note the verb *obrnit se*, represented twice in the data): the armor of "indifference" protects us because it reduces our sense of personal responsibility for the situation and, as a result, we avoid feeling at fault.[57] Yet another metaphor suggests that people may put on a "mask" of *lhostejnost* (*nasadit si masku lhostejnosti*), which points to the feigning scenario discussed above and which seems also to absolve them of responsibility for the matter. A final metaphor, represented a number of times in the data but in various lexical realizations and across parts of speech, is the association of *lhostejnost* with (emotional, intellectual, moral) lethargy or slumber.[58]

We may now turn to Havel's usage of *lhostejnost* and note that collocations in his texts largely conform to the picture evoked by the CNC data. The most frequent collocates in Havel's writings, already familiar to us from the CNC, include *rezignace* ("resignation") and *sobectví* ("selfishness") with four examples each as well as *sobecká* ("selfish") and *krunýř* ("armor") with two each. Negative associations with the concept are amply represented in Havel's texts, although the CNC collocates go further than Havel in this regard by providing a longer list of negative traits. As we noted earlier, the import of the concept also cuts across the personal/interpersonal divide for Havel: indeed, one of his main moves in *Letters to Olga* is

---

56 At least some of these are common metaphorical conceptualizations for a range of emotional concepts across different languages; ses Zoltan Kovecses, *Metaphor and Emotion: Language, Culture, and Body in Human Feeling* (Cambridge: Cambridge University Press, 2003).

57 A related one-off metaphor in the data is *obrnit srdce krunýřem lhostejnosti* "to fortify the heart with the armor of indifference," and another one-off metaphorical phrase conceives of *lhostejnost* as wrapping oneself in a "mental and emotional shell" (*duševní, citová skořápka*). These metaphors fit in well with the original sense of Greek *apatheia*.

58 For example, we can highlight the nominal collocates *spánek* ("sleep"), *lenost* ("laziness, sloth"), and *zapomění* ("oblivion").

to extend the meaning of *lhostejnost* from the personal domain (one of his bad moods) to the sociocultural sphere.

As we might glean from our earlier discussion of Havelian *lhostejnost*, he also agrees with the CNC data in not accepting "indifference" as a normal human response. It is instead a distortion of human identity in an impersonalized world. In a 1999 speech, he notes that we are "intrinsically disposed not to be indifferent [*lhostejný*] towards fellow humans and towards society" and that humanity "constitutes a subject of conscience, of moral order, of love for our fellow humans"; he suggests here that the cultivation of a vibrant civil society would provide an opportunity for human nature to "be exercised in its entirety, including its more subtle elements, which are more difficult to grasp, but are perhaps the most important of all."[59]

Even Havel's metaphors for *lhostejnost* largely match the CNC data in that he uses both "armor" and "slumber/lethargy" and also conceives of it as a force to be reckoned with. A Havelian metaphor that does not appear in the CNC and that Havel uses a number of times in different contexts conceives of *lhostejnost* as "waters" (a "sea" or an "ocean"), which threaten to overwhelm (and ultimately to drown) individuals and society.[60] This metaphor is reminiscent of one of Havel's lesser-known plays, *A Butterfly on the Antenna*, in which a failure to act threatens to cause a couple to drown from a leaky faucet—until the one character who can fix it wakes up from his nap.

Havel does, however, veer from conventional usage, and he does so in two prominent ways. Firstly, he downplays the feigning stance that we noted is strongly represented in the CNC data: it is entirely absent in Havel's essayistic texts, although we might arguably see

59 Václav Havel, "A Speech on the Occasion of 'Václav Havel's Civil Society Symposium'," 1999. For more on "civil society" as a key term, see Aspen Brinton's chapter in this volume.
60 See, for example, Václav Havel, "The Latin American Parliament," 1999, in which he wishes to "stir the stagnant waters of apathy [*apatie*]" that surround him.

hints of it in the dramatic tension evoked in his plays. Secondly and most significantly, Havelian *lhostejnost* collocates with three concepts, all related to each other, that are missing from the CNC data: *přizpůsobivost* ("adaptiveness, adaptability"), *kariérismus* ("careerism"), and *konformita* ("conformity"). I would argue that these are potential extensions from the baseline usage as implied by the CNC data, and Havel certainly develops this potential in earnest, especially, as we have already seen, in his letter to Husák. *Lhostejnost* is an "active social force" to the extent that people have conformed and adapted to the external circumstances of a normalized society and focus instead on their own careers and personal interests: it is these people that the state authorities leave alone to live a quiet life.

Conclusion

I conclude this study of *lhostejnost* as a key word in Havel's thought by summarizing its central points:

(1) Havel takes a concept grounded in the everydayness of human experience and raises it to the level of a concept with sociopolitical and philosophical import. Put another way, he takes the semantic-discourse associations with *lhostejnost*, as they are represented in the CNC data that we have examined, and weaves them into a much broader sociocultural and political analysis of his own particular time and place, an analysis that has implications beyond the borders of pre-1989 Czechoslovakia.

(2) In Havel's view, indifference is not merely a personal matter, but rather an active social force that emerges from the structural conditions of a modern-industrial society. It is an open question whether pre-1989 Czechoslovaks were, in fact, "indifferent" or rather if they simply did not see a viable pathway toward meaningfully empowered civic involvement. This question is arguably as true for us today who live in the post-1989 globalized world, although obviously in different terms than it was for Czechoslovaks under

Husákian normalization. In this regard, Jeffrey Goldfarb has argued that contemporary American society might represent not so much a case of mere indifference to civic matters than a much worse case of outright cynicism about them.[61] In some instances, certain political movements may actively cultivate widespread political cynicism because they stand to benefit from it, and this is disturbingly reminiscent, *mutatis mutandis*, of the situation in pre-1989 Czechoslovakia.

(3) The path-of-least-resistance translation of Czech *lhostejnost* as "indifference" is not fully adequate. The meaning of *lhostejnost* is grounded in the Czech semiosphere[62] in a way that distinguishes it from English "indifference," and I have suggested here how Havel's broader understanding of the concept's import emerges largely from these points of difference.

(4) *Lhostejnost* is a key word in Havel's thought that interacts with other such words, many of which are analyzed elsewhere in this volume: "power," "home," "civil society," "theater," "responsibility," and "truth."

Appendix

The texts in my sample, listed chronologically, are below; I also indicate the genre as well as the number of instances of appeal-oriented vocabulary in each.

"Básník dnešní doby [A Poet of Our Time]" (essay; 1956; 1)
"K otázce tzv. apolitičnosti [On the Question of So-Called Apoliticalness" (essay; 1957; 1)
"Address to the Congress of Writers" (address; 1967; 1)
"Letter to Dubček" (open letter; 1969; 3)
"Vystoupení v Československé televizi [Appearance on Czechoslovak TV]" (address; 1969; 1)

---

61 See Jeffrey Goldfarb, *The Cynical Society: The Culture of Politics and the Politics of Culture in American Life* (Chicago: University of Chicago Press, 1991).
62 For a discussion of the semiosphere, see Vladimír Macura, *Masarykovy boty a jiné semi(o) fejetony* (Prague: Pražská imaginace, 1993), 5.

"Dear Dr. Husák" (open letter; 1975; 12)
"Article 202" (essay; 1978; 1)
"Power of the Powerless" (essay; 1978; 12)
Letters to Olga (letters from prison collected in a book; 1979–1983; 35)
"Anatomy of Reticence" (essay; 1985; 1)
Disturbing the Peace (collaborative book; 1985–1986; 4)
"Anatomy of Hate" (address; 1990; 2)
Summer Meditations (book; 1991; 5)
"The George Washington University" (address; 1993; 1)
"World Congress of the International PEN Club" (address; 1994; 1)
"European Parliament" (address; 1994; 1)
"1995 Geuzenpenning" (address; 1995; 1)
"Technical University of Dresden" (address; 1995; 1)
"The Latin American Parliament" (address; 1996; 1)
"Státní svátek [State Holiday]" (address; 1996; 1)
"Address before the Members of Parliament" (address; 1997; 2)
"50th Anniversary of the Universal Declaration of Human Rights" (address; 1998; 1)
"Address in Acceptance of an Honorary Degree from Oxford University" (address; 1998; 1)
"A Speech on the Occasion of 'Václav Havel's Civil Society Symposium'" (address; 1999; 2)
"Address in Acceptance of 'Open Society' Prize" (address; 1999; 1)
To the Castle and Back (memoir; 2006; 8)

CIVIL SOCIETY: *OBČANSKÁ SPOLEČNOST*
Aspen Brinton

Introduction

When Václav Havel referenced *občanská společnost* in his political speeches after 1989, the phrase often appeared together with a list of his goals for post-Communist political life: democracy, the rule of law, human rights, a market economy, and pluralism. "Civil society" was almost always part of this list, and Havel rarely spoke of democracy without also speaking of "civil society."[1] There are two speeches during the 1990s where Havel moved beyond this list and developed an explicit definition of "civil society": his New Year's Address in 1994 and a keynote speech opening an academic conference about "civil society" in the United States at Macalester College in 1999.[2] There is, therefore, a documentary record of Havel giving detailed definitions of this key term, but there are also patterns of usage that suggest a complex associative context around his ideas. While his definitions in themselves are worthy of political-theoretical analysis, and will be treated here accordingly, in order to understand the wider context which gave rise to his understanding of "civil society," the words *občanská* and *společnost* are also examined partly as separate keywords, with an emphasis on the former. To divide the term (before reuniting it) helps us understand Havel's world of words from the different perspectives of his various life-chapters.

---

1 The list appears in these speeches: "World Economic Forum," 1992; "Wroclaw University," 1992; "George Washington University," 1993; "The Council of Europe Summit," 1993;" Chamber of Deputies of the Parliament of the Czech Republic," 1993; "New Year's Address to the Nation," 1994; "European Parliament," 1994; "Stanford University," 1994; "Five Years Later," 1994; "Czechs and Germans on the Way to Good Neighbourship," 1995.
2 Václav Havel, "A Speech by Václav Havel President of the Czech Republic on the Occasion of 'Václav Havel's Civil Society Symposium'," 1999.

As a justification of this separation and by way of a prelude, it must be noted that Havel rarely used the term *občanská společnost* (the two-word phrase to represent one concept) before 1989. He came to be known as a commentator on "civil society" because he frequently used *občanská společnost* in his presidential speeches after 1989, not because this phrase was oft-quoted in his plays, nor was this exact phrase used in his letters and essays. While both his plays and dissident writings contain many ideas about civic participation, political engagement, and the possibilities of civic and social openness beyond the purview of the state, the words he used to describe these phenomena vary much more widely in his earlier writings.[3] It could be said that his vision of the concept was not yet reified (or perhaps solidified) until his presidential speeches. Yet even if those earlier writings did not yet include the term, his explicit definitions of *občanská společnost* after 1989 developed at least partly out of his prior critiques of the Communist state in his dissident years. These connections can be traced through looking at his use of *občanský* as an adjective attached to other social and political phenomenon. *Občanský*, generally translated into English as "civic" or "civil," appears in his writings in many formulations related to (but not identical with) "civil society," including: civic bravery,[4] an active civic attitude,[5] civic responsibility,[6] the civic principle,[7] civic discontent,[8]

---

3 This generalization is based upon the digitized archive of the Václav Havel Library, which contains most all of the speeches and most of the major essays and plays written before 1989. I have not provided an exact number here because of the difficulties of searching archives that are not yet digitized with search features.

4 The Czech phrase is *občanská statečnosti*; see his play *The Memorandum* (1965).

5 The Czech phrase is *aktivní občanský postoj*; see his play *Protest* (1978).

6 The Czech phrase is *občanská spoluodpovědnost*; see Havel, "New Year's Address," 1994 and Havel, "Czechs and Germans on the Way To a Good Neighbourship," 1995. For more on "responsibility" as a key word, see Falk and Bouvier-Valenta in this volume.

7 For "civic principle," see the discussion below of the speech "New Year's Address 1994."

8 The Czech phrase is *občanská nespokojenost*; see Václav Havel, "The Power of the Powerless," chapter VIII and also his play *Protest*.

civic self-consciousness,[9] civic values,[10] civic action,[11] the structures of civic life,[12] civic participation,[13] and civic arrangement.[14] His uses of *společnost* are also not insignificant, and when he discusses a more preferred type of society, "democratic" society, "independent" society, and "open" society appear. Democracy, independence, and openness then became part of his specific definition of "civil society."[15] Before and after 1989, there are also many references to the "society" that was destroyed or "decimated" by Communism, and how it needed to be rebuilt or "reconstituted" with the right kind of social action, existential awareness, and community participation.[16] The following analysis will focus less on *společnost* and more on *občanský*, however, because it is Havel's notion of being and becoming "civic" that remains one of his most relevant and unique contributions to political thinking contemporarily, showing the wider path of his general thinking about politics and social action. This approach necessarily raises a few preliminary questions about the word *občanský* in Czech, also requiring a contextualization of the English term "civil society" and its translation into different languages.

9   The Czech phrase is *občanské sebevědomí,*"; see Havel, "The Power of the Powerless," chapter VIII. Note that "self-awareness and confidence" is also translated as "civic awareness."
10   The Czech phrase is *občanské hodnoty*; see Václav Havel, "O smyslu Charty 77," *Spisy* 4 (Prague: Torst, 1999 [1986]), 684.
11   "Civic action" appears in the English translation while *občanské i politické jednání* appears in the original Czech version; see Václav Havel, "What Communism Still Teaches Us," Project Syndicate, 2004 (https://www.project-syndicate.org/commentary/what-communism-still-teaches-us).
12   The Czech phrase is *struktury občanského života*; see Havel, "Address by Václav Havel, President of the Czech Republic, before the Members of the European Parliament," 2000.
13   The Czech phrase is *občanská účast na veřejném životě*; see Havel, "New Year's Address," 1994.
14   The Czech phrase is *občanské uspořádání*; see Havel, "A Speech by Václav Havel President of the Czech Republic on the Occasion of 'Václav Havel's Civil Society Symposium'," 1999.
15   Czech phrases here are *společenská emancipace* and *samostatný společenský subjekt*; see Havel, "O smyslu Charty 77," 684 and 685.
16   The word *společnost* is translated as "society," but can also be translated as "community." Another Czech word for "community" or "commonwealth" is *společenství*, which comes from the same root (*spolu* "together").

The civil, the civic, and "civil society"

In Czech, the word *občanský* ("civic") shares the same root with *občan* ("citizen").[17] This direct connection between *občanský* and the idea of a "citizen" means that the term has somewhat fewer ambiguities than the words "civil" and "civic" have in English—as well as French and Spanish. This matters today because the phenomenon that came to be called "civil society," *société civile*, and *sociedad civil*, respectively, suffered from definitional challenges in the 1990s that were never quite overcome or resolved. While *občanský* can be translated into English as either "civil" or "civic," the connection that ties *občan* to *občanský* was one that Havel used in Czech, but was not necessarily evident in the same way in the English discussion of "civil society." In German, more like in Czech, *bürgerliche Gesellschaft* became the term used to describe citizens' associations and activities separate from the official institutions of the state, and *Bürger* is a "citizen" in German.[18] So the Czech version of this concept shares with the German a greater specificity of meaning with a direct connection to the concept of a citizen, and makes "*civic* society" also a viable translation of the Czech phrase. Havel used *občanská společnost* to flesh out a vision of good citizenship and good governance, so "*civic* society" works at the level of generality in the etymology of the language, but is also true to Havel's specific theorizations of "civil/civic society," where he referenced how an individual *ought* to relate to the political world as a *good* citizen, as well as how political regimes *ought to* relate to their citizens as

---

17 The word *občan*, in turn, comes from *obec*, a "community" usually associated with the lowest level of governance (of a village or town) and thus on a more modest, cozy scale than the grand, imposing "city."

18 The German translation has a unique set of its own problems, however, in that *bürgerlich*, the adjective, can also mean "bourgeois," which could open up Marxist terrain, depending on usage, and that extra dimension complicates the meaning considerably. Czech *občan* does not have this association.

free human individuals. For Havel, these phenomena contained the *moral* weight of the word "civic," and were not simply "civil" (as in peaceful) or "civil" (as in being public or political).

With hindsight, if Havel's ideas could have entered the wider world without English translation, his useful and illuminating notions about being a good citizen might have avoided being connected to the muddle that is created when "civil" and "civic" face off in English. However, English is the language of global power, and even though the ambiguity in English brought the whole idea of "civil society" onto quite problematic definitional terrain, in languages like Czech, the concept necessarily had to track back through the English translations and related problems.[19] It is impossible here to summarize all the debates within the literature on civil society about these issues,[20] but much of it is already evident at the level of language: "civil" can imply being merely peaceful and polite, having nothing to do with citizenship, whereas "civic" implies by definition something about citizenship and politics; "civil rights" (*občanská práva* in Czech) are nonetheless related to citizenship and politics, and this seems why one might choose the term "civil society" instead of "civic society." Unfortunately, it then turns out that some forms of "civil society" can exist in some contexts without full "civil rights protections," as was the case for Havel and other dissidents before

19 In English, "civil" and "civic" are synonyms and come from the same Latin root *civilis*. Google Translate suggests that the Latin *civilis* can mean the following in English: "civil, civic, political, social, public, state, courteous, gracious, citizenly, national, political, affable." This brings too many concepts into discussion to maintain coherence of argument.

20 The "civil society literature" of the 1990s is too large to fully detail here. This limited sample of works would contain the relevant cross-references to trace the literature: Andrew Arato, *Civil Society, Constitution, and Legitimacy* (Landam, MD: Rowman and Littlefield, 2000); Adam Seligman, *The Idea of Civil Society* (New York: Free Press, 1992); Jean Cohen and Andrew Arato, *Civil Society and Political Theory* (Cambridge: MIT Press, 1992); Mark Warren, Democracy *and* Association (Princeton: Princeton University Press, 2001); Jeffery Alexander, *The Civil Sphere* (Oxford: Oxford University Press, 2001); Peter Wagner (ed.), *The Languages of Civil Society* (New York: Berghahn Books, 2006); Adela Cortina, *Covenant and Contract: Politics, Ethics, and Religion* (Dudley, MA: Peeters Leuven, 2003); Ernest Gellner, *Conditions of Liberty: Civil Society and its Rivals* (London: Penguin, 1994).

1989.[21] Theorists of civil society often argued that better civil rights protections provided for a better and more "robust" civil society,[22] but civic activity can still take place in authoritarian contexts in the absence of civil rights, as civic initiatives can turn into democratic revolutions that nonetheless started in non-democratic spaces.[23] Therefore, arguing a firm relationship between civil rights and the "robustness" of civil/civic society falls into a definitional morass at the same time as one is trying to sort out the more basic linguistic issues: all civil (public/political) activity is not civil (peaceful), then often there is civil (peaceful or public) activity that is not civic, and there is even civic activity that detractors would call uncivil (like certain forms of civil disobedience). It was perhaps too exhausting to keep redefining everything indefinitely, and the discussion declined.[24]

Despite all of this, and even if Havel's *občanský* might be closer to "civic" and less ambiguous than "civil," his translated speeches after 1989 used "civil" society rather than "civic" society for good reasons, and this is not to say anything was translated incorrectly, given the time. Words translate into a specific moment in history,

21 For a detailed analysis of the legal ideas circulating after the Prague Spring and before 1989, see Kieran Williams and James Krapfl, "For a Civic Socialism and the Rule of Law: The Interplay of Jurisprudence, Public Opinion and Dissent in Czechoslovakia, 1960s–1980s," in K. McDermott and M. Stibbe (eds.), *Eastern Europe in 1968* (Palgrave Macmillan, 2018).
22 The journal *Voluntas* traced the development of many of these policy indicators. *The Global Civil Society Yearbook* series from 2001 to 2012 also helped shaped this form of policy discourse. It was also argued that civil society could exist in a war zone, beyond all civility and any sense of the civil, by arguing that "islands" could be formed in war zones through a particular form of action that was civil and/or civic; see Mary Kaldor, *New and Old Wars: Organized Violence in a Global Era.* (Stanford, CA: Stanford University Press, 2012).
23 A. Brinton, "Association and Recognition in Authoritarian Societies: A Theoretical Beginning," *European Journal of Political Theory,* 11:3, July 2012.
24 Querying "civil society" (in English) in Google's Ngram Viewer shows these patterns fairly well. Usage is fairly level, and fairly minimal, until about 1985. Then it increases at a steep exponential rate until about 2000. Then a downward trend starts, and the Google records end in 2008. It looks a bit like it is on a downward trend heading for a bell curve shape with the peak at 2000, though something could change.

and the term "civil society" in English was flourishing with a life of its own after 1989, and Havel's ideas were important in building the reputation of the concept, even (and especially) in English-language conversations.[25] Havel and other Central European dissidents were celebrated in "the West" for how they used "civil society" to promote democracy and undermine Communism. Evoking "civil society" became a short-hand way to celebrate how civic engagement helped end the Cold War, as well as a way to extol the virtues of dissidents like Havel who helped bring about the global triumph of democracy.[26] The victory parade did not stop there, either. This enthusiasm for the role of civil society in democratic transitions later became a policy mandate, and "fostering civil society" came to be actively promoted around the world for old, new, and future democracies alike, advocated for by states, communities, and international organizations alike.[27] Throughout the 1990s, many policy-makers

25 For a very optimistic assessment of how civil society was involved in 1989, see Gale Stokes, *The Walls Came Tumbling Down* (New York: Oxford University Press, 1993).

26 Havel's pre-1989 work contains many insightful critiques of democracy, including at times placing it under the same problematic of technical-rationalized civilization as Communism. In some of the post-1989 triumphalist discourse, both Havel and his audiences seem to have become deaf to the memory of this critique. While Havel's speech on the state of democracy on the first anniversary of November 1989 was anything but triumphalist, by the time of his speech at Macalester College in 1999 (Havel, "A Speech by Václav Havel President of the Czech Republic on the Occasion of 'Václav Havel's Civil Society Symposium'," 1999), he had integrated "civil society" into most of his visions of democratic political solutions (see discussion below). The "post-1989 triumphalist discourse" had many outlets: it included the "new world order" proclaimed by George H. W. Bush, the idea of "there is no alternative" in the UK and Germany, the unending discussions of the "end of history" proclaimed by Francis Fukuyama, and the research industry around G. O'Donnell's and P. Schmitter's *Transitions from Authoritarian Rule* (Baltimore: John's Hopkins University Press, 1986) that advocated for more democratic transitions based on the Western model. More specifically, this set of ideas was also manifested in accounts of the 1989 revolutions, including Stokes' *The Walls Came Tumbling Down* and Timothy Garton Ash's *The Magic Lantern* (New York: Vintage, 1998). Some versions also appeared in international relation theory in the form of works like G. John Ikenberry's *After Victory: Institutions, Strategic Restraint, and the Rebuilding of Order after Major Wars* (Princeton: Princeton University Press, 2000), where it was argued that America's WWII victory had set the stage for the global success of its model of governance and foreign policy into the "long shadow" of the endless future.

27 There are departments at various national and international institutions which exist for the sake of "fostering civil society," and many of these have origins in the 1990s. A small set of

and academics (at times including Havel) treated "civil society" as a potential cure-all to pretty much every problem of global politics.[28] Concepts have larger-than-life moments, and the spotlight on "civil society" faded in the following decades, but in the late 1990s when Havel was giving many speeches and using the term regularly, "civil society" was all-the-rage, so-to-speak.[29]

Once both Havel (as president) and "civil society" (as concept) were in the limelight together on the global stage, translating *občanská společnost* to "civil society" meant borrowing from the aura of victory and hope. To translate Havel's speeches differently would have seemed awkward given the zeitgeist. Using "civil society" meant his words were included in conversations in other languages, also allowing him to comment on what kinds of governance might make democracy work and what kinds of social arrangements

examples: UN Civil Society https://esango.un.org/civilsociety/; European Commission Civil Society https://ec.europa.eu/europeaid/sectors/human-rights-and-governance/civil-society_en; USAID Europe and Eurasia Civil Society https://www.usaid.gov/europe-eurasia-civil-society.

28 Havel himself fell into this mode of overstatement: "In the world of today—enveloped by a global, essentially materialistic and widely self-jeopardizing civilization—one of the ways of combatting all the escalating dangers consists in the systematic creation of a universal civil society" ("Havel, "A Speech by Václav Havel President of the Czech Republic on the Occasion of 'Václav Havel's Civil Society Symposium'," 1999).

29 In the interests of full disclosure, I participated willingly and enthusiastically in this trendiness by entering graduate school in 2001 and choosing to write about "civil society" with a fellowship from a then-new institute called the "Center for Democracy and Civil Society." This center received a large initial grant in the late 1990s to launch, but then apropos of the situation, was unable to find much more financial support after that, and I was soon advised to reframe my own research to distance myself from what had become a problematic concept. My dissertation, "Civil Society Outside of Democracy: A Theory," was inspired by the writings of many different Central European dissidents, including Havel, but was incorporated into a book that did not have "civil society" in the title, for "strategic reasons." Trying to "make a contribution" in the academic sense to a literature that was spinning its wheels in definitional problems was seen at the time (after 2006) as a professional liability. While my singular experience should not be generalized too broadly, the overall trajectory and fate of "civil society" as a concept also affected Havel, especially as his own popularity in the Czech Republic declined and after a protracted debate with Václav Klaus about the concept of "civil society." In many ways, Havel staked his political career on the bundle of concepts linked together by his idea of "civil society," and then the world lost interest in the concept, as well as its interest in small eastern European countries, perhaps especially after 9/11/2001 marked the end of an optimistic era.

might better protect human rights, promote political pluralism, protect the natural environment, and help limit fanaticism.[30] For Havel and so many others, "civil society" became part of a package of ideas about how to fix the world, becoming an easily *recognized* term. Whether it was easily *understood*, however, was another matter. "Civil society" soon became part of the academic lexicon of political science and sociology, where there were many attempts to measure it and define it, and debates about its paradoxes and contradictions proliferated.[31] Other phenomena (some new, some old) came into discussion as possible alternatives or as tangential and collateral compliments: civic associations, uncivil society, civil disobedience, non-governmental organizations, non-state actors, civic community, global civil society, and so on. "Civil society" lost much of its initial aura through this evolution and fracturing, and academic interest declined.[32] Havel continued using the term, linking his notions of *občanská společnost* to being a good citizen in a post-Communist democracy, but also occasionally returning to earlier pre-1989 ideas about how to be a good citizen within a bad government.

With our current hindsight, and with the help of the Czech word *občan* ("citizen"), some of the chaos of the conversations about civil society in English in the 1990s, while necessary to acknowledge, can

---

30 In speeches where he discussed "civil society," he also often discussed these issues; see note 1.

31 Empirical data on the existence of civil society in the countries of the world was collected through many projects; for one example, see the *Global Civil Society Yearbook* series, published by the London School of Economics, (New York: Oxford University Press, 2001-2012).

32 A sample (not an exhaustive list) of skepticism from this period includes: Ariel Armony, *The Dubious Link: Civic Engagement and Democratization* (Stanford University Press, 2004); Gideon Baker, *Civil Society and Democratic Theory: Alternative Voices* (London: Routledge, 2002); Peter Wagner (ed.), *The Languages of Civil Society* (New York: Berghahn Books, 2006); Sarah Mendelson and John Glenn (eds.), *The Power and Limits of NGOs* (New York: Colombia University Press, 2002); Nancy Bermeo and Philip Nord, *Civil Society Before Democracy: Lessons from Nineteenth Century Europe* (New York: Rowman and Littlefield, 2000); Hakan Seckinelgin "Civil Society as a Metaphor for Western Liberalism", *Global Society*, 16:4, (2002); Stephen Kotkin and Jan Gross, Uncivil Society: 1989 and the Implosions of the Communist Establishment (New York: Random House, 2009).

be bracketed here, and it might become possible to explore instead what it meant to Havel to be a good citizen in civil or civic society, or civic communities, within the (very different) political situations he faced throughout his disparate life-chapters: some of his notions of being "civic" in a "society" as a "good citizen" were fostered in the dissident milieu of dark basements in Prague, where small groups of artists and intellectuals discussed samizdat texts while evading the secret police; some of his notions arose from thinking through the civic import of artistic integrity and freedom of speech as a playwright confronting a Marxist-Leninist regime; some ideas arose from the heady days of revolutionary exuberance in 1989; some ideas became tied together with local and global post-Cold War political debates that Havel might not have ever imagined initially, but nonetheless caused him (a head of state) to theorize his own version of global citizenship for the twenty-first century.

There are thematic resonances that tie together his ideas about being a good citizen of a "civil society," but there are also notional variations across the development of a complicated life, and his core ideas take on new conceptual nuances as the world changes around him. While it is impossible to show each slight shift of meaning in this short space, perhaps it is most illuminating to start with the end, represented by his 1999 definition of civil society offered at a Macalester College conference, then to work backwards through time to show how his notions of being "civic" (*občanský*) helped shape the fullness of his political ideas over several decades about a proper and good "society" (*společnost*). In Havel's non-linear universe, the categorizations offered here do not imply direct causation or a firmly linear genealogy from one idea to the next (therefore it is not wholly illogical to move backwards rather than forwards). The goal, rather, is to show a set of overlapping circles within which "civil society" came to matter for Havel as he moved through a changing world.

Presidential "civil society"

When Havel was invited to open a conference on the idea of civil society at an American university in 1999, he stepped into the role of an academic theorizer, replete with a detailed definition, a short history, and three pillars of policy. He started by explaining how Communism undermined civil society, or why "Communists knew very well why they needed to dominate and manipulate every bee-keepers' association," and then he described where civil society came from:

> Civil society is an intricately structured, very fragile, sometimes even slightly mysterious organism that grew for decades, if not centuries, out of a natural development, reflecting the continuous evolution of the human mind and morality, the degree of societal knowledge and self-knowledge, and a certain type of civic awareness and self-confidence.[33]

As a politician trying to regenerate civil society from a centuries-old tradition more recently undermined by Communism, at the moment of this speech Havel might have been trying to nurture the fragility of social institutions through a path of "civic awareness and self-confidence," but he also comes to a definition of civil society that has bullet-point policy recommendations, where he asserts that certain laws and state practices might help foster and rebuild this "mysterious organism." These policy recommendations become the substance of his description of civil society. He wants the state to support the "free association of people in different types of organizations, ranging from clubs, community groups, civic initiatives, foundations and publicly beneficial organizations up to churches and political parties."[34] After identifying these types of civil society

---

33 Havel, "A Speech by Václav Havel President of the Czech Republic on the Occasion of 'Václav Havel's Civil Society Symposium'," 1999.
34 Havel, "A Speech by Václav Havel President of the Czech Republic on the Occasion of 'Václav Havel's Civil Society Symposium'," 1999.

organizations, he then advocates policies of support: tax deduction for citizens' donations to these organizations, policies of oversight that are minimal and decentralized, and laws that help the post-Communist government overcome its resistance to decentralization. He expresses his disappointment that the central government had still refused to cede control of certain issues to municipalities and localities, citing centralization as detrimental to the redevelopment of civil society. Most of this policy discussion seems to be a glimpse into the presidential portfolio on his desk at that moment, making clear that in his mind, restoring civil society and restoring democracy and the rule of law were inextricably linked processes. In another telling moment, he hinted at the internal battles within Czech politics that came to involve problematic interpretations of the term: "Faith in civil society is still interpreted by many in the Czech lands as leftism, anarchism or syndicalism; someone has even called it proto-fascism."[35] The concept of "civil society" did indeed confuse traditional left-right categories,[36] and as the victory parade wore off after 1989, the term (and Havel himself) came under criticism for being the enemy of both the right and the left.[37]

In Havel's 1999 speech, and as a rejoinder to this problem of interpretation and misunderstanding, he ends by evoking a very different vision and definition of "civil society," one much less policy-oriented and much more concerned with ideas of existential humanism. He

35   Havel, "A Speech by Václav Havel President of the Czech Republic on the Occasion of 'Václav Havel's Civil Society Symposium'," 1999.
36   See J. Cohen and A. Arato, *Civil Society and Political Theory*: the opening chapters of this work explain the left-right tensions as well as the connections of the idea of "civil society" to Central European dissidents.
37   The story of Havel's disagreements with Czech Prime Minister Václav Klaus in the 1990s are described in John Keane, *Václav Havel: A Political Tragedy in Six Acts* (London: Basic Books, 2000), 438-476. Disagreements about interpretations of "civil society" were part of this. See also Martin Myant, "Klaus, Havel and the Debate over Civil Society in the Czech Republic," *Journal of Communist Studies and Transition* Politics, 22:2 (2005), 248-267; James F. Pontuso, "Transformation Politics: The Debate between Václav Havel and Václav Klaus on the Free Market and Civil Society," *Studies in East European Thought*, 54:3 (2002), 153-177.

comes to sound more like his earlier dissident writings, where "civil society" was about the cultivation of the moral citizen:

> The most important aspect of civil society is yet another thing—it is the fact that it enables people to realize themselves truly and entirely as the beings that they potentially are, that is, as the species called *zoon politicon*, or social animal. Human beings are [...] creatures who want to be with others, who yearn for various forms of coexistence and cooperation, who want to participate in the life of a group or of a community and who want to influence that which happens around them [...] Humanity constitutes a subject of conscience, of moral order, of love for our fellow humans. Civil society is one of the ways in which our human nature can be exercised in its entirety [...] Civil society, at least as I see it, is simply one of the great opportunities for human responsibility for the world [...] It seems to me that the most open arrangement—one that best enables all types of human self-identification to develop alongside one another—is an arrangement based on the civic principle, an arrangement founded on faith in the citizen and on respect for him. One of the most important expressions of such a civic arrangement is that which we call civil society.[38]

Here there are not only many references to responsibility, community, cooperation, and openness, but a "civic arrangement" (*občanské uspořádání*) stands over and above "civil society" (*občanská společnost*). This is a good example of Havel connecting prior notions of *občanský* and civic sensibility to a later definition of civil society. He uses the Greek term from Aristotle, *zoon politikon*, to evoke the social and political nature of human beings, intimating that certain groups or communities can become much more than the sum of their parts, also suggesting that we can become more

---

38   Havel, "A Speech by Václav Havel President of the Czech Republic on the Occasion of 'Václav Havel's Civil Society Symposium'," 1999.

human and more ourselves when we are in the right kind of social arrangements with others, or the right kind of "society."

From the tone of the speech, Havel seems more emotionally committed to this latter idea of civil society (as a moral and civic category) than he was to his basic policy recommendations. His 1994 New Year's address definition of "civil society," like the 1999 academic speech, also mixes newer democracy-related policy ideas with prior notions about the civically-minded moral citizen, doing so in the wake of the Velvet Divorce of the Czech Republic and Slovakia.[39] In 1994, Havel was highly concerned with the problem of nationalism being manifested in this separation, a concern made more acute by the nationalist conflicts in the Balkans at the same time.[40] Havel had already turned to civil society in 1994 to put forward ideas about the decentralization of state offices that he repeats in 1999, but he also used civil society in this earlier 1994 speech as a potential antidote to the problems of nationalism, thus connecting it to categories of moral and civic responsibility. Here Havel expresses two of his key ideas about civil society that repeat throughout his presidential speeches: the connections between civil society and democracy, and the importance of integration with European civil society as the future path of Czech democracy. Both concepts, notably, connect back to a robust notion of citizenship and what it means to be a proper citizen of a democratic state and to participate in civil society:

Democracy is a system based on trust in the human sense of responsibility. It ought to awaken and cultivate this responsibility. Democracy and civil society are thus two sides of the same coin. Today, when our very planetary civilization is endangered by human irresponsibility, I see no other way to save it than through a general

39 Havel, "New Year's Address to the Nation," 1994.
40 Havel, "Conclusion of the Month of Bosnia and Herzegovina in Prague," 1995. He contrasts the idea of civil society with the problem of nationalism in Bosnia, arguing that civil society could ameliorate the problems of nationalism

awakening and cultivation of the sense of responsibility people have for the affairs of this world [...] The development of civil society chiefly depends on the citizens themselves [...] It is essential that the expansion of possibilities that I am speaking of here will deepen in society a sense of civic solidarity, an interest in public affairs, and will give people the experience of participating in them, the feeling of responsibility for the whole and thus, indirectly, good relations with their own country [...] [The state] must offer citizens a wide variety of ways to become involved, both privately and publicly, to develop very different types of civic coexistence, solidarity and participation.[41]

While democratic institutions exist at the level of a national state, Havel goes on to argue in this speech that loyalty to the national state has not always been good for Europe, evoking fascism and the World Wars, and then explaining why the model of the European Union might, like civil society, mitigate the most harmful effects of nationalism:

Today, the only alternative to the programmatic national state as it has emerged in various forms in Europe over the past centuries is a state founded on the civic principle, a principle that unites people and does not separate them, without of course denying them any of their other affiliations. In fact, it is the only principle that makes it possible for people, freely and in peace with others, to give substance to their affiliations [...] A truly civic state, shored up by democratic law, is based on understanding for others, not on resistance to them [...] Building a state on the civic principle, however, can only be achieved by building a genuinely civil society [...]The basic principle that will make this integration at all possible is again, of course, the civic principle. It is a guarantee that national rancor will never again triumph over normal civic cooperation. The many different civil societies in the European democratic

41   Havel, "New Year's Address to the Nation," 1994.

countries will, together, create the great European civil society. I see no other and no better possibility for us than to accept this spirit of civic Europe. It is the only alternative that can rid us for good of the fear of others.[42]

The main theme here seems clarified by the repeated language: civic principle, civic cooperation, civic solidarity, civic state, civic Europe, and civic coexistence. In Czech, he uses some form of *občanský* in all of these terms, mapping a lexicon of "the civic" through imagining how European civil society and democracy were an antidote to nationalism. The "civic principle" was one way the nationalism might be overcome through a different type of solidarity, but also through a holistic vision of the citizen's good and proper relationship with the state, together with the state's willingness to provide for civic opportunities.

Whether or not "civil society" is actually an antidote to nationalism in a more general sense is one of the debates from the 1990s that was never resolved in a definitive theoretical or empirical way in the academic literature. For example, American political scientist Sheri Berman's widely-read article during the civil society exuberance of the 1990s put a severe damper on the kind of optimism Havel was expressing in his 1994 speech.[43] She argued convincingly that the Weimar years in Germany were a robust example of a fully engaged citizenry replete with prolific civic associations occurring in great numbers, but then showed how this social-political environment provided fertile soil for all types of political mobilization, including Nazism, and thereafter the collapse of a democratic regime. Some sobering-up followed, and her 1997 article was the beginning of much wider skepticism about the notion of civil society and its connection to democracy. Berman opened up the idea that the associations of

42 Havel, "New Year's Address to the Nation," 1994.
43 Sheri Berman, "Civil Society and the Collapse of the Weimar Republic," *World Politics* 49:3 (1997), 401-429.

"civil society" can be a vehicle of articulation for what is already there in a given society—civil or uncivil.[44] Then the circulation of the term "uncivil society" unleashed again the quagmire of definitional problems with civil-as-in peaceful and/or civil-as-in public/political. More importantly for Havel, this discussion led to a fracturing of the conversation towards categories that explicitly avoided moral or normative judgments, where terms like "non-state actors" or "non-governmental organizations" became more accepted than "civil society."

The Charta 77 civic citizen

The purported moral and ethical neutrality of this new stage of the discourse was not a place where Havel's ideas fit very well, especially given his dependence on normative judgments and moral categories to uphold his sense of what constituted the civil-civic and *moral* citizen. For Havel, morality was involved in sustaining and creating civic action, and vice versa. To be human was to be moral, and to be human was also to be political. Citizenship in a political entity defined by administrative status (like holding a passport or living in a municipality) was only a technicality; for Havel, being a citizen "in the strong and binding sense"[45] was not just about the rights granted to the citizen by the state, but about the duties of responsibility and obligation to your fellow citizens that came with political

44 See for example, Mark Kaldor and Diego Muro, "Religious and Nationalist Militant Groups" in Mary Kaldor, Helmut Anheier, Marlies Glasius (eds.), *Global Civil Society Yearbook, 2003* (Oxford: Oxford University Press, 2003); Petr Kopecky and Cas Mudde (eds.), *Uncivil Society: Contentious Politics in Post-Communist Europe* (London: Routledge, 2003); Morris P. Fiorina, "Extreme Voices: The Dark Side of Civic Engagement" in Theda Skocpol and Morris P. Fiorina (eds.), *Civic Engagement in American Democracy* (Washington, DC: Brookings Institution Press, 1999).
45 Havel, "O smyslu Charty 77," 672. The English translation of this document is not readily available in a published or online edition. Some of the same ideas are reiterated in two short essays in *Open Letters* that Havel also wrote about the Charter ("Two Notes on Charter 77"), but the full description of a good citizen and the moral grounding of the Charter is not in those, and is most fully elaborated in "O smyslu Charty 77."

and civic life.[46] Given his life as a dissident in a totalitarian state, he knew all too well that duty to the state could go terribly wrong, so he focused instead on a person's duty to other human beings as the basis of being a good citizen.[47] Under the surveillance of secret police in the bugged apartments of Prague where fear of state-sponsored persecution was the impetus for vulnerable dissidents to gather together, the basis of their community was explicitly moral and normative, where standing against the immoral practices of the ruling regime was pretty much the whole point. This was also a world that did not depend upon the state to do anything supportive—there were no tax deductions or decentralized municipalities or European Union helping out—but rather, being a "good citizen" meant a willingness to channel spontaneous discontent into a loose informal social gathering, and then eventually somehow find the "civic bravery" to jointly articulate that collective discontent at very high personal costs, such as going to prison or even dying. Havel directly articulated these ideas in his writings about Charter 77, but such gatherings had predated this specific civic initiative. Dissident groups had been a form of underground *civic community* since the Communists took power, and were less a form of *civil society*, especially given their conflictual relationship to the official government. Again, however, the English terms "civil society" and "civic community" are still confusing for the characterization of this situation, and it is probably clearer to say that Havel's conception of *the good citizen*

---

46 Havel, "The Power of the Powerless," chapter XXI: "Above all, any existential revolution should provide hope of a moral reconstitution of society, which means a radical renewal of the relationship of human beings to what I have called the 'human order,' which no political order can replace. A new experience of being, a renewed rootedness in the universe, a newly grasped sense of higher responsibility, a newfound inner relationship to other people and to the human community—these factors clearly indicate the direction in which we must go."

47 "I favor politics as practical morality, as service to the truth, as essentially human and humanly measured care for our fellow humans. It is, I presume, an approach which, in this world, is extremely impractical and difficult to apply in daily life", see Václav Havel, "Politics and Conscience," trans. Erazim Kohák and Roger Scruton, in *Open Letters: Selected Writings 1965-1990* (New York: Vintage, 1992), 269.

before 1989 was that of someone outside the state apparatus in their own autonomous community, and after 1989, Havel's *good citizen* was necessarily inside the state working to build democracy. These two types of gathering—state-supported institutions of "civil society" after 1989 in a democratic state, and dissident groups of 'civic community' before 1989 pushing against an authoritarian state—do, however, have in common for Havel a notion of an engaged citizen embedded in a moral order.

Havel's writings before 1989 have a rawness and honesty that political speeches by presidents in office can never have, and it is from this era of his life that his most lasting ideas about all that is civic—*občanský*—appear. The most illuminating usages of *občanský* are within the documents written about Charter 77, especially "The Power of the Powerless," "Politics and Conscience," and "The Meaning of Charter 77." Here he develops his ideas of civic responsibility, civic self-consciousness, and civic bravery; these ideas would become the core of what he came to call the "civic principle" later on (see above). The "civic principle" is a phrase that also repeats throughout the presidential speeches (as it did in the 1999 speech quoted above) and was already implicit within the dissident milieu of post-1968 Prague. After the Soviet invasion and the onset of "normalization" policies that renewed restrictions on freedom of speech and freedom of association, the role of the state was entirely adversarial for Havel and other dissidents and Chartists, so any sense of *občanský* as "civil" was decidedly *not* related to the public or to official political institutions. Dissidents' actions might have entailed civic responsibility in some understanding of the long-term future, but in daily practice it was more like huddling together nervously knowing Charter 77 would fail, but agreeing with other Chartists that it was morally necessary to do something anyway. As Havel asks in "The Power of the Powerless:"

Do not these small communities, bound together by thousands of shared tribulations, give rise to some of those special humanly meaningful political relationships and ties that we have been talking about? Are not these communities (and they are communities more than organizations)— motivated mainly by a common belief in the profound significance of what they are doing since they have no chance of direct, external success—joined together by precisely the kind of atmosphere in which the formalized and ritualized ties common in the official structures are supplanted by a living sense of solidarity and fraternity?[48]

These bonds of solidarity were an important part of what could constitute the "power of powerless" in an oppressive political situation. At the end of "Politics and Conscience," Havel cites Jan Patočka's idea of the "solidarity of the shaken" to reiterate the point that his type of solidarity had potentially global power:

When Jan Patočka wrote about Charter 77, he used the term "solidarity of the shaken." He was thinking of those who dared resist impersonal power and to confront it with the only thing at their disposal, their own humanity. Does not the perspective of a better future depend on something like an international community of the shaken which, ignoring state boundaries, political systems, and power blocs, standing outside the high game of traditional politics, aspiring to no titles and appointments, will seek to make a real political force out of a phenomenon so ridiculed by the technicians of power—the phenomenon of human conscience?[49]

The hopefulness in this idea, furthermore, is an extension of Havel's moral argument earlier in the essay:

---

48 Havel, "The Power of the Powerless," chapter XXII.
49 Havel, "Politics and Conscience," 271. For more on "power" as a key word, see Popescu in this volume.

We must make values and imperatives the starting point of all our acts, of all our personally attested, openly contemplated, and ideologically uncensored lived experience. We must trust the voice of our conscience more than that of all abstract speculations and not invent responsibilities other than the one to which the voice calls us. We must not be ashamed that we are capable of love, friendship, solidarity, sympathy, and tolerance, but just the opposite: we must set these fundamental dimensions of our humanity free from their 'private' exile and accept them as the only genuine starting point of meaningful human community. We must be guided by our own reason and serve the truth under all circumstances as our own essential experience.[50]

None of the actions undertaken by dissident civic communities would work, he claimed, unless participants were both moral and civic, basing their actions on values and conscience and seeking the truth.

Havel's ideas of civic community between Charter 77 and 1989 are infused with a sense of tragic anarchistic beauty, and elements of his ideas are admittedly both rather poetic and rather unstable. When he rhetorically asks in "The Power of the Powerless" if the community of dissidents huddled together facing the adversity of the post-totalitarian state might be a model of "post-democratic" politics able to bring about the reconstitution of society and humanity, he also points out how such gatherings are spontaneous communities that do not last and do not usually institutionalize themselves into the "ballast of hallowed traditions," but rather "emerge, live, and disappear." Then he asks, "[i]s not their attempt to create an articulate form of living within the truth and to renew the feeling of higher responsibility in an apathetic society really a sign of some kind of rudimentary moral reconstitution?"[51] While

50 Havel, "Politics and Conscience," 267.
51 Havel, "The Power of the Powerless," chapter XXII.

it might be hyperbole to put it this way, Havel seems to think that dissident civic communities might in some cases save our souls; turning to the reconstitution of morality (in both the self and the larger society) connects Havel's political action to ethical, normative, spiritual, and metaphysical concerns.[52] He sees choices about political commitments as choices about moral commitments, and moral commitments as capable of making us into whole human beings to stand against the falsities of totalitarianism.[53] He also sees the exercise of a personal "existential revolution" as happening within civic communities like Charter 77 that are fleeting and spontaneous, highly impermanent, and not anchored in ossified institutions. The truth which emerges in these spaces is also not an obvious truth pervasive at all times, but itself elusive and evanescent, a truth that must be actively sought out.[54] Havel wonders in "The Power of the Powerless" whether the togetherness and camaraderie of Charter 77 will disappear after the original adversity and pressure also disappears. With hindsight, his worries were justified; a general public sense of civic solidarity did not last

---

52 While there are many moments spirituality and politics intersect in his work, the beginning of "Politics and Conscience" has one of the clearest examples, where he sees reconstituting a vision of the natural world as the first step towards the form of political engagement he advocates: "We must draw our standards from our natural world, heedless of ridicule, and reaffirm its denied validity. We must honor with the humility of the wise the limits of that natural world and the mystery which lies beyond them, admitting that there is something in the order of being which evidently exceeds all our competence. We must relate to the absolute horizon of our existence which, if we will, we shall constantly rediscover and experience" (Havel, "Politics and Conscience," 267). See also David S. Danaher, *Reading Vaclav Havel* (Toronto: University of Toronto Press, 2015), in particular the chapter 4 on "spirituality" and other Havelian keywords in their original Czech and English translation. For a further account of the way morality works through Havel's political ideas, see Delia Popescu, *Political Action in Václav Havel's Thought: The Responsibility of Resistance* (Landham, MD: Lexington Books, 2012). Havel was also building on a sequence of prison letters from summer 1982; see Václav Havel, *Letters to Olga*, letter 143 (which calls for a renewed sense of human community or *pospolitost*) and letter 144.
53 For a comparison and a similar analysis of morality's relationship to politics and humanity in regard to Charter 77, see Jan Patočka, "Two Charta 77 Texts" in *Jan Patočka: Philosophy and Selected Writings*, trans. Erazim Kohák (Chicago: Chicago University Press, 1989), 340-347.
54 For more on "truth" as a key word, see Williams in this volume.

very far past 1989.[55] Yet for the Charter signatories themselves, their role became part of their personal identity, part of their own moral reconstitution, and part of history writ-large globally. As he wrote in "The Meaning of Charter 77": "history began to return among us [*dějiny se vracely mezi náma*]" and "the end opened anew [*konec se znovu otevřel*]" when a small group of people came together to undertake hopeless and absurd action against an unjust government.[56]

Co dělat? What to do?

Unlike his participation in the trendiness of the "civil society discourse" in the 1990s, Havel's dissident writings today seem more timeless, and thus also timelier. This timeless timeliness emerges from his ability to speak to existential and political conundrums far beyond his own century, even while doing so with ironic humility that does not point to itself as a timeless universal principle or "political theory." While his method is unconventional when held up to academic political theory and philosophy, his political thinking is nonetheless innovative and substantive: he zooms into the details of his own local situation—the common greengrocer, awkward office dynamics, the teenage rock band, the rude wine-bar bouncer, the smokestack polluting the heavens—and then asks his reader to zoom out—metaphysically far out—to see the broadest possible political significance of such quotidian details. Within this, the vision of civic community that emerges from Havel's intellectual process combines a concern for the morality of political action with meditations on the wistful fleetingness of dissident communities and activities.

---

55   For one example from an American political scientist, see Marc M. Howard, *The Weakness of Civil Society in Post-Communist Europe* (Cambridge: Cambridge University Press, 2003).
56   Havel, "O smyslu Charty 77," 685.

To paradoxically categorize the substance of his thinking that generally transcends categories, it could be said that his way of proceeding reveals a mix of Aristotelian virtue ethics (where politics is about shaping the virtuous citizen) and anarchism (where proper politics can only arise in voluntary spontaneous comings-together of responsible citizens in the absence of state authority).[57] While his version of virtue ethics is embedded into his ideas of a "good citizen" discussed above, the anarchism appears through his discussion of anti-organizational and anti-political dissidence:

> Rather than a strategic agglomeration of formalized organizations, it is better to have organizations springing up ad hoc, infused with enthusiasm for a particular purpose and disappearing when that purpose has been achieved [...] These structures should naturally arise from below as a consequence of authentic social self-organization; they should derive vital energy from a living dialogue with the genuine needs from which they arise, and when these needs are gone, the structures should also disappear. The principles of their internal organization should be very diverse, with a minimum of external regulation [...] Both political and economic life ought to be founded on the varied and versatile cooperation of such dynamically appearing and disappearing organizations.[58]

---

57 In their accounts of Havel's political thinking, both Delia Popescu and James Pontoso discuss Havel's use of political concepts such as anti-politics, parallel polis, decentralized civic action, and small-scale work to characterize the anti-statist and independent gatherings that Havel endorses. I have gone farther and beyond these interpretations in using a framework of "anarchism," because the limits and problems with the term "civil society" make it seem necessary to zoom outward to a wider framework. I am not, therefore, using "anarchism" here in a pejorative or negative sense, but in line with recent efforts in political theory to substantiate anarchism as a viable description of actual practices of dissidence and activism. See, for example, David Graeber, *The Democracy Project* (New York: Spiegel and Grau, 2013); Jean-Luc Nancy, *Being Singular* Plural, trans. R. Richardson and A. O'Byrne (Stanford: Stanford University Press, 2000); Jacques Ranciere, *Dissensus: On Politics and* Aesthetics, trans. Steven Corcoran (New York: Bloomsbury Academic, 2010); James Scott, *The Art of Not Being Governed: An Anarchist History of Upland Southeast Asia* (New Have: Yale University Press, 2010).
58 Havel, "The Power of the Powerless," chapter XXI.

This is, more or less, the evocation of an anarchist vision, a stance suspicious of not just the overarching power of the state, but of all formal power and organizational structures. Even though anarchism and Aristotelianism seem to share very little at first glance, as political theories, both have (each within itself) leftist and rightist versions.[59] If anarchism and Aristotelianism subvert reified political notions of "left" and "right" (anarchism perhaps more intentionally, as Aristotle just usefully predated these distinctions), so too does Havel share the same subversive tension. He reports in one essay how Charter 77 was disorienting to some onlookers because it was not traditionally "leftist" or "rightist." He then points out that the Chartists' unconventional mixing of ideas was indeed intentionally meant to overcome the "left-right" ideological farce of the Cold War.[60] To be a true dissident, then, Havel thought it necessary to dissent against both sides. Once he was president of an EU candidate state, he spoke in favor democracy and the free market (as well as attaching his idea of "civil society" to those ideas). Before that,

---

59   For example, rightist anarchism is shown in extreme libertarian movements in the United States, like the Montana Freeman, The Sovereign Citizens, and the newer examples of declarations of self-sovereignty in encampments by those refusing to cede authority to agents of the state or pay taxes; leftist anarchism is the final stage in Marx's theory, where the state "withers away" and becomes unnecessary because everyone is equal, self-governing, and there is no more need for the state to adjudicate conflicts. Rightist Aristotelianism would be focused on conservative preservation of moral traditions of virtue in established culture (see, for example, the work of Alasdair MacIntyre); leftist/leftish Aristotelianism comes in several forms, focusing on Aristotle's advocacy of civic engagement and democratic political involvement in *The Ethics* and *The Politics*—see, for example, Martha Nussbaum, "Aristotelian Social Democracy," in R. Bruce Douglass, Gerald M. Mara, and Henry S. Richardson (eds.), *Liberalism and the Good* (New York: Routledge, 1990).
60   Havel, "Two Notes on Charter 77," 326: "A kind of bi-polar thinking is becoming more and more common in today's politically polarized world [...] People who live in the world of such thinking have constant and understandable problems with Charter 77. If it is right-wing, then why isn't it properly, openly and consistently right-wing? If it is left-wing, then why isn't it properly, openly and consistently left-wing? [...] Such questions also spring from a misunderstanding of what the Charter really is. Charter 77 is neither left-wing nor right-wing, not because it is 'somewhere-in-the-middle,' but because it has nothing whatever in common with that spectrum, because in essence, it lies outside it. As a civic initiative [...] it is [...] 'above' it all [...] it is concerned with the truth, with truthful description of conditions, and with free and objective criticism of those conditions."

however, he critiqued both Communism and democracy as part of the same technological-rationalized automatism that undermined human autonomy and subjectivity.[61] He did believe Communism was worse, but before 1989, he identified traditional parliamentary democracy and capitalism as problematic in serious ways as well. He thought dissident civic communities addressed a larger problem that at once contained democracy, capitalism, Communism, and totalitarianism. His dissent against the "left," the "right," and the whole Cold-War structure reveals a reverence for the communitarian aspects of socialism as well as a reverence for individual human liberty oriented in opposition to the too-powerful state. There is both libertarianism and communalism within this mix.[62]

Thirty years after the end of the Cold War, such a tension is now an opportunity to ask, with Havel, "and why not?" *Why not* think with both anarchism and Aristotle at once? Why not put together communalism and libertarianism? Does the community that respects virtue, human subjectivity, and equality also *necessarily* have to be an institution that shuts down human liberties and denies us our freedom? Why did the Cold War force us to make this choice in these terms? How have our categories of political thinking been closed to new political imaginaries because we were told we must choose only from within this dichotomy in all of its forms: socialism

61   Havel, "Politics and Conscience," 267. "[I]t seems to me that all of us, East and West, face one fundamental task from which all else should follow. That task is one of resisting vigilantly, thoughtfully, and attentively, but at the same time with total dedication, at every step and everywhere, the irrational momentum of anonymous, impersonal, and inhuman power—the power of ideologies, systems, apparat, bureaucracy, artificial languages, and political slogans. We must resist its complex and wholly alienating pressure, whether it takes the form of consumption, advertising, repression, technology, or cliché—all of which are the blood brothers of fanaticism and the wellspring of totalitarian thought."
62   While this view can already be found in his earliest thoughts on politics in his teenage letters (around 1953), it was shaped in the 1960s by the revisionist Marxist philosopher Ivan Sviták. See also Jean Bethke Elshtain, "A Performer of Political Thought: Václav Havel On Freedom And Responsibility," *Nomos* 37 (1995), 464-482. Elshtain characterizes Havel's contribution to political thought as his ability to rise above ideological frameworks and get beyond the "legacy of the French Revolution," so her argument has some affinity with this one.

versus capitalism, small government versus big government, cosmopolitanism versus patriotism, environmental protection versus economic growth, and so on. Perhaps these supposedly "opposed" categories seem opposed to one another because they are tinged with the legacy of Cold War dualism. Havel's civic self-consciousness during his dissident years created one set of ideas involved in helping end the Cold War. Even if the triumphalism of "civil society" in the 1990s should be questioned, and even if it is admitted that "civil society" will always be too confused a concept to fix all problems everywhere at once, without civic initiatives, the civic principle, and such adjacent ideas, civically-minded citizens might not have gathered together in Prague's basements, and Havel's writings might not be here to be read.

Rereading Havel today, one can see that he used many forms of the civic—*občanský*—to call on his audiences to see beyond the over-simplified oppositions of left and right. Somewhere on a more distant horizon, taking this seriously might make possible the embrace of a vision of global citizenship wide enough to include community *and* liberty, virtue *and* independence, solidarity *and* progress. This might require, as the English collection of Havel's speeches was titled, engaging in "the art of the impossible."[63] Yet Havel also knew that when failure was inherent in the very act of impossible considerations, Sisyphus could, following Camus, come to be "happy."[64] So, as Havel might say were he still alive, let us end the Cold War yet again, and again, and again. Striving for a whole world where societies might be morally, existentially, and civically reconstituted according to Havel's vision is surely a Sisyphean task, but doing so in the small circles of quotidian life is entirely reasonable. Gather together a group of people that shares a vision for how part of the

63 Václav Havel, *Art of the Impossible: Politics as Morality in Practice Speeches and Writings 1990-1996*, trans. Paul Wilson (New York: Fromm International, 1998).
64 Albert Camus, *Myth of Sisyphus and other Essays.* (New York: Vintage, 1991).

world might be made better, use that community to undertake moral and civically-minded actions together, and so will follow a Havelian existential revolution. Both the world *and you* will be made better, because even when you fail at the immediate political task, and even after your anarchistic community properly disappears, you will have lived in the truth, a truth made civically (*občanský*) and together with the company of others (*společnost*). This is Havel's *občanská společnost*.

ABOUT THE AUTHORS

Daniela Bouvier-Valenta completed an M.A. in European and Russian Affairs at the University of Toronto's Centre for European, Russian, and Eurasian Studies in 2020. Her M.A. thesis focused on the Million Moments for Democracy civic organization in the Czech Republic in the context of the development of Czech civil society since the Velvet Revolution in 1989. Her research interests include the history and politics of Central Europe, memory studies, and civil society. She also holds a B.A. in political science and history from McGill University. Her other work on Václav Havel includes the forthcoming article "Václav Havel: Posthumous Reclamation of a National Hero?" co-authored with Barbara J. Falk.

Aspen Brinton is Associate Professor in the International Studies program at Virginia Commonwealth University. Her research interests include democratic theory, dissident movements, East-Central Europe, phenomenology, and the intellectual history of civil society and free speech. Her first book, *Philosophy and Dissidence in Cold War Europe* (2016), examines the philosophical legacy of Eastern European dissidents. Her second book, *Confronting Totalitarian Minds: Jan Patočka on politics and dissidence* (Karolinum Press, 2021) examines how the thought of Czech phenomenologist Jan Patočka might be relevant for the contemporary world.

David S. Danaher is Professor of Slavic Studies in the Department of German, Nordic, and Slavic at the University of Wisconsin-Madison. His most recent book is *Reading Václav Havel* (University of Toronto Press, 2015), and he regularly teaches an elective monograph course on Havel's writings to undergraduates.

Barbara Day arrived from the United Kingdom as a student in Prague in 1965, just in time to see the original productions of Václav

Havel's plays. She maintained her connections with Czechoslovakia through the years of the Soviet occupation and consequent "normalization", working with the "underground university" in her capacity as executive director of the Jan Hus Educational Foundation. Since 1994 she has lived in Prague, translating and teaching at a number of institutions. Her publications include *The Velvet Philosophers* (Continuum, 1999) and *Trial by Theatre: Reports on the Czech Drama* (Karolinum, 2019).

Barbara J. Falk is Professor in the Department of Defence Studies at the Canadian Forces College/Royal Military College of Canada, and a Senior Associate of the University of Toronto's Centre for European, Russian, and Eurasian Studies. She is the author of the first thorough and comparative account of dissident theory and activism under communism, *The Dilemmas of Dissidence: Citizen Intellectuals and Philosopher Kings* (CEU Press, 2003) and is now writing a book on comparative political trials across the East-West divide during the early Cold War.

Delia Popescu is Professor in the Department of Political Science at Le Moyne College. Her areas of interest include comparative political theory; Eastern European political philosophy as it relates to dissidence, resistance, totalitarianism and political ideology; Romani studies; and critical discourse analysis. Her publications include *Political Action in Václav Havel's Thought: The Responsibility of Resistance* (Lexington Books, 2011).

Jiří Přibáň is Professor of Law in the School of Law and Politcs at Cardiff University. He has published extensively in the areas of social theory and sociology of law, legal philosophy, constitutional and European comparative law, and the theory of human rights. Previous works published by Karolinum Press include *The Defence of Constitutionalism: The Czech Question in Post-national Europe*

(2017) and (with Karel Hvížďala) *In Quest of History: On Czech Statehood and Identity* (2019).

Jiří Suk is a Research Professor at the Institute of Contemporary History (Academy of Sciences of the Czech Republic) in Prague, specializing in the history of Communism, dissent, and the post-1989 changes. His many publications include *Labyrintem revoluce* (Through the labyrinth of revolution, Prostor, 2003), which won the Magnesia Litera prize for book of the year in 2004, and *Politika jako absurdní drama. Václav Havel v letech 1975-1989* (Politics as absurdist drama. Václav Havel in 1975-1989, Paseka, 2013).

Irena Vaňková is a specialist in Czech language and literature at Charles University's Faculty of Arts, Institute of Czech Studies for Foreigners and the Deaf. She has published widely in the fields of cognitive and cultural linguistics (also with a focus on audio-oral-scriptural and sign languages), ethnolinguistics, philosophy of language, cognitive poetics and interpretation of the artistic text, silence in language, communication and culture etc.

Kieran Williams is Associate Professor in the Department of Political Science at Drake University. His previous books include the biography *Václav Havel* (Reaktion Books, 2016) and *The Prague Spring and its Aftermath* (1997), which has become a standard work on the 1968 events in Czechoslovakia.

The **Václav Havel Series** aims to honor and extend the intellectual legacy of the dissident, playwright, philosopher, and president whose name it proudly bears. Prepared with Ivan M. Havel, and other personalities and institutions closely associated with Václav Havel, such as the Václav Havel Library and Forum 2000, the series focuses on modern thought and the contemporary world – encompassing history, politics, art, architecture, and ethics. While the works often concern the Central European experience, the series – like Havel himself – focuses on issues that affect humanity across the globe.

Published titles
Jiří Přibáň, *The Defence of Constitutionalism: The Czech Question in Postnational Europe*
Matěj Spurný, *Making the Most of Tomorrow: A Laboratory of Socialist Modernity in Czechoslovakia*
Jacques Rossi, *Fragmented Lives: Chronicles of the Gulag*
Jiří Přibáň & Karel Hvížďala, *In Quest of History: On Czech Statehood and Identity*
Miroslav Petříček, *Philosophy en noir: Rethinking Philosophy after the Holocaust*
Petr Roubal, *Spartakiads: The Politics of Physical Culture in Communist Czechoslovakia*
Josef Šafařík, *Letters to Melin: A Discourse on Science and Progress*
Martin C. Putna, *Rus - Ukraine - Russia: Scenes from the Cultural History of Russian Religiosity*
Ivo Možný, *Why So Easily ... Some Family Reasons for the Velvet Revolution*
Kieran Williams – David S. Danaher (eds), *Václav Havel's Meanings: His Key Words and Their Legacy*

Forthcoming
Marie Černá, *The Soviet Army and Czech Society 1968-1989*
Olivier Mongin, *The Urban Condition: The City in a Globalizing World*
Ivan M. Havel et al., *Letters from Olga*